HOUSE OF COⅠ		
LOCATION	R ᴐᴐ2-4(4)	
AUTHOR	BEGG	
Acc DAIE		

EMU:

**Prospects and Challenges
for the Euro**

TO BE
DISPOSED
BY
AUTHORITY

House of Commons Library

54056001011128

ABOUT THE EDITORS

David Begg is Professor of Economics at Birkbeck College, University of London, and a Research Fellow in CEPR's International Macroeconomics and Transition Economics research programmes. He is a recognized authority on monetary, fiscal and exchange-rate issues; has written extensively on the EMS and EMU, and undertook a major study for the IMF on monetary and exchange-rate policies in economies in transition. He has also served as an Adviser to the European Commission, the Bank of England, HM Treasury, and to Committees of the House of Lords and House of Commons. He contributes regularly to the annual CEPR Report *Monitoring European Integration*, most recently the 1997 Report *EMU: Getting the End-game Right*.

Charles Wyplosz is Professor of Economics at the Graduate Institute of International Studies, University of Geneva, and a Research Fellow in CEPR's International Macroeconomics and Transition Economics research programmes. He has published widely on exchange rates, macroeconomic policy and labour markets. He serves on the Scientific Councils of NIESR in London, EPRU at the University of Copenhagen, and CES University of Munich. He is member of the Editorial Board of the *Journal of the Japanese and International Economies, Annales d'Economie et de Statistique*, the *International Journal of Finance and Economics, Moneda y Credito* and *Weltwirtschaftliches Archiv*. He is an adviser to the government of the Russian Federation and has been consultant to the IMF, the World Bank, the French Government, the European Commission, the Harvard Institute for International Development, and the Committee for the Study of the Independence of the Bank of England.

Klaus F. Zimmermann is Professor of Economics and Director of SELAPO at the University of Munich; Co-Director of CEPR's Human Resources research programme; Associate Editor of the *European Economic Review*, the *Journal of Applied Econometrics, Labour Economics*, and *Recherches Economiques de Louvain*. He is also Editor-in-Chief of the *Journal of Population Economics* and a council member of the European Society for Population Economics and the European Economic Association. He has published on a variety of issues surrounding population change, migration, the labour market, education, technical progress, business survey analysis and microeconometrics. As a recognized authority in these areas he has also served as a consultant to the World Bank, the European Parliament, the German Parliament and the German Federal Government.

Jürgen von Hagen was Assistant and Associate Professor of Business Economics at Indiana University between 1987–92, and Professor of Economics at the University of Mannheim between 1992–6. He has been Professor of Economics and Director of the Center for European Integration Studies at the University of Bonn since 1996. He was the first winner of the Gossen Prize of the Verein für Sozialpolitik – the German Economic Association – in 1997. He has published more than 40 articles in international, refereed academic journals and over 60 contributions to non-refereed journals and books. He is Co-Editor of *Open Economies Review* and a member of the editorial board of the *Journal of International Finance and Economics* and the *European Economic Review*. His consulting activities include positions at the IMF, the European Commission, the Federal Reserve Board, and the Interamerican Bank.

EMU:

Prospects and Challenges
for the Euro

Edited by
David Begg, Jürgen von Hagen,
Charles Wyplosz and Klaus F. Zimmermann

This volume is a special issue of the review, *Economic Policy: A European Forum*. It contains revised versions of the papers presented at the Twenty-Sixth Economic Policy Panel Meeting held in Bonn on 17/18 October 1997, with the support of the Zentrum für Europäische Integrationsforschung.

The Economic Policy Panel meets twice annually to discuss papers that are specially commissioned by the editors to provide timely and authoritative analyses of the choices confronting policy-makers. The articles use the best of modern economic analysis, but are also easily accessible to a wide audience and highly readable. Each paper is discussed by a rotating Panel of distinguished economists whose comments are published to provide the reader with alternative interpretations of the evidence and a sense of the liveliness of the current debate.

Economic Policy is published in association with the European Economic Association for the Centre for Economic Policy Research, the Center for Economic Studies of the University of Munich, and Département et Laboratoire d'Economie Théorique et Appliquée (DELTA), in collaboration with the Maison des Sciences de l'Homme. The Senior Editors are Georges de Ménil, Richard Portes and Hans-Werner Sinn. The Managing Editors are David Begg, Charles Wyplosz and Klaus F. Zimmermann.

Copyright © CEPR, CES, MSH 1998

First published in 1998

Blackwell Publishers
108 Cowley Road
Oxford OX4 1JF, UK

and

350 Main Street
Malden
MA 02148, USA

All rights reserved. Except for the quotation of short passages for the purposes of criticism and review no part of this publication may be reproduced, stored in a retrieval system or transmitted, in any form or by any means, electronic, mechanical, photocopying, recording or otherwise, without the prior permission of the publisher.

Except in the United States of America, this book is sold subject to the condition that it shall not, by way of trade or otherwise, be lent, resold, hired out or otherwise circulated without the publisher's prior consent in any form of binding or cover other than that in which it is published and without a similar condition including this condition being imposed upon the subsequent purchaser.

British Library Cataloguing in Publication Data:
A CIP catalogue record for this book is available from the British Library

Library of Congress Cataloging-in-Publication Data applied for

This book is printed on acid-free paper.
Printed and bound by Page Bros, Norwich, UK

ISBN 0 631 20997 2

CONTENTS

CONFERENCE PARTICIPANTS

TORBEN M. ANDERSEN
Aarhus Universitet

CHARLES R. BEAN
London School of Economics

DAVID BEGG
Birkbeck College, London

OLIVIER JEAN BLANCHARD
Massachusetts Institute of Technology

OLIVIER DE BANDT
European Monetary Fund, Frankfurt

PAUL DE GRAUWE
Katholieke Universiteit Leuven

GEORGES DE MÉNIL
DELTA, Paris

RUDI DORNBUSCH
Massachusetts Institute of Technology

ANTONIO FATÁS
INSEAD, Fontainebleau

CARLO A. FAVERO
IGIER, Università Bocconi, Milano

INGO FENDER
ZEI, Universität Bonn

MARC FLANDREAU
OFCE and CNRS, Paris

HANS GENBERG
Graduate Institute of International Studies, Geneva

STEFAN GERLACH
Bank for International Settlements, Basle

FRANCESCO GIAVAZZI
IGIER, Università Bocconi, Milano

HOLGER GLEICH
ZEI, Universität Bonn

BERND HAYO
Universität Bamberg

MATTHIAS HERDEGEN
Universität Bonn

PATRICK HONOHAN
Economic and Social Research Institute, Dublin

ZORAN JASIC
Ambassador of Croatia, Bonn

SANDEEP KAPUR
Birkbeck College, London

BERND KEMPER
Universität Essen

JACQUES LE CACHEUX
OFCE, Paris

STEFAN LUTZ
ZEI, Universität Bonn

BERNHARD MANZKE
Deutsche Bundesbank

PHILIPPE MARTIN
Graduate Institute of International Studies, Geneva

ROBERT McCAULEY
Bank for International Settlements, Basle

THOMAS NOTHEIS
Landeszentralbank Nordrhein-Westfalen, Düsseldorf

MAURICE OBSTFELD
University of California, Berkeley

GIOVANNI PERI
University of California, Berkeley

RICHARD PORTES
London Business School and CEPR

LUCREZIA REICHLIN
ECARE, Université Libre de Bruxelles

HÉLÈNE REY
London School of Economics

KENNETH ROGOFF
Princeton University

ANDREW K. ROSE
University of California, Berkeley

ISA SCHEUNFLUG
Universität-Gesamthochschule Paderborn

FRIEDRICH SCHNEIDER
Universität Linz

KIM SCHOENHOLTZ
Salomon Brothers International Limited, London

URS SCHWEIZER
Universität Bonn

ROLF STRAUCH
ZEI, Universität Bonn

MARCEL THUM
CES, Universität München

BIRGIT UHLENBROCK
ZEI, Universität Bonn

JÜRGEN VON HAGEN
ZEI, Universität Bonn

AXEL WEBER
Universität Bonn

KATRIN WESCHE
Universität Bonn

CHARLES WYPLOSZ
Graduate Institute of International Studies, Geneva

KLAUS F. ZIMMERMANN
SELAPO, Universität München

FRÉDÉRIC ZUMER
Service d'Étude de l'Activité Économique, Paris

Editors' introduction

This special issue of *Economic Policy* is devoted to EMU. We asked contributors to focus not on problems during the initial transition to EMU, but rather on problems arising after EMU has begun. The seven papers in this issue were discussed at the 26th meeting of the Economic Policy Panel in Bonn on 17 October 1997. In view of the large number of papers commissioned for and presented in this special issue, we invited Jürgen von Hagen to reinforce the resident team of managing editors, and we take this opportunity to thank him for his efforts. Each paper is preceded by a summary of the argument and principal conclusions. In this editors' introduction, we place the papers in their wider context.

What immediate challenges will face the European Central Bank when it assumes responsibility for the common monetary policy at the start of 1999? Obviously, a comprehensive answer is beyond the scope of a single paper. Rudi Dornbusch, Carlo Favero and Francesco Giavazzi focus on three key problems: to what extent, and by what means, the ECB will develop a genuinely European perspective rather than simply reflect the aggregation of national concerns; whether consensus will be impeded (or even assisted) by possible asymmetries in monetary transmission that convert a common monetary policy into differential national or regional outcomes; and whether such asymmetries can be systematically related to differences in national institutions.

Developing a European perspective requires provision of information on an EMU-wide basis; getting this process started in advance of the establishment of the ECB is one of the tasks to be undertaken by institutions such as the European Monetary Institute and the European Commission, during the transition to EMU. However, provision of such information is far from sufficient. It is also necessary to analyse the political economy of how the ECB board is likely to vote. Here the authors draw many lessons from the operational history of the US Federal Reserve, examining the extent to which votes on interest rate decisions reflected the regional interests of individual board members and the (important) role that the Chairman has played.

During the last few years, there has been a steady flow of papers documenting cross-country differences in the speed and extent of the response of national economies to changes in interest rates by a given amount. Dornbusch, Favero and Giavazzi offer a useful assessment of what this research tells us and what it does not. For example, researchers' simulations often evaluate a unilateral change in the interest rate of a single country, then compare this with a unilateral change in the interest rate in a different country. Such isolated (sovereign) policy experiments do, of course, induce changes in exchange rates as capital markets respond to interest rate differences. Hence conclusions about national transmission mechanisms may conflate 'domestic' effects of interest rate changes and 'external' effects operating via the exchange rate. The key feature of EMU is that any interest rate change will be *common* to all participants.

While recognizing that EMU may change other aspects of economic behaviour – the famous Lucas critique – the authors try to control this and recompute national responses to common and simultaneous changes in interest rates. Generally, asymmetries are smaller than reported in some previous studies, but they do not vanish entirely.

The final part of the paper documents significant differences in the national structure of financial markets and financial services provision. For example, it is well known that the prevalence of variable-rate housing loans in the UK makes interest rate changes impact much more quickly on UK households than on their counterparts in, say, France or Germany. Interestingly, the paper shows that, even for the past, there is no easy correlation between observable financial structure and measured asymmetries in monetary transmission. Moreover, here the Lucas critique may bite quite hard: institutions that evolved in response to history (for example, a history of variable and uncertain inflation) may adapt quite quickly to a new environment if it is believed to be here to stay. On the key issues of how quickly institutions might respond, and what the consequences would then be for the symmetry of monetary transmission, there obviously remains a good deal of uncertainty.

One channel through which policy-makers have sought to diminish uncertainty, thereby increasing the credibility of the fledgling ECB, is through the Stability and Growth Pact, which gives concrete effect to the earlier objective of the Maastricht Treaty to provide incentives that inhibit excessive budget deficits and public debt. The Stability Pact lays out the circumstances in which deficits would be judged excessive and the financial penalties that might then be imposed. Barry Eichengreen and Charles Wyplosz agreed to examine the implications.

The benefit of the pact is that it enhances monetary credibility by limiting the circumstances in which the ECB chooses, or is forced, to print money. This benefit does not come free, since fiscal flexibility is impaired. Eichengreen and Wyplosz therefore ask two fundamental questions: could the benefits have been attained using other policies with fewer adverse side-effects; and, if the pact is indeed pursued, how large are the costs of diminished fiscal flexibility? With respect to the first question, the authors conclude that most of the alleged benefits of the pact could probably have been achieved more cheaply by other policies. One common fear is that cross-border spillovers are neglected. For example, excessive government debt in a brave new world without the option of inflating the burden away may eventually induce open default, which could precipitate a banking crisis not merely within that country, but in banks of other EMU countries, since they too are likely to be holding bonds of that member state.

Concern about a systemic banking crisis might then force the ECB to print money. The authors argue that, if EMU changes the risk characteristics of national bonds, the appropriate remedy is to change prudential regulation of banks' exposure to such positions. In similar fashion, the authors identify other alleged benefits of the pact and argue that most are misplaced; even where concerns are valid, a better medicine usually exists.

Does this mean that EMU promises chemotherapy merely to prevent nations catching cold? Are restrictions to fiscal room for manoeuvre as damaging as the pessimists fear? The authors endeavour to rerun history, asking what would have happened had the pact already been in place. This is no easy undertaking, and it is difficult to assess all the aspects of past behaviour that might have been influenced had the pact been in place. However, in trying to ask how frequently deficits would have triggered penalties, Eichengreen and Wyplosz give us two types of evidence. First, we have raw evidence, simply counting how frequently ceilings were actually breached. This, of course, is a poor guide to the future. Debt levels are now very different from the past, and, with low inflation expectations, we should expect nominal interest rates to be very different from in the past. The authors therefore offer us alternative calculations based on recent debt levels and nominal interest rates likely to prevail under EMU. Within a simple model of the evolution of national output, they calculate when the pact would have been binding and what cumulative effect this would have had on national output: their answer is 'not trivial but not huge'. Obviously, this conclusion reflects not merely the estimates of what fiscal policy would otherwise have been, but also the empirical estimates of the model of output evolution in each country.

Since these are subject to a range of uncertainty, Eichengreen and Wyplosz's conclusion is subject to quite a large margin of error. But, for now, it remains a good place to start. Members of EMU, in exchange for some benefits of enhanced monetary credibility, will bear some costs as a result of fiscal restrictions imposed by the Stability Pact. However, since the costs are not too big, the authors conclude that countries will manage their fiscal policies to avoid incurring explicit penalties triggered by the pact.

Much effort has been devoted to the study of monetary unions (like the USA or Canada) to draw lessons for Europe, an idea which has been exploited in several articles previously published in *Economic Policy*. One experiment that has been overlooked is the gold standard during 1880–1914. It is an interesting period from today's perspective, marked by a high degree of capital mobility and trade integration. To be sure, the gold standard was not exactly a monetary union, as currencies could be unhooked from their gold parities, but metal was still central and most large countries, and many smaller ones as well, remained on gold throughout the period. Economists and historians Marc Flandreau, Jacques Le Cacheux and Frédéric Zumer look into this period with fresh data and a modern eye. They come up with new and telling stories. Quite strikingly, they detect a core (consisting of the UK, France, Germany, the Netherlands, Belgium and Scandinavia) and a periphery, where the 'Club Med' and eastern countries figure prominently. Interestingly, the core countries managed to retain their gold parity throughout the period, while the periphery countries either never managed to be on gold or had to leave in the mid-1880s, re-entering later on. The more the world changes …

With the Stability Pact in mind, the paper's focus is on fiscal policy and supporting institutional design, including central bank independence. The authors show that the periphery skidded on mounting public debts. They also report that financial markets did not work as a restraining device. What makes this observation particularly important is that they detect a market-based penalty. Heavy borrowers did face increasingly high interest rates, but this visible and tangible sanction failed to rein in fiscal profligacy and could not prevent eventual exit from the gold standard. At this stage, the lesson would seem to be that both the Maastricht fiscal convergence criteria and the Stability Pact are vindicated. However, the authors also argue that institutions, no matter how well designed, did not stand in the way of fiscally strained governments. Central bank independence was much discussed at the time and very much seen as an essential component of macroeconomic stability. Yet cash-hungry governments reneged on previous commitments and forced debt monetization. On the other hand, when these countries recovered and finally aimed at fiscal rectitude, central bank independence was restored and the return to gold parities proved long-lived, with or without a corrective devaluation. Once this was done, low inflation, financial stability and fast growth characterized the last decade prior to the First World War.

Historians love to debate the past and reinterpret the facts, or to discover new facts. This article is therefore likely to be subject to criticism, some of which has already been found in the discussions that followed the presentation to our Panel. For modern readers, however, some lessons are worth pondering. That financial markets fail to check excessive debt accumulation effectively will sound very familiar, a confirmation of what we have seen over the last twenty years in Latin America, Europe and Asia. Are the various measures included in the Maastricht Treaty, particularly ECB independence and the Stability Pact, the appropriate response? This natural conclusion is challenged by the observation that institutions are not very robust.

Since the beginning of the debate over European monetary union in the late 1960s, many critics have argued that the loss of the exchange rate as a tool for adjustment to asymmetric shocks hitting the member states would cause severe tensions and problems in the monetary union. As emphasized by the theory of optimum currency areas, countries or regions adopting a common currency should be vested with sufficiently effective alternative instruments to deal with asymmetric shocks. The alternatives fall into two categories, market-based adjustment mechanisms and government interventions. Wage and price flexibility and labour mobility are the most important ones in the first category; fiscal transfer mechanisms are the most important ones in the second. Two papers in this volume deal with these issues.

Antonio Fatás's paper takes the more optimistic view. In line with a number of earlier studies of the US federal fiscal system, he argues that the proper substitute for exchange rate adjustment between EMU partners would be a transfer mechanism providing redistribution across EMU regions in response to transitory, asymmetric shocks. At the heart of his analysis is the distinction between 'insurance' against transitory relative income shocks across regions, smoothing income fluctuations over time, and more permanent 'redistribution' in response to permanent shocks that give rise to lasting income differentials. Fatás sets out a method of distinguishing empirically between insurance and redistribution, and tries it out on data for US states. He concludes that, because of the high correlation of shocks to state incomes, the insurability of state incomes against asymmetric shocks is low in the USA, and that the degree of insurance provided by the federal fiscal system is about ten cents in the dollar.

Fatás then shows that the insurability of the incomes of the EMU members is similarly low. Partners that are reasonably correlated with one another derive only moderate benefit from pooling income risks. Paradoxically, trade integration and emphasis on convergence, designed in part to reduce differences in political incentives across countries, thereby reduce the scope of a federal fiscal policy within EMU to insure against temporary country-specific shocks.

Dealing with redistribution has always been more difficult, since persistence of visible transfers across national borders can give rise to resentment and political difficulties in remaining committed to the redistributive mechanism. In practice, of course, any particular federal fiscal system would have both insurance and redistributive elements, depending on the persistence of shocks and the degree of their cross-country correlation. As such, it would be politically sensitive. Fatás observes that, since such a system would in any case achieve limited insurance, it might be unnecessary to proceed down this avenue. Rather, individual countries could continue to use bond markets to reallocate budget surpluses and deficits over time, thereby self-insuring against temporary shocks, although not, of course, against permanent shocks. This mechanism for intertemporal smoothing of income is not available to state governments in the USA, where tight restrictions on state deficits apply. Fatás thus concludes that the absence of a federal fiscal mechanism for transfers between EMU members in response to asymmetric shocks need not cause severe problems.

Obstfeld and Peri, who examine labour markets in Europe, are less optimistic about the ability of EMU countries to cope with asymmetric shocks. They offer a review of the relevant arguments and empirical evidence for European labour markets. Unsurprisingly, they find that, with little wage and price flexibility and low labour mobility, EMU's capacity to deal with asymmetric shocks without higher unemployment and large fiscal transfers is low. The authors take the conventional argument one step further, arguing that the emergence of sufficiently effective, market-based adjustment mechanisms can be prevented by the existence of a fiscal transfer system providing strong and lasting disincentives against labour mobility. Obstfeld and Peri substantiate this view by showing that labour mobility is high in the USA, a monetary union with relatively low transfers, and low even within European countries where unemployed persons receive relatively large and persistent transfers. The implication is that the implementation of an EMU transfer mechanism to help regions absorb asymmetric shocks might reduce rather than strengthen the monetary union's ability to cope with such shocks.

Since recent decades have seen major innovations in transactions technology, the demand for cash should have declined substantially. However, this is at odds with the evidence. The supply of OECD currency has actually grown as a share of OECD gross domestic product. It seems strange, at first sight, that this trend should be due to the developments in countries like the USA, Germany and Japan, but not, for instance, in Switzerland, the UK and France. Given the importance of the size of the stock of cash for the new policy of money supply of the European Central Bank, we wanted to understand the mechanisms behind this surprising phenomenon. Hence, we asked Ken Rogoff to explore the issue.

He concludes that it is the shadow or underground economy, both domestic and abroad, that is driving these results. Why is this so? Some part of this demand for cash is to evade taxation, some to accommodate criminal activities. Hence, a large and growing share of OECD currency, probably well over 50%, is held in the domestic OECD underground or shadow economy. Moreover, there is strong international demand from developing countries: a reasonable estimate is about 25–30% of all OECD currency. As a consequence, only about 20% of the overall currency is used for the designed internal purpose – a quite alarming figure. This trend seems to be fostered by the provision of large banknotes; indeed, their share of total currency is driving the overall rise in the stock of cash. Does this fuel the underground economy? 'Yes', says Rogoff, and central banks are happy to supply because of the expected seigniorage revenues obtained by issuing large-denomination notes.

How does this relate to European monetary union? The European Central Bank is expected to issue the euro in large denominations, including 100, 200 and 500 euro notes. This can be seen as an aggressive step towards grabbing a larger share of the developing country and underground demand for safe currencies, and hence challenging the current global dominance of the dollar in this market. But Rogoff points out that this may well be an accounting illusion, since the expected gains are likely to be offset by losses due to tax evasion.

From the day of its birth, the euro will be endowed with many blessings. For decades to come, it will be backed by one of the largest economic areas. It will be the currency of choice in some of the world's largest financial markets. The ECB will see to it that it is a strong currency in its own right, not just the successor to the Deutschmark. It is inevitable then to ask whether the euro will also emerge as a challenger to the US dollar as the world's premier currency, used in trade and financial transactions in distant parts of the world and held as cash in all troubled spots. Most discussions of this question have emphasized two issues. First, based on size and financial market depth, the euro has more than a fighting chance of being a strong competitor to the dollar. Second, habit and established position could make this a very slow process, spanning decades, not years. This is the so-called hysteresis phenomenon, the view that established patterns of payments do not change easily unless rocked by a sharp discontinuity.

Richard Portes and Hélène Rey offer a new way of looking at these questions. They base their analysis on a framework that takes into account the synergy between the use of a currency in foreign exchange transactions and in financial asset markets. The more a currency is used in one segment of the market, the lower the transaction costs and therefore the more widespread is its use then; the two markets interact. Portes and Rey also give empirical content to the hysteresis effect by focusing on costs of transacting in a particular currency. Based on this analysis and on new detailed estimates of transaction costs, they conclude that the days of dollar dominance are numbered, and sooner than commonly expected.

This bullish view of the euro's international future is open to many counter-arguments, many of which are taken up in the discussion that followed the Panel presentation. Yet, it is important to envisage the implications of this possibility. Some implications are clearly political, drawing on the symbolic power of a currency as a measure of a country's standing in world affairs. Other aspects are purely economic. They include seigniorage income, which Portes and Rey see as limited, in line with previous studies, although they add estimates for a commonly overlooked source of international seigniorage. Others consider the external value of the euro. Will its international use lead to appreciation? The authors lean toward this conclusion, but they admit that it rests on particular assumptions that the Panel did not find very convincing. More interesting perhaps is their assessment of the welfare effects of a new world monetary order where the euro shares the front seat with the dollar. They note that the widespread use of a currency provides those who primarily hold it with savings on transaction costs. Today, US citizens, firms and financial institutions spend less on unproductive transaction costs than their

European and Japanese counterparts and competitors. In a world where the euro assumes world status, these savings will accrue to Europeans. Portes and Rey put numbers on this effect and find that Europe's welfare may, indeed, rise by an amount larger than the seigniorage gains that have hitherto attracted most attention. In this view, the USA stands to lose non-negligible amounts, while Japan comes out about even. If this assessment is correct, then European authorities should do what they can to encourage widespread adoption of the euro. The article makes a number of proposals to that effect, mostly focusing on improving the width and depth of financial markets. Given the size of the City of London, this in turn makes UK membership of EMU a very important strategic step.

Immediate challenges for the ECB

Issues in formulating a single monetary policy

SUMMARY

This paper discusses a number of issues that the newly constituted board of the ECB will face early on. Conducting a European monetary policy will be very different from living under the protective umbrella of the Bundesbank. We discuss voting on the ECB board, and argue that the ability to communicate with the public will be critical for the success of the new institution. We also ask how a single monetary policy – a common change in the interest rate controlled by the ECB – is transmitted to the economy of each member country. We show that the monetary process differs significantly inside EMU: initially, at least, the cost of a disinflation episode could fall disproportionately on a few member countries, those with both a financial structure that spreads a monetary contraction widely and a wage–price structure that is relatively inflexible. This process, moreover, is sure to evolve, in part as a result of financial industry restructuring already under way, but in part accentuated by the common money. Furthermore, as the 'Lucas principle' suggests, the wage–price process itself will adapt to the changing focus of European monetary policy.

— Rudi Dornbusch, Carlo Favero and Francesco Giavazzi

Immediate challenges for the European Central Bank

Rudi Dornbusch, Carlo Favero and Francesco Giavazzi

MIT; IGIER, Università Bocconi; IGIER, Università Bocconi

1. INTRODUCTION

After a formal dinner hosted by Dr Tietmeyer on 3 January 1999, the board of the newly constituted European Central Bank meets on the morning of the 4th to assume its duties. In the chair is Jean Claude Trichet to welcome the members of the board to their important responsibilities. He underlines the historic occasion and reminds them that Europe and the world are watching, including, importantly, the bond market: 'You can make a first impression only once', the saying goes. He notes the importance of continuity in policy, after a decade of successful and often difficult convergence. But he also emphasizes the task of creating a *European* monetary policy, not a policy that just fits Germany. That does not mean a departure from the central criterion of price stability, but it does mean that Europe is now the focus. Needless to say, the chair is nervous and there is tension among the group. This is not the occasion for the chair to open up a discussion. He will have rigged the game way ahead, and the less reliable members of the board understand that a deal has already been struck behind their back. They might as well go along; this day belongs to the hard money crowd.

The critical agenda item is monetary policy: setting the short-term interest rate

We thank Luca Cazzulani for his help as a research assistant. Carlo Favero worked on this paper during a visit to the economics department of the University of California at San Diego. We are indebted to David Begg, Claudio Borio, Hans Genberg, Andrew K. Rose, Guido Tabellini and Robert Waldmann for their insightful suggestions.

(the ECB Funds rate). The Beige Book (by analogy with Federal Reserve practice) will have set out the economic conditions in the various member countries, and summary statistics will be available for decision making: current and prospective inflation, and the output gap. It will not occur to anyone to look at unemployment, which is understood to be substantially if not overwhelmingly structural. But the output gap helps summarize the cyclical situation and its prospective impact on inflation.

At the time of writing (November 1997), we estimate that the ECB board will initially face an environment in which the European output gap in 1998 will have declined significantly, with a further important reduction projected for 1999. In fact, by 1999, the output gap (ex-UK) will be only half that of 1996–7 and full utilization of productive capacity will be almost around the corner (Table 1 and Figure 1). Moreover, projections for growth in 1999–2000 run well above 2%: no slowdown will have appeared on the horizon. Inflation, after the trough of 1997, will have been on the rise with a further acceleration anticipated for 1999. With inflation above 2%, any restraint that has not happened under Bundesbank auspices in 1998 is overdue.

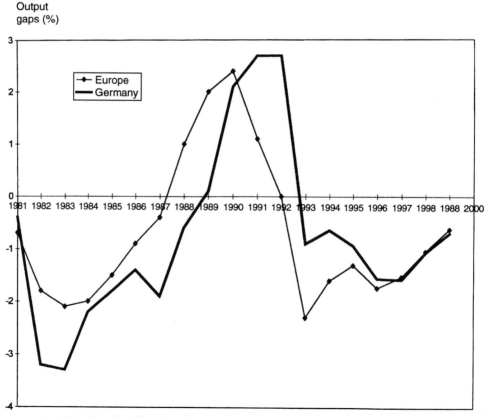

Figure 1. Output gaps in Europe and in Germany

Table 1. The EU output gap (%)

	1994	1995	1996	1997	1998	1999
Total EU	1.61	1.31	1.74	1.53	1.05	0.63
Ex-UK	1.63	1.37	1.89	1.84	1.28	0.77

Source: OECD.

The ECB board recesses at noon and a brief statement is released. The ECB Funds rate is being increased by 25 basis points to forestall an overheating of the European economy. The market reaction is prompt: the euro rallies against the dollar and euro long-bond yields fall by a full 10 basis points.

At a press conference later in the afternoon, ECB President Trichet remarks, in English, that monetary policy is overburdened by large budget deficits and long overdue deregulation. Observers note that his language is identical to that employed by President Tietmeyer on the occasion of the fiftieth anniversary of the Bundes-bank just six months earlier. But staffers clarify that this was thinking and language that has become the common stock of European monetary policy-makers. Press reaction is broadly favourable, with some notable exceptions. French former prime minister Rocard is quoted as deeply disappointed that the ECB did not repudiate the Bundesbank heritage vigorously and unambiguously; he says that a short working week had its logical counterpart in lower interest rates. In marked contrast, the *Deutscher Sparverein* deplores the ECB's failure to endorse a monetary aggregate target at this propitious opportunity, and expresses the view that the rate hike fell far short of what is needed to inspire confidence on inflation.

Conducting monetary policy in the boardroom of the ECB will be a very new game. The board will have to convince financial markets that the ECB is a serious institution. It will have to establish its political legitimacy, convincing the political community that it is European-minded and communicating this message to the European public. The board will also have to convince itself to look at EU-wide averages: learning about how the EU economy – a previously non-existent entity – works will be an immediate priority. This will take time, as the way in which monetary policy affects prices and output will change as a result of the introduction of the euro, and of the transition to a single central bank. Von Hagen (1997) has developed the full range of issues facing the EU monetary authority in a broad and definitive way. Our paper narrows the focus to several of the specific issues of monetary policy.

In preparing for EMU, a large number of studies have been written which ask the time-honoured question: is the EU an optimal currency area? (See, for instance, Maurice Obstfeld and Giovanni Peri in this issue.) These papers follow Mundell's (1961) traditional approach. They assume that the countries forming the currency union have similar economic structures, and ask how they can cope with asymmetric shocks once they lose the ability to set monetary policy independently. For example, a question that is often asked (see, for instance, Antonio Fatás in this issue) is whether the low degree of labour mobility inside Europe implies that some form of fiscal federalism among EMU members will be required to cope with the consequences of asymmetric shocks.

The focus of our paper is different. We examine how a *single* monetary policy – a common change in the interest rate set by the ECB – is transmitted to member countries. What if the cost of a disinflation episode fell disproportionately on the few countries with both a financial structure that spreads contractionary policy widely and a wage–price structure that is relatively inflexible? If such countries happened to share the German predilection for low inflation, such burdens might be tolerable; the outcome would be harder to accept if the country was, say, Fance, whose concerns about unemployment are relatively more important.

2. SOMETHING NEW IS COMING

So far, European monetary policy has been run by a board of German central bankers. The new team will comprise the central bankers of participating countries, veterans of the campaign against inflation in the past decade, plus six newcomers appointed by the EU Heads of State – probably from the staff of the current central banks. Even so, mere continuance of German stability-oriented policy is not an option: the ECB has Europe written all over it and hence must learn to operate in that dimension. The issues include what to target (inflation or aggregates), what intermediate targets to set (presumably short rates), and the key question of the objectives. How these will be measured (presumably as European averages) and how they are linked to policy instruments is uncertain at present. This is bound to be a major issue of controversy in the actual operation of policy.

The model of the past decade was straightforward: Germany set its own monetary policy on the basis of German inflation and unemployment rates. There is some question whether monetary targeting was actually taken seriously or whether some Taylor-style targeting was used, but the basic frame of reference was *German*.[1] The connection to the rest of Europe was provided by the EMS. The various partner countries within the context of the EMS had to translate German monetary policy moves into domestic monetary measures so as to be compatible with maintenance of the exchange rate margins. Over time that relation was not totally tight because increasing convergence provided some room for additional rate reductions on the soft periphery, and the presence of margins also yielded extra scope. But within the limits of these special factors, Germany made its own policy

---

[1] Among others, Clarida and Gertler (1996) most recently make the point that Bundesbank policy is well explained by a Taylor rule rather than well modelled as a monetary targeting experience.

and the rest scrambled along. By and large, in building a German reaction function, European (ex-Germany) conditions had no significance. By contrast, say in France, German variables would do better in explaining monetary policy than French conditions. Europe was on the Bundesbank standard.

In an EMU setting, joint decision making with an eye on European targets changes the process dramatically. The only plausible method is to look at European-wide averages (using GDP weights). For inflation the construction of this variable is under way. For a cyclical variable it is obvious that unemployment rates, even on a standardized basis, are useless. Their large structural component makes them an unreliable cyclical indicator. Spain's rate, in the 20+ percentage range, even scaled down by Spain's relatively smaller size, would impart an implausible expansionist bias to the numbers. More plausibly, weighted output gaps will be used (see Figure 1). These data are already available from the OECD (1997), though not apparently from Brussels. Table 2 makes it clear that, even looking at European averages, Germany remains the dominant player. But the game will definitely be different. The three large Latin countries combined carry far more weight than Germany.

Now consider the thoughts of members of the central bank board, looking at the same data on growth and inflation forecasts, and a cyclical indicator, both by country and Europe-averaged. Should the intermediate variable, the ECB Funds rate, be changed? If so, in what direction and by how much? The answer to this question will bring in the preferences of the individual board members in respect of inflation versus slack, judgements about the model – the monetary mechanism in this new universe, which is characterized by very different financial structures, and also different wage–price processes – and regional considerations over and above their reflection in the European averages.

Something very new is coming. Interest rates will simply no longer be set by

Table 2. Weights in Euro-GDP (%)

	EMU11	EMU15
Germany	34.3	27.6
France	22.3	18.0
Italy	17.5	14.1
Spain	8.5	6.8
Netherlands	5.7	4.6
Belgium/Luxembourg	4.0	3.3
Austria	3.3	2.7
Finland	1.8	1.4
Portugal	1.5	1.2
Ireland	1.0	1.0
UK	—	13.2
Sweden	—	2.9
Denmark	—	2.0
Greece	—	1.4

Source: European Economy, no. 63, 1997.

German authorities with German objectives in mind, and with the rest of Europe following. The change can be illustrated using a simple model of the interaction between interest rates and macroeconomic variables. Consider an EMU comprising two countries, say Germany and France (extending the countries would not change the argument), and suppose the ECB cares about a single macroeconomic objective (call it output; again the argument can be easily extended).

When the ECB cares about the EMU average, the common policy (the interest rate) optimally responds to a country-specific shock (say in Germany) by a larger amount (1) the larger the GDP weight of that country (since it has a greater effect on the average), (2) the less that country's macroeconomic response to changes in interest rates (since a larger policy effect is then needed), and (3) the less the other country's responsiveness to the interest rate change (since the ECB cares also about what happens there).

It is instructive to compare the EMS and the EMU regimes. Consider the effects of a German fiscal shock that raises demand in Germany and assume, for instance, that the Bundesbank cares about German output stability. In the EMS, the Bundesbank would set interest rates having in mind just the domestic objective, and would achieve full output stabilization by raising German interest rates appropriately. The cost for France of pegging to the DM after a German-specific shock has occurred is a fall in its output, caused by having to match higher German interest rates to defend the exchange rate parity.

Under EMU, the ECB raises interest rates by *less* than under the EMS, since the ECB internalizes the effect of the higher interest rates in causing a reduction of French output. In consequence, German output remains above its equilibrium after the expansionary German-specific shock, but French output falls by less than in the EMS regime. For this particular shock, France is better off inside EMU the larger its (GDP) weight relative to Germany (since the ECB then pays greater attention to what is good for French output). Moreover, for given weights, France gains more from membership in EMU the less responsive its transmission mechanism in comparison with that of Germany (for then interest rate rises necessary to have a particular effect on Germany have less side-effect on French output).

There are two lessons to learn from this simple example. First, it shows that, to set the ECB Funds rate, the bank needs to be aware of the characteristics of the transmission mechanism in member countries. But the example also confirms that Germany will lose the central role it has so far played in setting European interest rates. The extent to which this will affect the distribution of output losses across Europe will depend on the origin of the shocks, on the relative weight of the German economy, and on the relative extent to which interest rate changes affect output.

A dramatic way of illustrating this point is to ask just how a German fiscal expansion looks under the old regime – EMS with Europe following Germany – and EMU where Europe-wide data underlie policy making. The Federal Reserve has simulated just this exercise in its FRB/Global model.[2] Figures 2 and 3 show the impact of a German fiscal expansion of 1% of GDP, starting in 2000:1, on real GDP in Germany and France, respectively. Monetary policy is described by an active rule, linking short-term interest rates to deviations of output from potential and inflation from target. Under the EMS, Germany fights its own expansion with tight money, the output expansion is dampened by high interest rates and the rest of Europe is scrambling: the steep contraction imposed by the Bundesbank causes a sharp decline of output in France.

In EMU, the ECB uses an active monetary policy rule, in which the ECB Funds rate responds to the weighted average of output gaps and inflation deviations of member countries, assuming symmetric effects of monetary policy. This rule highlights the contrast with the previous regime, in which short-term interest rates in all member countries are determined by German output and inflation gaps. In EMU, monetary policy responds less vigorously to offset the fiscal shock. In fact, in the Fed simulation, interest rates rise by only 70 basis points rather than 150. That leaves room for Germany to have more of an expansion, and for France to avoid much of the recession, with favourable fiscal spillover mostly offsetting tight money.

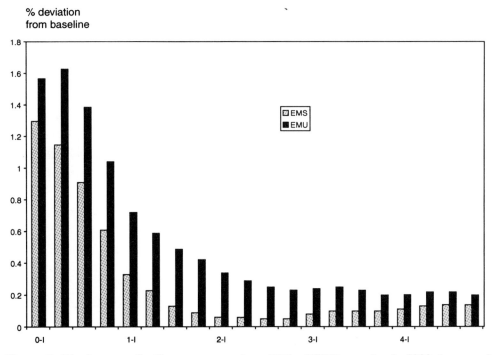

% deviation
from baseline

Figure 2. The impact of a German expansion of 1% of GDP, starting in 2000:1, on real GDP in Germany

[2] See Levin *et al.* (1997). We are indebted to the authors for graciously making their simulation data available.

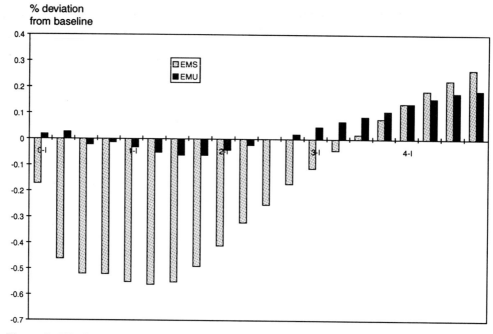

Figure 3. The impact of a German fiscal expansion of 1% of GDP, starting in 2000:1, on real GDP in France

If German unification had occurred in an EMU regime, the rest of Europe would have paid a lesser price.[3]

Is the EMU far more inflationary than a German/EMS scenario? The EMS setting imposes on France a drop in inflation at the peak of a quarter of a percentage point, while EMU keeps the price level largely unchanged (see Table 3). In Germany the EMS regime leaves the price level mostly unchanged while EMU involves somewhat more inflation – a half percentage point at the outset and gradually vanishing.

Table 3. Inflation effect of a permanent German fiscal expansion (absolute deviation from baseline, averages over four years)

	EMS regime	EMU regime
Germany	0.05	0.17
France	−0.15	0.03
EMU	−0.03	0.12

Source: Authors' calculations based on the Fed simulation.
Note: Here EMU is assumed to consist of France and Germany only.

[3] Of course, this presupposes that the country-specific shock originates in Germany. A purely French shock would not have been transmitted to Germany via interest rates under the EMS, but would spill over under EMU by affecting the interest rate chosen by the ECB.

Having introduced a number of different issues that need to be resolved in order to shape a European monetary policy, we now offer more detailed analysis of particular problems.

3. HOW WILL THE BOARD VOTE?

Will the regional or political background of board members influence their preferences regarding monetary policy? This possibility arises in two respects. First, the selection process that puts them in place may be systematically biased, so that they are 'hawks' or 'doves' chosen to be just that. Second, regional economic conditions may diverge significantly from the average of the monetary zone, and this may lead a particular board member to respond in a differential way. On both of these issues there is ample evidence from a long history of voting on the US Federal Reserve Open Market Committee (FOMC). Before going to the US evidence, however, it is worth clarifying the appropriate conceptual framework. The issue of centralized or regionalized decision making on the ECB board is the focus of a paper by von Hagen and Suppel (1994), who assume incomplete information. Centralized decision making, in a Barro–Gordon setting with principals and agents averse to inflation and employment variability, leads to offsetting of demand shocks and partial offsetting of supply shocks. In centralized decision making, regional shocks (with aggregate mean zero) are washed out. But when decision making falls to regional representatives, their parochial concerns affect policy reactions and induce inefficient choice in monetary policy. Of course, this is not the only way to model uncertainties and shocks, but it moves to centre stage the notion that this issue matters.[4]

The US FOMC comprises twelve voting members: seven are members of the Board of Governors and five, on a rotating basis, are presidents of the Federal Reserve District Banks. Of these five, the NY Fed has a permanent seat, and the Chicago and Cleveland Feds alternate. Faust (1996) summarizes the issue of divergent political interests controlled by the mixed influences getting together on the FOMC:

> The Fed was born in controversy. Farmers and small businessmen wanted a decentralised organisation under strong governmental control to counterbalance the power of eastern bankers. The financial community, on the other hand, feared that political control of the system would bring inflation.

Replacing 'eastern bankers' with 'the Bundesbank' makes the quote apply to control issues within the ECB.

---

[4] In the US case, board members represent the stable part, and the Reserve Bank presidents the flukes; by contrast, in the ECB the central bank presidents are the known quantities, hardened by a decade of convergence, while the new appointees, equivalent to board members in the US system, are the jokers in the deck.

A first point to note is the powerful influence of the chairman of the Federal Reserve. Much of the mystique surrounding Federal Reserve policy involves the uniquely powerful role of the chairman, his influence in shaping consensus, his never having been on the wrong side of the vote. Not all Fed chairmen have been as successful as in the myth; they have simply been forgotten. But where policy matters decisively, as at some stages of the Volcker and Greenspan years, the chairman's role in setting and communicating policy cannot be exaggerated. This central role has, of course, also contributed to the political debate about the Fed as an institution and the appropriate congressional control. If anything, this debate has strengthened the hand of the chairman and weakened adventurism or plain undisciplined talk on the part of board members. Moreover, as time passes, the chairman and his style and beliefs become a central institution of the capital market. As such, they become almost indispensable: their replacement is one of the most delicate tasks a president faces. Given the scrutiny with which the replacement will be viewed, a leaning towards the traditional and conservative is inevitable. Thus the cycle is closed. [5]

Consider next the members of the Board of Governors of the Fed, who are all political appointees. While they invariably have some credentials and are often highly qualified for the appointment (one was a lawn-mower manufacturer), they do clearly show the fingerprints of their patrons. Havrilevsky and Gildea (1996) show in detail that both board members and Reserve bank presidents reflect their political roots in their voting, and that they are swayed by the prevailing winds. The evidence is based on exploring those frequent instances where there are split decisions to determine on which side of the split a particular member of the FOMC votes. Economists, uniquely, are 'reliable' in that they vote a pattern rather than politics. But there are differences among governors and bank presidents. Specifically, 'bank presidents chosen under any Administration prefer less expansion than governors appointed by the same Administration'.

There are lessons for the ECB. The issue is *not* that governors or bank presidents take or solicit direct instructions from their patrons, but whether they are cloned and then sent on their mission. When an issue of difference arises, a French appointee would vote in the style of France, and a German, as predictably, in the way of the Bundesbank.

Going back to the Fed, the next issue is whether, in addition to national averages, regional conditions have an influence on the way bank presidents vote. The point here is that bank presidents are appointed by a local board (with heavy-handed supervision from the Fed board chairman) and are guided by their board, which includes predominantly local bankers and business people. It is therefore plausible to assume that these bank presidents would respond to local conditions either in a direct partisan way or else because local conditions, beyond the numbers, shape

---

[5] One is tempted to paraphrase James Carville's election-year aphorism, 'It's the bond market, stupid!'

their perception of the national situation. The evidence on this issue is not decisive. In a number of studies Havrilevsky and Gildea (1992, 1996; Gildea, 1992) conclude that there is, indeed, a decisive regional effect at work. But Tootell (1991, 1997), using a different methodology, finds that, given national variables as predictors of voting, regional variables do not add to the prediction.

Even if the issue remains undecided, the overriding presumption is that regional and political influences affect the FOMC meeting. This perception lies behind the various attempts to bring the FOMC under closer political control, either in respect of the appointments process for District presidents, or in widening the board to include Administration officials. What remains an issue for the FOMC will surely be a major issue for the ECB.

4. COMMUNICATING WITH THE PUBLIC

In its commitment to price stability, the ECB is equipped with an unambiguous charter. The independence from national governments – neither to seek nor take advice – further limits the scope for political dependence. Yet discussions continue, particularly in France, about moves to weaken this clear mandate by creating an offsetting political body to limit the independence and single-mindedness that the ECB is meant to enjoy. Where money is removed from immediate political control, the issue of accountability is inevitable in a democratic society, yet some account must be rendered of what policy is proposed and how well past targets have been met.

The ECB will need to do a lot of explaining. It will have to explain to all those who hoped that the transition from the Bundesbank Zone to EMU meant a more relaxed monetary policy that this cannot be so. It needs to establish the legitimacy of a serious monetary policy as a desirable European objective rather than an automatic continuation of Bundesbank policy. At the same time, the ECB has to offer decisive assurance to the sceptics, demonstrating its commitment to price stability without compromises. Most importantly, to be successful the ECB needs to create a constituency that understands and supports its conception of policy.

It is immediately clear that there is a role model and precedent. It is the Bundesbank. Week after week, in Germany and throughout Europe, the top layer of the Bundesbank shows up at public events of industrialists, savers, bankers and every conceivable civic or commercial association to explain the importance of sound money, the immediate challenges ahead, the instruments used to achieve and sustain price stability, and the risks of veering from the true path. Over time, direct communication with the public has paid off. The Bundesbank is probably less questioned in Germany than any other institution from government to church or university. It has created broad support, most fervently from the die-hard savers, for price stability and policies to support just that.

The ECB leadership will have to do just the same in a very intensive fashion. If it succeeds in creating an understanding, acceptance and support for its policies, it will become politically independent. If it relies on the narrow script of the Maastricht Treaty, it will soon feel the influence of political pressures even if they are not directly represented at the table.

The idea of a political body that interacts with the ECB is shocking: Europe and the world have moved a healthy distance from short-term political control of monetary policy. But there is obviously a gap to be filled. Hearings before the European Parliament may be useful, but only to inform not to direct. Meetings with finance ministers may be useful for discussion (the Fed chairman has a regular breakfast with the Secretary of the Treasury). None of these things amount to 'control' – the little extra bit that unreconstructed expansionists would like to bring on the scene. There is a vacuum, which the ECB needs to fill from day 1 or someone else will. Accountability comes down to effective communication to the broad and concerned public: once that is in place and gains depth, the vacuum is filled and political meddling is fought off by a broad constituency.

The experience of the UK makes the point of how transparency and an effective communication strategy change completely the scope for political meddling. The first step was the publication of the minutes of the monthly meeting between the Chancellor and the Governor of the Bank of England. After the Bank espoused the inflation targeting approach and started publishing an Inflation Report, the scope for the government to control monetary policy, while legally still present, became smaller and smaller. Independence became the logical next step. The success of a communication strategy has a lot to do with a simple message. Formal and explicit inflation targeting is, of course, a far better story than monetary aggregates, which are alien to the everyday experience of the average citizen.

5. THE MONETARY MECHANISM

Soon ECB board meetings will ask 'What do we know? How much will 50 basis points on the ECB Funds rate dampen EMU-wide demand? How different, in both timing and magnitude, will the impact be across member states?'

5.1. Regional effects and initial conditions

The regional impact of monetary tightening is rarely at the forefront of debate. Some studies have addressed the issue in the USA. Carlino and deFina (1996) find that monetary policy has an above average effect on the Great Lakes states and a below average impact on the South West and Rocky Mountain states. Most other regions, accounting for about 70% of US income, respond like the country-wide average. Perhaps the Fed has been fortunate that the regional discussion remains fairly muted. It is bound to be of central concern in the ECB, whose member states have become accustomed to discussing the appropriateness of the single monetary policy, albeit selected by Germany within the EMS, for the regions of Europe that we call France or Italy.

What would be the effect of an ECB decision to tighten interest rates? Those countries with a relatively large share of GDP in construction, capital goods and consumer durables will be more exposed, other things equal. Some regions absorb most of the shock simply because, by economic geography, industrial activity may be clustered. But do these differential *regional* effects translate into a significant effect across *countries*? Germany is a producer of capital goods and durables *par excellence*, Luxembourg is not. Of course, these are extremes. In between lie most countries, such as France, Italy and Spain. Reviewing the category 'machinery and equipment' as a share of GDP in the OECD *Historical Statistics* suggests that differences are in fact minor among EU economies. For construction, the other credit-sensitive component of spending, broadly the same conclusion applies.

Interest rate changes will, of course, operate also by changing the external exchange rate of the euro, creating another channel for differential effects across countries.[6] A rise in euro interest rates, other things equal, will lead to appreciation and hence to both a loss of competitiveness and a real income gain from terms of trade improvements. These effects may be differentially distributed across member states.

Openness across European countries differs significantly. Part of this involves intra-European trade and does not interest us here. But the part that involves extra-European trade is large enough to be of interest (Table 4). The UK and Ireland, and to some extent Germany, are relatively more exposed to fluctuations in cross-Atlantic competitiveness. Monetary policy will therefore have a differential impact. Countries that are more open will experience more of the loss in competitiveness that comes with tight money, and more of the terms of trade improvement.

Where exchange rate and interest rate exposure overlap, this focuses the impact further on particular countries. But this is not always the case. Sometimes openness and sensitivity to credit differ, in which case exposure to the common monetary policy is diluted.

Even more important is the role of initial conditions. Tight money hurts large debtors far more than it affects countries with moderate debt levels and good balance sheets. These differences are well documented in Europe. Belgium and Italy stand out with mega debts and special vulnerability. This problem is compounded, at least for Italy, by the below average quality of bank balance sheets (see section 8.1). Moreover, the consequences of higher interest rates for debt service then impact on budget flows, potential failure to comply with the Stability Pact, and the possibility of fines and a deterioration of credit rating.

---

[6] For a discussion of the exchange rate policy of the euro, see CEPR (1997).

Table 4. Openness of EMU members

	Overall	% of exports			
		Outside EMU7	Outside EMU15	To North America	To central Europe
Austria	24.2	59.0	41.0	4.1	4.9
Belgium/Luxembourg	51.4	51.0	29.0	7.9	0.1
Denmark	26.5	—	—	4.1	2.0
Finland	27.5	—	39.0	7.6	1.8
France	18.2	68.0	38.0	7.5	0.5
Germany	19.7	69.0	44.0	8.1	4.5
Greece	16.1	—	46.0	6.2	1.0
Ireland	58.9	65.0	28.0	13.0	0.1
Italy	20.0	—	45.0	7.0	0.2
Netherlands	37.5	47.0	25.0	7.0	0.1
Portugal	27.6	—	20.0	4.3	0.1
Spain	18.4	—	29.0	5.9	1.1
Sweden	28.4	—	44.0	6.0	1.4
UK	22.7	—	47.0	13.2	0.9

Source: European Economy. Data refer to 1995.
Note: Central Europe is Czech Republic, Hungary and Poland.

5.2. Lessons from the pre-EMU experience?

Once the board has come to a consensus on EMU-wide inflation prospects, and on the appropriate response, the next step is to decide by how much interest rates should be changed. What this requires is a lot of experience of how the economy works, what the lags are, and the extent to which spending responds to a change in interest rates, and wages to a change in demand. Even for the much studied USA, answers to these questions remain uncertain. In fact, the ground is shifting faster than the rate at which previous questions are being answered.

The ECB will be reminded of the Lucas critique: if 'something very new is coming', there may be little to be learned from past history. The ECB reaction function will be very different from that of the previous national central banks; the way national economies respond to monetary policy will also change. Yet it is unhelpful to tell the ECB that the only way to learn is by experimenting; it needs to know how uneven the distribution of the sacrifice ratio could be. Uncertainty about this distribution, or even awareness that it will be unevenly distributed, may bring the board to a standstill, as the coalition of losers protests the unfair distribution of the burden.[7]

---

[7] We are not aware of any study that attempts to estimate regional sacrifice ratios for the USA. It would be interesting to learn what they look like.

Moving from the EMS to the EMU is a big change in regime, but this does not imply that the data from the EMS years are of no use. In this section we show that they contain information valuable to the ECB. Consider the EMS regime. Behaviour of a typical EMS member (country i) can be captured by a pair of equations. The first (the economic structure) describes how a set of endogenous variables Y_i (including, for example, inflation and output in country i) are related to a set of variables X_i outside the control of its central bank, to current and past values of R_i, the interest rate set by its central bank, and to a random shock u_i. The second equation (the reaction function) describes how the central bank chooses R_i (in deviations from its long-run equilibrium R_i^*) to reflect anticipated deviations of inflation, real output and the exchange rate from their target levels. In the EMS regime, reaction functions differed across countries: the Bundesbank targeted domestic objectives, which possibly included the $/DM exchange rate; other countries followed Germany by using, as targets, the values of the German targets (see Clarida *et al.*, 1997).

A stylized view of the change from EMS to EMU is that it will leave the economic structure equations essentially unaltered, but will change the reaction functions, replacing the entire set of previous reaction functions with a single reaction function, describing how the single interest rate is (optimally) set given anticipated deviations of EMU inflation, EMU output and the (external) EMU exchange rate from their target levels. Both expected levels and targets are expressed as EMU averages using GDP weights.

Moving to EMU thus changes the reaction function. Even if the ECB objectives coincided with those of the Bundesbank, the *weights* in the reaction function will change. As discussed in section 2, optimal weights will have to allow for differences in the transmission mechanism across the EMU.

Although the economic structure equations remain essentially unchanged, we have to take care of one particular difficulty. Under the EMS, the effect of country i's interest rate R_i on its own endogenous variables Y_i in principle includes induced exchange rate effects against other EMS countries; under EMU such country-specific changes in interest rates are precluded by the common monetary policy. The next task is to show how to deal with this, and thereby to use EMS data to produce estimates of relevant parameters of the new economic structure equations under which EMU will operate. Such estimates, when coupled with anticipated levels of the variables outside central bank control, will then allow the construction of a monetary conditions index for the ECB.

5.3. The empirical evidence available

The available information on the monetary mechanism in Europe comes in two forms: there is evidence based on 'large' econometric models, and evidence based on 'small' econometric models. The first is available in compact form thanks to a project organized by the Bank for International Settlements (BIS, 1995). The goal of the BIS exercise was to detect cross-country differences in the effectiveness of monetary policy, and to ask whether they could be related to cross-country differences in financial structure. The tools used are the large econometric models developed by the national central banks and the multicountry macroeconometric model built by the staff of the Board of Governors of the Federal Reserve, which covers the G7 countries. All models considered quarterly data and are used to run the same policy experiment: a temporary (eight quarters) 1% increase in the interest rate directly controlled by the local central bank. Recent attempts at evaluating the impact of monetary policy shocks in different countries using small econometric models are the structural VAR models estimated by Gerlach and Smets (1995) and by Barran *et al.* (1997), and the Small Stylized Dynamic Model estimated by the staff of the Bank of England (Britton and Whitley, 1997). These studies differ in the identifying restrictions they impose on the data, but are based on a similar statistical structure: namely, a reduced form.

If these experiments are to be useful in evaluating the monetary mechanism in EMU, the simulations considered should reproduce conditions inside EMU as closely as possible. Three points are relevant. First, the direct effects on prices and output of a change in interest rates should be separated from the indirect effects working through the exchange rate movements that are induced by the change in interest rates. Exchange rate movements should then be separated into an intra-EMU channel and an extra-EMU (mostly a dollar) channel, as only the first will disappear inside EMU. This is an important point because, in the EMS regime, we could observe cross-country differences in the transmission mechanism that are simply the consequence of movements in intra-European exchange rates induced by a change in monetary policy. Second, the exercise should consider the response to a simultaneous change in interest rates in all countries, as this will be the case inside EMU. Third, it should be possible to test the statistical significance of the cross-country differences that are observed in the response of prices and output to a change in interest rates: given point estimates of the parameters that characterize the monetary transmission mechanism in different countries, we should be able to construct a test of the hypothesis that such parameters are equal across countries.

Unfortunately, simulations with these characteristics are not available. In the BIS exercise, only for France, Belgium, Italy and the Netherlands are the simulations run under the assumption of exogenous intra-European exchange rates. For other countries it is impossible to partial out the intra-European exchange rate channel – in particular, for Spain, Austria and the UK. Most simulations also consider a change in interest rates occurring in one country at a time, and in none of them is it possible to test the hypothesis of homogeneity in the monetary mechanism. We shall review this evidence, ask how far it can bring us, and then attempt to overcome some of its limitations, presenting some new evidence.

5.3.1. Evidence from large econometric models.

Table 5 presents the response of output and inflation to a 1 percentage point increase in interest rates lasting two years, estimated using the national central bank models. In a first group of countries (Germany, Austria, the UK, Spain and the USA, which we report for comparison), the exchange rate is endogenous; in the second group (France, Holland, Belgium and Italy), intra-European exchange rates are maintained fixed. Thus the two sets of simulations are not directly comparable. Two facts emerge. The UK and Italy appear to be the countries where monetary policy has the strongest impact on output, Spain the country where the impact is smaller. In the UK, the fall in output is twice as large as in Germany in the first year of the monetary contraction, three times as large in the second. In Spain the increase in interest rates has virtually no effect on output.

Comparisons among the countries in the second group are more informative, as these simulations assume constant intra-ERM exchange rates. The effect on output of the monetary contraction is smaller in Belgium and Holland, largest in Italy. The Italian response is twice as large as that in Holland both on impact and three years after the change in monetary policy. The impact on inflation is largest in Belgium and Italy, surprisingly small in Austria. The perverse response of UK inflation in the short run depends on the presence of housing mortgages in the CPI basket considered: it takes three years for the price of mortgages to work its way through the CPI. When the effect is over, the response of UK inflation is relatively strong; stronger than in Germany.

The data in Table 5 can be used to compute output–inflation trade-offs. These are shown in Table 6. Looking at the four countries for which results are available under the assumption of fixed intra-ERM exchange rates, the trade-off appears to be relatively more favourable in the small open economies, Belgium and Holland, compared with France and Italy. The effects of a monetary tightening estimated

Table 5. Monetary transmission, based on models of national central banks (% change in output and inflation, after 1 percentage point rise in short rates)

Exchange rates	Output			Inflation		
	Year 0	Year +1	Year +2	Year 0	Year +1	Year +2
Endogenous						
USA	−0.1	−0.5	−1.2	0	−0.2	−0.7
Germany	−0.2	−0.4	−0.3	0	−0.1	−0.3
Austria	−0.1	−0.1	0	0	0	−0.1
UK	−0.4	−0.9	−0.6	+0.9	+1.3	−0.5
Spain	−0.1	0	0	−0.1	−0.1	−0.2
Fixed within ERM						
France	−0.2	−0.4	−0.2	−0.1	−0.2	−0.3
Netherlands	−0.1	−0.2	−0.2	−0.1	−0.4	−0.4
Belgium	0	−0.1	−0.2	−0.1	−0.5	−0.8
Italy	−0.2	−0.4	−0.3	−0.2	−0.4	−0.5

Table 6. Output–inflation trade-offs: central banks' models
((% fall in output/% fall in CPI inflation)
after 1 percentage point rise in short rates)

	Year 0	Year +1	Year +2
France[a]	3.6	2.4	0.8
Netherlands	0.8	0.5	0.4
Belgium	0.2	0.3	0.3
Italy[b]	1.1	1.0	0.6

[a] Exchange rate fixed only *vis-à-vis* the six main ERM partners.
[b] Exchange rate fixed *vis-à-vis* all ERM partners except the UK.

using the Fed MCM model (Table 7) are more similar across countries, suggesting that some of the differences observed when using the national models may be due to the different specification of such models. The Fed simulation, however, leaves exchange rates endogenous, and is thus not very instructive in view of EMU. Finally, none of these experiments provides a statistical criterion to judge the significance of the observed cross-country differences.[8]

5.3.2. Evidence from small econometric models. Estimating the effects of a monetary contraction using small econometric models results in less pronounced cross-country differences. The model used by Gerlach and Smets (1995) is a trivariate vector autoregression (VAR) in prices, output and the short-term interest rate; a similar model is estimated by Barran *et al.* (1997), who augment the specification by including the exchange rate.[9] The structure of the model is much richer in Britton and Whitley (1997), who include domestic demand, imports, exports, short and long rates, inflation, the nominal exchange rate and some

Table 7. Monetary transmission: Fed MCM model
(% change in output and CPI inflation, after 1 percentage point rise in short rates)

	Output			Inflation		
	Year 0	Year +1	Year +2	Year 0	Year +1	Year +2
USA	−0.5	−0.6	−0.2	−0.1	−0.2	−0.1
Germany	−0.7	−0.7	0	−0.5	−0.4	−0.1
UK	−0.9	−1.2	−0.3	−0.2	−0.2	−0.3
France	−0.7	−0.7	−0.1	−0.5	−0.4	−0.2
Italy	−0.4	−0.3	−0.1	−0.4	−0.3	0

Note: Exchange rates endogenous.
Source: BIS (1995).

[8] In principle such a test could be run in the Fed model, which is a simultaneous multicountry model.
[9] The way in which the identification problem is solved in this model is less than fully convincing: the model includes both interest rates and exchange rates, and identification is recursive.

exogenous variables, including the oil price and tax rates. Gerlach and Smets use quarterly data covering the period 1979–93, while Britton and Whitley consider a longer period spanning from 1964 to 1994, also using quarterly data. Gerlach and Smets include all the G7 countries, while Britton and Whitley consider a subset formed by France, Germany and the United Kingdom. Neither model allows for simultaneity across countries.

Identification is the crucial step in the interpretation of a VAR. Gerlach and Smets assume that monetary policy affects output with a lag, but neither contemporaneously nor in the long run. This is problematic: the imposition of long-run restrictions requires that all the dependent variables in the estimated system are stationary – otherwise the long-run responses cannot be constrained because they are explosive – but this condition is unlikely to be satisfied by the variables used. The imposition of long-run restrictions in misspecified models can result in misrepresentations of the data-generating process (see Faust and Leeper, 1997): the Gerlach and Smets model describes the whole economy with only three variables, and is therefore likely to be under-parameterized. Moreover, monetary authorities in all countries are assumed to react to the same set of variables: this is an obvious potential source of misspecification, and one that could lead to misrepresentations of monetary policy shocks. The possibility of misspecification also raises an identification problem. Suppose the Bank of Italy reacted to changes in German monetary policy: omitting German rates from the specification of the Italian reaction function would lead to identifying as an exogenous Italian monetary policy innovation what is instead the endogenous response of the Bank of Italy to an innovation in German monetary policy. The reported response of the economy would thus be the response to a wrongly identified impulse. The very limited choice of variables also does not allow us to distinguish a domestic channel from the exchange rate channel, thus making the exercise of little use for our purposes. More importantly, the simulation exercise of interest – namely, a co-ordinated change in interest rates for all countries in EMU – cannot be performed with this model.

In the small structural model estimated by Britton and Whitley, identification is instead achieved by imposing on the data the Dornbusch overshooting model. However, in the core European countries the spread between local interest rates and German interest rates has been strongly positively correlated with the DM exchange rate, in particular since the 1992 ERM crisis, and until the start of the convergence trade in 1996. This evidence – a widening of the spread paired with depreciation of the weak currencies relative to the DM – is hardly compatible with the Dornbusch model, thus raising doubts about the identifying restrictions imposed on the data. [10]

---

[10] Another question concerns the stability of money demand over the long sample (1964–94) used in their estimation. An identical specification for money demand is adopted for the three countries, and no tests for structural stability are provided. An incorrect specification of the money demand equation would imply the confusion of money demand shocks with money supply shocks, a crucial issue for the analysis at hand.

5.3.3. Summing up the evidence to date. The available empirical evidence points to an important difference between the results based on large econometric models and on small econometric models. The latter do not detect cross-country differences in the monetary transmission mechanism, contrary to what seems to be the evidence from large, country-specific econometric models. Small models are subject to misspecifications and depend on the identifying restrictions they impose on the data. Estimates from large models are not statistically comparable across countries, and can only investigate the consequences of a local change in monetary policy. Still the simulations run by the individual central banks contain useful information because they are likely to incorporate the 'local wisdom' on the monetary mechanism in a particular country.

5.4. New empirical evidence

In this section we provide new evidence on the monetary mechanism in Europe.[11] We begin by estimating reaction functions for each country, then we turn to the equations describing economic structure. We use similar (small) models for all countries to try to limit the effects of differences in model specification. We also control for the effect of changes in intra-European exchange rates, thus replicating the conditions that will prevail inside EMU. Finally, we provide a statistical test of cross-country differences in the impact of interest rate changes on output.

We consider six countries representative of the EMU group: Germany, three 'core' European countries (France, Italy and Spain), and two 'non-core' countries (the UK and Sweden). The difference between core and non-core countries depends on the role of the DM as the nominal anchor in our sample EMS period: core countries pegged their currencies to the DM, whereas monetary policy in non-core countries was largely unconstrained by German monetary policy. This does not preclude a non-core country pegging from time to time to the DM; it rules out a policy of consistent pegging, which is what defines a core country. We use monthly data starting in 1985, allowing us sufficient observations while excluding a period (up to the mid-1980s) when exchange controls in Europe were widespread and monetary sovereignty was greater even in core countries.

Our estimated monetary policy reaction functions assume that within each monthly decision period the central bank has a target for the nominal short-term interest rate that depends on the state of the economy as described by expected inflation, the level of output and the nominal exchange rate.[12] As pointed out by Clarida *et al.* (1997), whether central banks respond to an additional percentage point of expected inflation by raising nominal interest rates by more or less than a

---

[11] Full details are available in Dornbusch *et al.* (1998).
[12] This extends to an open economy the closed-economy specification adopted by Taylor (1993), Clarida and Gertler (1996), and Clarida *et al.* (1997).

percentage point reveals the central bank's attitude towards inflation: in the former case, the target real rate adjusts to stabilize inflation; in the latter case, some inflation is accommodated. The magnitude of this parameter thus provides a yardstick for evaluating the central banks' attitude towards inflation – information relevant to a view of how different preferences will contribute to the outcome of the votes taken on the ECB board.

In estimating reaction functions for our six countries, we recognize central banks' tendency to smooth changes in interest rates, a common practice justified by the fear of disrupting capital markets, by the potential loss of credibility that could result from sudden policy reversals ('whipsawing' the markets), and by the need to build consensus in support of a policy change (Goodfriend, 1991). We therefore assume partial adjustment: in each period, actual interest rates adjust to close some fraction of the gap between the desired interest rate and the interest rate inherited from the previous period.

We estimate simultaneously the reaction functions for the six countries, selecting lags according to Hendry's (1995) general-to-specific strategy.[13] To estimate the system we separate our six countries into three groups: Germany, the European core, and Sweden and the UK. We use the short-term interest rate (three-month eurocurrency rates, except in Sweden where we use the call money rate) as the variable from which to extract information on monetary policy.[14] We measure inflation as yearly CPI inflation, and we use industrial production as the indicator for real activity. We treat the three groups differently in the specification of targets and relevant exchange rates. For Germany, the target level of output is a quadratic trend,[15] while the target exchange rate is the trade-weighted exchange rate vis-à-vis other European countries.[16] The core of Europe targets the German values of inflation and output growth; central banks are also assumed to react to fluctuations in the $/DM exchange rate, as these are associated with tensions in their own

---

[13] In the reaction function reported in Table 8, we use current and lagged variables as instruments for expected future variables. Since we are interested in equilibrium parameters, the identification of a forward-looking reaction function from a backward-looking one is not relevant to our estimation problem. If in equilibrium expectational errors are not relevant (in econometric terms, all we need is stationarity), the model specified in terms of expected rather than observed variables yields the same elasticities. Our results could thus be interpreted, alternatively, as a reduced form of a forward-looking model – in which combinations of present and past variables are proxies for expected future variables – or of a genuine Taylor-type, myopic rule, in which present and past variables are all that matters for the central bank. Nor need we take a view on the horizon for the forward-looking central bank: current and lagged observed variables are instruments for future variables at any future date, providing a data-based criterion for the parsimonious choice of instruments.

[14] The correlation between the level of the relevant policy rate in each country (the tender rate in Germany, France, Spain and Italy; the rate on outright purchases in the UK; and the central bank marginal loan rate in Sweden) and the level of the three-month money market rate is high (although the correlation between first differences is sometimes much smaller). Between the mid-1980s and the mid-1990s it was 0.99 in Germany (0.68 in first differences), 0.90 in France (0.24), 0.93 in Spain (0.37), 0.94 in Italy (0.81), 0.99 in the UK (0.87), 0.85 in Sweden (0.95) : see BIS (1995). On the use of three-month rates as a proxy for the policy rate, see Bernanke and Mihov (1996).

[15] A Hodrick–Prescott filter produces essentially the same results.

[16] We have also tested the significance of the $/DM exchange rate, and of the Federal Funds rate, without finding an independent significant role for these variables.

exchange rate relative to the DM. German variables also play a role in the determination of the Swedish reaction function. For the UK instead we consider, as in the German case, a quadratic trend as the proxy for target output, and we find an important (although limited to the short run) role for German interest rates. Because we use different instruments for different countries, we estimate the system by FIML. Estimates of the full specification are available in Dornbusch *et al.* (1998): Table 8 reports estimates of the key parameters.

Leaving aside the UK, where interest rates have a unit root, Table 8 shows that all central banks raise interest rates when expected inflation increases, when expected output gaps increase and when the DM appreciates against the US dollar. This third effect arises because in such circumstances other European currencies typically depreciate against the DM, prompting some consequent tightening of interest rates in these countries. With respect to inflation, the first column shows coefficients significantly below unity for France, Italy and Sweden, implying that higher inflation does not induce an equivalent rise in nominal interest rate targets; nor, since interest rates eventually adjust to target, does it induce an equivalent rise in actual interest rates in the long run. These estimates therefore provide evidence of inflation accommodation in these countries during the period since 1985. This seems a good description of policy in Sweden and Italy, at least until recently, though less obvious as a description of the strong franc policy pursued in France.

We decompose interest rate changes into expected and unexpected components,

Table 8. Reaction functions
(Short-term interest rate $R = \rho R^* + (1-\rho)R_{-1} + e$)

	Effect on R^* of expected deviation from target of			German short-term interest rate	Effect on R of R_{-1}	σ
	Inflation	Output	DM/$			
Germany	0.91	0.32	—	—	0.89	0.26
	(0.15)	(0.09)			(0.03)	
France	0.50	0.12	0.13	0.95	0.60	0.68
	(0.13)	(0.07)	(0.12)	(0.13)	(0.06)	
Italy	0.34	0.11	0.45	0.76	0.74	0.62
	(0.20)	(0.07)	(0.20)	(0.18)	(0.05)	
Spain	1.96	0.45	1.03	1.50	0.94	0.64
	(0.97)	(0.44)	(0.97)	(0.70)	(0.02)	
UK	—	—	—	—	0.98	0.44
					(0.04)	
Sweden	0.39	0.38	0.48	0.75	0.75	0.87
	(0.14)	(0.08)	(0.27)	(0.21)	(0.06)	

Notes: Estimated monthly 85(5)–95(4); 95(5)–96(7) retained for out-of-sample forecast test. Standard errors within brackets. σ measures standard errors of the residuals of each equation, reported in hundreds of basis points (0.26 reads as 26 basis points). The unit root in the UK equation does not allow identification of the long-run parameters of its reaction function. We have estimated short-run UK elasticities as 0.64 with respect to the German rate, 0.28 with respect to the output gap, and 0.20 with respect to inflation (further details from authors).

using fitted values and residuals from Table 8. However, a closer inspection of the residuals of our models cautions against interpreting unexpected interest rate changes as monetary policy shocks: in all countries but Germany, during periods of exchange rate turbulence we observe very big residuals, probably associated with shocks to the risk premia rather than exogenous monetary policy innovations.[17] In other words, short-term rates contain information on the reaction function – under the maintained hypothesis that the supply for reserves is flat – but are also affected by shocks to the exchange risk premium, which have nothing to with the reaction function. Because such shocks primarily affect the residuals of the reaction function, they do not appear in the anticipated component of interest rates. One important reason that we estimate reaction functions, and subsequently use fitted value of interest rates in the 'output equations' describing economic structure, is precisely to gauge more accurately the economy's response to *policy-induced* variations in interest rates, rather than its response to shocks from changes in the exchange-risk premium or from 'peso problems'.

Are the reaction functions that we estimate stable over the sample? The UK and Italy left the ERM in September 1992, and Sweden faced two speculative attacks before the 1992 devaluation. There is a clear possibility of a change in regime within our sample. We do not have enough data to run a proper stability test. Looking at the residuals of our fitted model during the EMS crisis suggests that the estimated reaction functions fail to track the data during the period of exchange rate turbulence, but come back on track as soon as the turbulence disappears. To shed further light on parameter stability we retained a number of observations at the end of our sample period and performed out-of-sample forecasting. The results are particularly good for Italy and Spain, but less satisfactory for France and Sweden. The observed values of the variables are always within the 95% confidence interval of the out-of-sample forecast, apart from a few observations for France.

We turn now to the equations for economic structure. We estimate these equations with a very specific question in mind: 'In EMU, will the effect of monetary policy on output be different in different countries?' To simulate the conditions that will prevail in EMU, our dynamic specification controls for the intra-European exchange rate channel. For each country we regress real output growth on (1) past values of its own output growth, (2) past values of each of the other countries' output growth, (3) present and past values of its own interest rate, both expected and unexpected, using fitted values and residuals from Table 8, and (4) present and past values of its bilateral exchange rates against the DM and the dollar. We can view this specification as the natural extension to small open economies of the set of

---

[17] Contrary to the USA, where the interpretation of SVAR residuals as exogenous monetary shocks is independent of exchange rate fluctuations, more care is required when a similar exercise is applied to small open economies such as Italy, France and Spain.

variables traditionally considered in the analysis of the monetary transmission mechanism in the USA. Fiscal variables are not included: if monetary policy is independent of fiscal policy shocks, their omission does not affect the estimates of the impact of monetary policy. The model is estimated by FIML to allow for simultaneity in the determination of European output.

In our preferred dynamic specification, the impact of monetary policy on output growth can be traced only to the *fitted* values of the interest rate: unexpected components of interest rates are insignificant.[18] Anticipated monetary policy has an initial impact, with a lag varying from eight to twelve months, and is always significant, except in Spain.[19] Note, finally, that because our estimated equations *always* include the exchange rate of the local currency against the DM, it will be possible, in assessing EMU, to switch off this channel, thereby asking questions about the transmission mechanism of a *common* monetary policy.

Within this framework we can also use the estimates for the different countries to test the hypothesis of a *common* effect of monetary policy (both anticipated and unanticipated) on output. Two tests are of interest: that the *impact* effect of monetary policy is the same, and that the *long-run* effect is the same. In fact, we tested for equality of both the impact effect and the effect after two years. The results are shown in Table 9, which reports the absolute values of the elasticities derived from our estimated structural model. These elasticities refer to a co-ordinated permanent rise in interest rates, having controlled for the exchange rate.

Our findings can be summarized as follows. First, the impact effect of a change in the short rate becomes significant only after eight months in Italy, Spain, Sweden and the UK, nine months in Germany, and twelve months in France. Note that the degree of persistence in our estimated model is such that the effect after two years coincides with the long-term effect for all countries.

Second, the impact effect on output is always significant, but differs across countries. We find similar impact elasticities in Germany, France and the UK (around −0.5), less impact in Spain (−0.4), and more in Sweden and Italy (−1.0 and −1.1, respectively). However, the hypothesis that all these elasticities are equal is not rejected at the 10% critical level.

Third, for the effect after two years, cross-country differences are more marked. The hypothesis of equal impact is now rejected at the 1% critical level, pointing towards clear (but not dramatic) differences in the effect of monetary policy on

---

[18] We tested for the significance of the unexpected component of interest rates in all six countries, obtaining a value of 1.81 for a χ^2 with six degrees of freedom, which does not allow us to reject the null hypothesis. This evidence can be related to our previous comment on risk premia, in the sense that the unexpected component captures shocks to the exchange rate premium rather than monetary policy shocks.

[19] Our proxy for monetary policy is a generated regressor, so that the coefficients on these variables are consistently but inefficiently estimated (see Pagan, 1984). The inconsistency problem could be solved by using instrumental variables, but the cost, in terms of fewer degrees of freedom, is not affordable in our case. Moreover, given the significance of all coefficients, the correction for the generated regressors problem should strengthen rather than weaken our empirical results.

Table 9. Elasticities of output with respect to interest rates (for an expected, permanent, common change; at constant exchange rates within Europe)

	Impact effect (within 8–12 months)	Effect after 2 years
Germany	0.54	1.40
France	0.46	1.54
Italy	1.11	2.14
Spain	0.35	1.54
UK	0.47	0.90
Sweden	0.95	2.36

Wald Test of equality across countries of impact effect:	$\text{Chi}^2 (5) = 9.1389\ [0.1037]$
Wald Test of equality of effect after 2 years:	$\text{Chi}^2 (5) = 21.245\ [0.0007]$
Standard errors available on request.	

Table 10. Estimated weights in a European Monetary Conditions Index (imposing constant exchange rates within Europe)

	Output elasticity w.r.t $/DM exchange rate (1)	Output elasticity w.r.t common EMU interest rate (2)	MCI weight (2)/(1)	95% confidence interval MCI weight
Germany	1.0	1.4	1.4	[0–2.8]
France	0.7	1.5	2.1	[0.4–3.9]
Italy	0.7	2.1	2.9	[0.6–5.3]
Spain	1.1	1.5	1.5	[0–2.9]
Sweden	0.3	2.4	8.1	[−3.0–19.2]
ECB			2.2	[0.1–4.3]

Note: Relative weights for UK omitted, since exchange rate not significant in estimated UK output equation.

output in the countries considered. Sweden and Italy still stand out (-2.4 and -2.1), while Germany, France and Spain lie between -1.4 and -1.5. The two-year impact is least in the UK (-0.9), partly because UK output is less strongly related to the European business cycle: spillover effects of a co-ordinated monetary policy are less important for the UK. Interestingly, in Spain monetary policy becomes effective over this longer horizon. The sharp change in the results for Spain should not come as a surprise, given the high degree of openness of the Spanish economy.

5.5. Building a monetary condition index (MCI) for the ECB

The concept of an MCI, originally developed at the Bank of Canada, is currently used by the IMF, the OECD, central banks and investment banks. Designed to measure a country's monetary stance, an MCI is computed as the weighted sum of a short-term interest rate and the external exchange rate. Weights reflect the effect of a change in interest rates and in the exchange rate on the objective(s) of the central bank, typically some measure of real output. For Canada, for instance, the weights are 3 to 1: a 1% increase in the interest rate has the same impact on output as a 3% appreciation of the Canadian dollar. The weights are derived from econometric evidence on the impact of interest rates and the exchange rate on aggregate demand, based on single equation models. [20]

MCIs for the countries in our sample can be easily derived from our estimated model. We first compute by country the relevant (long-run) weight on interest rate versus DM/$ exchange rate in determining national output *once we impose constant exchange rates against the DM to reflect common monetary policy*. These weights are derived from the static long-run solution of the estimated dynamic model of output described in section 5.4. Table 10 reports the weights thus implied country by country. Relative weights on interest rates versus external exchange rate range from a minimum of about 1.3 for Germany and Spain to a maximum of over 8 for Sweden.

The estimates in Table 10 could also be aggregated *across countries*, using GDP weights, to construct an MCI for the ECB (more precisely for this subset of EMU, which covers 70% of EMU 15 GDP). The implied relative weight (exchange rate to interest rate) is 2.17 (with a confidence interval ranging between about 0 and 4). [21]

This discussion is intended to be indicative not exhaustive. For example, rather than using weights based on steady-state parameter estimates, which therefore indicated the long-run effect of current monetary conditions, it would be possible to use estimated impact effects to estimate a short-run index of monetary conditions. For some purposes, notably the immediate pressures on monetary policy in the ECB, this might be more relevant. Some of these short-run issues are taken up in the following section.

Similarly, before the ECB is likely to allow any index built on econometric estimation much weight in relation to more familiar subjective assessment, it will be necessary to undertake considerable sensitivity analysis of the underlying econometric equations. Nevertheless, tried and tested intuition may usefully be supplemented by more formal analysis precisely because, initially at least, the ECB (like everyone else) will lack experience of how EMU will operate.

6. WHY IS THE MONETARY MECHANISM DIFFERENT ACROSS EUROPE?

Given the significant differences in the monetary mechanism across EMU members documented above, three questions naturally arise. What are the sources of these asymmetries? Will they disappear once monetary union takes off? If so, how quickly? The ways in which a change in interest rates affects the economy – the 'monetary

---

[20] Ericcson *et al.* (1997) report such models, including that for Canada by Duguay (1994).
[21] Building the MCI using the ratio of the weighted averages, rather than the weighted average of the individual countries' ratios, yields a very similar number: 1.92.

mechanism' as Modigliani referred to it in his 1963 article – depend essentially on the working of two blocs in the economy: the financial market and wage settlements. In this section we discuss financial structure and its relation to the monetary mechanism. We then ask how quickly it will change and what role labour market institutions will play.

The empirical evidence in section 5 points to the importance of financial structure: effects of monetary tightening in countries such as France and Germany, characterized by a bank-centred financial system, are systematically weaker than in the UK, where the capital markets play a central role in the financing of industry.

6.1. Channels of monetary transmission in Europe

How does the monetary transmission mechanism depend on financial structure? When the central bank changes short-term interest rates, its actions are transmitted to the economy through two main channels. The first is the textbook channel: the change in interest rates affects new marginal spending by modifying borrowing conditions and by affecting asset prices, and thus the market value of wealth. In terms of the simple IS-LM-AS model, monetary policy shifts the LM schedule. But a change in interest rates can affect spending decisions through two additional channels related to a country's financial structure: the 'credit' and 'broad credit' channels (Bernanke and Gertler, 1995). When loans and bonds are imperfect substitutes in the balance sheets of banks, a liquidity squeeze makes banks reduce the amount of loans they supply. Firms could turn to the bond market, but if bonds and loans are imperfect substitutes, the external finance premium will go up, amplifying the effects of the monetary tightening. A second channel is associated with the credit constraints that may arise when firms' ability to borrow depends on the availability of collateral. An increase in interest rates reduces the market value of collateral (e.g., real estate values), thus affecting the firm's access to bank lending (Kiyotaki and Moore, 1997).

The credit channel will be relevant in EMU because, especially in continental Europe (see Tables 11 and 12), banks provide the bulk of firms' credit. The contrast with the USA and the UK is particularly striking: British and American firms raise on the capital market three or four times as much funds as a typical continental European firm, with the possible exception of France where securities markets have recently developed quickly.

Evidence on the role of collateral in the provision of bank loans points to significant differences across Europe (see Table 13). Sweden and the UK stand out: more than one-half of total loans are backed by collateral, suggesting that in these countries a change in interest rates may have a stronger effect on real activity. The ratio is also high in France, as witnessed by the collapse of Crédit Lyonnais following the fall in French real estate prices.

One reason why the role of banks could give rise to asymmetries in the monetary

Table 11. Liabilities of non-financial enterprises

	Securities as % of (loans + securities)		% of bank loans in total debt liabilities	
			All non-financial enterprises	239 of world's largest manufacturing firms
	1993	1983	1993	1995
Germany	6	2	85.1	63.1
Netherlands	3	4	78.6	47.8
Austria	2	3	—	—
Belgium	7	12	89.9	—
France	15	8	80.2	46.8
Spain	9	10	77.3	—
Italy	5	7	94.6	73.1
Sweden	4	5	80.9	46.8
UK	19	17	49.4	36.0
USA	20	17	32.4	11.0

Notes: Private placements of long-term securities, whose status lies somewhere between loans and market instruments, in USA counted among securities, in some other countries counted among loans. 1995 entry for Netherlands is in fact for Benelux.
Source: BIS (1995), R&S (1997).

Table 12. Financial structure (1996, % of GDP)

	Debt and equity	Bank assets
EU	147.8	175.6
USA	246.3	68.9

Source: Authors' calculations based on IMF data.

mechanism relates to the special relationship between a bank and its customers. When lending is organized in a competitive securities market, lenders have no reason to cushion the effect on the borrower of a change in policy-determined interest rates. A bank, instead, cultivates a long-term relationship with its customer: it will thus be prepared to absorb, at least temporarily, some effects of an interest rate hike, anticipating that it will be able to make this up in the future (Allen and Gale, 1997). Another important reason is the lack of competition in the European banking industry. The evidence in Table 14 points to significant differences in the

Table 13. Collateral (% of total loans backed by real estate, households and firms, 1993)

Germany	36	Belgium	34	Italy	40
Austria	31	France	41	Sweden	61+
Netherlands	36	Spain	33	UK	56
				USA	66

Source: BIS (1995).

Table 14. Response of bank lending rates (in basis points) to a 100 basis point rise in central bank interest rates

After:	One month	One quarter	Two quarters	One year
Germany	0	36	53	74
Netherlands	71	95	102	103
Belgium	63	95	93	93
France	51	53	55	58
Spain	0	100	104	105
Italy	19	72	97	106
UK	100	100	100	100
USA	70	77	83	85

Source: BIS (1995).

magnitude, and especially in the timing, of the response of bank lending rates to a change in the interest rate controlled by the central bank. The adjustment is instantaneous and complete in the UK. In Germany, one quarter after the change in the policy rate, only a third of such change has been translated into the loan rate, and the adjustment is still far from complete after one year. This evidence confirms the tight relationship between banks and firms in Germany. The response is even slower in France, where a year after the change in policy rates only one half has made it to the lending rate. Sluggishness is lower in Italy, Spain, Belgium and the Netherlands.

A similar exercise run by the IMF (1996c) confirms these findings. In the IMF estimates, a 100 basis point increase in the policy rate raises bank lending rates by 45 basis points in Germany, 51 in France and 73 in Italy.

6.2. Asymmetries in the income effect of monetary policy

When consumers face liquidity constraints, and hold significant net asset positions, a change in interest rates can affect their ability to spend. European consumers differ a great deal in their net asset positions. In northern countries (Table 15), especially in the UK and Sweden, consumer borrowing is widespread, and households have substantial financial liabilities. In southern Europe, consumer credit is underdeveloped. It is in the high-debt states, Belgium, the Netherlands and Italy, that the need to finance large budget deficits has impeded growth of the consumer-debt industry. Germany's relatively higher level of consumer debt mainly reflects housing mortgages. The maturity of household debt affects the impact on individuals' cash flows of a change in short-term rates. Italy stands out on three accounts: the low level of consumer debt, its predominantly short-term nature (the share of consumer debt at adjustable interest rates is very high also in the UK), and the high level of net interest income as a share of total disposable income, the result of the very large share of public debt directly held by households.

Table 15. Household balance sheets, 1993

| | Household financial liabilities (% of disposable income) | Debt composition | | % of total borrowing at adjustable rate | Mortgages (% of disposable income) | Net interest received by households |
		Bank loans	Long-term debt			
Germany	77.9	100.0	72.4	36	90	4.2
Netherlands	64.9	75.8	59.0	8	90+	10.1
Belgium	41.5	n.a.	23.5	18	majority	6.1
France	51.0	82.2	43.9	13	5[a]	0.2
Spain	58.0	88.3	n.a.	n.a.	80	4.2
Italy	31.4	94.6	14.7	59/69	75	11.4
Sweden	100.3	90.2	57.3	n.a.	10	−5.5
UK	102.0	97.5	77.6	90	90	5.2
USA	92.0	39.2	67.9	34	15	7.3

[a] The lender retains discretion over the time and size of adjustments.
Source: BIS (1995).

An increase in interest rates will depress consumption where households' financial liabilities are high, as in the UK and Sweden (but also in Spain), but will raise disposable income and spending in Italy, Belgium and the Netherlands. In the UK, for instance (see the Bank of England simulation discussed in section 5), following a 1% increase in short-term rates, consumption falls 27 basis points below the baseline; in Belgium and the Netherlands, it initially remains essentially flat, independently of the exchange rate regime assumed.

6.3. Asymmetries in the credit channel: is the relevant lending rate short or long?

We have documented above the different speed at which banks adjust lending rates to a change in policy rates. The numbers in Table 14 refer, however, to interest rates on short maturity lending. But the share of bank lending at short, or adjustable, rates is very different across Europe, partly reflecting the inflation history of the various countries. In two countries, the UK and Italy, most company borrowing is short term, either because, as in Italy, the nature of the contract is short term, or because contracts are indexed to short-term interest rates, or in any case are adjustable at relatively short frequencies. In contrast, in countries with 'universal' banks, lending is predominantly at fixed rates.

The relevant lending rate is important because a decision by the ECB to change the policy-relevant interest rate can have different effects at the short and at the long end of the yield curve. For instance, if the ECB reacts to an 'inflation scare' by raising the short rate, the long rate may actually fall. It thus makes a great deal of difference if a firm borrows long or short. Given the distinction between Italy and the UK, on the one side, and the rest of continental Europe on the other, a common monetary impulse from the ECB should thus translate relatively faster into changes in spending in the first two countries.

Table 16 documents the conditions of lending contracts in Europe and, for comparison, in the United States. The share of lending at short-term rates is particularly high in Italy, Austria and the UK. Lending terms also appear to be short in Spain – a finding that seems at odds with the evidence indicating a very slow transmission mechanism in that country. Borio (1996) notes that Spanish lending rates, although adjustable at short intervals, really tend to behave like long-term rates because of the Spanish banks' sources of financing.

6.4. Summing up the evidence on financial structure and the monetary mechanism

The empirical evidence presented in section 5 suggested the following ordering in the impact of an EU-wide change in interest rates on real activity. The impact is largest in Italy and Sweden, smaller in France and the UK, and smallest in Germany and Spain. The characteristics of the financial system documented above go some way towards explaining the observed asymmetry in the transmission mechanism, thus raising the question: will EMU foster financial integration in Europe, and thus eliminate the current asymmetries?

In Sweden, the fast transmission of monetary policy to output could be related to the importance of bank credit, and thus of the credit channel; to the short maturity of lending contracts; to the important role of collateral; and to the balance sheet position of households, whose financial liabilities exceed 100% of disposable

Table 16. Credit at adjustable interest rates (% of total credit)

	By sector			By instrument: bank loans
	All sectors	Households	Firms	
Germany	39	36	40	45
Austria	74	—	—	76
Netherlands	25	8	37	35
Belgium	44	18	67	51
France	44	13	56	—
Spain	43/64[a]	—	—	47/70
Italy	73	59/69	77	79
Sweden	35	—	—	70
UK	73	90	48	85
USA	34	31	35	35

[a] 43% indexed to short-term rates, 64% adjustable within a year.
Source: BIS (1995).

income. In Italy, short-term bank credit and the balance sheet position of households work in opposite directions, but the first must clearly dominate.

In the UK and, although to a lesser extent, and only recently, in France, the speed of the transmission could be related to the role of the capital markets in the financing of firms. Collateral could also be important, especially in France.

Germany and Spain show surprisingly low responses, although the response in Spain increases when the change in interest rate is EU-wide because the Spanish economy is very open. The importance of bank credit, and of relationships between banks and industry, must underlie the slow and small impact of interest rate changes on German output.

7. THE MONETARY MECHANISM: IMPLICATIONS FOR THE ECB

From our discussion of the monetary mechanism in the EMU, we draw the following two implications for ECB behaviour.

First, asymmetries in the transmission of a change in policy-determined interest rates to real variables cannot be neglected. A monetary tightening by the ECB will produce an uneven distribution of output losses across the monetary union. For instance, and importantly, we documented how an EMU-wide increase in interest rates affects output by a relatively smaller amount and with longer lags in Germany, compared to other countries (with the exception of Spain). This would result in Germany being partially sheltered from the effects of monetary tightening, and possibly experiencing higher than average inflation. These asymmetries are related to the financial structures of EMU members. The speed at which financial structures will converge – for instance, with the development of an EU-wide liquid market for corporate bonds, thus reducing the role of banks in the intermediation of savings – will be an important factor in eliminating such asymmetries. For some time, the ECB will have to live with the consequences of these asymmetries. There is, however, important room for policy here. For example, as suggested in Pennant-Rea *et al.* (1997), differential capital adequacy requirements could encourage banks to shift from variable-rate to fixed-rate loans and mortgages. Tax changes could also be used to reduce gearing in countries where household debt is relatively high, and to encourage companies to shift from debt to equity financing.

Second, computation of a Monetary Condition Index for the ECB suggests that the exchange rate of the euro will remain an important factor in setting monetary policy. We have computed a relative weight of 2.2, which means that inside EMU the effect on output of a 1% change in interest rates will be equivalent to that of a 2.2% appreciation of the euro relative to the dollar. The corresponding number for the United States is roughly 10 (IMF, 1996a), indicating a very weak impact of the dollar exchange rate on US output. The number for Germany is 1.4, indicating a much stronger effect of fluctuations in the external value of the DM on the German economy. The ECB will care about the euro/$ exchange rate less than the

Bundesbank cares about the DM/$ rate, but its concern for the exchange rate will remain much greater than that of the Fed.

8. CHANGING STRUCTURE

It is hard enough to enact monetary policy without the benefit of continuity, except in the broadest terms as the commitment to price stability; it is even harder when policy targets suddenly turn European, and with an economic structure that remains largely to be explored. The simple question 'What is the effect of a 100 basis point increase in the ECB Funds rate on European output, and over what time period?' does not have an answer at present. Our effort in exploring the monetary mechanism has attempted to put a first guess on that issue. But the problem for policymakers is certain to be more complicated for two reasons.

First, the euro will change the way financial markets work, inducing corresponding changes in the monetary mechanism. In addition to pervasive deregulation already under way and innovation, the introduction of the euro will revolutionize the financial structure of Europe. Europe will in a short period become more nearly like the USA, and that, of course, has a bearing on the operation of monetary policy. Assuredly, any notion of a stable relationship between a monetary aggregate and target variables is not going to last; this, by the way, is an important argument against relying on monetary aggregates as indicators for monetary policy.

Second, but less definitely than financial restructuring, the wage–price process may well evolve as economic actors adjust to operating more clearly in a single market with a common currency. While the arrival of these changes is certain or plausible, the details of the dynamics are altogether unknown. Without question, monetary policy suffers an extra handicap as a result.

8.1. The demise of European banks

In making the case for a common money, the European Commission highlighted the benefits of a wide and deep European capital market taking over from narrow, illiquid, repressed and segmented national markets. As we have seen, banks at present play a large role in continental Europe, and the capital market almost none; this may be an overstatement for the government sector, but not for business. What are the plausible features of this new capital market?[22] A suitable comparison might be with the USA, where there was both deregulation that opened the capital market via competition and structural change that continues to lead to massive merging. Europe's financial system differs substantially from country to country, and it differs still from the highly deregulated and competitive system in the United States. This is

---

[22] These questions are addressed in Prati and Schinasi (1997), and McCauley and White (1997).

what we should expect with the creation of the euro, the accompanying deregulation, and internal market legislation that eases cross-border competition:

- Large firms will move into a euro CD market and a euro bond market.
- Depositors will shift from traditional deposits to money-market fund accounts.
- Households will find they can borrow in a new euro consumer credit market.
- Real estate lending will move into a euro securitized market.
- Wholesale business will shift from banks to specialized institutions, including possibly a few banks; this includes, in particular, foreign exchange and distribution of securities.

This transformation is dramatic for banking systems in Europe. How fast the transition is going to be, and whether the speed of change will be different across Europe, are very relevant questions for the ECB. The banking systems of some European countries are already fragile before the competition even starts. For fragility of the banking system, what matters is not the average but the outliers. Europe has fat tails (Table 17).

Having relied on captive customers for both loans and deposits, these banks will suddenly face more competition than they have ever imagined. There is little question that the role of banks in the financial sector will decline, and that mergers on a vast scale will be inevitable. The surviving players will surely have to be European in scale.

The situation is worsened by the fact that those banks that already have a weak financial situation will be worst placed to stay in the game. They will have the highest funding costs and therefore will be the first to lose prime customers. In a vicious circle, their credit ratings will worsen until they are ripe for takeover by the government. Unless governments take precautionary measures by a pre-emptive merger policy, banking problems will be important and they may affect macroeconomic performance, as in the USA in the 1980s, Sweden in the early 1990s, and most recently east Asia. For monetary policy, in particular, latent banking problems provide an important complication.

If a need for monetary tightening arises, the robustness of the banking system in

Table 17. Financial strength of banks (1996, % of banks in each group)

	A	B+	B	C+	C	D+	D	E+	E
USA	1.0	7.1	23.0	38.2	27.0	3.7	0	0	0
Europe	6.5	11.1	22.2	20.9	22.2	10.5	3.2	0.7	2.6
Germany	11.5	7.7	15.3	30.7	23.0	11.5	0	0	0
UK	3.7	18.5	33.3	18.5	18.5	3.7	0	0	0
Italy	0	0	16.6	33.3	22.2	11.1	0	5.5	11.1
France	3.7	7.4	18.5	14.8	18.5	18.5	14.8	0	3.7
Spain	8.3	25.0	41.7	8.3	16.7	0	0	0	0

Source: Authors' calculations based on IMF (1996b, p. 77).

transmitting monetary policy will be significant. Since the quality of banking systems differs substantially across countries, with financially repressed regimes lagging badly, monetary policy will be severely complicated by the political fall-out.

Monetary policy operates via the interest rate channel and the credit channel, including credit-rationing effects. Financial liberalization tends to shift the balance more towards interest costs, while financial fragility adds credit-rationing effects for those customers for whom banks are the natural credit agents. In the transition to a new financial structure, the net effects are not obvious.

8.2. The wage–price process

The other area of changing structure that interfaces with monetary policy is the wage–price process. A plausible description of the existing mechanism is that German labour understands the limited inflation tolerance of the Bundesbank and therefore practises wage restraint to avoid unemployment. Because the Bundesbank reacts directly to prospective price inflation foreshadowed by current wage settlements and productivity developments, there is nothing diffuse in the link between wage hikes and unemployment.

But how will German labour act once central bank policy is geared to European-wide inflation rather than German wages? Now the cost of a German wage hike is less directly reflected in German unemployment. In fact, unless there is a matching inflationary increase in wages everywhere, European inflation will not rise one-for-one with German wage hikes, and thus the need for disinflationary policy is less. Even to the extent that there is a disinflationary reaction from the ECB, the cost is not fully borne by German workers: unemployment will rise everywhere and other countries' increased wage discipline may provide scope for additional German aggression in pursuit of wage increases, especially if, as discussed in earlier sections of the paper, Germany will be partially sheltered from the consequence of monetary tightening.

Of course, the story does not end here. In fact, the solution is likely to be a complicated game in cross-border wage hikes. The presumption must be that the disruption of a direct link between wage hikes and unemployment will remove much of the discipline now in place, at least until a new equilibrium pattern has emerged that involves translation to the European level of the current game between the Bundesbank and German labour. But the new game could be very different. In Germany, wages are bargained at the industry level on a regional basis, but settlements are driven by the wage agreement in the metal industry, which typically sets the pattern for the entire country. This may happen in the EMU one day, but for some time wage bargaining will remain much more decentralized. The new cross-country game among different national unions could worsen the output–inflation trade-off that the ECB faces, compared with the trade-off currently faced by the Bundesbank.

The point that the degree of centralization of wage bargaining affects the outcome in terms of wage inflation has been made by Calmfors and Driffill (1988). In a recent paper, Cukierman and Lippi (1997) show that the strategic interaction among many uncoordinated unions and a single central bank results in the monetary authorities facing a worse output–inflation trade-off than they would if they were confronted by a single union. The output–inflation trade-off faced by the central bank worsens as the number of unions it faces increases.

9. CONCLUSIONS

Questions such as 'Will EMU happen? Will it be a large EMU? How will the Maastricht criteria be fudged?' are history. EMU is around the corner and in a little less than a year a brand new European central bank will be conducting European monetary policy. The challenge is nothing short of formidable.

So far, the Bundesbank has been running German monetary policy and the rest tagged along as well as they could. In conducting monetary policy, the new ECB will face three major issues all connected to the fact that the bank will conduct a 'European' monetary policy. Nobody has ever done that. Conducting a European monetary policy involves three challenges.

First, the ECB has to tread the narrow path between an institutional revolution and uninterrupted continuity with the Bundesbank. The capital markets will be unforgiving if they see anything less than Bundesbank policy. But the political community will be unforgiving if they do not see a genuine preoccupation with being European, creating a language and constituency that goes beyond German savers and monetary hawks. The legitimacy that the ECB must build depends critically on its understanding that its constitution in no way guarantees its political effectiveness. Success relies critically on developing successful communication.

Second, the ECB must conduct a European policy. It cannot get itself to accept solving every local problem by excessive regionalization of its policy; it must work on the broad picture of stabilizing European prices, not putting a lid on German inflation or a floor under French deflation. The challenge is to shift the discussion to European averages and to work credibly with these.

Third, the ECB has to develop a grip of the monetary mechanism in the European economy. This task is complicated because financial structures and the wage–price process differ widely. Our research shows that the monetary process differs significantly across countries. Moreover, this process is sure to evolve in part as a result of the financial industry restructuring that is already under way, and that is accentuated by the common money. Furthermore, as the Lucas principle suggests, the wage–price process itself will adapt to the changing focus of European monetary policy. Shooting at a moving target in the fog is no easy task.

The list of problems does not stop there, but these seem the most pressing for the success of the new institution.

▬▬▬▬

Discussion

Hans Genberg
Graduate Institute of International Studies, Geneva

The paper by Dornbusch, Favero and Giavazzi addresses a crucial practical issue that the future European Central Bank (ECB) will have to face as of 1 January 1999; namely, the nature of the monetary mechanism linking policy instruments and policy targets in the EMU. This issue is important because it conditions questions like 'How will the ECB board vote?', 'Will a common monetary policy have different impact on different regions in the EMU?', 'What will be the effect of different financial structures on the transmission mechanism of monetary policy?' and 'Do wage–price processes differ in the EMU countries, and how will that affect the conduct and effects of monetary policy?' These are indeed *the* questions to ask in the context of the changeover from national monetary policies to a common ECB policy, and the authors give us many elements of the answers, based on experiences from the Federal Reserve System in the USA, from an insightful analysis of the existing structure of the financial systems of the likely member states, and from a sophisticated empirical analysis of the EMS period. The problem with looking at the past to draw inferences about an entirely new system like EMU is that the 'Lucas critique' looms larger over the problem than over just about any other monetary policy issue that it has been applied to since it was articulated. The authors are, of course, aware of this, but rightly, in my view, they do not let this prevent them from trying to find answers.

1. How will the ECB board vote?

Under this heading the authors discuss two separate issues: will the members of the executive board reflect country-specific preferences regarding the trade-off between unemployment and inflation, on the one hand, and will they take into account regional differences in business cycle positions when they 'vote' on the conduct of the common monetary policy, on the other? To the first question the authors answer, yes. They say: 'The issue is *not* that governors or bank presidents take or solicit direct instructions from their patrons, but whether they are cloned and then sent on their mission. When an issue of difference arises, a French appointee would vote in the style of France, and a German, as predictably, in the way of the Bundesbank.' The implicit suggestion is that the nationality of the board members will make a difference for the average inflation rate of the monetary union because nations differ in their tolerance of inflation. Putting it bluntly, if Italy and Spain are members of the union, and therefore represented on the board, the suggestion is that the average inflation rate in the EMU will be higher than if they are not.

But are there really national psyches when it comes to evaluating the costs of inflation? The hyperinflation in Germany is said to have determined the attitudes towards inflation of an entire German generation. Is this true also for the current generation, which did not experience this inflation itself? What about the Swedes? In much of the postwar period, the monetary policy in Sweden has been one of accommodation to wage pressures in the form of currency devaluations. The current leadership and perhaps public opinion is of the view that such a policy is no longer (if it ever was) in the interest of the country, and that a policy of low-level inflation targeting is preferable. So would a Swedish board member vote according to the old school of Swedish monetary policy or according to the current orthodoxy? Attitudes change over time, so what seemed to be a particular nation's attitude towards inflation yesterday is no longer relevant today.

Institutions and incentives may be more important explanations of inflation performance than national characteristics. New Zealand provides a good example. Before the recent changes in the laws that govern the Reserve Bank, this country was not a model of price stability. After the new law and the new incentive schemes facing the management, the country has achieved a very significant reduction in inflation, even though the population of New Zealand remains what it was before.

So I do not believe that the country of origin of a member of the ECB executive board will matter much for the average inflation rate that it will deliver. If this is correct, but if the 'bond market', like Dornbusch *et al.* believes it does, then there is a danger that the ECB will have to be stricter than otherwise in order to establish a reputation for monetary stability. If long-term rates build in a premium for some inflation due to the presence on the board of so-called inflation-prone countries, then Europe will have to live with high real interest rates for some time after 1999. The communication problem of the ECB that the authors rightly emphasize will thus be to convince markets that bygones are bygones as far as attitudes towards inflation are concerned, and that all board members are pulling in the same direction.

On the second issue concerning how the board will vote, the authors draw on evidence from the US Federal Reserve System to argue convincingly that ECB board members will take regional economic conditions into account when they discuss the appropriate stance of monetary policy. Although it might lead to heated discussions at their meetings, attention to regional differences in business cycles is exactly what we would like to see because it spreads the burden of adjustment to idiosyncratic shocks. The authors make this argument formally in section 2 of the paper and state the conclusion succinctly: 'If German unification had occurred in an EMU regime, the rest of Europe would have paid a lesser price.' Likewise, if cyclical conditions in all EMU member countries, and not just in the centre, are taken into account when monetary policy is determined, then it is likely that EMU will be the truly symmetric system that the EMS was designed to be but never was.

2. Does the monetary transmission mechanism differ across EMU candidates?

The authors work hard to convince us that a common monetary policy by the ECB after 1 January 1999 will have different effects across countries. In my view they overstate their case. Differences in the economic structure of the potential members as well as previous econometric studies do not point strongly to major differences across countries, and the empirical evidence in the paper itself is not conclusive.

Initial conditions and previous studies. One way to determine whether monetary policy is likely to have a differential impact on regions is to think of them as having particular industrial structures, and to ask whether it is likely that individual industrial structures respond idiosyncratically to a common monetary policy. The authors' answer to this question is that industrial structure is not different enough across countries (although it might be across *regions*) to make a prima-facie case for different responses to the same policy-induced interest rate shock. This is good news on two accounts: it means that conflicts at the ECB board will be less likely as a result of the consequences of monetary policy, and it also means that asymmetric real shocks that are not policy induced are unlikely to be a major problem to grapple with.

But the structure of the financial sector and of the financial position of households and firms may also be reasons why a common monetary policy would impact on countries differently. The authors document several potential sources of these differences, such as the response of bank lending rates to interest rates controlled by the Central Bank, the balance sheet position of households and the importance of collateral in banks' lending decisions. Although they identify considerable differences across countries, they are much less successful in matching these differences with their empirical evidence on the speed and strength of the impact of monetary policy. One reason for this is that the impact effects of monetary policy are not statistically different across countries.

Previous cross-country empirical studies of the monetary transmission mechanism come in two forms: those that are based on large multi-equation econometric models, and those that are based on small VAR-type models. The former seem to point to significant differences across countries, while the latter do not. The authors put more emphasis on the results from the larger models. In fact, they discount the evidence from the small VAR models because of the difficulties associated with structural interpretation of reduced-form relationships. This begs two questions, however: are the identifying restrictions imposed on the large multi-equation models any more 'credible' than those used in smaller VARs; and are the restrictions imposed by the authors on their (even smaller) model sufficient to allow a structural interpretation of the results? Neither question receives a satisfactory answer in the paper, and I have some doubts on both grounds.

The new empirical evidence. With the hope of resolving the ambiguity of previous studies, the authors carry out their own empirical investigation of the monetary mechanism in six EU countries, four of which are likely to be part of the initial EMU group (France, Germany, Italy and Spain), and two of which are not (Sweden and the UK). The objective is to infer from the past how the central banks in these countries react to macroeconomic developments, and how the economies react to monetary policy initiatives. These estimates are then used to discuss how the EMU might function and what challenges the ECB executive board will face.

Of course, as I have already mentioned, the Lucas critique is present with a vengeance when we try to extrapolate from the past about the future under EMU. But this should not prevent us from trying, and the authors make a nice effort here. However, the interpretation of the results leaves some room for discussion.

My reading of the evidence presented in Table 5.9 is that the response of output to a common interest rate shock is remarkably similar, especially when we look at the countries that are likely to be part of the first group of EMU countries. In fact, the short-run effects of interest rate shocks are not statistically different between all countries. For longer-horizon effects, statistical tests do show significant differences when all countries in the sample are taken into account, but I suspect that if Sweden and the UK (two almost certain non-members initially) are removed, it will not be possible to reject the hypothesis that the influence of a common monetary policy is the same in all four remaining countries. For the countries that will be represented on the ECB board from the beginning, the problem of asymmetric effects of the joint monetary policy is hence likely to be minor.

I therefore interpret the empirical evidence as telling us that there is not much empirical justification for differences across countries in the effects of monetary policy. But this does not mean that the president of the ECB can relax. As the authors emphasize, the introduction of EMU is likely to modify the financial structure of the member countries' central banks, and changing structure means changing transmission mechanisms, especially in the early years of EMU. It is therefore essential for the ECB not to tie its monetary policy to particular intermediate targets or indicators that may rapidly become obsolete as the financial and real structures of the EMU members evolve. For example, a strategy of strict monetary targeting would be a mistake.

For the same reasons, as well as others referred to by the authors, I have serious misgivings about basing monetary policy on some mechanical index such as an MCI that the authors construct and propose as a guide for monetary policy. An eclectic inflation-targeting strategy is much to be preferred. Such an approach would, of course, take into account indicators such as short-term interest rates, the external value of the euro, and the monetary and credit aggregates in EMU as a whole, but it would not elevate any one combination of them as *the* official index of monetary conditions. Putting monetary policy into such a strait-jacket would unnecessarily reduce the scope for adaptation to changing circumstances, which will be essential in the early days of EMU.

Andrew K. Rose
Haas School of Business, University of California, Berkeley, CEPR and NBER

Dornbusch, Favero and Giavazzi are to be congratulated for tackling a potentially important problem. They address some of the key issues that the newly appointed European Central Bank (ECB) will have to confront immediately upon taking office in 1999. In particular, they focus on the question 'Does the ECB face a serious problem because of asymmetric effects of monetary policy?'

Potentially this is a topic of vital concern. Consider the scenario of an asymmetric shock hitting a country that has surrendered its monetary sovereignty by joining EMU. Since European labour is immobile and no substantive system of fiscal transfers exists, the costs of this shock are entirely borne by the country. To make things concrete, consider a precipitous decline in the demand for, say, Finnish high-tech goods. The ECB is pursuing tight monetary policy, either to establish credibility or because of the state of the European business cycle. A fringe nationalist party contests an election on an anti-Europe platform, arguing that the Finnish recession stems from a tight money policy pursued by the dark forces of Frankfurt, in blatant disregard of Finland's woes. Indeed, if the authors are right, the recession may stem from the uneven incidence of tight European monetary policy. The party is swept to power on a platform of repatriating power to Helsinki. The worst-case scenario is that Finland drops out of EMU. After all, what goes in can come out; currency arrangements are anything but permanent, as shown by the 1992 departures from the EMS. Of course, joining a common currency is a much more serious commitment than fixing an exchange rate. But even if the Finns retain the euro, they have any number of protectionist measures open to undermine the single market. Then again, the ECB may kowtow to the Finns, leading to inappropriate loose European monetary conditions.

The best solution to this problem is to avoid it in the first place. Thus I certainly agree with the authors that developing European-wide support for the ECB and its goal of low inflation is an immediate and important policy objective.

Problems like this are conceivable. But are they likely? I have considerable doubts about the relevance of my secession scenario, and therefore of the likely importance of the issues raised by the authors. My scepticism can be stated in the form of four questions:

- Has monetary policy really had large asymmetric effects?
- How relevant are the historical data?
- How enduring will the issue be?
- Will the ECB need to change monetary policy?

1. Is the evidence of historical asymmetries compelling?

It is by no means clear that monetary policy has had substantially asymmetric effects in Europe. But this is not to say that the evidence in favour of uniform effects is any more compelling. A Scottish verdict of 'not proven' is most appropriate.

As the authors readily admit, there is not much work that can be used to shed light on the issue. Many of the existing models have endogenous exchange rates, and are therefore irrelevant. When exchange rates are exogenous – as in the lower panel of Table 5 – the effects of monetary policy seem broadly similar across countries. The new evidence provided by the authors in Table 9 shows similar impact effects of monetary policy across countries. And while the effects of monetary shocks are statistically distinguishable after two years, all the action comes from Sweden and the UK. While financial channels point to Italy, Sweden and the UK as being disproportionately affected by monetary policy, the evidence is weak.

In any case, not all countries are equal, at least *vis-à-vis* the ECB. The evidence presented by the authors under-emphasizes the small countries, which constitute much of EMU. Further, the strongest evidence of asymmetries concerns Sweden and the UK, which are of limited concern to the ECB. After all, for a region to be of concern it must be: (1) in EMU; (2) asymmetrically affected by monetary policy; and (3) a country. The last point is of consequence; the issue of concern is the *national* effect of monetary policy. Mundell framed the optimum currency area theory in terms of specialized *regions* that are vulnerable to idiosyncratic shocks. Currencies are aligned with countries, not regions; and it is countries that can respond to secessionist pressures. Are countries regions? Usually not. The evidence in the literature (e.g., Obstfeld and Peri in this issue) indicates that many European countries are larger than regions (areas within which labour is mobile). Certainly large countries like Italy and Germany seem to have a number of different regions; even Belgium seems to have different regions. And some regions span countries: northern Italy may have more in common with southern Germany than with southern Italy. Regional effects of monetary policy are less threatening if regions are not aligned with countries.

In any case, how large do asymmetries have to be for them to worrisome? What's the benchmark? Carlino and deFina (1996) find large regional differences in the response of output to monetary shocks for three of eight American regions. But while academics sometimes ask whether the United States is too large to be an optimum currency area, there has been no serious talk of splitting the country into different currency zones. In any case, Bayoumi and Eichengreen (1993) find that the congruence of the EC core was roughly comparable to that of US regions, well before EMU and the continuing integration of European markets.

I conclude that we simply do not know if monetary policy has really had strong asymmetric effects in Europe. But even if we did have such evidence, would it be relevant?

2. Is history bunk?

As the authors are aware, the 'Lucas critique' states that history may be irrelevant in the face of a substantial change in policy. EMU surely counts as the policy regime *par excellence*. Do we believe that statistical evidence gleaned from a regime of fixed but adjustable exchange rates is valuable for the EMU era? On the one hand, EMU has been widely anticipated and the shift in monetary objectives is clearly specified. On the other hand, nature does not make jumps.

While it is hard to be sure, I am inclined to agree with Henry Ford: the endogeneity of the economy's structure is not an issue of academic (read 'trivial') importance. The authors discuss the potentially important effects that EMU will have on integration in financial and labour markets. These changes may be large and fast; then again, they may be small and gradual. Unfortunately, the dearth of comparable experiments does not provide evidence one way or another.

In any case, goods markets may be as profoundly affected by EMU as labour and capital markets. Two countries that surrender their national currencies will surely trade more, as the European Commission has stressed. As trade increases, business cycles change. Reduced trade barriers will lead countries to specialize more in their industries of comparative advantage. If shocks are mostly industry-specific, then business cycles will become more *asynchronized*, making my 'secession' scenario more likely. But if intra-industry trade dominates inter-industry trade, or if common (demand) shocks are larger than industry-specific shocks, then increased trade will result in greater business cycle *synchronization*. The impact of EMU on the synchronization of European business cycles is thus uncertain, at least theoretically. But the ambiguity turns out only to be theoretical. Jeffrey Frankel and I have found empirically that reduced trade barriers have been associated with greater trade and increased business cycle synchronization (Frankel and Rose, 1998). As EMU leads to more trade and more synchronized European business cycles, the 'secession' scenario becomes less likely.

3. A bubble on the tide of empire?

The differences in the monetary transmission mechanism are likely to be mostly transitory. As the authors stress, financial and labour market structures will adjust; certainly inflation convergence of inflation is already leading to more uniform patterns of long- and short-term finance. While I agree with them that the increased competition may take a while to have an effect, the dangers will certainly diminish with the passage of time. The problems that the authors raise are short term.

This short-run problem will exist only if EMU starts with the joining countries either (1) out of phase or (2) close to capacity, so that inflationary pressures are building. Is there reason to be concerned?

Table 18. OECD forecasts of output gaps

	1997	1998
Austria	-1.3	-0.9
Belgium	-2.4	-1.7
Denmark	-0.8	-1.7
Finland	-0.4	0.3
Germany	-1.2	-0.8
France	-2.3	-1.6
Ireland	0.7	1.1
Italy	-2.3	-2.3
Netherlands	0.1	0.3
Portugal	-1.1	-0.8
Spain	-2.3	-1.9
Europe	-1.6	-1.2

Note: All figures are annual percentages.
Source: OECD.

Currently, the business cycles of the 'ins' seem to be broadly in synch; Table 18 provides recent evidence. Synchronization is no great surprise. First, it has been the historical regularity. Even the enormous effect of German unification led to only a slight asymmetry, as the authors' Figure 1 shows. Also, both inflation and expected inflation (as measured by the long-term interest rate) have converged, which is presumably why these criteria are in the Maastricht Treaty. Third, countries which are out of phase are less likely to choose to enter EMU; the UK is the most obvious example.

The remaining question is then: are the 'ins' running too hot? How likely is a non-trivial tightening of monetary policy during the early, fragile part of EMU?

4. Genesis or Exodus?

'In the beginning God created the heavens and the earth. And the earth was formless and empty' (Genesis 1:1–2). Is the ECB in a similar situation, creating European monetary policy from a void? If Europe is overheating in 1998, then a monetary contraction is all the more likely in the dangerous early years.

But is 1999 really a monetary Genesis? A better analogy may be Exodus: the ECB is leading Europe into the promised land out of the bondage of the Bundesbank.

Clearly the job of the ECB will be much easier if the monetary conditions are reasonable in late 1998. A Bundesbank gift of tight monetary policy going into EMU will mean a longer honeymoon for the ECB.[23] Europeans may yearn for the

---

[23] More accurately, a Bundesbank bequest.

bad old days if the ECB is forced to raise interest rates quickly. Is the ECB likely to have a trial by fire because the Bundesbank leaves monetary policy too loose?

It is conceivable, but unlikely. The ECB would be forced to tighten monetary policy only if European conditions demand tighter money than is dictated by the German conditions that concern the Bundesbank. But, to reiterate, business cycles seem synchronized across Europe. And the Bundesbank tends to err on the side of tight money in any case. It is thus hard to believe that the ECB will be forced to raise interest rates more than the token amount needed to start the long process of building credibility.

Conclusion

I expect business in Frankfurt to be much the same in 1999 as in 1998. The decisions will be made in a different way in a different building by different people. But a dramatic difference in monetary policy is unlikely. Of course, a smooth monetary transition is to be hoped for, not to be sneered at. The real effects of EMU will emerge with time, and are likely to surprise (and inform) economists.

The short-term effects of EMU are just as likely to be political as economic. European politicians have spent their best energies of late making painful sacrifices on the altar of EMU. Millions of Europeans may become quickly disillusioned when a common currency proves not to be the magic bullet that ends a decade of high unemployment and slow growth.

General discussion

Richard Portes thought the paper had overplayed the secessionist scenario under monetary union. Secession was highly unlikely, and one could not compare situations in which a few countries left the ERM to secession. Once a country is in the monetary union, the costs of leaving it would be very high and any attempt to do so would certainly result in a constitutional crisis. Furthermore, he wondered if differences in business cycle conditions are going to cause particular problems for monetary policy after the start of EMU.

Lucrezia Reichlin called for a comparison of the dynamic profile of business cycles for different countries. She thought that the dynamic profile was fairly homogeneous across Europe, except for the cases of Greece and the UK. The asymmetries between countries are not enormous and the bulk of variance in output is due to common shocks. This raises the question of how the different dynamic profiles should enter a future target for aggregate output.

Olivier Blanchard expressed his concern that countries with little weight in the decisions of the ECB will be at a disadvantage when fluctuations are not highly correlated among countries and decisions are based on Europe-wide averages. He wondered whether these small countries have any means to protect their interests and, if so, whether these measures will lead towards necessary structural reforms of financial markets.

Jürgen von Hagen was critical of the empirical analysis of the transmission process. Evidence from the USA suggests that the transmission effects of monetary policy differed across sectors that differed in the size composition of firms. Small firms depend on banks more than large firms and, therefore, were affected to a greater extent by monetary policy. The transmission argument could be applied to different regions – as done in the paper – only if there were regional differences in the portfolio of industries. The extent to which these regional differences are likely to matter depends on the model of decision making on the ECB board. It was not clear that the median voter would decide. The Bundesbank history, for instance, showed that decisions were usually made almost by consensus. Hence, it would be very interesting to simulate different voting rules: in particular, as regional representation mattered only during times of severe crises and not so much for everyday monetary policy.

Patrick Honohan thought that the distribution of voting powers would not play a large role as the six executives in the ECB board would be able to dominate the governors, who are the national representatives.

Maurice Obstfeld argued for better modelling of the wage-setting process. First, if more unions were involved in the wage-setting process, things might even get better and not worse. Second, there were wide differences in wage-setting institutions across Europe. In Austria, for instance, the bargaining process was highly centralized, which helped to keep unemployment low. Hence, the labour markets in the EU countries would be affected differently by a change in the monetary system. Georges de Ménil agreed with Maurice Obstfeld that the wage-setting mechanism will change and that the outcome is not yet clear. He added that, whatever the effect on the wage-setting institutions, the increased price competition would limit the power of trade unions. Marc Flandreau felt that the credibility problem was overemphasized. Market participants have formed expectations about the behaviour of the ECB and its rules even before the euro has been launched. Hence, there will not be a drastic break, as suggested by the 'red-letter day'.

Axel Weber criticized the formulation of policy reaction functions which, in his opinion, led to implausible predictions and inconsistent results. A more general approach would allow each country's interest rate to react to output, inflation and other domestic variables, and thus help to isolate the reaction to foreign policy changes.

Stefan Gerlach thought that the responsiveness of Swedish output to monetary policy may have been artificial, as Sweden experienced an extraordinarily large recession in the sample period.

REFERENCES

Allen, F. and D. Gale (1997). 'Financial markets, intermediaries, and intertemporal smoothing', *Journal of Political Economy*.

Barran, F., V. Coudert and B. Mojon (1997). 'La transmission des politiques monétaires dans le pays européens', *Revue Française d'Economie*.

Bayoumi, T. and B. Eichengreen (1993). 'Shocking aspects of European monetary unification', in F. Giavazzi and F. Torres (eds.), *The Transition to Economic and Monetary Union in Europe*, Cambridge University Press, New York.

Bernanke, B. and M. Gertler (1995). 'Inside the black box: the credit channel of monetary transmission mechanism', *Journal of Economic Perspectives*.

Bernanke, B. and I. Mihov (1996). 'What does the Bundesbank target?', *European Economic Review*.

BIS (1995). *Financial Structure and the Monetary Policy Transmission Mechanism*, Basle.

Borio, C.E.V. (1996). 'Credit characteristics and the monetary policy transmission mechanism in fourteen industrial countries', in K. Alders *et al.* (eds.), *Monetary Policy in a Converging Europe*, Kluwer, Amsterdam.

Britton, E. and J. Whitley (1997). 'Comparing the monetary transmission mechanism in France, Germany, and the United Kingdom: some issues and results', *Bank of England Quarterly Bulletin*.

Calmfors, L. and J. Driffill (1988). 'Bargaining structure, corporatism, and macroeconomic performance', *Economic Policy*.

Carlino, G. and R. deFina (1996). 'Does monetary policy have differential regional effects?' Federal Reserve Bank of Philadelphia, *Business Review*.

CEPR (1997). 'Options for the future exchange rate policy of the EMU', Occasional Paper no. 17.

Clarida, R. and M. Gertler (1996). 'How the Bundesbank conducts monetary policy', NBER Working Paper no. 5581.

Clarida, R., J. Gali and M. Gertler (1997). 'Monetary policy rules in practice: some international evidence', paper presented at ISOM Conference.

Cukierman, A. and F. Lippi (1997). 'Central bank independence, centralization of wage bargaining, inflation and unemployment', unpublished manuscript.

Dornbusch, R., C. Favero and F. Giavazzi (1998). 'Red letter day', CEPR Discussion Paper.

Duguay, P. (1994). 'Empirical evidence on the strength of the monetary transmission mechanism in Canada: an aggregate approach', *Journal of Monetary Economics*.

Ericsson, N.R., E.S. Jensen, N.A. Kerbeshian and R. Nymoen (1997). 'Understanding a monetary condition index', unpublished manuscript.

Faust, J. (1996). 'Whom can we trust to run the Fed? Theoretical support for the founders' views', *Journal of Monetary Economics*.

—— and E.M. Leeper (1997). 'When do long-run identifying restrictions give reliable results?', *Journal of Business Economics and Statistics*.

Frankel, J. and A.K. Rose (1998). 'The endogeneity of the optimum currency area criteria', *Economic Journal* (forthcoming).

Gerlach, S. and F. Smets (1995). 'The monetary transmission mechanism: evidence from the G-7 countries', BIS Discussion Paper.

Gildea, J. (1992). 'The regional representation of Federal Reserve Bank presidents', *Journal of Money, Credit and Banking*.

Goodfriend, M. (1991). 'Interest rates and the conduct of monetary policy', *Carnegie-Rochester Series on Public Policy*.

Havrilevsky, T. and J. Gildea (1992). 'Reliable and unreliable partisan appointees to the Board of Governors', *Public Choice*.

—— (1996). 'The biases of Federal Reserve Bank presidents', *Economic Inquiry*.

Hendry, D.F. (1995). *Dynamic Econometrics*, Oxford University Press, Oxford.

IMF (1996a). *World Economic Outlook*, May, Washington, DC.

—— (1996b). *International Capital Markets*, September, Washington, DC.

—— (1996c). *World Economic Outlook*, October, Washington, DC.

Kiyotaki, N. and J. Moore (1997). 'Credit cycles', *Journal of Political Economy*.

Levin, A., J. Rogers and R. Tryon (1997). 'A guide to FRB/Global', unpublished manuscript, Board of Governors of the Federal Reserve.

McCauley, R.N. and W.R. White (1997). 'The euro and European financial markets', in P. Masson, T. Krueger and B. Turtleboom (eds.), *EMU and the International Monetary System*, IMF, Washington, DC.

Mundell, R.A. (1961). 'A theory of optimum currency areas', *American Economic Review*.

OECD (1997). *Economic Outlook*, Paris.

Pagan, A.R. (1984). 'Econometric issues in the analysis of regressions into generated regressors', *International Economic Review*.

Pennant-Rea, R. *et al.* (1997). *The Ostrich and the EMU*, Centre for Economic Policy Research, London.

Prati, A. and G.J. Schinasi (1997). 'EMU and international capital markets: implications and risks', in P. Masson, T. Krueger and B. Turtleboom (eds.), *EMU and the International Monetary System*, IMF, Washington, DC.

R&S (1997). *International Financial Aggregates*, Ricerche e Studi, Milan.

Taylor, J.B. (1993). 'Discretion versus policy rules in practice', *Carnegie-Rochester Series on Public Policy*.

Tootell, G. (1991). 'Regional conditions and the FOMC votes of district presidents', *New England Economic Review*.

——(1997). 'Reserve banks, the discount rate recommendation, and FOMC policy', unpublished manuscript, Federal Reserve Bank of Boston.

von Hagen, J. (1997). 'Monetary policy and institutions in the EMU', *Swedish Economic Policy Review*.

—— and R. Suppel (1994). 'Central bank constitutions for federal monetary policy', *European Economic Review*.

Stability Pact
More than a minor nuisance?

SUMMARY

The Stability and Growth Pact will lead member countries to aim for cyclically balanced budgets. Until this steady state is reached, Europe will continue its efforts at deficit cutting. While so doing, politicians are less likely to undertake the difficult labour market reforms that are really needed. Is further fiscal retrenchment wise? The paper reviews the reasons that have been advanced in favour of a Stability Pact and finds them wanting. The most serious justifications, such as the systemic risk of bank crisis following a government's failure to service its debt, can be better dealt with in other ways: for example, by prudential limits on banks' exposure to public debts. Moreover, our analysis reveals that the macroeconomic costs of the Stability Pact, while sizeable, are not as dangerous as often believed. The costs will be barely visible once the steady state is reached. The true macroeconomic costs are front loaded; they concern the next few years, after a decade already dominated by convergence efforts.

— Barry Eichengreen and Charles Wyplosz

The Stability Pact: more than a minor nuisance?

Barry Eichengreen and Charles Wyplosz

IMF, University of California, Berkeley, CEPR and NBER; Graduate Institute of International Studies, Geneva, and CEPR

1. INTRODUCTION

The Maastricht Treaty provides the institutional framework for Europe's monetary union. Its essential features have been the subject of extensive discussion: these include the three-step transition, the creation of a European Central Bank, procedures for shaping the conduct of fiscal policy (the Excessive Deficit and Mutual Surveillance Procedures of Art. 103, 104 and 109) and the no-bailout rule prohibiting the ECB from acquiring public debt directly from the issuer (Art. 104 of the treaty and Art. 21 of the Protocol on the European System of Central Banks).

The one post-Maastricht element, finalized at the June 1997 meeting of the European Council in Amsterdam, is the Pact for Stability and Growth.[1] The pact clarifies the provisions of the Excessive Deficit Procedure. It calls for fiscal

For help with data we thank Tamim Bayoumi, Herve Daudin, Paul De Grauwe, Tom Fernley, Morris Goldstein, Patrick Honohan, Alessandro Missale, Th. Papaspyrou, Ole Marius Tideman, Giuseppe Tullio, Bill White and Geoffrey Woglom. Xavier Debrun, Arjan Kadareja, Darren Lubotsky and Matthew Olson provided efficient research assistance. Financial support was provided by FNRS in Switzerland and the Center for German and European Studies of the University of California as well as the National Science Foundation in the United States. The opinions expressed are not necessarily those of the International Monetary Fund. Without implicating them in our conclusions, for helpful comments and guidance we would like to thank Donogh McDonald, the members of the Economic Policy Panel, our discussants, the journal's referees and David Begg.

[1] The 'growth' part was added at the request of the French authorities as a face-saving device after they were forced to soften their previous opposition.

positions to be balanced or in surplus in normal times so that automatic stabilizers can operate. It urges stronger surveillance of medium-term fiscal positions with the goal of providing an early warning signal that the 3% reference value for budget deficits is at risk. It clarifies the conditions under which participants in the monetary union will be allowed to exceed the 3% deficit ceiling without being determined to have an excessive deficit. Countries will be automatically exempt only if their GDPs have declined by 2% and the excess deficit is temporary and small. Those in which GDP declines by between 0.75% and 2% could also be exempt, but only with the concurrence of the Council of Ministers. Countries with even milder recessions will be found to have an excessive deficit and forced to make mandatory deposits that are transformed into fines if the fiscal excess is not eliminated within two years.

Although this new transparency is welcome, it also reveals a more restrictive set of provisions than those laid down by the Maastricht Treaty. The treaty says only that the general government deficit may not exceed its reference value (3% of GDP) unless the deficit has declined significantly and continuously to where it is close to that reference value, or the excess of the reference value is only exceptional and temporary and the deficit remains close to the reference value. It says nothing, in other words, about the size of the output decline producing that exceptional and temporary excess deficit, or the period over which it must occur. In this sense the Stability Pact implies less flexibility than the Maastricht Treaty.

The Stability Pact has not received the same systematic analysis as other aspects of the Maastricht Treaty.[2] Providing that analysis is our purpose in this paper.

Our conclusion is that the Stability Pact will have some effect. Governments will adjust their fiscal policies just enough to avoid incurring fines. EU authorities for their part will give countries just enough leeway to avoid having to fine them. Actually imposing fines would worsen conditions in the adversely affected member state, lead to recrimination and deal a blow to EU solidarity. Actually incurring fines would subject a government to serious embarrassment and loss of political face. Hence, the pact is likely to alter fiscal behaviour just enough to avoid these outcomes.

This will reduce the extent of automatic stabilization. Estimates based on historical data suggest that automatic stabilization may increase in the output gap, but by only a fraction of a percentage point. Hence the 'minor nuisance' of the title. But even a fraction of a percentage point on the growth rate can become important when allowed to accumulate over time. Our simulations suggest that, after accumulation over the last two decades, levels of real output would have ended 5% lower in France and the UK, and 9% lower in Italy.

---

[2] See, however, Artis and Winkler (1997), Beetsma and Uhlig (1997) and Buti et al. (1997).

The critical question, therefore, is how hamstrung automatic stabilizers will be. Will the Stability Pact weaken them as much in the future as it would have in the past, had it been superimposed on actual experience? The answer hinges on how far below the 3% ceiling budget deficits are when Stage III begins. If budgets move significantly into surplus relative to past experience, there is no reason why automatic stabilizers will be much affected. But in the present climate, where electorates lack the appetite for further spending cuts, significantly smaller deficits require significantly faster growth. The danger is thus that the Stability Pact will divert effort from the fundamental reforms needed to step up the pace. In particular, without fundamental labour market reform, Europe will fail to grow by at least $3-3\frac{1}{2}$% a year, and deficits will not decline. The Stability Pact will grow more binding, and the operation of Europe's automatic stabilizers will remain feeble, increasing the volatility of output, further depressing growth, and making the provisions of the pact even more binding than before. Through the operation of this vicious spiral, Europe could be condemned to a low-level equilibrium trap.

Our view is that leaders have a fixed amount of political capital that they can allocate to politically costly fiscal reform or politically costly labour market reform. To the extent that they invest in one, they have fewer resources left to devote to the other. In practice, they are likely to compromise, doing a little of each. For example, those European countries that have made the most progress in eliminating budget deficits and increasing labour market flexibility (Ireland and Finland spring to mind) have allocated their adjustment effort evenly to fiscal consolidation and labour market reform.

Our conclusion will be that the Stability Pact may have some slight benefits in terms of fiscal discipline, but may have significant costs, both in diverting political effort from more fundamental problems and indeed in making those fundamental problems worse than before.

2. WHAT THE STABILITY PACT SAYS

The Stability Pact consists of two Council regulations, one on the Excessive Deficit Procedure and another on surveillance, and a European Council resolution that provides guidance to the Council and member states on the application of the pact. The two Council regulations have the force of law. They clarify the meaning of the Maastricht Treaty's provisions regarding excessive deficits, in particular in respect of exceptional and temporary circumstances under which the 3% reference value for the general government deficit can be exceeded without a determination that the deficit is excessive. In addition, under the pact's provisions, participants in the monetary union commit themselves to a medium-term budgetary stance 'close to balance or surplus'.

The pact will consider a deficit in excess of 3% to be exceptional if a country's GDP declines by at least 2% in the year in question. In addition, a recession in which real GDP declines by less than 2% but more than 0.75% may qualify with the concurrence of the Council. The country will have to show that its recession was exceptional in terms of its abruptness or in relation to past output trends. Countries with annual output declines smaller than 0.75% will not be able to claim exceptional circumstances. These provisions thus clarify the Maastricht Treaty's clauses regarding the exceptional circumstances under which the 3% reference value can be exceeded without leading to the determination of an excessive deficit.

The pact also includes provisions concerning further exemptions. While countries are obliged to correct excessive deficits 'as quickly as possible after their emergence' and to 'launch the corrective budgetary adjustments they deem necessary without delay', they will probably be able to run deficits in excess of 3% of GDP for at least two years in a row without incurring fines. The Commission will receive definitive data that a country's deficit in year t exceeded 3% around March of year $t+1$. By the end of May it will have issued a recommendation for eliminating that excess in accordance with Article 103(4). The country will then have to take corrective action such that the excess is eliminated by year $t+2$. If no corrective action is taken by the end of year $t+1$, financial sanctions will be imposed. But presumably corrective action that will eliminate the excess in year $t+2$ will suffice to eliminate this threat. Thus, two successive years of budget deficits in excess of 3% (and possibly more – see below) will be permitted.

Moreover, the passage specifying these time limits ends with the qualifying phrase 'unless there are special circumstances'. The nature of those special circumstances is not specified. But presumably a country like Finland in the early 1990s, which suffered budgetary difficulties reflecting special circumstances largely beyond its control, would be allowed to take even longer to bring its deficit back down to 3%. Nor does the pact clarify a third provision of the Excessive Deficit Procedure, that the budget must remain 'close' to the reference value to avoid the determination of an excessive deficit.

Sanctions, when required, will take the form of non-remunerated deposits, which start at 0.2% of GDP and rise by one-tenth of the excess deficit up to a maximum of 0.5% of GDP. Additional deposits will be required each year until the excessive deficit is corrected. If the excess is not corrected within two years, the deposit will be converted into a fine; otherwise it will be returned.

Thus, a careful reading does not imply that fines will be levied as soon as budget deficits exceed 3% of GDP. The pact is rather more flexible. It allows temporary exemptions for countries experiencing 'severe' recessions. More generally, it allows time for excessive deficits to be corrected; in the case of undefined 'special circumstances' it allows unspecified amounts of time. Clearly, one needs to think harder about the political economy of EU policy making to forecast how strictly the fines and sanctions of the Stability Pact will be applied.

3. RATIONALES FOR THE STABILITY PACT

For an argument favouring the Stability Pact to convince, it must satisfy three conditions. The effect on which it hinges must be first order (on the principle that controversial policies with potentially important side-effects should not be adopted in response to negligible problems). It must have Europe-wide repercussions (on the principle that, if its effects are purely national, there is no justification for a Europe-wide response). And, arguably, it must be a consequence of monetary union rather than a corollary of European integration (on the principle that the Excessive Deficit Procedure and the rest of the Maastricht Treaty apply to member states whether in or out of the monetary union, whereas the sanctions of the Stability Pact apply specifically to participants in EMU).[3]

3.1. To prevent inflationary debt bailouts

The most compelling argument for the Stability Pact is as extra protection for the ECB from pressure for an inflationary debt bailout. The scenario might run as follows. The government of an EMU country gets into fiscal trouble, from which it cannot extricate itself. Investors fear suspension or (more likely) modification of payment on its public debt , and therefore sell its bonds. Its bond prices start to plummet. Banks holding those bonds find their capital impaired, inciting depositor runs. Bond markets (and indirectly banks) in other EMU countries suffer adverse repercussions, as investors in public debt of other European states become demoralized. To prevent the collapse of Europe's banking and financial system, the ECB buys up the bonds of the government in distress. As the costs are being borne by the residents of the EMU zone as a whole rather than the citizens of the responsible country, governments have an incentive to run riskier policies in the first place, and investors have less reason to apply market discipline.

This scenario is more than hypothetical: in 1994–5 something similar occurred in Mexico (see Box 1). But is it relevant to Europe? Recent debt problems, not just in Mexico but in Thailand, South Korea and elsewhere, suggest that the monetary authorities (the ECB in Europe, the IMF in the broader international context) come under intense pressure to extend a debt bailout when two conditions hold: debt problems place the banking system at risk; and they threaten to spread contagiously to other national markets.[4] Banks are the weak link in the chain of macroeconomic and financial stability: their core business, maturity transformation, renders them

---

[3] The point is arguable because other pact provisions, such as medium-term surveillance and the precise conditions under which a deficit will be found as excessive, will apply to EU countries whether or not in EMU.

[4] The probability of bailouts is further enhanced by serious imbalances in the vertical structure of taxation and spending, when the centre collects the taxes but subcentral governments receive transfers and do the spending. This works against the likelihood of a debt bailout in Europe, where member states collect the bulk of their own taxes, and where transfers from the EU remain relatively small. We develop these points further in Box 2.

illiquid. Operating in an environment of asymmetric information, they are vulnerable to runs when depositors lack confidence. The Great Depression reminds us that widespread bank failures can have serious macroeconomic repercussions. Contagion provides major motivation for IMF intervention in countries like

---

Box 1. Should Stability Pact proponents fear that Europe will be another Mexico?

A precedent for the bailout scenario feared by European policy-makers is the Mexican crisis of 1994–5 (for an overview and analysis on which we draw, see Sachs *et al.*, 1995). That episode points to four factors that magnify bailout risk. First, a significant share of Mexican public debt, the notorious *tesobonos*, was foreign-currency indexed. Since the Bank of Mexico could not print dollars and was committed to holding the exchange rate within a band, once investors began selling its bonds, the Mexican government was in the same predicament as a member of a monetary union. It could purchase what was being sold only in so far as it possessed dollar reserves. Since its reserves were limited, it had to solicit a bailout from the USA and the IMF.

Second, much of Mexico's debt was short term. The *tesobonos* and their domestic-currency equivalents, *cetes*, ran only 30, 60 or 90 days to maturity. Not only did the government have to service its debts, but it had to redeem a significant quantity if investors failed to roll them over. Since it lacked the dollars to do so and might print pesos to finance redemptions, the spectre of inflation loomed. Doubts about the government's willingness or ability to service its debts could therefore ignite a run.

Third, significant quantities of public debt were held by the Mexican banking system, whose stability was critical for the macroeconomy. The outbreak of the crisis was followed immediately by withdrawals by domestic and foreign depositors. Fear of collapse of the banking system was a powerful motive for the rescue by the USA and IMF.

Fourth, there were fears of contagion. The Mexican crisis led to extensive reserve losses and deposit withdrawals in Argentina and repercussions as far afield as Thailand, Hong Kong and Sweden. US officials cited danger of contagion and systemic risk as a rationale for the Mexican bailout.

Each of these points has an analogy in EMU. National central banks will be mere operating arms of the ECB, unable to print euros. Some candidates for EMU have significant amounts of short-term debt, held in important part by the banking system. And as European banking systems and financial markets more generally become increasingly integrated and interdependent, worries of contagion will grow.

Box 2. Sooner or later? When will bailout risk be greatest?

At what stage in the construction of EMU will bailout risk be greatest? McKinnon (1996) suggests it will be most intense at the start; von Hagen and Eichengreen (1996) argue that bailout risk will be least at the outset.

McKinnon's conclusion follows from assuming that bailout risk is minimized when four conditions are met:

- *monetary separation* (the government neither owns nor controls the central bank). Monetary separation hardens budget constraints, discouraging governments from recklessly accumulating debts.
- *fiscal separation* (little co-mingling of revenues of different levels of government, so lower levels of government cannot expect additional transfers from higher levels when they overspend). When lower levels of government receive transfers, their budget constraints are softened, and they may be tempted to run reckless fiscal policies.
- *factor mobility*, intensifying tax competition and limiting the size of the public sector. This, in McKinnon's view, will limit the size of the public sector debts that member states accumulate.[5]
- *low debt/GNP ratios*, so that governments do not pressurize the monetary authorities to use the inflation tax on optimal-taxation grounds.[6]

The first three conditions will be met from the outset. The single market, by encouraging factor mobility, will intensify tax competition. No national government will have its own central bank. Revenue sharing will be minimal. If there is bailout risk, it will arise from failure to meet the final condition, a failure that will be most egregious in the short run. This implies that the need for the Stability Pact is most pressing in the early years of EMU but less so subsequently (when debt overhangs have been removed).

Von Hagen and Eichengreen emphasize that bailout risk will depend on the vertical structure of the tax base: in other words, on the extent to which subcentral – in the context of EMU, member state – governments collect their own taxes versus relying on transfers from the centre. Contrast two situations. In scenario A, all taxes are raised by a central government that provides grants to subcentral governments. If a subcentral government experiences difficulties, its

Continued

[5] The counterargument, which we regard as more plausible, is that tax competition will put downward pressure on revenues, but its impact on expenditure may be less than one for one. For this reason it may be associated with larger deficits and debts, not smaller ones.

[6] A clear analysis of how high debt burdens lead governments to press for use of the inflation tax in the Ramsey model is De Grauwe (1996).

Box 2. *continued*

only options are to default or obtain a bailout. If default is not politically palatable, then a bailout will be forthcoming. A subcentral government that knows this will have an incentive to run risky policies.

In scenario B, subcentral governments control their own taxes. If they experience difficulties, they can be asked to raise the tax rates they control, reinforcing their financial position. Since in this case there exists a lower-cost alternative to default, the central bank can credibly promise not to provide a bailout.[7]

It follows that pressure for a bailout will be intense in the early years of EMU. The European Union lacks a highly developed system of fiscal federalism. Its budget is small, and the vast majority is earmarked for the common agricultural policy and Structural Funds (leaving it unavailable for treating debt- and deficit-related problems). The member states control the taxes levied on their citizens. This will give national governments a third, low-cost, alternative to default and bailout: namely, adjusting their own tax rates to redress their own financial problems. The ECB, aware of the existence of this third alternative, should be able to resist the pressure for a bailout.

Eventually there may develop pressure for a European system of fiscal federalism to smooth the operation of the monetary union, in which case the vertical structure of the tax base will be transformed and with it the severity of bailout risk. But this is a long-run prospect. Thus, in contrast to McKinnon, who sees bailout risk as most intense in the short run, von Hagen and Eichengreen and the present authors see it as more pressing later.

Correctly choosing between these models is important, for erroneously accepting one could aggravate the very problems forecast by the other. Say that one accepts McKinnon's interpretation and adopts strict limits on fiscal policy. If member states are then prevented from operating their automatic fiscal stabilizers in response to business-cycle disturbances, they will press the EU to do so for them. They will lobby for an expanded EU budget with automatic-stabilization capacity and transfers from the EU to the member states. Ultimately this could lead to precisely the bailout problem about which the proponents of the Stability Pact are so concerned.

---

[7] Von Hagen and Eichengreen test this hypothesis by estimating a probit regression on cross-country data for 1985–7. The presence or absence of fiscal restrictions on subcentral governments, which will be needed where bailout risk is most intense, is modelled as a function of the share of subcentral government spending financed out of own taxes. (Per-capita income is also included as a control.) The results confirm that the vertical structure of taxation matters for the incidence of fiscal restrictions and by implication for bailout risk.

Mexico, Thailand and South Korea; if a crisis in one country has major international externalities that national policy-makers have little incentive to internalize, there is an obvious argument for multilateral intervention (in the European case, by the ECB).

We take seriously the rationale for the Stability Pact based on the spectre of an inflationary debt bailout. But the Maastricht Treaty already contains a no-bailout rule that prohibits the ECB from purchasing public debt directly from the issuer. To justify reinforcing this rule with a Stability Pact, it is necessary to show that the factors heightening bailout risk – threats to the banking system and bond market contagion – will operate in EMU: in other words, that the risks to Europe's banking system and bond markets are sufficiently intense that the ECB will be unable to resist importuning by heavily indebted countries. We provide evidence on these questions below.

3.2. To neutralize inflationary pressure more generally

A second popular rationale for the Stability Pact is to offset other sources of inflationary pressure. The ECB, concerned to maximize economic efficiency, will seek to balance the deadweight cost of the inflation tax against the deadweight cost of other taxes. Where the total resources required by the public sector are large, all taxes, including the inflation tax, will be high. If governments of EMU countries run large deficits and accumulate high debts, the ECB will permit more inflationary monetary policies to reduce the deadweight losses associated with *other* taxes. Since product and factor market taxes fall on the residents of each country, while the inflation tax will be shifted to the residents of the whole euro zone, national incentives to run deficits will be increased by EMU membership.

This analysis, as in De Grauwe (1996), presupposes that the ECB will be simply a Stackelberg follower to the fiscal lead of different member governments. However, there are convincing reasons to think that the ECB will not act as a myopic follower of fiscal fashion, but will engage in a repeated game in which it seeks to convince governments and markets of the credibility of its commitment to price stability. It will keep inflation low even if this means that other taxes have to be higher.[8] Governments, finding the deadweight loss of taxation to be higher, may then pursue lower government spending. They will be Stackelberg followers, not leaders.

Thus, there is good reason to think that any inflation bias in ECB policies produced on optimal taxation grounds will be small. This is a weak reed, hardly first order in magnitude, on which to rest any justification for the Stability Pact.

---

[8] If EMU members appoint independent central bankers who attach overriding importance to the goal of price stability, even a myopic ECB will be reluctant to trade off higher inflation tax revenue for reductions in distortions from other sources of tax revenue.

3.3. To offset political bias towards excessive deficits

A third widely voiced rationale for the Stability Pact is to offset Europe's bias towards excessive deficits (Beetsma and Uhlig, 1997). Years of deficit spending have saddled governments with debt/GDP ratios in excess of 70%. High debts make the public finances more fragile, reduce the effectiveness of monetary policy (Giavazzi *et al.*, 1997), increase fiscal crowding out (since additional government spending, by raising interest rates, thereby raises debt service costs), raise the deadweight cost of taxation, and make funding social security liabilities more difficult.

The solution is to move Europe's budgets towards balance sufficiently to stabilize the debt/income ratio or to allow it to decline. Thus, the Stability Pact sees Europe's budgets as broadly balanced or in modest surplus in expansions, with deficits widening to as much as 3% of GDP in contractions. With real GDP growing at 2–3% per year, this should suffice for debt/income ratios to fall over the medium run.

The obvious objection to this rationale for the Stability Pact is that it suppresses the symptoms without eradicating the disease. If EU policy-makers fail to remove the underlying disorder – identified by the 'institutional school'[9] as excessively decentralized fiscal procedures that aggravate free-rider problems – then imposing numerical caps on budget deficits only encourages devious behaviour to meet the letter but not the spirit of the law. We need only note the operation of the Excessive Deficit Procedure. While some progress has been made in curbing deficits in Stage II, the EDP has also encouraged fiscal fiddles like refundable 'euro taxes', sales of central bank gold reserves and one-off appropriations of public enterprise reserves. It remains to be seen how much recent progress is sustainable. Pessimists (including one of the authors) worry that, in the absence of an effective remedy for the underlying disorder, 'Maastricht fatigue' will set in once countries are admitted to EMU, as refundable euro taxes are refunded and, more generally, as countries previously forced to suck in their stomachs to squeeze into Maastricht's tightly tailored trousers then expel their breath violently.[10]

However, suppressing the symptoms is standard practice when the disease is untreatable. Doctors administer powerful pain-killers to patients with untreatable cancers. If excessive deficits can be prevented only by using the EU's authority to impose a credible external constraint, there is no reason not to try.

3.4. To internalize international interest rate spillovers

Another popular justification for the Stability Pact is to internalize the cross-border interest rate spillovers associated with uncoordinated fiscal policies. Policy-makers,

---

[9] See Alesina and Perotti (1994), von Hagen and Harden (1994) and Alesina *et al.* (1995).
[10] See Eichengreen (1997).

in this view, have inadequate incentive to take into account the impact of their borrowing on interest rates in other member states when formulating their national fiscal policies. The Excessive Deficit Procedure and the Stability Pact offset this bias. However, European countries borrow in global not national financial markets: it is unclear how fiscal policy in Italy and Spain has significant effects on interest rates in Germany or France.

Even if they did, in the absence of other distortions, changes in interest rates are purely redistributive. They redistribute income from debtors to creditors, within and across EU states. Table 1 suggests that higher interest rates would mean redistribution from the Nordic countries, Spain and Italy towards Germany and the Benelux countries. Ironically, core members of the future EMU should be the last countries to worry about redistributive effects of high interest rates! In any case, in so far as these externalities are pecuniary, they do not warrant intervention on standard efficiency grounds (Buiter *et al.*, 1993).

Of course, in the presence of other distortions, such as rigid wages, changes in interest rates can have cross-border effects on the level of output and employment. But these are unlikely to be significant, not least because two effects substantially offset one another: deficit spending at home boosts the demand for imports and therefore output and employment in neighbouring countries, but also drives up interest rates and therefore depresses output and employment abroad. The two effects roughly cancel out (Oudiz and Sachs, 1984).

At this stage, this case for the pact is unproven: we return to the evidence in section 6.

3.5. To encourage policy co-ordination

A fifth argument for the pact invokes the advantages of policy co-ordination in an integrated Europe. It is desirable both that national fiscal policies be co-ordinated (as explained in section 3.3) and that monetary and fiscal policies be co-ordinated with one another. A bad policy mix of loose fiscal policy and tight monetary policy may lead to high real interest rates, low investment, a chronically overvalued exchange rate and slow growth (Debrun, 1997). Medium-term surveillance under the pact will serve the useful purpose of focusing European governments' attention on the need for a balanced policy mix.

Not only do most studies of policy co-ordination suggest, however, that the

Table 1. Net foreign assets, 1994 (% of GDP)

Sweden	−57	Austria	−12	Germany	10
Finland	−56	Italy	−11	Belgium	11
Denmark	−29	France	−7	Netherlands	26
Spain	−20	UK	−2		

benefits are slight, but numerical deficit limits like those of the Stability Pact are far from an ideal basis for encouraging policy co-ordination. By limiting the flexibility of national fiscal policies, they may actually impede efforts to co-ordinate policies. In the long run, the non-cooperative equilibrium in recessions is as likely to be inadequately expansionary budgets as excessively expansionary budgets, with European countries failing to take into account the locomotive effects of their deficit spending on neighbouring states (much like the states of the USA). Numerical deficit ceilings are the wrong instrument for addressing the general problem. If the Stability Pact is seen as a way of putting flesh on the bones of the Mutual Surveillance Procedure of the Maastricht Treaty (Art. 103, under which the Council develops guidelines for the economic policies of member states, monitors their performance and issues recommendations), then it is misguided.

3.6. Summing up

The most compelling rationale for the Stability Pact rests on the need to buttress the no-bailout rule of the Maastricht Treaty. That need will be most pressing where debt problems place banking systems at risk and where bond market contagion is pervasive. It is to these questions that we therefore turn.

4. WOULD A DEBT RUN DESTABILIZE EUROPE'S BANKING SYSTEM?

Imagine a heavily indebted government, which, unable to borrow in the markets and subject to the no-bailout rule for the ECB and EU institutions, has to default. Its bond prices collapse, causing a loss of asset values for commercial banks holding this debt. Fears that banks are at risk triggers runs by depositors (King, 1997). Although this crisis originates in one country, banks in other countries are linked by the interbank market, and by payments and settlement systems. In the worst-case scenario, banking panic infects much of Europe, leading the ECB to monetize debt to prevent a meltdown.

EMU membership may alter the incentives of governments in undesirable ways. When rescue operations are conducted by national central banks, the domestic taxpayer ultimately foots the bill. Within EMU the burden will be borne by EMU taxpayers. In effect, the defaulting country will obtain a transfer from its fellow EMU members. This ability to 'shift the bill' provides a perverse incentive to run risky policies. The role of the Stability Pact, in this view, is to limit moral hazard.

How likely is a debt crisis to infect the banking system? How exposed are banks to public debt? Data on public debt holdings by banks are hard to obtain. Table 2 shows data for 1992. We focus on national public debt as a share of bank assets (in the first panel), although the picture is essentially the same when we consider bank holdings of public debt as a percentage of GDP (in the second panel). The share of public debt in bank portfolios tends to be higher where the government is heavily

Table 2. Bank exposure to national public debt (NPD) and real estate loans (REL), 1992

Bank holdings	% of bank assets		% of GDP		% of public debt		Memo item: Public debt as % of GDP
	NPD	REL	NPD	REL	NPD	REL	
Austria			23		48		52
Finland							39
France	1	14	2	19	5		39
Germany	4		9		31		34
Greece			9		12		105
Ireland	8	6	11	8	12	8	92
Italy	17		20		19		106
Netherlands			11		17		62
Norway	2	32	1	25	42	108	23
Spain	12	14	17	20	42	48	41
Sweden	2	35	3	71	8	160	67
Switzerland		29		72			16
UK	1	10	2	24	3	70	34

Notes: For Ireland real estate is personal house mortgage finance; for Sweden data concern all credit institutions. Final column refers to central government debt.
Source: National central banks; government statistical yearbooks.

indebted, as in Italy and the Netherlands, although there are exceptions to the rule. [11]

How much public debt is too much? One comparison is with house price fluctuations in the late 1980s and early 1990s, exposure to which created serious problems for European financial institutions; in Nordic countries it forced governments to rescue the banks. Table 2 compares bank exposure to real estate loans with bank exposure to public debt. By this measure, exposure to public debt is not obviously a problem. At the time of the Nordic crisis in 1992, the BIS estimates that the share of bad loans in banks' portfolios was 7.7% in Finland, 8.3% in Sweden and 9.3% in Norway (BIS, 1993). Suppose we conclude that the loss of 5% of bank assets was enough to cause severe distress and force the authorities to intervene. [12] Were a government fully to default on its debt, exposure of 5% or more would be dangerous. Of course, governments rarely repudiate their debts; more typically they restructure, limiting capital losses for bondholders. Even if the capital loss associated with restructuring were 50% of the face value of the debt, only bank exposure in excess of 10% would be dangerous. By this measure, only Italy and Spain face significant risk of bank failure for debt-related reasons.

Debt default could still be a problem if the banks' customers rather than the banks themselves hold the bulk of the debt. Default might incite households and

[11] Central government debt is 12% of bank assets in Spain and 8% in Ireland, yet such debt is 105% of GDP in Ireland, but only 23% in Spain.
[12] These are averages for all banks (for more details, see Dalheim *et al.*, 1992).

non-bank firms holding bonds to scramble for liquidity, and the ensuing withdrawal of deposits might create liquidity problems. It is instructive to consider the response of the Federal Reserve to the collapse of stock prices in 1929 and again in 1987. In both instances monetary policy was eased *despite* the fact that US financial institutions directly held only small amounts of stock. The Fed's fear on both occasions was that financial distress would lead to defaults by brokers and other bank customers that would impair the capital position of the banks. In both cases, however, the liquidity injected into the financial system was smoothly withdrawn once the crisis passed; the consequences were deflationary, not inflationary.[13] Similarly, banking crises in Sweden, Norway and Finland and serious problems for the banking system in France, Spain and Switzerland were all associated with deflation, not inflation, despite pervasive intervention by governments to rescue the banking system.

5. WOULD DEFAULT BY AN EMU MEMBER DEMORALIZE EMU BOND MARKETS?

A second channel through which debt problems in one jurisdiction can spill over to another is contagion in the bond market itself. If information is asymmetric, one debtor's default may lead investors to revise downwards their expectations of maintenance of debt service by others. Debtors will find themselves having to accept higher yields to place new issues or to induce investors to roll over maturing ones. In so far as adverse consequences follow for the entire European bond market and not just the market in assets of the country in which the problem originates, pressure for the ECB to head off the problem will be intense.

This seems unlikely in Europe. Compared, say, to Latin America, information about governments' willingness and ability to pay is relatively complete. It is unlikely that default or near default by one EMU country will *per se* lead investors to sharply higher expectations of default in another. This is logically distinct from the question of what might *cause* debt problems in an EMU country (election of a fiscally irresponsible politician, an asymmetric shock or an asymmetric response to a common shock); here we are concerned not with the causes of default, but with the scope for contagion.

From this point of view, a good analogy for post-EMU Europe may be the US market in state and municipal bonds. Not only is information relatively complete,[14]

---

[13] Subsequent research has found no role for fiscal profligacy in either crisis; indeed, scholarly accounts of the Great Depression blame excessively contractionary monetary policy. Neither suggests that a stability pact would have been helpful.

[14] Especially in so far as tax advantages lead the vast majority of a state's bonds to be held by its residents, who are in a good position to monitor the state's economy and government.

but the USA is also a monetary union and individual states lack individual central banks to underpin their bond markets. The US market for state bonds has been analysed extensively: Goldstein and Woglom (1994) and Bayoumi *et al.* (1995) have studied yield spreads on state bonds issued between 1981 and the 1990s.

An objection to the use of these state and municipal data is that they pertain to lightly indebted governments. Both because 49 of the 50 state governments operate subject to statutory and constitutional fiscal constraints of varying severity and because their tax bases are relatively mobile, they have a limited capacity to incur and support high volumes of debt. Gross state debt to gross state product ratios are around 3%, far below the 70% debt ratio that characterizes the EU. Without substantial debts, US states have not experienced substantial debt problems; one would not expect to observe contagion. Yet US states rely on a smaller tax base than the European governments. Table 3 shows statistics on the ratio of public debts to the tax base (approximated by public spending). The difference between the two sets of governments remain sizeable, but less than the debt/income ratios.

While this objection has merit, US data are the only game in town. Nor is it true that statutory and constitutional restrictions prevented states and municipalities from running into trouble – recall New York City in the 1970s and Orange County in the 1990s. US states might have light debt loads, but having highly mobile tax bases, they also have limited capacity to raise taxes once a fiscal problem arises. Bayoumi *et al.* (1995) estimate that states get rationed out of the capital market when their debt/gross state product ratios approach 9%.

5.1. Event-study analysis

If contagion is present in a bond market like the USA, it may be a danger in post-EMU Europe. We therefore look for evidence that state-specific interest rate shocks have indeed been transmitted to neighbouring US states. Ideally, the original shock should be large, exogenous and state specific. We identified the ten largest changes in annual yield spreads (i.e., those at least two standard deviations above the mean change).[15] All spreads are defined relative to the yield on New Jersey's general

Table. 3 Public debt as % of public spending

	Average	Minimum	Maximum
51 US states (1990)	15	3	41
EU14 (1996)	158	102	250

Note: EU14 is without Luxembourg.
Sources: Bayoumi *et al.* (1995) and OECD.

[15] Alabama, Michigan, Minnesota, Rhode Island, Washington and Wisconsin in 1982, New Hampshire in 1983, Texas in 1986, Louisiana in 1987 and Massachusetts in 1990.

obligation bonds, since this is how they are provided by the source. In most cases we were able to identify events leading to extraordinary increases in yields. Some of these were plausibly exogenous (the effect of the downturn in the auto industry on Michigan in 1982, the effect of falling oil prices on Louisiana in 1987). But neither the recession of the early 1980s nor the oil price decline of the late 1980s had effects limited to an individual state. For these, sympathetic increases in bond yields elsewhere could reflect that common shock rather than contagion *per se*.

One case where the shock was large, exogenous to the bond market *and* plausibly state specific was Washington State in 1982, where a major power district ran into serious trouble, servicing bonds issued for the construction of nuclear power plants (see Box 3). We concentrated on this case. We re-estimated the equations of Bayoumi *et al.* (1995), explaining the determinants of yield spreads to control for observable economic and demographic characteristics of states, and examined the residuals.[16] Washington State had a large positive residual of 57 basis points in 1982. There was also a large positive residual for Oregon (20 basis points), consistent with contagion, even after controlling for changes in the debt burden,

---

Box 3. Whoops! Washington State under nuclear stress

The 1982 shock to the Washington State bond market emanated from problems with servicing the obligations of the Washington Public Power Supply System (WPPSS). While these were not general obligation bonds, they represented one of the largest US bond defaults in history, and there was considerable uncertainty for a time about whether the state would assume responsibility for these obligations. WPPSS had been established in 1957 by a consortium of some two dozen small municipal utilities, whose initial goal was to build a hydroelectric plant and a steam generating plant, among other projects, to serve the member utilities. In 1970 WPPSS made a huge leap in scale and technology, beginning construction of five nuclear power plants. The small utilities involved had no experience of large-scale power projects, much less nuclear power. By the early 1980s they had incurred enormous cost overruns. In 1982 the bonds issued to finance the construction of Nuclear Units 4 and 5 lapsed into default. The event found immediate reflection in the yields on Washington State's bonds. These increased by more than 70 basis points between 1981 and 1982, in the single largest increase in the ten-year sample.

---

[16] Bayoumi *et al.* (1995) relate the observed yield spread to the level of debt (as a percentage of gross state product, or GSP), the taxation of state bonds, the rate of unemployment and the strength of constitutional controls on state borrowing.

unemployment, tax rates and so forth. But several other states also had positive residuals in 1982 at least as large as Oregon's, including Delaware, Florida, Massachusetts, Michigan, Minnesota and Rhode Island; it is hard to see why any of them should have been especially strongly affected by difficulties in Washington State.

Other, unobservable, characteristics of states influencing yields could conceivably account for these patterns. To control for unobservables that are constant over time, we examined the *change* in the residuals from the yield spreads equation between 1981 and 1982. While the increase in the residual from the spreads equation is large and positive for Washington (51 basis points), it is now *negative* for Oregon. Positive increases of at least 25 basis points in the residual were also observed in Minnesota, Michigan and Rhode Island; decreases of at least 25 basis points in Pennsylvania as well as Oregon. As a final test, we examined states other than Washington that were also constructing nuclear power plants. Again the results were negative: there were neither unusually large residuals nor unusually large changes in the residuals in such states in 1982. Nothing in this analysis provides much evidence of interstate contagion.

5.2. Econometric analysis

To analyse contagion in the US state and municipal bond market more systematically, we re-estimated the Bayoumi *et al.* model, adding a measure of interest rate shocks in 'economically contiguous states'.[17] If the coefficient on the relevant measure of economic contiguity, when interacted with interest rates in neighbouring states, is positive, we have evidence of contagion. The critical step, obviously, is to measure economic proximity, the economic neighbours from which interest rate spillovers are most likely to spread. We consider a variety of specifications, appending them to Bayoumi *et al.*'s basic specification (column (1) of Table 4). In this basic specification, the spread increases with the ratio of debt to gross state product (heavier debt burdens increasing default risk), declines with the highest marginal tax rate in the state (a higher tax rate creating a captive market for bonds, income on which is tax exempt for local investors), rises with the state unemployment rate (in so far as this implies less tax capacity) and falls with the stringency of self-imposed fiscal restrictions (which imply less debt accumulation in the future). All four regressors included in the basic specification are significant at conventional confidence levels.[18]

---

[17] Bayoumi *et al.* are concerned with non-linearities in the relationship between spreads and the level of debt; but while their non-linear specification allows them to capture the possibility of credit rationing, it also introduces instability into the model. We therefore focused on a linear version of their preferred specification. The basic results turn out to be quite similar to those of Bayoumi *et al.*
[18] We also estimated, but do not report, the constant term and a vector of dummy variables for years.

Table 4. Bond market contagion in US states

	Baseline	Similarity: debt/GSP	Similarity: Federal aid	Similarity: govt size	Similarity: fiscal restraints		
					$N<6$	$N<7$	$N<10$
	(1)	(2)	(3)	(4)	(5)	(6)	(7)
Debt	7.5	13.5	7.5	7.7	3.8	8.3	5.4
	(4.4)	(2.5)	(4.3)	(4.6)	(1.3)	(3.2)	(2.7)
Tax	−2.2	−3.0	−1.6	−2.1	−1.8	−3.2	−1.3
	(2.0)	(2.0)	(1.4)	(1.9)	(1.3)	(2.7)	(1.0)
Unemployment	5.8	6.2	6.3	5.8	6.6	6.1	5.7
	(8.8)	(8.3)	(9.1)	(8.3)	(7.0)	(9.3)	(8.4)
Fiscal restraints	−3.5	−3.7	−3.7	−3.4	4.4	−7.2	−6.7
	(8.3)	(8.0)	(8.4)	(7.9)	(1.5)	(4.7)	(5.8)
Economic similarity		−0.8	−0.6	0.1	2.6	−1.0	−1.0
		(1.2)	(1.8)	(0.4)	(2.7)	(2.4)	(2.0)
SER	19.2	20.8	20.1	19.1	20.7	22.9	20.7

Notes: t-statistics in parentheses. Debt is debt/GSP. Tax is highest marginal tax rate in states that impose different tax rates on in-state and out-of-state bonds. Fiscal restraint indexed from 0 (none) to 10 (maximum). Unemployment and fiscal restraints treated as exogenous. Estimated by 2SLS using as instruments: average household size, population, change in population, proportion of young and old, trend GSP. All statistics computed with White heteroscedastic consistent procedure. 380 observations.
Source: Bayoumi *et al.* (1995) pooled time series (1981–95) over 33 US states.

In the first of our augmented regressions (column (2)), we assume that interest rate spillovers are most likely to spread from states with similar debt burdens (as a share of gross state product): markets may interpret higher debt costs in one state as a signal of impending difficulties in states with similar debt levels. For each state in each year, we calculate the average yield in the four states with the most similar debt burdens, taking the two states just below and the two states ranked just above, using the debt/GDP ranking. We treat the average spread in these neighbouring states as endogenous to reflect common shocks as well as spillovers from a state to its neighbours. In column (2) the coefficient on 'economic similarity', having the wrong sign and being insignificantly different from zero, lends no support to the hypothesis of contagion.

In column (3) we consider a second definition of economic proximity based on federal aid per capita received. We apply the same procedure as for debt (selecting the two states immediately above and the two immediately below, using this ranking). Again we fail to detect significant contagion. The same result obtains using a third definition of proximity: the size of the state government measured as the ratio of state spending to GSP, in column (4).

Columns (5)–(7) focus on institutional constraints on fiscal policies, specifically the stringency of statutory and constitutional balanced-budget and debt-limitation provisions. The hypothesis, which seems plausible a priori, is that states are most subject to contagion from other states that use similar institutional procedures to formulate their fiscal policies, since such states would be expected to respond similarly to similar disturbances. Bayoumi *et al.* (1995) utilize an index of the stringency of institutional restraints on fiscal policy constructed by the Advisory Commission on Intergovernmental Relations (discussed further in Eichengreen, 1990), which ranges from 1 to 10 in increasing order of severity. Unfortunately, states are not uniformly distributed over this interval. Of the 38 states in Bayoumi *et al.*'s sample, seventeen have the maximum score of 10, while another seven have a ranking of 8 or 9. Hence, using the same procedure as before to identify states would yield indeterminate or arbitrary results. We therefore consider states only with rankings N and below, assigning a value of zero for states ranked above, and then we allow N to take several values from 5 to 9.

The results are in columns (5) to (7). For $N = 5$, we detect some evidence of contagion via our economic similarity measure, but for larger values of N the effect is negative not positive: higher yield spreads in states with similar budgetary institutions lead to lower yields in states with similar fiscal arrangements, as if the markets, when they grow concerned by a state's finances, shift their holdings so as to maintain a balanced portfolio of risks.

We also investigated whether there is contagion between 'politically similar' states.[19] We define political proximity by the party affiliation of the governor, and construct a proximity dummy that takes a value of 1 when two governors are both Democrats or both Republicans (and zero otherwise). We then multiply the previous economic proximity variables by this dummy. Since rerunning the regressions in Table 4, replacing economic proximity by the above measure of economic and political proximity, made little difference to the broad pattern of results, we do not report these results separately. Indeed, in the few cases in which proximity variables that had previously been insignificant now became significant, their sign was *negative*, again suggesting *portfolio diversification* rather than *contagion*. The experience of US states provides no evidence to justify European-wide fiscal restraints to protect against contagious bond market crises.

6. WOULD EXCESSIVE DEFICITS PUSH UP EMU INTEREST RATES?

In EMU, within which capital is mobile, borrowing by one country is likely to have only a small effect on EMU interest rates: European countries borrow on global capital markets, relative to which they are individually small. Even if a country's actions raise its own interest rates – for example, through a larger risk premium – there is little reason (contagion apart) why this should imply substantial cross-border spillovers.

---

[19] Note that we condition political proximity on economic proximity. Unconditional political proximity is unlikely to be a sharp classification if about half the governors are Democrats and the other half are Republicans.

6.1. Evidence from the financial markets

The ideal way to verify this hypothesis would be to build a structural model of savings and investment for each European country, taking account of the influence of both domestic and foreign variables, and distinguishing rest-of-Europe and rest-of-world magnitudes. This is ambitious to say the least. Here we take the simpler tack of estimating the reduced-form relationship between interest rates, asking whether interest rates in a particular European country are affected mainly by own values, rest-of-Europe values or rest-of-world values.

The straightforward way of implementing this analysis is with Granger causality tests. Two prior decisions that must be made are what countries and what interest rates to analyse. But no one would be surprised if our results showed that interest rates in Luxembourg were affected by interest rates in the rest of the world and in the rest of Europe, but that interest rates in Luxembourg affected those in neither the rest of Europe nor the rest of the world. We therefore bias the results against our own hypothesis by considering the impact of rest-of-world and rest-of-Europe interest rates on Germany, and the impact of German interest rates on those of the rest of the world and the rest of Europe.

Similarly, if the analysis concerned itself with co-movements in short-term interest rates, no one would be surprised if we found evidence of Granger causality running in both directions, since these timing relationships could reflect not just market spillovers but also the induced policy reaction of central banks, which use short-term interest rates as policy instruments (Wyplosz, 1990). We therefore focus on the behaviour of long-term interest rates, whose co-movements are less likely to be dominated by induced central bank reactions and are more likely to convey information about market spillovers.[20]

Table 5. Causality tests on long-term interest rates, 1973:1 to 1997:5

	Germany causes Europe?	Germany causes ROW?	Europe causes Germany?	Europe causes ROW?	ROW causes Germany?	ROW causes Europe?
F-statistic	1.9	1.4	2.2	2.0	3.2	2.4
Probability (%)	3.9	14.4	1.3	2.8	0.0	0.7

Notes: Tests with 12 lags (choice implied by Akaike and Schwartz criteria). Europe is GDP-weighted average of Austria, Belgium, Denmark, France, Ireland, Italy, Netherlands, Spain, UK. Rest of the world (ROW) is weighted average of Canada, Japan and USA.
Source: IMF, *International Financial Statistics.*

---

[20] Since long rates are an average of the current and expected future short rates, this does not eliminate the possibility that the correlations we pick up are in part central bank reactions, but it should minimize that possibility.

We used monthly data, current and lagged up to twelve months, on treasury bond rates for Germany, the rest of Europe (a weighted average of nine European countries listed in the note to Table 5, weighted by 1985 GDP) and the world (proxied by interest rates for the USA, Canada and Japan, again weighted by 1985 GDP). At the 1% level, we can reject all spillovers except that rest-of-world interest rates affect European interest rates and that rest-of-world interest rates affect German interest rates: once we control for world interest rates, innovations in German rates do not affect interest rates in the rest of Europe, and innovations in rest-of-Europe rates do not affect German rates. The only other relationship that approaches significance at the 1% level is the impact of rest-of-Europe rates on Germany. In each case, then, it is the larger entity whose interest rates affect those of the smaller economy.

These tests confirm that European countries borrow on a global capital market, with only small interest rate spillovers between EMU members. They hardly justify a stability pact to internalize cross-border interest rate spillovers of national fiscal policy.

7. WOULD THE PACT INCREASE THE VOLATILITY OF EMU OUTPUT?

We address this question in two steps. We use retrospective evidence to ask how frequently the Stability Pact would have been binding, and we use counterfactual simulations to estimate how European output would be affected if binding Stability Pact ceilings were imposed. Inevitably this exercise is subject to the Lucas critique: evidence from the past may not be a reliable guide to the future. We go some way towards answering this objection by adjusting historical debt ratios and interest rates to the levels likely to prevail at the outset of EMU, basing our simulations on these adjusted values.

7.1 Retrospective evidence

Figure 1, which shows budget balances for OECD countries since 1955, documents that the 3% barrier has been breached quite frequently.[21] (A similar analysis, reaching the same conclusions, is provided by Buti et al., 1997). Table 6 shows that this has been the case 34% of the time for the OECD as a whole, and 40% of the time in Europe.

Of the 241 cases when the deficit was more than 3% of GDP, in only 7 was the concurrent decline in GDP more than 2%, and in only 28 was it more than 0.75%.

---

[21] The Maastricht Treaty includes a particular definition of deficits that may differ slightly from the data from *International Financial Statistics* used in the figure.

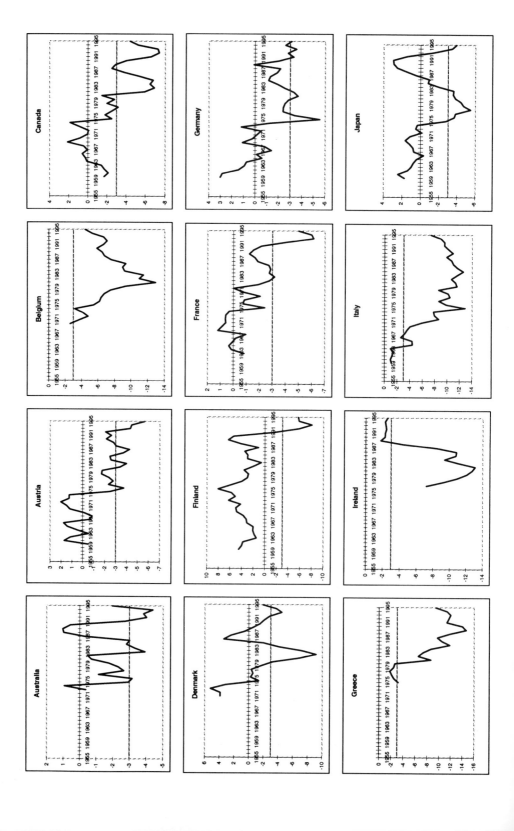

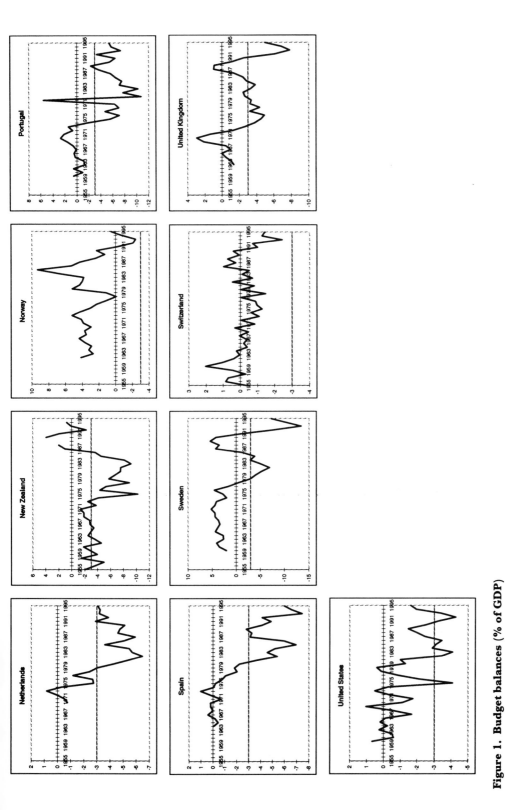

Figure 1. Budget balances (% of GDP)

Source: OECD.

Table 6. Number of times the deficit exceeded 3% of GDP

	Number of years	Total observations	Percentage above 3%	Recession years	
				Above 0.75%	Above 2%
(a) Actual budget (OECD countries, 1955–96)					
Australia	7	23	30.4	1	0
Austria	9	36	25.0	0	0
Belgium	25	26	96.2	3	0
Canada	13	36	36.1	2	1
Denmark	7	36	19.4	1	0
Finland	4	36	11.1	2	1
France	5	33	15.2	1	0
Germany	7	36	19.4	3	0
Greece	16	21	76.2	1	0
Ireland	12	19	63.2	0	0
Italy	30	36	83.3	2	1
Japan	10	36	27.8	0	0
Luxembourg	0	13	0.0	0	0
Netherlands	16	26	61.5	1	0
New Zealand	17	39	43.6	1	1
Norway	0	34	0.0	0	0
Portugal	19	36	52.8	3	1
Spain	14	32	43.8	1	0
Sweden	9	36	25.0	2	1
Switzerland	0	41	0.0	0	0
UK	13	33	39.4	2	0
USA	8	36	22.2	2	1
All countries	241	700	34.4	28	7
EU countries	186	455	40.9	22	4
(b) Budget assuming 1995 debt and 6% interest (1960–95)					
Australia	9	22	40.9	0	0
Austria	12	26	46.2	0	0
Belgium	27	27	100.0	3	0
Canada	21	36	58.3	2	1
Denmark	10	25	40.0	1	0
Finland	4	35	11.4	2	1
France	9	26	34.6	1	0
Germany	21	36	58.3	2	0
Greece	20	21	95.2	1	0
Ireland	13	19	68.4	0	0
Italy	36	36	100.0	1	1
Japan	8	36	22.2	0	0
Luxembourg					
Netherlands	12	26	46.2	1	0
New Zealand					
Norway	0	21	0.0	0	0
Portugal	17	34	50.0	2	1
Spain	18	32	56.3	1	0
Sweden	10	26	38.5	2	1
Switzerland					
UK	12	26	46.2	1	0
USA	17	36	47.2	3	1
All countries	276	546	50.5	23	6
EU countries	221	395	55.9	18	4

Note: Recession years are counted only when the budget deficit exceeds 3% of GDP.
Source: OECD *Economic Outlook.*

Had OECD countries been operating with the Stability Pact, 85% of the deficits that exceeded 3% of GDP would have been judged excessive.[22] Put differently, we can calculate the probability of observing a deficit in excess of 3% of GDP *conditional on* there being no recession. When a recession is defined as a decline in annual real GDP of at least 0.75%, the conditional probability is 32%, rising to 34% when recession is defined as a 2% decline (Table 7). If the past is a guide, we can expect violations every third year. The constraint imposed by the Stability Pact appears even more stringent when we realize that the conditional probability of observing a recession when the budget deficit exceeds 3% is only 12% if the recession corresponds to the 0.75% definition, and 3% for the 2% definition.

One can argue that this record is evidence of the need for constraints to prevent misbehaviour. Indeed, the common interpretation of the Stability Pact is that it will lead member countries to aim at budgets that are on average in balance, or slightly positive. With a budget in surplus at the peak of cycle, it will be possible to use fiscal policy as a counter-cyclical tool. What is wrong with that? A first response – the second one is presented below in section 8 – is that the 'misbehaviour' documented in Table 7 did not have the dramatic inflationary consequences of concern to proponents of the Stability Pact. Average annual inflation for the same sample of countries was a relatively moderate 6% over the period. This 6% may be more inflation than some Europeans would like, but it is hardly the inflationary disaster feared by some EMU-sceptics. Pooling the data for all countries, the partial correlation between inflation and the budget deficit is *negative* (though not significant), contradicting the assumption that deficits are associated with inflation.

Table 7. Conditional probabilities of excessive deficits

Event	Conditional upon	Conditional probability
Using actual budgets 1955–96		
Deficit > 3%	No recession (0.75%)	0.32
Deficit > 3%	No recession (2%)	0.34
Recession (0.75%)	Deficit > 3%	0.12
Recession (2%)	Deficit > 3%	0.03
Assuming 1995 debt level and 6% interest rate		
Deficit > 3%	No recession (0.75%)	0.49
Deficit > 3%	No recession (2%)	0.50
Recession (0.75%)	Deficit > 3%	0.08
Recession (2%)	Deficit > 3%	0.02

Source: Authors' calculations based on Table 6.

---

[22] Our approach does not exactly match the criteria of the Stability Pact which apply to the previous four quarters, since we have to look at calendar years (fiscal data are widely reported only on an annual basis).

7.2. Counterfactual evidence

Can we gauge the consequences of having subjected the European economies to the Stability Pact for the last 30 years? One approach involves estimating, for the four largest countries (France, Germany, Italy and the UK), a simple structural model. The simplest structural macroeconomic model of all, of course, is the textbook model of an upward-sloping aggregate supply curve and a downward-sloping aggregate demand curve in the output–price space. Fiscal policy, among other variables, shifts the demand curve. We measure the fiscal stance by the fiscal impulse, the year-to-year change in the cyclically adjusted budget deficit. This allows us to minimize the risk that an observed correlation between the deficit and output captures the impact of output on the budget, rather than the impact of the budget on output, with which we are concerned. Allowing for some inertia in both relationships, we get the reduced form for output and inflation in Table 8.[23] In order to impose the restriction that fiscal policy has no steady-state effect, we use the output gap and the change in the inflation rate along with the fiscal impulse measure. The output gap and the cyclically adjusted budget are taken from the OECD *Economic Outlook*.

Table 8. Models used for counterfactuals

Coefficient (*t*-statistic)	France		Germany		Italy		UK	
	Output gap	Change in inflation	Output gap	Change in inflation	Output gap	Change in inflation	Output gap	Change in inflation
(Output gap)$_{-1}$	0.87	0.35	0.85	0.42	0.87	0.21	0.89	0.58
	(6.18)	(1.61)	(4.52)	(3.40)	(6.43)	(0.61)	(7.26)	(2.25)
(Inflation change)$_{-1}$	−0.31	−0.02	−0.59	−0.15	−0.13	0.23	−0.15	−0.16
	(2.38)	(0.09)	(1.84)	(0.71)	(1.28)	(0.95)	(1.73)	(0.88)
Fiscal impulse	−0.68	0.09	−0.58	−0.33	−0.43	1.28	0.69	0.51
	(3.03)	(0.26)	(2.11)	(1.79)	(1.73)	(2.52)	(2.03)	(1.07)
Adjusted R^2	0.71	0.43	0.51	0.39	0.74	0.12	0.69	0.26
SER	0.01	0.02	0.02	0.01	0.01	0.03	0.02	0.04

Source: OECD.
Notes: Fiscal impulse is change in cyclically adjusted budget surplus; for France and the UK this variable is contemporaneous; for Germany and Italy it is lagged one period.

[23] Note the parallel between these reduced forms and standard VARs, since output and inflation both depend on their own lagged values. The policy inferences that we make from these equations are subject to standard critiques (see Cochrane, 1994). We finesse some but not all of these objections by using the cyclically adjusted budget as opposed to the actual budget deficit. In addition, we worry about the possibility that the fiscal impulse variable is systematically correlated with monetary policy, thus biasing the estimate of its coefficient. A check is to look for subsample stability. Performing Chow tests with a break in 1985, to account for a change in the policy mix when monetary discipline was introduced in the EMS, we can reject at the 5% confidence level (and in most cases at the 1% confidence level) the hypothesis that the estimates change from one subperiod to the other.

The coefficient on the fiscal impulse shows the impact of the budget on the output gap. This coefficient is similar across our sample, ranging from −0.43 in Italy to −0.68 in France; thus, for each of the four countries, an increase in the cyclically adjusted surplus by 1% of GDP lowers the output gap by roughly 0.5% of GDP.

These equations are used for counterfactual simulations in which the budget deficit is capped at 3%, as if the Stability Pact had been strictly binding. The top row of Figure 2 shows the actual budget balance in our four countries (the solid line) and the counterfactual deficits capped at 3% of GDP (the broken line). French deficits would have been different only in the early 1980s, under the first Mitterrand government, and in the 1990s. German deficits would have been smaller in the wake of the two oil shocks and to a lesser extent following unification. Italy, the high-deficit country in our sample, would have had very much smaller deficits since the early 1970s, while the UK would have had somewhat smaller deficits over the same period, with the exception of the second half of the 1980s.

The bottom row of Figure 2 shows the effect in our estimated model of restricting the budget deficit to a maximum of 3%. It displays the actual output gap (the solid line) and the counterfactual gap from a simulation where the deficits are capped at 3%, as shown in the top row (the broken line). A fair characterization is that Stability Pact ceilings on deficits would have mattered for output, but not dramatically so. (Box 4 discusses the extreme cases.) Table 9 compares the average actual and simulated output gaps. In each country but Germany the output gap is lower when the deficit is capped; while the slowdown is not large, even a fraction of a percentage point on the annual growth rate can become a big effect when it lasts over decades. This is shown by cumulating the gaps over the 22-year period 1974−95: the output losses range from about 5% in France and the UK to 9% in Italy, significantly larger than optimistic estimates of favourable output effects to be expected from EMU. For example, the EU Commission's report *One Market, One Money* (1990) set its central estimate of the gross gains at 9.8% of GDP. Furthermore, in each case but Germany, the variability of output as measured by the standard deviation is higher under the counterfactual. The tempting political-economy inference is that Germany is particularly insistent on a 3% cap on deficits because historically it alone among the four large EU member states would not have suffered too seriously from the imposition!

It can be objected that these simulations do not provide a reliable guide to the future because historical time series do not capture fiscal conditions as they will exist at the beginning of EMU. Simulations and conditional probabilities based on historical data are an imperfect guide to the future because debts are higher now than historically and because (nominal) interest rates will be lower at the start of EMU than over the last twenty years. If we adjust debts and interest rates to levels likely to prevail in 1999 (we use 1995 debt/GDP ratios and nominal interest rates of 6% (2% inflation + 4% real interest), this has the predictable effect of raising the probability of a deficit in excess of 3%. The bottom part of Table 7 showed that,

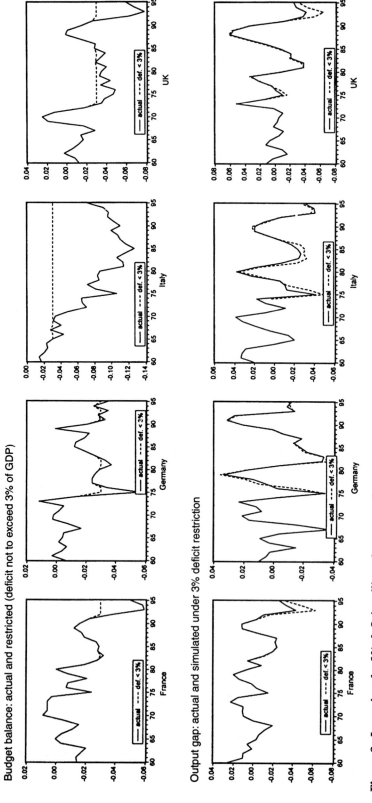

Figure 2. Imposing the 3% deficit ceiling: the counterfactuals

Sources: OECD and authors' calculations.

Table 9. Counterfactuals: the effect of a 3% deficit ceiling, 1974–95

		Actual output gap (%)	Counterfactual output gap (%)	Cumulative output difference (%) by 1995
France	Mean	−0.7	−0.9	−4.7
	Standard deviation	1.7	2.1	
Germany	Mean	−0.3	−0.3	−0.2
	Standard deviation	2.1	2.1	
Italy	Mean	−0.6	−1.1	−9.3
	Standard deviation	2.3	2.4	
UK	Mean	−0.1	−0.3	−4.8
	Standard deviation	3.1	3.5	
Assuming 1995 debt level and 6% interest rate				
France	Mean		−0.8	−2.6
	Standard deviation		2.0	
Germany	Mean		−0.3	1.3
	Standard deviation		2.3	
Italy	Mean		−0.9	−6.7
	Standard deviation		2.5	
UK	Mean		−0.3	−4.9
	Standard deviation		3.5	

Sources: OECD and authors' calculations.

when a recession is defined as a decline in annual real GDP of at least 0.75%, the conditional probability is 49% (up from 32% when historical data are used), rising to 50% (up from 34%) when recession is defined as a 2% decline. This suggests violations every second year.

We can also revisit our simulations under these assumptions. The top row of Figure 3 shows (as a fraction of GDP) the actual budget surplus (solid line) and the counterfactual budget under these assumptions (broken line); predictably, higher debts would have led to larger deficits in the early part of the sample period for France, Germany and Italy. The bottom row of Figure 3 assumes 1995 debt levels and a 6% interest rate, and contrasts the actual output gap (solid line) with the counterfactual simulation under the assumption of a 3% deficit ceiling (broken line). Output losses and increased variability are lower than when actual debt and interest rate levels are used. In Germany, output is actually higher and only slightly more variable. Again, our simulation provides unexpected insight into why Germany is such a strong advocate of the Stability Pact compared to its neighbours.

Had the Stability Pact been in place over previous decades, it would not have had a devastating impact on the level and variability of output. The future, of course, will differ from the past; recessions within EMU may be deeper and more protracted than those of previous decades. Our calculations suggest that they would have to be very much deeper before the Stability Pact began to make a major difference. But if an unusually protracted recession qualifies as a 'special' circumstance, even then the Stability Pact may not bind.

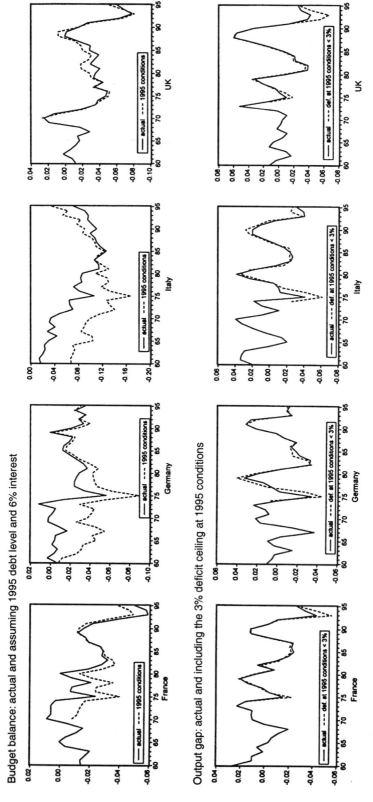

Figure 3. Imposing the 3% deficit ceiling with 1995 debt levels and a 6% interest rate: the counterfactuals

Sources: OECD and authors' calculations.

Box 4. Extreme recessions

Table 6 reveals that, over the 42 years spanning the period 1955–96, recessions deeper than 2% occurred only seven times. These cases are Canada (−3.2% in 1982), Finland (−7.1% in 1991 followed by −3.6% in 1992), Italy (−2.7% in 1975), New Zealand (−2.3% in 1991), Portugal (−4.3% in 1975), Sweden (−2.2% in 1993) and the USA (−2.2% in 1982). Figure 4 shows the average growth rate for these seven cases during the seven years surrounding the bottom of the recession. In all cases but the Nordic countries, these were snap recessions often followed by a rebound the next year. The quick rebound may imply that OECD recessions are typically rare and very short-lived, the impact effect of unusual events (the dates point to the oil shocks and bursting bubbles). Alternatively, it could be that macroeconomic policies have been actively used, and have successfully limited the extent and duration of the recessions. The behaviour of budget balances, however, shows that after three years the deficits are still significantly deeper than before the recession. Would a Stability Pact have prolonged the recession?

One way of dealing with this issue is to perform a counterfactual experiment. Since Italy turns out to be among the deep recession cases, this is shown in Figure 1. The deep recession of 1975 is indeed visible. The simulation suggests that, even if Italy had not been awarded exceptional suspension of the Stability Pact, the output gap would not have been immensely worse.

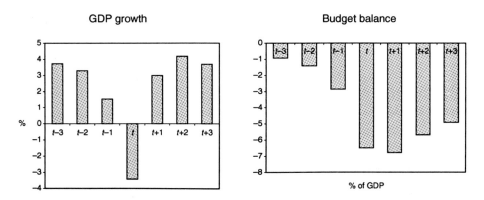

Figure 4. The seven deepest OECD recessions

8. EUROPE'S FISCAL PROSPECTS

Economic outcomes may also influence politics. If the Stability Pact prevents Europe's automatic stabilizers from operating and increases the severity of recessions, it may undermine support for free and open markets. Will member states manage to attain a budgetary position that on average is in balance or even in surplus, thereby leaving scope for customary levels of automatic fiscal stabilization to be provided in recession without triggering penalties under the Stability Pact? The answer comes in two parts: how much endogenous fiscal improvement should be expected as Europe continues to recover from its mid-1990s recession; and how extensive will be the discretionary changes in policy that work to reduce budget deficits further?

8.1. Growing out of deficits

Current OECD estimates for Europe put 1997 budget deficits at 3% of GDP. With potential output rising at between 2 and $2\frac{1}{2}$% per annum, that much growth is required to hold the output gap steady and prevent growing budget deficits. The elasticity of the fiscal balance/GDP ratio with respect to growth is about 0.5% − for every additional percentage point of growth, the deficit ratio falls by half a per cent. The precise elasticity varies with the structure of the national tax and expenditure system, although it tends to be higher in Europe's smaller, more open economies. DG II of the European Commission puts these elasticities at 0.8 for the Netherlands, and 0.5 for Germany and France, with an average of 0.5 for the EU as a whole; OECD estimates are similar. IMF staff estimates suggest somewhat higher average elasticities, of the order of 0.6, with those for Denmark, the Netherlands, Sweden and the UK around 0.75.[24]

For Europe to reduce its budget deficits from 3.0% in 1997 to 2.5 or 2.6% in 1998 (OECD forecasts; see Table 10) without further discretionary changes in fiscal policy, output will have to grow by between 3 and $3\frac{1}{2}$%. As of mid-1997, the OECD forecast for 1998 growth in OECD Europe was 2.7%, the J.P. Morgan forecast 2.9%. The IMF forecast for the EU, released in its September 1997 *World Economic Outlook (WEO)*, split the difference at 2.8%. This is consistent with an average EU deficit ratio of 2.8 or 2.9%, as the *WEO* forecasts. For the OECD forecast of 2.5−2.6% to be right, there will have to be substantial discretionary cuts in public spending or further increases in taxes in 1998.

This implies that, if growth proceeds at the expected pace, Europe will enter

---

[24] 'Box 3: The European Union's Stability and Growth Pact,' *World Economic Outlook* (October 1997). Bayoumi and Eichengreen (1995) put the elasticity at 0.51 for the Netherlands, 0.44 for Germany and 0.41 for France (for consolidated government budgets, including social security funds).

Table 10. OECD forecasts of EU budget balances (surplus (+) or deficit (−) as a % of nominal GDP)

	1995	1996	1997[a]	1998[a]
Germany	−3.6	−3.8	−3.2	−2.7
France	−5.0	−4.2	−3.2	−3.8
Italy	−7.0	−6.7	−3.2	−3.8
UK	−5.5	−4.4	−2.8	−1.8
Austria	−5.3	−3.9	−3.0	−3.4
Belgium	−4.1	−3.4	−2.8	−2.7
Denmark	−1.9	−1.6	0.0	0.7
Finland	−5.1	−2.6	−2.0	−1.4
Greece	−9.2	−7.4	−5.2	−4.0
Ireland	−2.1	−0.9	−1.2	−1.0
Netherlands	−4.1	−2.4	−2.3	−1.7
Portugal	−5.0	−4.0	−2.9	−2.8
Spain	−6.6	−4.5	−3.0	−2.6
Sweden	−7.7	−3.6	−2.1	−0.2
EU average[b]	−5.2	−4.4	−3.0	−2.6

[a] Projected figures.
[b] Excluding Luxembourg.
Source: OECD.

EMU in 1999 with a budget deficit somewhat greater than 2%. Assuming growth continues at 3% a year, it is unlikely that the endogenous response of revenues and expenditure alone will eliminate budget deficits even by 2002. And if a recession intervenes due to, say, the end of the already long-lived US expansion, even less progress can be expected.

8.2. Discretionary initiatives

The elimination of budget deficits could be accelerated by additional discretionary tax increases or expenditure cuts. Since 1992 France and Germany have reduced their cyclically corrected budget deficits at an annual average rate of 0.4% of GDP per year, while in Italy the improvement has been nearly $1\frac{1}{2}$% per annum. If fiscal consolidation continues at this pace, Europe's budgets may move substantially towards balance by about 2002.

There are several reasons to question this rosy scenario. There are already signs of fiscal fatigue in Europe after successive years of tax increases, and (in fewer cases) spending cuts, without readily visible benefits. The French elections of mid-1997 are only the most visible indication of public resistance to further austerity. Consistent with this diagnosis, European governments have relied on one-off measures – central bank sales of gold, refundable euro taxes, appropriation for the general budget of public enterprise pension reserves, and sales of strategic petroleum reserves – to meet the Maastricht fiscal criteria for 1997. Moreover, further discretionary cuts in public spending will depress the rate of growth and therefore slow the endogenous closing of the fiscal gap. Nor are demographic trends favourable: even ten years hence, one begins to worry about the fiscal consequences of an ageing population, especially in countries where health services are publicly provided. OECD (1996) suggests that these effects may become quite substantial within ten years of the start of EMU, especially for the Netherlands and the Nordic countries.

None of this rules out further discretionary cuts in spending or discretionary tax increases that will move Europe's budgets towards balance more quickly. In our estimation, however, taxes are already prohibitively high, and public support for radical expenditure cuts is absent.

Could deficit reduction become more popular because it actually boosts growth? According to the recent literature on the anti-Keynesian effects of fiscal policy (e.g., Giavazzi and Pagano, 1995), cutting the deficit can be expansionary when it boosts consumer confidence and therefore consumer spending. If a country was previously on an unsustainable fiscal trajectory, returning to a stable fiscal path can increase confidence, much as stepping on the brakes of a car hurtling towards a brick wall can increase the confidence of the passengers. This effect is most likely when deficit reduction is significant, sustained and credible, and when it takes the form of spending cuts rather than tax increases (Alesina and Perotti, 1995). These, of course, are precisely the conditions lacking in Europe. Deficits of 3% and debts of 70% may be too high, but they are not obviously unsustainable. Refundable euro taxes and other one-off measures hardly build confidence that fiscal correction will be sustained. The Jospin government's stated intention of paring the French deficit just enough to qualify for EMU hardly creates confidence that the budget will be cut significantly from recent levels. So far, the majority of adjustment has taken the form of increased taxes rather than reduced spending on social programmes and other entitlements. We should not expect deficits to become more popular because of an anti-Keynesian effect in boosting output.

8.3. Stepping up the pace

Ensuring that Europe's fiscal stabilizers are unconstrained by the Stability Pact requires stepping up the pace of growth to accelerate endogenous deficit reduction. If Europe grew at 4% a year, the rate projected for the USA in 1997 by the IMF, this would lop off between $\frac{3}{4}$ and 1% of its deficit per year through the endogenous response of revenues, assuming that restraint was exercised on fiscal spending.

Faster growth without inflation requires more flexible markets, and more flexible labour markets in particular. The danger here is that excessive energy devoted to fiscal consolidation and to the Stability Pact will sap the energies of reformers. Leaders, having invested most of their political capital in pushing through deficit-cutting measures, may have little left to invest in labour market reform. Truck drivers, farmers and employees of Air France are already feeling the pinch of budget cuts; further cuts in sick leave or annual holidays will be one more insult.

The reduction of hiring and firing costs, among the most important labour market reforms, will meet with considerable resistance in a slowly growing economy, where the odds of a dismissed worker finding another job are relatively slim; yet fiscal consolidation in Europe is making for slow growth.[25]

Less rigid preoccupation with fiscal consolidation will improve the prospects for labour market reform, for two reasons: European leaders will retain more political capital to devote to the issue; and a more buoyant macroeconomic environment will reduce public opposition to the reduction of hiring and firing costs. If successful, labour market reform will reinforce the buoyancy of the macroeconomic environment and hasten the pace of fiscal consolidation.

9. POLICY IMPLICATIONS

We have sought in this paper (1) to identify the economic problems that prompted adoption of the Stability Pact and (2) to assess its costs and benefits. Our assessment is that enforcement of the pact will be relatively loose, but still tight enough to affect some member states' deficits. EU officials will be reluctant to levy fines and lose goodwill. Member states will be reluctant to incur fines and suffer embarrassment. As in most EU affairs, a negotiated settlement just acceptable to both sides is the likely outcome.[26] EU decision-makers will compromise, allowing the 3% ceiling to be violated. Governments will compromise, eliminating deficits that egregiously violate the Stability Pact. They will modify their fiscal policies just enough to avoid forcing their neighbours to impose fines.

9.1. The pact's fiscal implications hinge on Europe's growth performance

If member states quickly move their budgets to balance or surplus, the Stability Pact will become a non-issue. If they run surpluses of 2% of GDP in expansions, they will be able to provide customary levels of automatic stabilization in response to an increase in the output gap of as much as 10% of GDP. It is hard to see that the Stability Pact could bind.

But except for clearly unsustainable fiscal trajectories, governments are reluctant to impose sharp discretionary shifts in the fiscal balance. In the United States, where circumstances have been relatively normal, a shift in the fiscal position of 0.25% of

---

[25] To date fiscal progress has been piecemeal. Coe and Snower (1997) argue that this explains both why the results have been disappointing and why there is public resistance to further reform. And policies (like work sharing and early retirement) that reduce measured unemployment rather than increase the demand for labour impede faster deficit reduction.

[26] Theorists would attribute the prevalence of successful negotiations, and absence of breakdown and sanctions, to the repeated-game nature of the interaction, the relatively complete nature of the information environment, and the fact that the EU has built institutions to minimize transaction and negotiation costs over the course of its 40-year history.

GDP is a big deal politically. Throughout Europe, the backlash against fiscal austerity is evident. It is not clear that the political will exists to go faster.

If Europe is to eliminate deficits and move budgets into surplus, it will have to do so by outgrowing them. Even if one adopts an optimistic forecast of economic growth (3% a year), Europe's deficits will only fall to $2\frac{1}{2}$% by the time EMU begins, *unless other discretionary changes are adopted*, which for the above-mentioned reasons seems unlikely. If, contrary to our expectations, governments attempt to reduce their deficits more quickly, growth will slow. Two pounds of fiscal effort will thus be needed to obtain an extra pound of fiscal results. And if a recession intervenes, little if any progress will be made.

9.2. Concern with fiscal stability should not divert attention from labour market reform

There is a real danger that preoccupation with fiscal consolidation is hindering labour market reform, and hindering more general reforms to enhance economic flexibility and boost productivity growth. As explained above, more fiscal flexibility in the short run may improve the prospects for labour market reform. If successful, labour market reform will reinforce the buoyancy of the macroeconomic environment and on balance hasten rather than slow the pace of fiscal consolidation.

The remaining implications of our analysis flow from the principle that efficient intervention should take place as close as possible to the source of the problem in order to avoid creating more distortions than it eliminates. Those implications are as follows.

9.3. Better public debt management would permit greater fiscal flexibility without aggravating bailout risk

If the danger is a financial crisis, such as struck Mexico in 1994–5 when investors refused to roll over the government's maturing debts, the efficient solution is to lengthen the maturity structure of the debt and smooth the distribution of maturing issues, not to limit governments' fiscal flexibility. Debt runs occur when large amounts of debt mature suddenly and investors refuse to roll it over. This likelihood can be minimized by efficiently managing the term structure, lengthening maturities and avoiding bunching.

Lengthening maturities may seem easier said than done for countries with large debts. However, Table 11 shows no correlation between the size of debts and their maturity structure. High debts have been no barrier to lengthening maturities for countries that have made this a priority.

To be sure, countries that lengthen the term structure force themselves to shoulder a larger term premium. This implies higher taxes, lower spending or larger

Table 11. Structure of central government debts in Europe

	Debt as % of GDP	Short-term as % of domestic debt	Foreign-held debt as % of total	Year
Austria	52.4	0.4	19.1	1993
Belgium	131.1	21.1	15.8	1993
Finland	38.7	27.9	65.1	1992
France	38.7	42.4	n.a.	1994
Germany	33.7	3.9	48.7	1994
Greece	104.9	50.0	21.5	1992
Italy	105.8	39.4	14.5	1992
Luxembourg	3.9	45.5	6.9	1992
Netherlands	61.6	4.9	21.3	1994
Norway	23.2	35.4	29.9	1992
Spain	41.3	52.7	17.0	1992
Sweden	66.7	15.3	50.5	1994
UK	34.0	29.6	17.1	1992

Sources: Government statistics; IMF.

deficits, other things equal. But the real danger is not debts so heavy that European countries will repudiate them, all but unprecedented in peacetime, but rather that investors will refuse to roll over maturing debts, creating a more serious and sudden problem that European governments lack the resources to address. If the problem with lengthening the term structure is that this heightens the temptation to inflate, the appropriate response is to index the debt.

Since less debt is also better than more from this point of view, measures to limit debt accumulation may also be desirable. The longer and smoother the term structure, the looser can be application of the Stability Pact, because the risk of problems in the market for public debt will be lower.

9.4. Better bank regulation would permit greater fiscal flexibility without aggravating bailout risk

If the problem is that the ECB will come under pressure to intervene when the crisis spreads to the banking system – because bank failures destabilize the macro-economy or because the banking system is a channel for contagion – the efficient policy response is to strengthen the banks, not to limit fiscal flexibility. This was the lesson drawn by the Argentine government from the country's debt-cum-banking crisis in 1995, when Mexico's bungled devaluation led investors to withdraw their funds, placing Argentina's bank system at risk. In response, the government raised capital and liquidity requirements for the banks; by limiting their ratio of liquid liabilities to liquid assets, it limited the resources that had to be raised in the event of a run.[27]

[27] For further details on the spread of instability from Mexico to Argentina and how the Argentine government responded by strengthening the position of its banking system, see Caprio *et al.* (1997).

In Europe, the fear is that the costs of a bailout of a national banking system would be borne by the residents of the whole EMU zone, not just the offending country, inducing moral hazard. If so, the solution is to raise capital and liquidity requirements for the banks – perhaps to even higher levels than mandated by the BIS Accords (which are designed for countries with their own central banks). If European policy-makers believe that the banks' investments in government bonds are a threat to financial stability, the efficient solution is to limit the banks' ability to hold such bonds, not to limit governments' ability to issue them. The BIS allows banks to adjust their capital holdings for risk using proprietary models; if European officials feel that those models underestimate the risks of holding public debt (because they neglect externalities associated with, *inter alia*, contagion and systematic risk), then the efficient policy response is to change how those capital standards are calculated, not to prevent governments from issuing debt. More generally, if the underlying problem is instability in the banking system, national governments and the EU should tighten supervision and inspection of Europe's banks rather than placing fiscal authorities in a straitjacket. The stricter is prudential supervision and the higher are capital and liquidity requirements, the looser can be the Stability Pact, because the risk to the banking system will be less.

We conclude that the Stability Pact is a minor nuisance if European countries succeed in moving their budgets into balance or, better, into surplus, making room for their automatic stabilizers to work. But if their deficits remain right up against their 3% reference values when EMU begins, the pact becomes more of a problem. Since much of Europe lacks the appetite for radical fiscal consolidation, reducing deficits means outgrowing them. Here labour market flexibility is key. In this connection, the Stability Pact should not be allowed to become a diversion. Europe needs more attention to labour market reform, not single-minded preoccupation with fiscal retrenchment. If its politicians do not devote all their political capital to contentious fiscal cuts, they will have more resources to push through needed labour market measures. And to the extent that debt management and financial sector reforms encourage them to apply the Stability Pact more flexibly, faster deficit-reducing growth, not interrupted by recessions, becomes easier to sustain.

Discussion

Charles Bean
London School of Economics

This paper could just as easily have been entitled 'The costs and benefits of the Stability Pact'. Eichengreen and Wyplosz conclude that the benefits are probably minimal, and could have been achieved in other ways. I agree. They also argue that the costs will be small. I am less convinced.

As far as the benefits go, Eichengreen and Wyplosz list five possibilities. The first, and potentially most important, is to prevent inflationary debt bailouts. Of course, there is already a 'no-bailout' clause in the Maastricht Treaty, but questions remain as to whether that is an entirely credible commitment on the part of the signatories. If, say, Italy were to find itself unable to fund its debt obligations, is it really likely that its European partners would not come to its aid? The first point to note is that, if a bailout did happen, the European Central Bank would not be the main agency involved; rather it is the IMF and national governments that would have to organize any rescue package. The ECB enters the picture only if there is a risk of contagion and a flight to liquidity that threatens the stability of the financial system. Here the authors undertake a brave attempt to draw lessons from US experience. The fiscal position of US states is so different from that of the EU nations that it is tempting to dismiss the exercise as irrelevant, but one should look where one can for evidence. In this respect, surely the Latin American experience of the 1980s, and that of the Far East today, provide better laboratories for investigating contagion effects. Clearly, excessive debt levels generating financial instability are a cause for concern, but provided any injection of liquidity by the ECB is temporary, and is withdrawn as financial stability is restored, it need have no effect on inflation. Furthermore, the risk of such a scenario can be reduced in a sharper and more direct way by limiting the exposure of financial intermediaries to risky sovereign debt.

As for the other arguments for limiting debt and deficits, the argument that high-debt countries will press for higher inflation so as to reduce the real value of their outstanding debt obligations ignores the fact that the members of the Governing Council of the European System of Central Banks are not supposed to act as representatives of narrow national interests. Moreover, if there were genuine concern that this might happen, the voting rights of high-debt countries could be limited, as suggested by Paul De Grauwe.

As far as dealing with the political bias towards excessive deficits goes, there is no reason why this should be a matter for supranational action. If indeed it is the case that deficits are excessive, and have the adverse effects enumerated by the authors – all of which are internal to the country – then national governments could tie their hands by passing into law a Code for Fiscal Stability that constrains fiscal policy along appropriate lines. Such a code is presently in force in New Zealand and is currently being introduced in the United Kingdom. There is a case for supranational action only if there are adverse spillovers from these excessive deficits on to other countries.

Indeed, spillovers on to interest rates provide the fourth argument for constraining deficits. Aside from the fact that such spillovers appear to be small – although in their empirical work the authors confuse a lack of statistical significance with a lack of economic significance – there is surely a widespread misunderstanding of the theoretical case here, which the authors do a service by exposing. If a country chooses to borrow beyond the point at which the opportunity cost of funds equals the (social) returns, the costs of that inefficiency are borne by the taxpayers of the borrowing country. At most there is a distributional issue, as countries that are net lenders (borrowers) will gain (lose) from higher interest rates. As most European countries have a net asset position that is quite close to balance, such distributional considerations are marginal.

Finally, as far as the policy co-ordination argument goes, the literature shows that fiscal policy could just as easily be too tight as too loose, and that consequently the Stability Pact is ill-designed for achieving a more efficient outcome.

Let me now turn to the costs of the pact. Its architects believe that countries will be sufficiently far-sighted and will run surpluses in good times, so as to give room for the automatic fiscal stabilizers, and other discretionary fiscal action, in bad times. To anyone who has observed the shameless fiscal bribery of the electorate by successive UK governments as election time draws near, this is hopelessly Panglossian. The problem with the pact as presently framed is that it is all stick and no carrot; rewarding good fiscal behaviour in booms rather than, or in addition to, punishing bad behaviour in slumps would surely make better sense. This could easily be done by relating payments to the EU budget or the distribution of euro seigniorage to fiscal positions.

Eichengreen and Wyplosz seem to subscribe at least partially to the Panglossian view, while simultaneously arguing that sufficient discretion exists to ensure that fines would in any case not be imposed. Surely there is an inconsistency here − if governments do not believe fines will be imposed in bad times, why should they run fiscal surpluses in good times?

The authors undertake an interesting counterfactual exercise in asking how different the past would have looked if the Stability Pact had been in force over the past 22 years, and conclude that the cumulated output losses for France, Italy and the UK would be somewhere between 5 and 9% of GDP, i.e. the equivalent of an annual loss of $\frac{1}{4}$–$\frac{1}{2}$% of GDP, which is significant but not disastrous. However, their methodology is flawed in that, to carry out the simulations, they calculate the historical excess deficit and then assume that this is the amount by which the cyclically corrected deficit (their fiscal impulse measure) also needs to change. But in practice a one percentage point decline in the cyclically corrected deficit requires a reduction in the actual deficit of more than one percentage point because the fiscal contraction lowers taxes and boosts transfers. In fact, using the estimates in the paper for the elasticities of output with respect to the deficit, and of the deficit with respect to output (Table 11), suggests that the output losses are at least half as much again as the authors suggest.

Looking forward, the authors note that further fiscal retrenchment is required if member countries are to have sufficient room to allow the fiscal stabilizers to operate, and for any supplementary discretional fiscal action, during recessions. What to my mind the authors do not bring out sufficiently clearly is that improvements in the fiscal position due purely to faster cyclical growth will be of little help here, since what is required is an improvement in the cyclically corrected fiscal position; at best, more robust cyclical growth buys a little more time. Instead what is required is a permanent and sustainable increase in the level of output – something that is harder to achieve.

Finally, the most serious criticism of the Stability Pact, and indeed of the drive towards the single currency, is that it has served as a distraction from tackling some of Europe's more serious structural problems: in particular, high and persistent unemployment and the need for pension reform. As far as unemployment goes, some people argue that monetary union will hasten labour market reform as countries will no longer have access to the quick fix of devaluation. But since Europe's unemployment is primarily structural rather than cyclical, devaluation is in any case only a temporary solution. Furthermore, the political reality of labour market reform is that it is easier to reduce firing costs, cut unemployment benefits, etc. in a booming economy. Getting the agreement of the various social partners to such policies will therefore be easier if macroeconomic policies are free to support the structural reforms, thus ensuring the gains from reform come hard on the heels of the necessary pain. Having greatly reduced their room for manoeuvre on the monetary front, European governments are now in danger of doing the same on the fiscal front.

As far as pension reform goes – one of the biggest challenges on the horizon for most European governments – the Maastricht debt numbers make no allowance for the accumulated pension obligations under the current pay-as-you-go arrangements. Given increasing longevity and the fall in the birth rate, the tax rate necessary to finance these obligations is set to become unacceptably high, and greater reliance on funded schemes is unavoidable. However, a major problem with switching from an unfunded to a funded arrangement is that at least one generation of taxpayers has to bear the double burden of saving for their own pensions as well as paying for the pensions of their parents. The equitable way of undertaking the transition is, of course, for the government to borrow to finance the pensions of the final generation of pay-as-you-go retirees, so that the burden is borne by future taxpayers as well as current ones. The Stability Pact makes this all but impossible to do.

Stefan Gerlach
Bank for International Settlements, Basle

For those of us who have read past papers by Barry Eichengreen and Charles Wyplosz, this paper comes as no surprise: it provides a clear and careful analysis of an important policy question, and draws a provocative conclusion that the Stability Pact is something between a minor nuisance and a major problem. In my comments, I argue that the paper underestimates the risks and consequences of a public debt crisis and the likelihood of interest rate spillovers, that it downplays the inflationary consequences of high public debt, and that it is thus too quick to conclude that the Stability Pact (SP) is not desirable.

The paper starts with a review of a number of claims that have been made in support of the SP. After analysing each in turn, the authors conclude that only two of them may be valid: (1) the SP could reduce the likelihood of an inflationary debt bailout, and (2) it could limit the risk of interest rate spillovers within the euro area. The authors argue that whether the SP actually will have these benefits is an empirical question, and they go on to analyse these two claims more thoroughly before rejecting them. For reasons of space, I focus much of my discussion on their analysis of these arguments in favour of the Stability Pact. I conclude with a brief analysis of why the SP could be helpful in reducing inflationary pressures – an argument that the authors reject without much discussion.

Debt bailouts

While the authors recognize that the SP may reduce the likelihood of a public debt crisis and therefore the need for an inflationary bailout, they do not believe that in practice this justifies the pact. They study the extent to which banks experienced losses on their real-estate lending in past banking crises, and compare these losses with banks' exposure to government debt. They argue that banks actually hold relatively little public debt and note that any debt crisis would only partially reduce the value of government bonds.[28] They therefore conclude that a public debt crisis is not likely to endanger the banking system. The authors argue, furthermore, that past banking crises have been deflationary rather than inflationary, and emphasize that any liquidity infusion by the central bank in a future crisis is likely to be temporary.

I have several reservations regarding these arguments. First, I doubt that past banking crises that were caused by poor real-estate loans provide much information about the likelihood that a public debt crisis would trigger a banking crisis. One reason for this is that real-estate loans, in contrast to bonds, are not marked-to-market and it is therefore easier for banks to keep problems related to such loans out of the public view for some time, which may reduce the risk of a bank run. Some opaqueness provided that it is temporary and that the supervisory authorities are kept informed at all times may be desirable from a systemic perspective, since it gives banks some time to resolve problems without at the same time having to endure a crisis of confidence. Second, I have some concerns regarding the authors' data on the exposure of the banking system. My colleagues Bob McCauley and Bill White have recently presented some calculations suggesting that banks are about twice as exposed as Table 2 of this paper suggests.[29] If this is correct, it seems that

---

[28] It is implicit in the paper that a public crisis, if it were to occur, would take the form of a forced exchange of short-term for longer-term debt, perhaps with a reduction of the applicable interest rate. Thus, a debt crisis would only partially reduce the value of the debt.
[29] See McCauley and White (1997, table 20, p. 377).

the authors may have underestimated the consequences of a public debt crisis for the stability of the banking sector. Third, while banking crises may well be deflationary, there are of course many other reasons – in particular, their effect on output and employment – why they should be avoided.

More fundamentally, however, I think the authors underestimate the potential systemic implications of a forced conversion of the public debt. It is important to recognize that a drastic fall in the value of government bonds could lead to a systemic crisis even if banks hold no public debt directly. A collapse of bond prices may lead to a collapse of non-bank financial institutions that are counterparties to banks in a number of markets. Thus, any crisis that erupted would spread to banks sooner or later. Moreover, for a systemic crisis to start, it is not necessary for a public debt crisis actually to occur. The mere suspicion that banks hold government bonds of questionable value may lead depositors to withdraw funds and counterparties to take their business elsewhere, which in turn could trigger a financial crisis.

Interest rate spillovers

The second argument that the authors consider to be potentially correct is that the SP could reduce the risk of interest rate spillovers. Such spillovers could arise if, for instance, overly lax fiscal policies in one country lead to higher interest rates in other countries, or if a confidence crisis in one country triggers confidence crises elsewhere. The authors argue that, since governments are price-takers in integrated financial markets, it is difficult to believe that there would be large spillovers. They also provide some econometric evidence suggesting that there is little evidence of such spillovers among individual US states and in Europe.

However, I think it questionable whether the US evidence contains much information relevant to the likelihood of interest spillovers in Europe. First, debt/income ratios are much smaller for individual US states than for European countries. Second, there are apparently no cases of a 'near-default' in the US data, and it is therefore difficult to see what can be learned from them.[30] Third, since the income on bonds issued by the state of residence tends to be tax free, there are strong clientele effects in the markets for state debt in the USA, which are likely to reduce the possibility of interest rate spillovers. Since the US data are likely to be uninformative, it would be instructive to consider whether there were spillover effects in other episodes in which there was some uncertainty in the market for public debt. One episode of potential interest is the period surrounding the referendum in Quebec at the end of October 1995.

[30] The same argument would seem to hold for the European data.

Inflation and the public debt

The 'standard' justification of the SP it that it is necessary to ensure the achievement and maintenance of price stability in the euro area. Viewed from this perspective, it is particularly striking that the authors apparently find no merit in the argument that large public debts can be inflationary.

There are at least two reasons why large public debts may be inflationary. The first is that large public debts carry with them a temptation to reduce the real value of the debt by generating an unexpected burst of inflation. However, since a significant part of the public debt in many countries is of short maturity, and since some borrowing may be in foreign currency, the practical relevance of this argument is negligible, at least in Europe.[31] The second argument is based on the observation that the maintenance of low inflation may sometimes conflict with the stability of the debt/GDP ratio. Suppose that the ECB cares about inflation and financial stability, and therefore the size of the public debt. A tightening of monetary policy not only raises the real interest rate (and hence debt service), it also reduces real growth (hence, at given tax rates, raising the primary deficit). Higher deficits lead to the accumulation of higher debt in the numerator, and lower output directly reduces the denominator: through both channels, tighter monetary policy will increase the debt/GDP ratio.

The monetary policy implications of this stem from the fact that at any point in time there are likely to be differences of opinion between the members of the Governing Council of the ECB regarding the appropriate stance of policy: some members might argue for a tightening of policy, others might prefer to leave interest rates unchanged, while still others might view a relaxation of policy as appropriate. While it is not clear what, in practice, the decision-making process in the ECB will be like, it is plausible that policy will be heavily influenced by the views of the 'average' member. The fact that a tightening of policy is likely to worsen the debt situation and increase the risk of financial instability may lead the average council member to be marginally less willing to tighten, or marginally more willing to relax, monetary policy. Large public debts could therefore impart an inflation bias to the ECB's monetary policy. While it is difficult to speculate how large this inflation bias could be, a few per cent seems plausible. If correct, this would provide a good reason for limiting public debt in Europe.

General discussion

Maurice Obstfeld thought that Canadian experience, more than that of the United

---

[31] Persson *et al.* (1996) show that an increase in inflation would impact positively on government finances in Sweden. However, these gains stem not from the real depreciation of the government debt and increased seigniorage, but rather from nominal features of the tax and transfer system.

States, could provide a useful guide to the future evolution of the Stability Pact. Canadian provinces have substantial debts and also greater leeway in their financing methods. One could test the validity of the bailout story by studying the debt ratios of provinces: do higher levels of debt push up the provincial interest rates? Importantly, such a test should concern itself with real interest rates rather than nominal ones. Finally, he noted that high growth is not a panacea for the problem of fiscal adjustment. A buoyant economy may allow us to postpone the hard decisions needed on the fiscal front, but it cannot do so indefinitely.

Kenneth Rogoff felt that concerns regarding the anti-inflationary ability of the European Central Bank were exaggerated. In his opinion, the real issue was the ECB's regulatory ability: in particular, its ability to co-ordinate and supervise banks.

Jürgen von Hagen, in contrast, doubted that the ECB could always resist the pressure to inflate away debt. Regardless of the constitution of the ECB, it may be tempted to allow higher inflation in exceptional circumstances. He noted that the deterioration of deficits is often caused not by the fiscal stance, but as in the case of Italy, by increased transfer payments and high interest rates. Moreover, judging from experience, fiscal restrictions in periods of recession tend to result in cutbacks in some crucial areas, such as infrastructure and education. If volatility in expenditure patterns in these sectors is costly, fiscal restrictions imposed by the Stability Pact will prove to be more than just diversions. Finally, simulations suggest that the impact of negative fiscal stimuli on an economy depends on the fiscal stance in other countries as well. Fiscal stimuli that affect many countries could have more pronounced effects than isolated ones.

Olivier Blanchard wondered how austere a government needed to be in the long run in order to keep room for manoeuvre against an occasional but significant recession. How much below the 3% level would the budget deficit have to be to provide this cushion? He expressed the view that fiscal restrictions imposed by the Stability Pact may lead to structural activism: reform and intervention in areas other than monetary and fiscal policy, most notably in labour markets. The UK had carried this out successfully, while France had not, so the results could well be mixed. In Klaus Zimmermann's opinion, the 3% deficit criterion was chosen to exclude Italy, which was somewhat unfair. If Italy's shadow economy were taken into account, we would come to a different judgement of its true position.

Andrew Rose thought the paper was concerned excessively with the size of the public debt, whereas the Stability Pact is designed around budget deficits. Torben Andersen thought that the Stability Pact focuses on the deficit norm because of perceived political myopia. Perhaps politicians do not realize that large persistent deficits lead to higher debt levels. He argued that the paper captured only the effects of discretionary changes in fiscal policy and left out the automatic stabilizers. Automatic stabilizers play a significant role in European economies, and if they were eliminated by the deficit criterion, the Stability Pact might prove to be costlier than expected.

Paul De Grauwe also stressed the role of automatic stabilizers. The Stability Pact aimed to move countries towards balanced budgets. It was not clear that the 3% deviation from balanced budget would provide enough room for automatic stabilizers to work properly. If not, the Stability Pact would restrict the efficacy of automatic stabilizers. Second, behind the Stability Pact lay the assumption that default and bailout risks were greater under monetary union. One could argue, to the contrary, that Italy's default risk is higher outside the EMU than inside it. Likewise evidence suggests that most bailouts have been carried out between countries that are not part of a common currency area.

Richard Portes stressed that the ECB definitely can intervene when liquidity problems are at stake. However, as far as solvency is concerned, there is nothing in the monetary process that requires European taxpayers to solve other countries' solvency problems. Robert McCauley felt that the paper ignored the considerable structural change that had occurred in the last 25 years. For instance, the change in the German long-term interest rate was certainly affected by German unification.

REFERENCES

Alesina, A. and R. Perotti (1994). 'Budget deficits and budget institutions,' unpublished manuscript, Harvard University and Columbia University.
—— (1995). 'Reducing budget deficits', paper presented at conference on Growing Government Debt: International Experiences, Economic Council of Sweden, Stockholm, 12 June.
Alesina, A., R. Hausmann, R. Hommes and E. Stein (1995). 'Budget institutions and fiscal performance in Latin America', unpublished manuscript, Interamerican Bank.
Artis, M.J. and B. Winkler (1997). 'The Stability Pact: safeguarding the credibility of the European Central Bank', CEPR Discussion Paper no. 1688.
Bayoumi, T. and B. Eichengreen (1995). 'Restraining yourself: the implications of fiscal rules for economic stabilization', *IMF Staff Papers*.
Bayoumi, T., M. Goldstein and G. Woglom (1995). 'Do credit markets discipline sovereign borrowers? Evidence from US states', *Journal of Money, Credit and Banking*.
Beetsma, R. and H. Uhlig (1997). 'An analysis of the Stability Pact', unpublished manuscript, Tilburg University.
BIS (1993). *Annual Report*, Basle.
Buiter, W. (1985). 'A guide to public sector debt and deficits', *Economic Policy*.
——, G. Corsetti and N. Roubini (1993). 'Excessive deficits: sense and nonsense in the Treaty of Maastricht', *Economic Policy*.
Buti, M., D. Franco and H. Ongena (1997). 'Budgetary policies during recessions – retrospective application of the 'Stability and Growth Pact' to the post-war period', Economic Paper no.121, European Commission, Brussels.
Caprio, G., M. Dooley, D. Leipzinger and C. Walsh (1997). 'The lender of last resort function under a currency board', *Open Economies Review*.
Cochrane, J. (1994). 'Comment on "What ends recessions?"', *NBER Macroeconomics Annual*.
Coe, D. and D. Snower (1997). 'Policy complementarities: the case for fundamental labor market reform', *IMF Staff Papers*.
Dalheim, B., G. Lind and A.K. Nedersjö (1992). 'Bank results in Sweden and other Nordic countries', *Quarterly Review*, Bank of Sweden.
Debrun, X. (1997). 'Monetary stability in the European Monetary Union: inflation-adverse central bank and budgetary arithmetic', unpublished manuscript, University of Geneva.
De Grauwe, P. (1996). 'Discussion', in H. Siebert (ed.), *Monetary Policy in an Integrated World Economy*, Mohr, Tübingen.
Eichengreen, B. (1990). 'One money for Europe? Lessons from the US currency and customs union', *Economic Policy*.
—— (1997). 'Saving Europe's automatic stabilizers', *National Institute Economic Review*.
EU Commission (1995). *One Market, One Money*, Brussels.

Giavazzi, F. and M. Pagano (1995). 'Non-Keynesian effects of fiscal policy changes: international evidence and the Swedish experience', paper presented at IMF Research Department seminar, 16 November.

Goldstein, M. and G. Woglom (1992). 'Market-based fiscal discipline in monetary unions: evidence from the US municipal bond market', in M.B. Canzoneri, V. Grilli and P.R. Masson (eds.), *Establishing a Central Bank: Issues in Europe and Lessons from the US*, Cambridge University Press, Cambridge and New York.

King, M. (1997). 'Debt deflation: theory and evidence', in Forrest Capie and Geoffrey Wood (eds.), *Asset Prices and the Real Economy*, Macmillan, London.

McCauley R.N. and W.R. White (1997). 'The euro and European financial markets', in P.R. Masson, T.H. Krueger and B.G. Turtelboom (eds.), *EMU and the International Financial System*, IMF, Washington, DC.

McKinnon, R.I. (1996). 'Monetary regimes, government borrowing constraints, and market-preserving federalism: implications for EMU', unpublished manuscript, Stanford University.

OECD (1996). 'Labor market performance, budget control, and social transfers', *Economic Outlook*, Paris.

Oudiz, G. and J.D. Sachs (1984). 'Macroeconomic policy coordination among the industrial economies', *Brookings Papers on Economic Activity*.

Persson, M., T. Persson and L.E.O. Svensson (1996). 'Debt, cash flow and inflation incentives: a Swedish example', IIES Seminar Paper no. 613.

Sachs, J., A. Tornell and A. Velasco (1995). 'The collapse of the Mexican peso: what have we learned?', *Economic Policy*.

von Hagen, J. and B. Eichengreen (1996). 'Federalism, fiscal restraints, and European monetary union', *American Economic Review, Papers and Proceedings*.

von Hagen, J. and I. Harden (1994). 'National budget processes and fiscal performance', *European Economy, Reports and Studies*.

Wyplosz, C. (1990). 'EMS puzzles', *Revista Española de Economía*.

Stability pacts
European lessons from the gold standard

SUMMARY

The gold standard was a system of fixed exchange rates that offered little opportunity for carrying out monetary policies, short of suspending gold convertibility. Trade integration and capital mobility were very high. It is worthwhile asking whether there are useful lessons to draw for EMU from European experience during that period. One clear lesson is that debts matter. Another basic finding is that the stability of the European gold standard depended on the underlying price trend. Deflation prior to 1895 resulted in rising public debt burdens, which forced some countries to leave the system. Once gold was discovered and deflation gave way to inflation, real interest service fell, debts grew more slowly and a high degree of convergence allowed most countries to return to gold. For EMU, this result implies that stability will hinge on the ECB's policy not being too restrictive. Other lessons concern the fragility of institutions in the face of deep public finance difficulties, the risks for the single market of leaving out countries that have not fully converged, and the existence of a virtuous cycle including low real interest rates, fast growth and debt reduction.

— *Marc Flandreau, Jacques Le Cacheux and Frédéric Zumer*

Stability without a pact? Lessons from the European gold standard, 1880–1914

Marc Flandreau, Jacques Le Cacheux and Frédéric Zumer

EHESS, OFCE, OFCE

1. INTRODUCTION

Since the early years of the Industrial Revolution, European countries have, collectively or separately, tried various economic arrangements. These efforts include insulation: commercial protectionism until the Cobden–Chevalier Treaty of 1860, capital controls from the 1930s to the 1970s, and the free float of the 1930s. They also include periods of openness: fixed exchange rates with the ERM, free capital mobility during the nineteenth century, and increased free trade since the Treaty of Rome. The latest step, European monetary unification, stands as an

We wish to thank Jérôme Legrain for his excellent work as a research assistant in the first phase of the project. Special thanks are due to Roger Nougaret, who heads the Archives of the Crédit Lyonnais, for his kind help in the investigation of sources. We are also grateful to a long list of colleagues either for their contribution in supplying directions to appropriate sources, or for their comments on earlier drafts, or both: Pablo Martin Acena, Michael Bergman, Michael Bordo, Steve Broadberry, Felix Butschek, Forrest Capie, Elio Cerrito, Olga Christodoulaki, Jean-Pierre Dormois, Barry Eichengreen, Curzio Giannini, Paul Gregory, Tim Hatton, Ingrid Henriksen, Lars Jonung, Anton Kausel, Charles Kindleberger, John Komlos, Jacques Mélitz, Leandro Prados de la Escosura, Jaime Reis, Andreas Resch, Hugh Rockoff, Annalisa Rosselli, Max-Stefan Schulze, Pierre Sicsic, Jan-Pieter Smits, Peter Solar, Nathan Sussman, Giuseppe Tattara, Bruno Théret, Jan-Luiten Van Zanden and Vera Zamagni. We also thank Charles Wyplosz, the Editors of *Economic Policy* and our discussants, whose comments helped to improve the paper's focus. We are especially grateful to the OFCE Documentation Staff (Gwenola de Gouvello and Christine Paquentin) and to the *Sciences-Po* crew, who were kind enough to ship us unusually large numbers of volumes of the *Statesman's Yearbook* during the early stages of the project. The Editors thank Michael Bordo for detailed advice.

unparalleled experiment. Or does it? In a sense, it doesn't. On the eve of the First World War, such heterogeneous countries as wealthy Britain, France and Germany, small open Belgium and Netherlands, the Scandinavian nations, uneven Italy with its leading industrial north and underdeveloped south, backward and agricultural Greece, and even catching-up Russia, all found themselves on a common gold standard with essentially free capital and labour mobility as well as low levels of commercial protection. These countries, which hardly formed an optimum currency area, had undergone a common process of institutional reform that resulted in central banks' statutes being designed to foster institutional independence from governmental interference. Some contemporaries even dreamt of a common central bank – although we know the rest of the story.

The relevance of the European side of the gold standard for current debates remains to be fully grasped (Foreman-Peck (1991) is a contribution). In sharp contrast to the current strategy of convergence, which proceeds along agreed common rules (the Maastricht Treaty, the Stability and Growth Pact), the spread of the gold standard to Europe was a highly decentralized process. It was triggered by a lack of co-operation between France and Germany, which led in the early 1870s to the demise of silver and bimetallic standards in western, central and eastern Europe (Flandreau, 1995a, 1996). Decentralization was again visible as various European countries hopped on and off gold convertibility in the period between 1880 and 1914 (Eichengreen and Flandreau, 1996). The many international monetary conferences that took place between 1865 and 1892 called for extensive policy co-ordination, but they failed to achieve very much, if anything (Russell, 1898; Gallarotti, 1995). Yet most of Europe ended up on gold, without collectively agreed targets for debt, deficits, inflation, exchange rates or long-run interest rates. To the extent that it succeeded, the European gold standard appears as a case of stability without a pact.

Is it true to say that policy-makers of the time harboured a benign view of monetary policy and public finance? Quite to the contrary, the economic literature of the time shows that contemporaries *did* worry about the level of public debts, deficits, etc., which were very much at the heart of policy debates (see, e.g., Baxter, 1871). Moreover, the statistical apparatus to assess monetary and fiscal policy was readily available, so the absence of formal criteria cannot be explained by 'technological' limitations. Acceptable measures of activity would start to be constructed only in the years preceding the First World War, but several substitutes existed. General surveys were frequently conducted, and various industrial indices were used to assess the economic situation, providing contemporaries with a fair notion of national income. They also had very precise figures on exports and population, and often computed ratios of public debts or flows of interest payment per head in an attempt to compare national debt burdens in a more systematic manner (see, e.g., Théry, 1887). Another view is that the gold standard acted as a kind of invisible (to modern economists) hand, which provided a number of implicit mechanisms that substituted for our modern formal criteria. This traditional interpretation, which dates back to the interwar years, sees the classical gold standard as a coherent system of rules and policies. (For critiques of this view, see Bloomfield (1959) and Triffin (1964); for links with current debates in Europe, see Eichengreen and Flandreau (1997).) Recent work has refined this interpretation by specifying the nature of restraints.

A first view emphasizes the political mechanism. Gallarotti (1995) stresses that the ruling European bourgeoisie wanted stable prices and exchange rates over the long run, because it held a large fraction of its wealth and pensions in the shape of fixed-interest domestic and foreign bonds. The conservative policies that preserved the gold standard are seen as the by-product of the conservatism of élites. However, in a democratic society, decision making must be transparent. Monetary stability cannot rest on an arrangement that empowers a specific interest group with the ability to set fiscal or monetary targets. Formal rules are needed to prevent changes in political majorities resulting in fiscal misconduct. The Maastricht 'formal rules' approach would be a democratic equivalent of the gold standard 'political' mechanism as a way to deliver stability.

An alternative view emphasizes the market mechanism. According to Bordo and Rockoff (1996), the gold standard rule worked as an incentive mechanism. Lenders monitored fiscal and monetary misconduct, using gold convertibility as a signal of orthodox policies. Because leaving the gold standard implied higher interest rates, each country had an incentive to adopt disciplined policies. Bordo and Rockoff's point is that this mechanism was stabilizing because disciplined countries were rewarded through lower interest rates: 'countries chose to join the gold standard bloc, even though being on gold imposed restraint on their fiscal and monetary behaviour'.[1] However, nothing in this reasoning is specific to the gold standard. The same incentives should in principle exist under *any* regime: indeed, the modern literature on financial markets discipline (Bishop *et al.*, 1989) stresses that markets perform the job of providing governments with appropriate incentives. Under this view, therefore, the market mechanism will be an essential ingredient of stability in the euro zone.

The institutional and market mechanism views of the gold standard correspond to two alternative perceptions of the requisites for a successful functioning of the euro zone. This paper looks into the historical precedent of the gold standard to determine whether lessons can be drawn for today's Europe. We begin with an investigation of the record of the European gold standard (section 2). Our key conclusion is that the gold standard comprised two subperiods. The first period, starting in 1880, ended with a severe exchange crisis in the 1890s. The second period began with exchange rate instability, but then evolved after the turn of the

---

[1] Private correspondence from Hugh Rockoff, which neatly summarizes their view.

century towards the stable European gold standard. We also find that exchange rate instability coincided in an intriguing way with the record of European debt/GDP ratios.

Section 3 looks at the role of institutional design. Focusing on the record of central bank independence, we find that monetary authorities did not always enjoy the respect and awe that has been portrayed in the literature. Central bank independence was constantly tested, and repeatedly violated, especially when recurrent fiscal difficulties were experienced. It was only after 1896 that central bank independence was gradually reconstructed, suggesting that the degree of insulation of monetary authorities is not exogenous.

Section 4 evaluates the market discipline hypothesis. We contribute to the literature (see Mélitz, 1997) by adding to studies that have looked at existing monetary unions (see, e.g., Bayoumi *et al.*, 1995) a situation where European debt burdens were found at levels that are close to current ones.

Section 5 looks at price movements that affected the opportunity cost of being part of the gold standard. When prices were falling, debt service costs rose and many debt-laden countries suspended gold convertibility. By contrast, countries found it easier to participate in the gold standard when prices rose. To a large extent, divergence and convergence within the gold area can be traced to trends in rates of inflation.

The conclusion sums up the evidence and discusses policy implications. In particular, we suggest that stability will hinge on the ECB's policy not being too restrictive.

2. LIVING WITH HIGH DEBTS: STYLIZED FACTS ABOUT THE EUROPEAN GOLD STANDARD

2.1. European integration and globalization, 1880–1914

While this paper focuses on Europe as a regional entity, it should be kept in mind that the European gold standard developed in the context of global integration, both real and nominal, and was one aspect of the international gold standard. Capital, as is often the case, was perhaps the most mobile factor and flowed swiftly across borders. Numerous empirical studies have demonstrated that extremely close links existed between regional financial centres in Europe and elsewhere. Short-term capital, in the shape of exchange bills, circulated rapidly from country to country, and short-term interest rates exhibited considerable covariations at both the European (Flandreau, 1995b) and international levels (Zevin, 1992), even during financial crises. Goschen, a contemporary observer, called it the 'solidarity of international financial centres'. Long-term capital also travelled rapidly. Large and well-organized capital markets (the leading centres had a capitalization that represented several times the national product of the corresponding country) provided borrowers with a huge pool of funds on which they could tap. Private and public issues took place in co-ordination with banking syndicates that provided underwriting facilities, and became an important outlet for individual savings. As a result, national investment was not limited by domestic resources, thus giving rise to a disconnection between saving and investment. When implementing Feldstein–Horioka's test of the saving–investment correlation, Bayoumi (1990) and Taylor (1996) found recently that the period 1880–1914 was one of greater disconnection between saving and investment than any subsequent period. These findings are hardly surprising in view of the limited obstacles to financial flows. Even if some governments reportedly attempted to manipulate financial markets for political reasons, they were countered by the competition between lending centres, mostly London, Paris and Berlin. Minor price differences between asset returns are generally traceable to differences in tax systems or other minor frictional costs.

Labour mobility was high too. European immigration laws were usually not very restrictive, and some intra-European mobility existed. Such migrations, however, remained mostly local (workers crossing the border on a daily basis) and often seasonal. These movements were in any case dwarfed by the massive flows of migrants between the old and the new worlds, a factor which, according to Williamson (1996), contributed to the convergence of real wages. Migrants leaving Italy, Germany or Scandinavia helped to relieve the downward pressure on the regions where European wages were lowest.

While capital and to a certain extent labour markets were largely globalized, markets for commodities had a regional bias. European trade was based on short distances, similarities in tastes (Verley, 1997) and generally low levels of protection. The proportion of trade coming from and going to European countries as a share of total European trade generally stood above 50%, in some periods, even above 60%. Bairoch (1974) notes, however, that European trade became slightly less Euro-centred as it progressed. Rising incomes were accompanied by an increased demand for greater variety in imports, and this trend was accentuated by the decline of transportation costs over the period 1870–1914.

Like today, globalization aroused fears of economic decline, especially after the 1890s. For instance, economist Théry warned that 'emerging countries, newcomers to modern civilization, equipped thanks to the investments of Old Europe, organized by [its] engineers and industrialists, having lands of an incomparable fertility and an almost free labour force, exempt from unions and strikes, [were] on their way to the economic conquest of the world' (Théry, 1894). Contrary to the current situation, the European response to these challenges was not the deepening of the European market, but rather some partial sheltering of domestic economies behind protective barriers. The movement towards extended free trade that had developed after 1860 stalled in 1879, and started receding in the 1890s. According to Bairoch (1993), the period after 1892 should thus be portrayed as one of gradually rising protectionism in continental Europe. Yet indices of protection before the First World War reveal that Europe was no fortress. Measured as a ratio between customs revenues and imports, protection rates were about 8% for Europe at large and 10% for the continent alone (Bairoch, 1993). This was less protectionist than, say, the USA, Canada or Australia.

2.2. Gold parities and exchange rates: entry, exit and the spread of the gold standard

Participation in the gold club was not the outcome of any negotiation. A country only needed to define a gold parity for its currency: that is, the quantity of pure gold in national coins. As long as they effectively maintained convertibility (i.e., stood ready to exchange their notes against coins), central banks indirectly pegged their bilateral exchange rates *vis-à-vis* other gold convertible currencies within the so-called gold points. These may be thought of as target zones, whose centre coincided with the official parity and whose bandwidth corresponded approximately to bullion shipping charges between countries. This was the situation in countries like Britain, France, Germany and the Netherlands. Other currencies, while not strictly convertible, behaved as if they were pegged to gold, because the central bank held foreign exchange reserves and used them to stabilize the exchange rate each time it threatened to exit notional gold points. This was the case in Austria. In other countries, such as Greece in the years immediately preceding the First World War, the national currency was related to gold through what was essentially a currency board arrangement: domestic units were created on a one-for-one basis as a counterpart of foreign exchange reserve holdings.

Since these measures were implemented at the country's convenience, they could always be suspended without international agreement: the option was always available to suspend convertibility, discontinue stabilizing foreign exchange interventions, or quit gold standard arrangements. In this case, the country was effectively dropping off gold and its exchange rate could fluctuate. Historically, such decisions tended to follow periods of crisis, during which money creation had been large and capital inflows low, so that the amount of gold (or reserves) required to settle the country's external obligations was larger than the quantity available in the vaults of the central bank. Once off gold, countries found themselves effectively on a paper standard with a floating exchange rate. The official gold parity represented a floor for exchange rate appreciation, because the central bank that could not sell gold against notes could still sell notes against gold. A country could either undertake to return the exchange rate to its gold parity (a course adopted during the period under study by Portugal, Greece, Italy and Spain), or bring the parity into line with exchange depreciation, accepting a permanent devaluation (a course adopted by Russia and the Austro-Hungarian Empire in the 1890s).

Figure 1 summarizes the spread of the gold standard in Europe. There is, of course, a degree of arbitrariness in deciding where to put the boundary between shadowing a gold standard and not being on a gold standard, but the general pattern would survive alternative definitions. This figure reveals a dichotomy between a European 'core' comprising Britain, France, Germany, the Netherlands, Belgium and Scandinavia, and the European southern and eastern 'peripheries'. In the core, the gold standard was a durable regime of unquestioned exchange rate stability. However, in the periphery, adherence to the gold standard was less robust.[2] Traditional descriptions of the evolution of the gold standard tend to characterize it as a continuous process of extension. More careful scrutiny reveals two periods. The first phase, from 1880 to the mid-1890s, witnessed increasing fragility with fewer countries on gold at the end of the period than at the beginning. Only during the second phase did the gold standard generalize to the periphery of Europe, still leaving aside Spain and Portugal. The era of monetary stability in Europe was in fact circumscribed to the ten years immediately preceding the First World War.

Figure 2 displays the evolution of European exchange rates in terms of end-of-period gold parity, so that a value above unity means the exchange rate is temporarily depreciated. The three key European currencies (sterling, franc and Reichsmark) are excluded from the diagram because they remained within their assigned gold points throughout the period. The general pattern exhibits a bell shape. Nearly all exchange rates are located in a narrow 10% interval. The only exception is Portugal, for which the depreciation was around 20%. For several countries, depreciation was considerable during the 1890s and early 1900s, and was followed by appreciation as the currencies returned to the gold standard.

The general pattern conceals three different groups. Small economies, such as Belgium, the Netherlands and Scandinavia, display a very high level of exchange

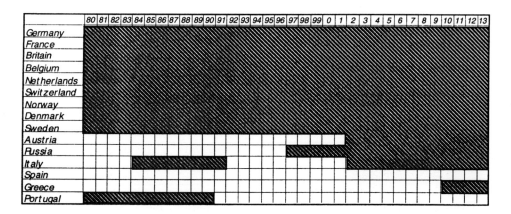

Figure 1. Countries on gold, 1880–1913

----

[2] This feature echoes the descriptions of other peripheral areas, such as Argentina (Ford, 1962).

rate stability throughout the period. The second group comprises the central and eastern European empires (Russia and Austria-Hungary). While the exchange rate depreciation that had characterized these countries until the mid-1880s had come to a halt, their currencies still fluctuated wildly at short frequency (Yeager, 1969). In the early 1890s, the rouble and the florin eventually stabilized around a new, devalued gold parity, which acknowledged the depreciation that had occurred since the 1870s. In both cases no effort was made to go back to the mid-century gold parity, and the devaluation was substantial (about 30% in the case of Russia). The third group comprises the southern European countries (Greece, Portugal, Spain and, to a lesser extent, Italy). For these countries, depreciation began and accelerated after 1890, reaching considerable levels (about 80% for Greece in 1895, above 65% for Spain and Portugal in 1898). In the early 1900s, however, their exchange rates stabilized and then regained lost ground. Only Greece and Italy went back to gold, but Spain and to a lesser extent Portugal experienced a substantial stabilization of their currencies in terms of gold.

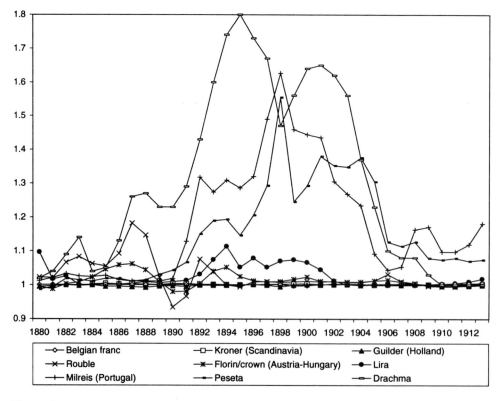

Figure 2. Exchange rates (ratio to end-of-period parity), 1880–1913
Source: Schneider *et al.* (1991).
Notes: Key currencies (the French franc, pound sterling and Reichsmark) which remained at par over the whole period are excluded from the diagram. The pesata and milreis did not return to par towards the end of the period as these countries remained outside the gold club. The Russian and Austro-Hungarian gold club parities were devalued in the 1890s (this is why the rouble and florin exchange rates cross their end-of-period parity in 1890).

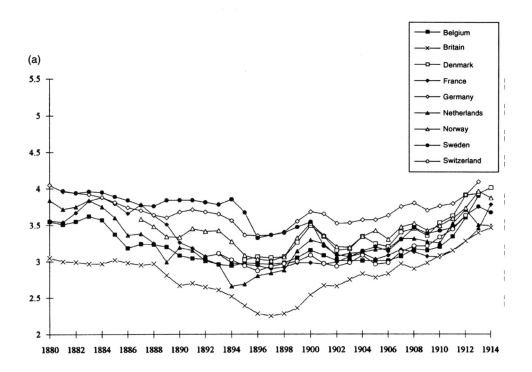

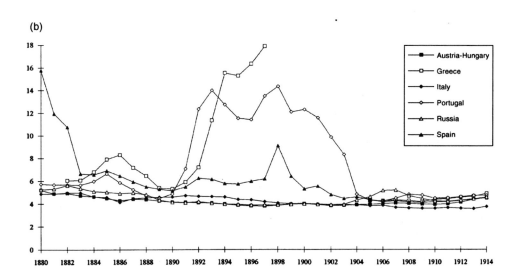

Figure 3. Long-term interest rates, 1880–1914
Source: See Appendix A.

Thus the European gold standard was not the strict regime often portrayed in the literature; or if it was, then its rules were repeatedly broken. Moreover, once the rules were broken, there was no reason to expect a quick return to the old parity, as exemplified by Russia and Austria-Hungary. A more adequate picture of the gold standard comprises a stable core with southern and eastern peripheries – an intriguing reminder of today's divisions.

2.3. Long-term interest rates

The long-term interest rates shown in Figure 3 were computed as the implicit return on government-funded long-term debt. The corresponding bonds typically bore gold coupons and thus provide us with a measure of the various governments' default risk, because such instruments were not subject to exchange rate depreciation (technically, paying the coupon in paper rather than in gold would amount to a partial default). The diagram shows that interest rates converged only between 1905 and 1913. Among the core countries, convergence was achieved as early as 1880, and was sustained throughout the period, although some narrowing of the range is perceptible in the final years. The other countries faced much higher rates, but they all tended to converge towards the core countries until the late 1880s. Then a split occurred. While central and eastern European countries (Russia and Austria-Hungary) converged further, southern Europe exhibited an opposite trend. During the 1890s, 1900s and early 1910s, the spread between central and eastern Europe and the European core continued to decline, only interrupted by the Russo-Japanese war, which caused a relatively mild upsurge in Russian rates. In contrast, in the early 1890s, interest rates in Portugal, Greece and Spain, and to much more modest extent Italy, bounced up.[3] A steady decline came later, after the turn of the century: to the Reich's disappointment, Italy's long-run interest rate even fell below that of Germany.

2.4. Debt/GDP ratios

The ratios of total debt to gross domestic product are shown in Figure 4. We can observe considerable differences across countries, with ratios ranging from 200% (Greece, 1890) to 3% (Switzerland throughout the period).[4] At the beginning of the period, large debtors (in terms of national income) included Spain (160%), which defaulted in 1881–2, Italy and France (around 95%), Portugal, the Netherlands

---

[3] The estimated interest rates that we report take into account the reduction in interest service that these countries implemented. The maintenance of high interest rates after the partial defaults suggests that they did not substantially improve these countries' prospects.

[4] For Switzerland, we report only the federal debt. Including cantonal debt would not change the picture much. Note, however, that for other 'federal' or 'confederal' countries such as Germany and Austria-Hungary, the figures we report are inclusive of all regional debts.

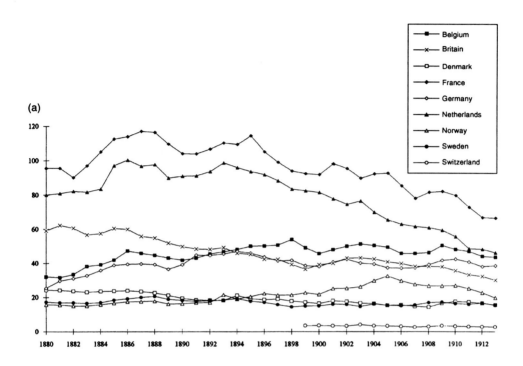

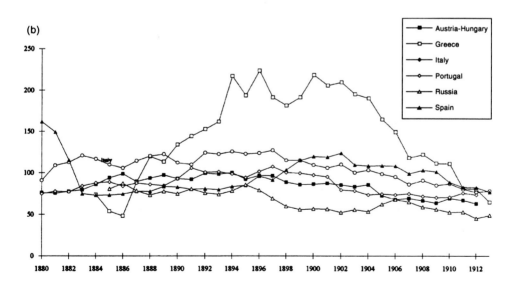

Figure 4. Debt/GDP ratios (%) in Europe, 1880–1913
Source: See Appendix A.

and Austria-Hungary (75%). Greece and Russia, for which debt/GDP ratios can be computed only after 1885, also entered the scene with ratios around 75%. Thus, more countries were found above a hypothetical 60% threshold, where the UK roughly lay, than below it: only Germany and some small countries (Belgium, Scandinavia and Switzerland) were found substantially below that level.

Pre-First World War levels tended to be slightly lower. With the exception of Spain and Italy (around 100%), France and Greece (at about 80%) and Portugal (120%), debt/GDP ratios were below 60%. Yet, some initially low-debt countries (such as Germany and Belgium) had experienced a mild increase in their ratio, so that intra-European differences were smaller than they had been in the past. This evolution, far from continuous, conceals a general trend of initially increasing and then declining ratios (the exception being Britain, where the decline was steady). The coincidence between this movement and the post-1900 process of long-term interest rate convergence observed in Figure 3 is striking. It suggest that long-term interest rates are a broad measure of default risk. This pattern contradicts the received wisdom – based on the American and British experiences – according to which public debts rose in periods of war and declined in periods of peace. With peace prevailing during the period, military shocks were relatively few. Even when wars occurred and led to debt accumulation, the broad trends were not reversed, as can be seen from the case of Russia during its war against Japan, or of Greece at the time of the Balkan crises after 1900. Conversely, debts rose before domestic or external unrest, as exemplified by Spain and Portugal until the mid-1890s. The rise of continental debts in the midst of the *pax britannica* suggests that current European concerns with high debts in fact have very old precedents.

Summarizing, we find that during the period of the gold standard, European countries went through a largely common trend of rising and then declining debts. This process was accompanied by co-movements in long-term interest rates and by exchange rate depreciation. The heyday of the gold standard was in fact circum-scribed to the years between 1900 and 1913, when spreads between exchange rates, interest rates and debt/GDP ratios were decreasing. It does not cover the whole period between 1880 and 1913, as is often assumed. As we reconsider the overall experience, we seek to determine the common causes of varied experiences, in contrast to the traditional focus on the common causes of an alleged common success.

3. INSTITUTIONAL FIXES: DEMOCRACY, CENTRAL BANK INDEPENDENCE AND THE SPREAD OF THE EUROPEAN GOLD STANDARD

In this section, we document the contribution of institutional arrangements to monetary stability under the European gold standard. Our goal is to try to assess the extent to which the features documented above can be ascribed to institutions.

3.1. Politics and institutions: the gold standard record

As shiny as gold may be, it cannot be used to stabilize debts that have been monetized. Fiscal misbehaviour inevitably leads to a gradual depletion of gold reserves, usually accompanied by a speculative attack and exchange depreciation (Flood and Garber, 1984). What matters is the decision-making process *within* the gold standard, hence the importance of relations between monetary authorities and the polity. It is often believed that, before 1914, monetary authorities remained largely insulated from politics and were able to commit themselves credibly to the maintenance of stable exchange rates. This claim (which can be traced back to Polanyi (1944)) has taken a variety of forms. Some authors have argued that the pre-1914 period was one of universal central bank independence. For instance, Capie *et al.* (1994) have argued that monetary *laissez-faire* (by which they mean limited government intervention) emerged in the nineteenth century and dominated throughout the years 1880–1914, until it was repealed during the war. Under this view, most analyses tend to focus on the relationship between central and commercial banks (see, e.g., Goodhart, 1988). Very few recent studies document the long swings in central bank independence (partial exceptions include Holtfrerich (1988) and Bouvier (1988), who briefly discuss the pre-1914 period for Germany and France; Capie *et al.* (1994) also discuss the issue briefly, and it is dealt with more extensively in Capie (1997)).

The modern prejudice is that central banks were *de facto* in the hands of the financial establishment, which thus implemented its preferred policies independently of what the public felt (Gallarotti, 1995). Eichengreen (1992, 1996) further suggests that the restrictive electoral franchise, the limited strength of trade unionism and the dearth of parliamentary labour parties helped to reduce distributional conflicts because those who were in charge of monetary policy were those who suffered least from its effects. Painful adjustments that resulted in wage contraction were always feasible, since workers did not have a say. Table 1 reports estimates of the registered electorate as a proportion of the enfranchised age group (see Flora *et al.* (1983) for a discussion of the methodological problems involved in this measurement).[5] The extension of the franchise in the latter part of the nineteenth century corresponds to the gradual elimination of exclusions based on income as well as reductions in the list of requirements. By the turn of the century, remaining exclusions for men included the homeless, convicts, those with criminal records or in asylums, and

---

[5] The figures are (politically incorrectly) constructed on the basis of the male population only, since such was the way universality of voting rights was understood at that time. From the point of view of our argument this restriction matters only if potential female voters would have systematically favoured less conservative interests. Yet as Scandinavian socialists would learn to their cost in the 1900s, women's right to vote often resulted, in the short run, in more conservative outcomes, not more leftist ones.

Table 1. The extension of the franchise:
those eligible to vote as a % of the adult male population

	1880	1890	1990	1910	1913
Britain	35.8	62.4	61.5	62.2	62.4
France	86.4	86.6	90.0	91.5	90.5
Germany	91.3	92.3	94.2	94	86.8
Belgium	8.2	8.1	90.7	91.6	91.6
Netherlands	12.2	25.6	51.6	62.6	67.0
Switzerland	79.2	80.2	78.1	76.4	75.8
Denmark	78.3	84.2	85.4	87.9	87.8
Norway	23.7	32.2	89.7	95.0	95.0
Sweden	23.5	22.9	27.5	77.5	76.5
Italy	9.0	32.0	26.5	32.2	89.8
Spain	n.a.	n.a.	n.a.	n.a.	n.a.
Portugal	n.a.	n.a.	n.a.	n.a.	n.a.
Greece	n.a.	n.a.	n.a.	n.a.	n.a.
Austria-Hungary	24.8	30.5	34.3	94.5	94.5
Russia	n.a.	n.a.	n.a.	n.a.	n.a.

Source: Flora *et al.* (1983), vol. I, pp. 89ff.

those who had recently changed residence; for them, and for women, democracy would have to wait. But workers were in general no longer excluded.

Table 1 does not suggest a direct link between limitations on democracy and the stability of the gold standard. In fact, the trend towards extended franchise coincides after 1900 with the decline in debt/GDP ratios. For instance, in Italy, universal suffrage was granted only in the early years of the twentieth century, after the lira was firmly stabilized, and it did not weaken the lira. It is during these years that the yield on Italian bonds fell below the German level. Similarly, exchange rate instability in Austria coincided with a restricted franchise, while stability again coincided with an extended franchise. Conversely, core countries such as Germany and France had granted universal and equal suffrage well before the period under study (in 1871 and 1848 respectively). Many authors may have been influenced by the case of Britain, where a restricted franchise did indeed coincide with monetary stability. But on this dimension, when all of Europe is taken into account, Britain stands as an exception.

3.2. Central bank independence, 1880–1914: doctrines and features

No view could be more distant from the concerns of economists in the 1890s and 1900s than the modern prejudice that central bank independence was the normal state of affairs during the gold standard. In the years *immediately* preceding the First World War, the protection of central banks against political pressures was indeed high. However, this was perceived by contemporaries as being the result of a patient construct which, in a large number of European nations, had only recently been completed. Summarizing in 1911 a view that had developed in the profession over the past half century, leading monetary expert Raphaël-Georges Lévy refers to the 'theory that calls for the separation of the central bank from the State' (Lévy, 1911). This theory has a surprisingly familiar ring: according to Lévy, central bank independence was an absolute prerequisite for exchange rate stability, because a non-independent bank would lead market participants to expect eventual debt monetization. As a result, central banks or banks of issue serve public treasuries better if their 'existence [is] more independent, and their administration more separate, from that of the State. The less public authority gets involved into the management of the banking system, the better national credit and wealth are protected.' On the eve of the First World War, Lévy wrote approvingly of the progress of central bank independence.

Central banks initially developed as the interface between the banking and industrial communities and the state. On the one hand, the banking and industrial community needed a central bank to implement some minimum level of co-ordination among financial institutions, most importantly to provide lender of last resort functions in periods of crisis. For this purpose, co-operation of state bodies was necessary, as special laws and decrees had to be passed. On the other hand, the state wanted easy access to credit, as well as influence over monetary policy: for instance, favouring certain groups or making credit more abundant in a proto-Keynesian way (as argued by Kindleberger (1988), public works and fiscal stimuli were not an invention of the 1930s). States and banking or industrial communities had thus both common and divergent interests, and central banks' charters were the locus where the balance of power both crystallized and could be renegotiated.

Governments could extract seigniorage in two ways. They could force the central bank to monetize the debt and they could directly circulate government notes independently of the central bank. Following Cukierman's (1992) distinction between limitations on lending and ways to influence decisions, two features of central banks' charters are of interest. Direct political control is linked to the ownership of the bank (privately or state owned), the appointment of the board (governor, sub-governor(s) and council), as well as rules governing the cover system. Obviously, the greater the private sector ingredient in the decision-making process, the more constrained was the government (Capie (1997) makes a similar point). Indirect control rests on rules governing the government's right to obtain short-term advances, to monetize securities, or to issue its own paper. One should not take a nominalist view of such features. Statutes were not resources lying exclusively in the hands of central bankers or governments. They were the endogenous outcome of negotiations that codified state–bank relations when charters were drafted, and their adjustment over time followed, rather than preceded, actual changes in underlying power relations. Leads and lags existed between printed norms and actual behaviour. For instance, the central bank's need to obtain on occasions a renewal of its charter, especially in the presence of a potential competitor, reduced its actual bargaining power well *below* what statutes suggested, especially as the renegotiation of the charter approached. Moreover, 'invisible' threats could very well distort actual practices. On the other hand, the need for the government to secure a minimum level of co-operation from the banking community (for instance, when large public loans were floated) certainly checked its incentive to exploit the bank of issue.[6]

3.3. The good guys

Table 2 summarizes the information for the three core countries (Britain, France and Germany) and Table 3 focuses on smaller economies (Belgium, the Netherlands and Scandinavia). For these eight countries, which were steady members of the gold club, we find substantial balances in the relationship between government and the central bank. Statutory limits usually applied to automatic credit lines, which were kept to a minimum, when they existed. Issues backed by government securities were tightly regulated. Additional requirements pertained to the cover system. Taken together, these measures made sure that the bank would always have enough free resources to invest in private bills (as opposed to government paper), while providing for an appropriate cover ratio. These protections were often further supported by the balance of power on the board. Because the central bank was often a private corporation, it had to include some representation of the shareholders. Interestingly, in Sweden, the only country in this group where it was state owned, the central bank was explicitly made responsible not to the Treasury but to Parliament, to which it had to report. In all eight countries, parliamentary audits of central bank action and accounts generalized over time.

This general pattern, however, conceals national idiosyncrasies. Britain, the Netherlands, Belgium and the Scandinavian countries had the most independent central banks. All combined a fair amount of independence in the decision-making process with statutory requirements regarding their cover system, advances to the state, and issues on the basis of government securities. In France, however, almost no formal rule existed regarding either the cover system or limitations on government credit. Since parallel issues were not authorized, reserve ratios and investment in public securities depended on the balance of power on the bank's board (the Conseil Général). The independence of the Bank of France thus rested on the ability of shareholders to impose their decisions during board meetings. They were indeed able to outvote government officials, but the checks and balances that

---

[6] Posen (1994) supports the endogeneity view largely held among economic historians. Alesina (1994) presents the mainstream economists' counterview.

Table 2. Central bank independence: core countries

	Britain: Bank of England	France: Banque de France	Germany: Reichsbank
Status	Private	Private	Private
Head Appointed by	Governor and 1 deputy governor Shareholders	*Gouverneur* and 2 *sous gouverneurs* Government	President Imperial government
Council Appointed by	24 directors Shareholders	*Régents* Shareholders	4 curators, the Chancellor and three delegates 1 curator appointed by the Chancellor, the others by the Federal Council 3 delegates appointed by the shareholders participate in board meetings (no vote)
Cover system	Act of 1844: 100% specie backing in the issue department, plus fixed issues on 'securities' Suspension of the Act of 1844 required to issue beyond this limit	No formal rule (limits on aggregate issues are regularly revised upwards)	Fixed limit against which reserve of 1/3 must be held Remaining 2/3 to be issued on the basis of first-class bills Issues beyond this figure must have 100% cash backing Penalties beyond
Parallel issues	No	No	No
Statutory advances	Yes But very limited: 'deficiency advances' in the Banking Department under parliamentary control	No obligation	Possible (discount of government bills)
Statutory issues on govt sec.	Upper limit	No obligation	Possible
State's treasurer	Yes	Yes, partly	Yes (for free since 1909)
Profits	Shared	Rent to the state	Shared
Monopoly	Yes (quasi-monopoly)	Yes (since 1848)	Yes (quasi-monopoly since 1876, reinforced in 1899)
Charter/revised	1833/1844	1857/1897	1875/1889/1899/1909
Legal tender	Act of 1844	Since 1870	Not until 1909

Sources: Lévy (1911); Conant (1915).

Table 3. Central bank independence: small countries

	Netherlands: de Nederlandsche Bank	Sweden: Riksbank	Norway: Norgesbank	Denmark: Nationalbanken	Belgium: Banque Nationale de Belgique
Status	Private	Government owned	Private, but state is large shareholder	Private	Private
Head	President (7 years)	Commission that is not responsible to the executive govt	President and vice president	5 members in board of directors	Governor (5 years)
Appointed by	Government		Government	1 by govt, 5 by shareholders	Government
Council Appointed by	5 regents Shareholders	and controlled by the Diet	5 members Shareholders	15 members Co-opted	6 *Directeurs* Shareholders
Cover system	Reserve >40% of circulation	Reserve >40m kronor	35m kroner unbacked issue	Reserve >50% issue	Reserve (=specie + bills) >33% of issues
Parallel issue	No	No	No	No	No
Statutory advances	Yes, but very limited	No	No	Yes, but ceiling	No
Statutory issues on govt sec.	Limited to a fraction of the reserve and capital	Yes, but limited to 3/8ths of the 40m reserve	No	Yes, but very limited	Yes, but very limited (<5m)
State's treasurer	Yes	No	Yes	Yes (state's cashier office)	Yes
Profits	Yes: profits in excess of dividends	Yes: all profits (state bank)	Yes: profits in excess of dividends +retained earnings	Yes: fixed duty + profits in excess of dividends	Yes: profits in excess of dividends
Monopoly	Yes	Yes, since 1904	Yes, if convertibility maintained	Yes, since 1818	Yes, since 1850
Charter/revised	1863/1889/1903	1887/1897/1904	1816/1900	1818/1907	1850/1872/1900
Legal tender	Yes	Yes	Yes	Yes	Yes, since 1873

Table 4 Central bank independence: central and eastern Europe

	Russia: Bank of Russia Before 1894	Russia: Bank of Russia After 1894	Austria-Hungary: Österreichisch-Ungarischen Bank Before 1892	Austria-Hungary: Österreichisch-Ungarischen Bank After 1892
Status	State	State	Private	Private
Head Appointed by	Governor Imperial government	Governor Imperial government	Governor and 2 deputy governors Jointly appointed	Governor and 2 deputy governors Jointly appointed
Council Appointed by	Board of civil servants	Board of civil servants	Council General (12 members) Shareholders	Council General (12 members) Shareholders
Cover system	None	1894: limit on issues 1887: without gold backing 1897: 50% gold backing for issues under 600m roubles, 100% cover beyond this point	200m florins unbacked issues Reserves >40% circulation	400m crowns unbacked issues Reserves (1900)
Parallel issue	Yes, unlimited	No	Yes	No
Statutory advances	Yes, unlimited	No	Yes, since 1873 overdraft to both Austria and Hungary	Very limited
Statutory issues on govt sec.	Yes, but limited	Yes, but limited	Yes	No
State's treasurer	Yes	Yes	Yes	Yes
Profits	100% go to the state	100% go to the state	Shared	Shared
Monopoly	Yes	Yes	Yes	Yes
Charter/revised	(statutes) 1860/1894/1897	(statutes) 1860/1894/1897	1878/1887/1897/1907	1878/1887/1897/1907
Legal tender	Yes	Yes	Yes	Yes

Sources: Lévy (1911); Conant (1915).

prevailed in some other countries were lacking.[7] Ironically perhaps, Germany had the least independent central bank of the group. Large powers rested in the hands of the Chancellor of the Empire, who effectively directed the bank through a technocrat. The shareholders' role was limited to auditing and certifying the bank's accounts. Their delegates could participate in board meetings, but their votes were not taken into account. Most checks rested on the set of formal rules governing note issues (see James (1997) for a congruent view). Much of the discipline was exercised through the cover system, which put a lower limit on the specie reserve. The fact that the Chancellor needed shareholders' support from time to time (for instance, when the capital of the bank had to be increased) also fostered compliance to these agreed rules.

3.4. Central bank independence in the European periphery

3.4.1. Central–eastern Europe.

In eastern and southern Europe, state–bank relations changed over time and differed from those prevailing in core countries (Table 4). In Russia the bank was owned and controlled by the state. The cover system, initially modelled on the British system, nominally imposed tight limits on the issue of banknotes. These limitations quickly lost significance as the Treasury started to circulate its own notes. Moreover, while issues based on government bonds were limited, short-term advances to the state were unlimited. Several schemes were tried as the rouble depreciated in the 1870s and fluctuated in the 1880s, but reform had to await the consolidation of Russian finances in the early 1890s. While the central bank remained under state control, a number of decrees provided for strict limits on note issues by the government. The Russian Treasury borrowed on international markets to purchase the bank's gold reserve. In 1897 the system took its final shape with a regime that provided for one of the highest cover ratios on the continent, and ruled out parallel issues. Contemporaries were generally impressed. For instance, Conant (1915) concluded that 'the history of the Bank of Russia is of interest, because it is the most successful instance on a large scale of a bank of issue owned by the State, and because it carried through in the closing decade of the nineteenth century the most serious operations ever undertaken in Europe for the restoration of stability of exchange upon a gold basis'. Of course, this policy could be reversed in a matter of days by a few decrees. The Bank of Russia's independence was credible only inasmuch as nobody expected the Treasury to change its policy stance.

---

[7] The absence of formal constraints left more space for bargaining. This has led historians of the relations between the Bank of France and the state (Bouvier, 1988; Plessis, 1985) to conclude that the bank was not very independent. That the Bank of France was able to implement deflationary policies when needed, and even when this did not suit the government, is in our view the proof of its effective autonomy.

The Austro-Hungarian case reveals some similarities. Until the late 1870s, the central bank was the Bank of Austria. While private, it operated under the control of the Austrian Treasury, which could obtain short-term advances and force the bank to take up its securities. As in Russia, the Treasury could short-circuit the bank and issue government notes: in 1877 these issues had reached 350 million florins at a time when central bank note issues totalled about 300 million. This situation created considerable uncertainty and the exchange rate fluctuated widely. In 1878 the statutes of the Austrian central bank were redrafted. Under pressure from Hungary, the central bank, renamed the Austro-Hungarian Bank, came under joint control of both Austria and Hungary. This situation was further consolidated in 1887 with the introduction of a combined system of fractional reserve and minimum cover ratio, which provided tight limits on direct government seigniorage. In 1892 a set of monetary laws laid the foundations for the adoption of the gold standard. The outstanding government paper money would have to be repurchased gradually, and the Treasury would no longer be allowed to issue notes. Statutory advances were kept to a minimum and government bonds were not allowed to be part of the reserve. The Austro-Hungarian Bank was gradually converging towards western European standards.

3.4.2. Mediterranean countries. Southern European countries provide a graphic illustration of how easily independence can be suspended in the face of serious fiscal difficulties (Table 5). Treasuries in the four southern European countries usually refrained from directly issuing notes. They preferred to use statutory advances and automatic credit on government bonds. While initially limited, these facilities were gradually extended during the second half of the 1880s. For instance, in 1887 both Portugal and Greece loosened the constraints on short-term advances. The process accelerated in the early 1890s. The Spanish government decided that the bills issued to finance the Treasury's overseas expenses would be discounted by the Bank of Spain, which was further forced in 1891 to grant a large credit to the state. In Portugal, Greece and Italy, short-term advances were made to the Treasury in exchange for the deposit of government bonds, sometimes almost at will. Limits on note issue were repeatedly raised.

Italy was the first country to take decisive remedial steps. In 1893 it imposed tight limits on government credit and added a 40% cover system to its central bank. Greece followed suit in 1898 after the international rescue package, put together to help Greece pay its indemnity to Turkey, led to a shift in the balance of power between the bank (which had in the past unsuccessfully sought to resist government intervention) and the Treasury. Now under close creditor control, the Treasury's ability to pressurize the central bank was substantially reduced. Additional automatic advances were ruled out in 1899 and, finally, investment in public securities was kept to a statutory maximum.

In Spain, reform started under the Villaverde ministry, at the turn of the century. In 1902 it was decided that short-term advances to the Treasury should be

Table 5. Central bank independence: southern Europe

	Portugal: Banco de Portugal	Greece: National Bank of Greece	Spain: Banca d'España	Italy: Banca Nazionale/ Banca d'Italia
Status	Private	Private	Private	Private
Head	Governor, vice-governor	Governor, 2 sub-governors and one commissaire royal	Governor	*Direttore Generale*
Appointed by	Government (Governor 3 years), vice-governor from list supplied by directors	Elected by shareholders' general assembly	Government	Shareholders with government approval
Council	10 directors	Administrators	Board	Board
Appointed by	Shareholders	Shareholders	Shareholders	Shareholders
Cover system	Reserve ratio rules Dismantled in the late 1880s and early 1890s, never reimposed	1877: limits on note issues 1885: 1/3 of issues backed by gold	1874: specie = 1/4 note issue and max. issue = 750m ptas 1891: reserve >1/3 note issue, gold >1/2 reserve, and max. issue = 500m ptas 1898: max. issue = 2500 m ptas	1874–84: under the *Consorzio* limits on the circulation of each bank of issue 1891: each bank's max. issue is raised 1893: gold and foreign bills >40% note issue After 1897 reserve must be >300 then 400m lire
Parallel issue	No	Yes	No	No

Advances	Limit of 2000 contos until 1887 Since 1887: ceiling renegotiated every year	1885: government credit in exchange for larger note issues Existing advances converted into government securities in 1898	Yes: Whole period: up to 125m ptas (law of 1874) 1890s: credit by discounting ultramar's *pagarés* 1891–3: extra credit of 150m ptas 1902: advances (except for the 150m ptas credit) must be reimbursed by 1911	Yes: 1874–84: advances from *Consorzio* against government securities (up to 1bn lire) 1884–93: advances of banks of issue against deposit of government securities After 1893: limited. Advances up to 115m lire only
Statutory issues on govt sec.	Limited until 1887 Yes, since 1887	1/3 of note issues according to law of 1885 Short-term debt consolidated in 1898 must be amortized	Yes: no limit	Before 1893: yes, banks can take government bonds in portfolio After 1893: yes, but not beyond 75m
State's treasurer	Yes	Yes, some treasurer role	Yes	Yes (increased responsibilities over time)
Profits	Shared	Shared until 1892	Nothing goes to the state	Only tax on circulation
Monopoly	8 July 1891	Quasi monopoly in 1899	1874	Quasi monopoly in 1893
Charter/revised	1846/1887	1841/1866/1903	1856/1874/1899	1893
Legal tender	1887–91: 5 km around the bank 1891: Portugal	Yes (1885)	Yes (1874)	Yes (1893)

Sources: Lévy (1911); Conant (1915); private communication to the authors by Elio Cerrito (Italy), Olga Christodoulakis (Greece) and Jaime Reis (Portugal); see also Cerrito (1995).

gradually reimbursed. While investment in public securities was still unlimited, the Treasury made a substantial effort to consolidate its balance sheet and repurchase the former advances, and this in turn succeeded in consolidating the bank's reserves. The proportion of specie in the reserves grew at the expense of government bonds. In Portugal, efforts at separating the central bank from the state remained elusive. Until the end of the period, the Portuguese Treasury continued to draw on the Bank of Portugal by depositing depreciating government securities in exchange for short-term credit. This easy door to monetization was never shut, and the political turmoil of the last years before the war led to a return to automatic central bank credit and exchange rate fragility. On the eve of the First World War, Portugal had the least independent central bank and was not in sight of the gold standard.

3.5. Conclusion

It is clearly impossible to claim that central bank independence was the European gold standard's recipe for monetary stability. Rather, poor exchange rate performance was associated with low levels of central bank independence. Much like today, contemporary observers concluded that central bank independence was the exogenous source of stability. Yet the evidence suggests that institutions were extremely fragile and never resisted the pull of fiscal problems. The evolution of Mediterranean central banks' statutes in the 1890s demonstrates that the protective walls that appeared so safe in core countries could very well crumble. Eventual efforts towards better protection of monetary authorities were in fact led by governments (Raffalovich, 1900). Central bank independence thus came and went as fiscal needs changed. Public finance problems led to the collapse of Mediterranean currencies in the 1890s, and their resolution led the way out. The consolidations in Italy, Spain and Greece had not been imposed on the Treasury by a powerful central bank. Rather, the increased autonomy of the central bank resulted from the Treasury's ability to balance its accounts, or in Russia and Austria, from the desire to accumulate gold reserves. In the next section, therefore, we consider how constraints on debt accumulation might have influenced both exchange rate stability and central bank autonomy.

4. IN SEARCH OF THE MARKET MECHANISM

4.1. Market discipline: the weak, the strong and the ugly

According to the market discipline hypothesis, lenders charge higher interest rates to borrowers whom they consider riskier, which in turn discourages risky behaviour. The question, of course, is to determine what defines risky behaviour.

Bordo and Rockoff (1996) ask whether adherence to the gold standard was the signal that markets used to judge countries. They find that long-term interest rates are indeed statistically lower in countries on the gold standard, once account is taken of fiscal and monetary conditions.[8] Faced with higher interest rates, countries with a poor record of adherence to gold felt the incentive to put their house in order. In other words, the gold standard acted as a 'good housekeeping seal of approval'.

The market mechanism is undoubtedly an important part of any comprehensive picture of the gold standard, but its implications for EMU must be considered carefully. It is not only membership of a given club (the gold standard then, EMU tomorrow) that markets monitor, but more broadly the credibility of policies which in turn permit the participation in that club to be maintained. This distinction matters a lot for EMU because a strict interpretation of Bordo and Rockoff's results could be that, once countries commit to a permanently fixed exchange rate, the seal of approval mechanism is lost. Yet there are grounds to believe that markets will discriminate among EMU member governments – as opposed to countries – paying particular attention to fiscal policies.

In this section, consistent with modern analyses of market discipline (e.g., Bishop et al., 1989), we focus on the pricing of government bonds. Three possible patterns are tried, as explained formally in Box 1. The first pattern may be interpreted as the weak form of the market discipline hypothesis. It posits a linear relationship between risk premia (measured by the spread between the country's long-term interest rate and a (risk-free) British consul) and debt levels (measured by debt/GDP ratios). This specification assumes that increased indebtedness is costly, but that the marginal cost of increased indebtedness is constant. Supply-side incentives for fiscal orthodoxy do not change as debt accumulates. We will refer to this weak version of the market discipline hypothesis as the 'linear form'.

We consider two additional specifications. Both assume that the relation between debt levels and interest rates is non-linear: more specifically, that the marginal cost of borrowing increases with the debt level. The 'credit punishing' specification – the strong form of the market discipline hypothesis – posits that borrowing costs grow exponentially with the debt level. This specification assumes that debt accumulation increases the probability of default. In contrast to the linear form, the growth of the marginal cost of borrowing creates a growing disincentive for debt over-accumulation. Finally, the 'ugly' form of the market discipline hypothesis considers that there exists a debt threshold beyond which the sovereign is no longer able to borrow because lenders react to the risk of default by rationing borrowers (Stiglitz and Weiss, 1981). Technically, the credit supply schedule has an asymptote (an infinite limit) at the level of indebtedness where rationing occurs. We refer to this last

---

[8] The sample used by Bordo and Rockoff only partly overlaps with ours.

Box 1. The linear, punishing and rationing models

The following arbitrage relation states that, for a risk-neutral investor, the expected return for a risky bond must equal the expected return for a risk-free bond, say a British consol (s_{it} represents the risk premium charged on currency i at date t):

$$(1 + R_{UKt} + s_{it}) \cdot P(H_t) + 0 \cdot (1 - P(H_t)) = 1 + R_{UKt} \tag{1}$$

where $R_{it} = R_{UKt} + s_{it}$ stands for the interest rate charged to country i at date t (s_{it} is the default premium, $P(H_{it})$ is the probability of default, $P'(H_{it}) < 0$, and H_{it} is a variable summarizing the determinants of default (we abstract from taxation as a large proportion of the bonds studied here were exempt from tax duties). Getting rid of the country and time indices, assuming that $P(H)$ is a logistic function $(P(H) = 1/(1 + \exp(H)))$, and writing $H = \alpha B/GDP + X'\beta$ (where B/GDP is the debt/GDP ratio and X is a vector of exogenous variables influencing the probability of default), we obtain:

$$s = \exp\left(\alpha \frac{B}{GDP} + \beta_0 + \beta_1 \frac{EX}{GDP} + \beta_2 \frac{GDP}{POP}\right) + \varepsilon \tag{2}$$

which is non-linear. We call (2) the 'credit punishing' equation. EX/GDP is the exports to GDP ratio, and GDP/POP is real GDP per head converted at PPP prices. In this formulation, the default premium grows exponentially with the debt level, but there is no absolute limit to borrowing.

Alternatively, the default premium can be modelled as an increasing function of B/GDP, but with an upper limit on debt accumulation. This can be done if one assumes that the whole debt is reimbursed and reissued at every period (see Bayoumi *et al.*, 1995). This allows us to identify the marginal cost of borrowing (R_i) with the average cost of servicing the total debt (the interest burden on the outstanding debt). In this case, the formula assumes that the derivative of the cost of borrowing with respect to the debt/GDP ratio converges towards infinity when the debt/GDP ratio approaches a certain threshold (equal to $1/\gamma$). Formally:

$$s = \left(\alpha \frac{B}{GDP} + \beta_0 + \beta_1 \frac{EX}{GDP} + \beta_2 \frac{GDP}{POP}\right) \cdot \frac{1}{1 - \gamma \dfrac{B}{GDP}} + \varepsilon \tag{3}$$

We call this equation the 'credit-rationing hypothesis' as it shows that the default premium rises to infinity when the debt/GDP ratio approaches $1/\gamma$: borrowers are prevented from increasing their debt beyond $1/\gamma$. These two formulations are to be contrasted with an alternative linear relation between the default premium and the debt/GDP ratio. Formally:

$$s = \alpha \frac{B}{GDP} + \beta_0 + \beta_1 \frac{EX}{GDP} + \beta_2 \frac{GDP}{POP} + \varepsilon \tag{4}$$

which is referred to in the text as the linear form of the market discipline hypothesis.

version of the market discipline hypothesis as 'credit rationing'.[9] Clearly the linear mechanism provides weaker incentives to borrowers than the punishing or rationing ones for high debt levels.

4.2. Estimation results

We use our panel of European countries to examine the link between indebtedness and the cost of borrowing by regressing the spreads of government bond yields over a risk-free bond on the debt/GDP ratios. Our regressions also capture the effect of economic fundamentals that may influence debt sustainability. These include the exports/GDP ratio and levels of economic development measured by using real GDP per head converted at PPP prices. We also included an 'on gold' variable, which takes the value 1 when the country is on gold in any given year, and zero otherwise. This variable may be interpreted as either capturing the additional effect of market discipline in rewarding countries adhering to gold (the seal of approval view) or reflecting a number of factors that were known to market participants, but which are not included in our data set and which were correlated with adherence to the gold standard (e.g., political shocks).

The results of pooled cross-section regressions are shown in Table 6. We use instrumental variables (see Appendix B for details) with explanatory variables alternatively included in and excluded from the estimation. The results range from the most parsimonious specifications (only debt ratios are included) to the most extensive ones (all exogenous variables are included). In all regressions, the parameters are generally found statistically significant and their signs correspond to economic intuition. The negative effect of per-capita income reflects the fact that economic development is typically accompanied by a greater ability to tax, and hence improved debt sustainability. The negative effect of openness captures the fact that in nineteenth-century Europe, capital exporting countries were also the most open ones. Open countries were usually capital lenders and had a greater ability to retain foreign investment; hence they were better able to deal with external payment problems (Bairoch, 1974). The signs of the debt and 'on gold' variables clearly fit the previous discussions.

Judging from the fit (adjusted R^2), the non-linear specifications (panels a and c) do a better job than the linear specification (panel b). This conclusion can be rigorously tested when comparing the 'rationing' and 'linear' specifications, since the latter can be seen as imposing on the former the restriction that the 'debt rationing' coefficient is zero. This restriction is clearly rejected. Additional tests presented in Appendix B

---

[9] This latter form of the market discipline hypothesis was applied to US states by Bayoumi *et al.* (1993). Their findings imply that American states are rationed at relatively low debt ratios, all below 10% of gross state product. These thresholds are far below what was observed under the gold standard, and far below current European debt levels. This suggests that the overall economic and institutional context in which US states accumulate debts is quite different from the European one, past, present and future.

Table 6. Assessing the market mechanism

(a) 'Rationing'

	Debt/ GDP ratio	Export/ GDP ratio	Per-capita GDP	On gold	Rationing	Implied debt threshold (% of GDP)	R^2 adj.	Hausman	Sargan	SBIC
1	1.732	−0.958	−1.627	−0.528	0.356	281%	0.67	$\chi^2(3) = 89.26$	$\chi^2(1) = 0.01$	708.1
	(3.06)	(−0.98)	(−2.39)	(−3.22)	(10.18)			$(P = 0.00)$	$(P = 0.92)$	
2	1.949	−0.041	−2.052	—	0.343	292%	0.66	$\chi^2(2) = 61.54$	$\chi^2(1) = 0.03$	710.2
	(3.18)	(−0.04)	(−2.81)		(9.47)			$(P = 0.00)$	$(P = 0.87)$	
3	2.037	−0.886	—	—	0.338	296%	0.65	$\chi^2(2) = 9.19$	$\chi^2(2) = 0.25$	712.6
	(3.15)	(−1.01)			(9.32)			$(P = 0.01)$	$(P = 0.88)$	
4	1.949	—	−2.054	—	0.343	292%	0.66	$\chi^2(2) = 25.58$	$\chi^2(2) = 0.01$	707.2
	(3.17)		(−2.92)		(9.52)			$(P = 0.00)$	$(P = 0.99)$	
5	2.044	—	—	—	0.335	299%	0.65	$\chi^2(2) = 18.90$	$\chi^2(3) = 0.45$	709.7
	(3.07)				(9.27)			$(P = 0.00)$	$(P = 0.93)$	

(b) 'Linear'

	Debt/ GDP ratio	Export/ GDP ratio	Per-capita GDP	On gold	R^2 adj.	Hausman	Sargan	SBIC
1	5.645	3.838	−1.708	−0.398	0.62	$\chi^2(2) = 12.40$	$\chi^2(1) = 0.02$	735.6
	(4.69)	(2.94)	(−2.36)	(−1.36)		$(P = 0.00)$	$(P = 0.90)$	
2	5.877	4.287	−1.929	—	0.62	$\chi^2(2) = 10.42$	$\chi^2(1) = 0.01$	733.8
	(5.27)	(3.36)	(−2.42)			$(P = 0.01)$	$(P = 0.91)$	
3	6.315	3.326	—	—	0.61	$\chi^2(1) = 6.83$	$\chi^2(2) = 0.13$	733.7
	(6.24)	(2.69)				$(P = 0.01)$	$(P = 0.93)$	
4	5.768	—	−1.569	—	0.61	$\chi^2(2) = 9.12$	$\chi^2(2) = 0.13$	733.2
	(5.15)		(−2.00)			$(P = 0.01)$	$(P = 0.94)$	
5	6.160	—	—	—	0.61	$\chi^2(1) = 2.19$	$\chi^2(3) = 0.06$	732.3
	(6.16)					$(P = 0.14)$	$(P = 0.99)$	

(c) 'Punishing'

	Debt/ GDP ratio	Export/ GDP ratio	Per-capita GDP	On gold	R^2 adj.	Hausman	Sargan	SBIC
1	1.449	−16.426	−3.213	−0.345	0.81	$\chi^2(1) = 20.19$	$\chi^2(1) = 0.03$	595.5
	(6.28)	(−3.43)	(−5.08)	(−3.39)		$(P = 0.00)$	$(P = 0.87)$	
2	1.490	−15.451	−3.652	—	0.80	$\chi^2(2) = 15.08$	$\chi^2(1) = 0.01$	601.0
	(6.32)	(−3.03)	(−6.43)			$(P = 0.00)$	$(P = 0.91)$	
3	2.025	−10.06	—	—	0.72	$\chi^2(1) = 12.05$	$\chi^2(2) = 0.48$	665.8
	(7.75)	(−2.66)				$(P = 0.00)$	$(P = 0.79)$	
4	1.471	—	−3.476	—	0.79	$\chi^2(3) = 31.90$	$\chi^2(2) = 0.35$	610.6
	(5.91)		(−5.74)			$(P = 0.00)$	$(P = 0.84)$	
5	2.041	−1.457	—	—	0.72	$\chi^2(3) = 7.93$	$\chi^2(3) = 1.14$	666.7
	(7.36)	(−5.89)				$(P = 0.05)$	$(P = 0.77)$	

Notes: Number of observations: 398. Not shown are the country-specific constants. The instruments used were a constant term, a time trend, the rate of growth of the country's population, the first lag of the debt/GDP ratio for each country, and the burden of interest service for each country (IR/Rev where Rev is government revenue and IR is interest payment on the public debt). Regressions involving different sets of instruments are reported in Appendix B.

Numbers in parentheses are heteroscedasticity consistent Student t statistics (corresponding standard errors are computed from a heteroscedastic-consistent matrix). Frequently in practice, some elements of the difference in the covariance matrices of the two sets of estimates are negative on the diagonal. If this is the case, the Hausman test should be computed only for those parameters corresponding to positive diagonal elements, with a corresponding correction for the degrees of freedom, which is what our program does. (One has to use a generalized inverse in the many cases in which the covariance matrix of the vector of contrasts does not have full rank. See Hausman and Taylor (1982).)

do not discriminate clearly between the two non-linear specifications. In fact, for our current purpose, it is enough to observe that both specifications point to similar conclusions. The rationing hypothesis suggests precise but very high rationing thresholds. This means that rationing, even if it took place, occurred at such high debt levels that the difference between the 'punishing' and 'rationing' views is a matter more of taste than of substance.

In order to study the robustness of our results, we performed a full series of tests reported in Appendix B. These include tests for pooling, tests of coefficient stability allowing for country-specific effects, excluding problem countries (e.g., Greece and Portugal), tests of sub-sample stability over the two periods identified in the paper (before and after 1895) as well as checking for the validity of our instruments.

The conclusion that emerges from the previous statistical exercises is that the gold standard experience by and large supports the view that markets react to increases in debt burdens by inflicting increasingly higher risk premia. On the other hand, countries had to plunge quite deep into debt before they started feeling the pain. This can be illustrated by the fact that long-term interest rates converged after 1900, while debt levels remained as high as 100% of GDP in some countries, implying that at this level, markets did not inflict massive punishments. That debt burdens seriously mattered only when they reached fairly high levels suggests that the market mechanism, while certainly a strong incentive, did not provide absolute discipline. The same market mechanism was in fact in place both during the period of rising public debts and at the time of steady decline during the *Belle Époque*. Clearly some other factor must have driven the flow and ebb of European public debts.

5. CONVERGENCE BY OTHER MEANS: LOST RECIPES FROM THE GOLD STANDARD

In this section, we argue that price movements constitute a key factor in the behaviour of public debts. In the late nineteenth century, price trends went through two subperiods which interestingly coincide with the evolution of public debts. Prices moved down between 1873 and 1896, and then up until the war – a tendency perceptible in all countries adhering to gold, in Europe and elsewhere. There is general agreement that these trends can be explained by the supply of gold. Gold was too scarce to avoid deflation in the wake of the decline in the monetary role of silver after 1873, but it suddenly became abundant following discoveries in South Africa and Klondike in the 1890s. While it obviously matters how central banks reacted, for our purpose it is enough to assume that they were essentially passive as they stuck to gold. Indeed, Barsky and De Long (1991) show that gold output was a good predictor of inflation in gold standard countries, implying that central banks in the gold zone did not fully sterilize the effects of gold discoveries.

The considerable degree of covariation of price levels across gold standard countries is abundantly documented. For instance, McCloskey and Zecher (1984) even argue that the observed price correlation was responsible for the smooth operation of the gold standard: countries on gold were like the 'regions' of a single area. Having shown, however, that the gold standard did not operate particularly smoothly in Europe, we need to revisit the role of price fluctuations. Price dynamics could generate pleasant or unpleasant fiscal arithmetics, depending on whether prices were moving up or down. A fall in the general price level meant, other things being equal, rising levels of debt ratios. With constant GDP and tax revenues, falling prices meant an increase in the burden of interest service on outstanding long-term debt. In contrast, a rise in prices would reduce the burden of the outstanding nominal debt. In other words, governments were collecting an inflation tax when prices were steadily rising, and paying a deflation premium when prices were steadily falling.

To illustrate the mechanism at work, we decompose the dynamics of the debt/GDP ratio into its components: the ratio of primary deficits to GDP (that is, the deficit before interest service is taken into account), the *ex post* real interest service and, finally, real GDP growth. Higher real interest service or higher primary deficits contribute to raising the debt burden, whereas higher growth contributes to reducing it.[10] Figure 5 describes the evolution of these three components for the set of countries for which data on public debt service were available. Several features emerge. First, primary deficits did not change dramatically at the turn of the century. Indeed, the five-year averages that we report indicate that, for a number of countries, there was a deterioration rather than an improvement. Debt reduction must have come from somewhere else. This is especially visible for peripheral countries such as Austria-Hungary, Italy and Russia, where debt ratios went down by substantial amounts. The improvement in debt ratios can be traced back to a combination of drastic declines in real interest service and an acceleration of growth. Real interest service fell from rather high levels in the early 1880s to record lows after 1905: they went from 8% to 1% in Italy, from 5% to 3% in Austria, from 6.5% to 1.5% in Germany, etc. Even without the contribution of improved growth prospects, as inflation progressed, public debt sustainability improved, and the default risks that sovereign borrowers faced declined. The acceleration of growth that some countries experienced at the turn of the century helped further. However, this tendency was perhaps less systematic than the effects of gold inflation. For instance, growth was marked in Austria, Russia and Germany, but much less so in Britain and France.

---

[10] Let $b(t) = B(t)/GDP(t)$ be the ratio of nominal debt B to nominal GDP, $r(t)$ the real (*ex post*) interest rate, $g(t)$ the real growth rate, and $def(t)$ the primary deficit divided by GDP. Then the total deficit or accumulation of debt is: $db(t) = def(t) + (r(t) - g(t))b(t)$.

This mechanism was amplified by the predominance of the long-term component in European sovereign debts: the inertia of the interest service on this fraction of public debts was the channel through which price movements affected public finances.[11] Through their effect on public finances, price trends in turn influenced governments' incentives to participate in the gold standard. Deflation forced a difficult choice between deteriorating borrowing conditions and painful adjustments. Countries starting with relatively low debt levels could compromise, letting their debt drift slightly and making only partial fiscal adjustments. But for those that already had fairly high debt levels, such

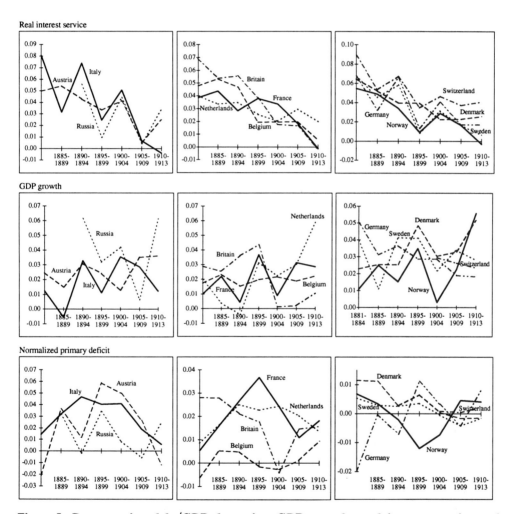

Figure 5. Decomposing debt/GDP dynamics: GDP growth, real interest service and GDP-normalized primary deficit, five-year averages, 1880–1913

[11] We do not have a precise breakdown of the proportion of short- and long-term debts for all countries in the sample. Various indications suggest that long-term 'funded' debt represented more than 90% of the aggregate public debt in countries like Britain, Germany and France, and even Russia and the Austro-Hungarian Empire. It fell to lower levels (still above 50%) in other peripheral countries.

as the southern European countries, the adjustment cost required for continued participation in the gold standard could be very large, especially since the market mechanism implied that a sustained deterioration in public debts meant accelerating premia for new loans. The opportunity cost of being part of the gold standard was becoming very substantial, increasing the pressure to switch to seigniorage finance, and go on inconvertible paper to escape gold deflation. On the other hand, when prices rose, countries were suddenly able to reduce the cost of new loans (as debt levels decreased), while facing a lower real cost of interest service on existing indebtedness. Thus inflation provided an additional reason for participating in the gold club.

Summarizing, price trends, of which no single country had control, strongly affected incentives to belong to the gold club. Indeed, club membership followed the trends: deflation until the mid-1890s, inflation afterwards. Moreover, in periods of deflation, as public finances tend to deteriorate, the price of central bank independence rises. Central bank independence did not survive in the most heavily indebted and economically vulnerable countries. Markets were trapped when falling prices pushed the highly indebted countries to breaking point. Under these circumstances, market discipline and central bank independence could only be self-defeating. By contrast, after the mid-1890s, governments could both better listen to the markets' wishes and reduce default risk. The second factor facilitating consolidation of the gold standard after the mid-1890s was improved growth in a number of countries (most notably members of the periphery) at the turn of the century. Of course, it is likely that inflation and growth trends were related, since the decline in long-term real interest rates facilitated investment and growth. With growth rates rising above interest rates, debt burdens receded, bringing about the golden age of the European gold standard.

6. CONCLUSION

Economists have long scrutinized the gold standard sphinx, trying to understand its riddle in the hope of discovering lessons that could help bring back the golden age. In fact, the gold standard heyday was a rather limited period, extending from the late 1890s or early 1900s to the First World War, not the whole 1880–1913 era, as is often believed. This evolution, so far little noticed, conveys several interesting lessons. First market-imposed discipline was a very important aspect of the gold standard and will certainly matter under EMU. However, it cannot be relied upon exclusively to provide borrowers with appropriate incentives. Incentives even become destabilizing when unexpected deflation adversely affects public finances. This lesson supports formal limitations on debts or deficits. On the other hand, debt ratios above 60% are not a hindrance provided that they are on a declining trend. The European gold standard could survive with high and varied debt levels, but its consolidation coincided with a period of general decline in debt ratios.

The second lesson for EMU is that denying admission into the euro zone may not be the best way to solve the systemic risk of debt over-accumulation. Externalizing that risk may create other problems. Left to themselves and to the imperfect discipline of financial markets in the early 1890s, southern European countries borrowed too much and were found high and dry when the cost of borrowing surged. Depreciation in turn created protectionist pressures in those countries of the European core which still had a large agricultural sector, such as France. This is a clear reminder that the benefits of externalizing fiscal discipline by limiting the euro zone to a small number of countries must be balanced against the costs of endangering the single market.

Our third lesson concerns the successful record of eastern and central European peripheries. Even under the most lenient application of optimum currency area criteria, these relatively backward countries would not have qualified for gold area membership. Yet the exceptional growth that Russia and Austria-Hungary experienced after 1900 suggests that continued adherence to the gold standard provided them with all the benefits of low interest rates, including declining debts and better growth prospects. It might well be that, by the same mechanism, some countries of the current European periphery will be among the big winners of EMU.

Finally, our analysis highlights the importance of finding a proper balance between discipline and incentives. The gold standard turned out to be hostage to the exogenous evolution of prices. Over the period 1873–96, the declining price trend exacerbated the public finance problems of the periphery to breaking point. After 1896, by contrast, inflation made convergence and steady participation in the gold zone much more attractive. Governments became more eager to conform to the discipline that markets required. The clear implication for EMU is that its stability will hinge on the ECB's policy not being too restrictive.

In the end, the heyday of the European gold standard was an accident of history. It came about when steady gold inflation moderated national incentives to extract seigniorage and brought about a reduction of debt burdens that contributed to lower interest rates. This in turn facilitated growth and the convergence process. Exchange stabilization and the spread of central bank independence followed. To what extent could such a regime survive? The whole construct was quite dependent upon features such as price trends that in a gold standard would have to be reversed over the long run. It was not very well equipped to face the major shock that the war and its aftermath represented. The bad and good fortunes of the gold standard should, in fact, serve as a reminder that we are all accidents of history.

Discussion

Rudi Dornbusch
Massachusetts Institute of Technology

Economic historians are never shy: this paper purports to stand traditional understanding of the gold standard on its head. It did not start when you thought it started; it did not start for the reasons you thought. This paper is as provocative as it is thorough. Only people thoroughly in love (and endowed with an army of research assistants) can and will make such a contribution. One must hope that the full data set will ultimately become available, so that this fruitful direction of research can be pursued further. The paper offers two central theses and a thorough portion of econometric research. I will comment on each.

The first thesis is that, contrary to the established doctrine that dates the gold standard to the period 1880–1913 (the golden age of liberalism), the *European* gold standard started only in the late 1890s. It was only then that *all* of Europe was on board – among the late comers were Italy, Austria-Hungary, Spain and Portugal as well as Russia. This thesis is both correct and uninteresting. It is factually correct that various European countries hopped on and off gold for quite a while, staying on for an extended period only starting in the late 1890s. This fact is, of course, well known from the vast historical literature on the subject. For example, Bloomfield (1963) notes: 'The span of the international gold standard, stretching from about 1880 to 1914, was a relatively brief one. In 1880 the following were the main countries on the gold standard or some variant thereof: Great Britain, France, Germany, the United States, Belgium, Holland, Switzerland, Norway, Sweden, Denmark, Finland, Canada, Australia, South Africa and New Zealand. They were joined in 1890 by Romania, at the turn of the century by Russia, Japan, India, Argentina, Italy, and Austria Hungary.' The thesis of Flandreau, Le Cacheux and Zumer is peculiar in two respects. It obviously adds nothing to the facts as we know them. Anyone who thought that Russia was on gold in 1881 just because that was the gold standard period simply had not done their homework. But in a deeper sense their thesis is misleading. First, it would have occurred to no one at the time to think of a *European* gold standard. This was the period of internationalism *per se* and Australia, Canada and even Japan were part of the relevant world. Second, and more importantly, the fact that Austria-Hungary (by then a side show to the German empire) or even more so Spain were not yet in gold was absolutely irrelevant to what Europe was doing. It was just as irrelevant as their presence or absence from EMU next year is to people's perception that Europe has a common money.

The periphery just does not matter; the issue is what the big players do. The big players were on gold and that is why economic history, rightly, puts the dates 1880–1913 on the gold standard. What the big players were doing set the trend and showed the standard to aspire to; the periphery, whether Latin America or central Europe and the Club Med, gradually made their way to it. The fact that Italy slipped in 1992 from the convergence process in the ERM does not mean that a grand European convergence was not under way. The fact that even now the UK cannot make up its mind surely does not mean that there will not be a European Monetary Union. The same goes for talking of the gold standard in the 1880s and beyond. There is another chapter to the story: how did the stragglers ultimately get on gold? That is what, more modestly, this paper might claim as its subject.

The second hypothesis offered by the authors is that the gold standard could not work until the late 1890s, when under the pressure of gold discoveries, real interest rates turned negative and debt burdens of peripheral high-debt countries started declining. This is an interesting hypothesis indeed, but it is not plausible, at least not in the way in which it is offered – that expected real interest rates declined, seigniorage increased and thus public finance improved. The fact that debt might have played an important role is suggested by the debt per capita data in Figure 6. Some of the laggards were, indeed, high-debt countries. But so were some countries that went on gold early and successfully. More specifically, centring on expected real interest rates as the trigger for going on gold is unconvincing. It is unclear why the periphery should have anticipated the shift towards inflation while the creditors did not: if they had been on a par, interest rates would have increased along with inflation expectations and nothing would have been gained. It is also unclear how inflation, on a gold standard, increases seigniorage. There might be such a possibility, but it is more the case for paper currencies on floating rates than for gold standards.

It is certainly correct that a period of low real interest rates and steady growth, such as the 1890s, puts battered debtors in a better financial position. Accordingly, it allows them to shape up debt service and restore normality in public finance, including going on gold as a show of confidence for their creditors. In fact, they might get a loan to get on gold. In this sense, the 1890s surely helped. But was the crucial factor the actual debt reduction, the countries on gold held up as an

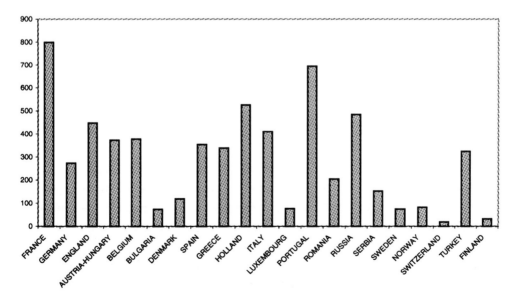

Figure 6. Debt per capita (1892, FF)
Source: Haupt (1894).

example, or the authors' story of expected low real interest rates? Surely the first two are more relevant. In any event, the hypothesis is muddled and no direct test of the ways in which the post-1895 inflation might have helped is ever conducted. There is a paper to be written on normalization of debt situations and its connection to gold, but this is not it.

It might be interesting to draw the parallel with the post-1982 experience – from debt default to stabilization and liberalization around the world in emerging economies and the Club Med. In a broad way, the late 1890s might have been the same. If so, it is interesting to understand the relative roles of ideas, real interest rates and the stability of the world economy in bringing about this situation. Work by Gallarotti (1995) is suggestive of this approach.

A significant and fascinating part of the paper deals with the question of whether capital markets during the gold standard functioned effectively in assuring fiscal probity. At first sight the answer might be no, as the authors document huge debt/GDP ratios well above 100%. The formal tests of credit rationing are tested using a rich source of interest rates. Work by Neisser (1929, 1930) and Morgenstern (1959) might have been mentioned in this context, just to note the integration of capital markets. There are a few important questions to be asked of this empirical work. One concerns the accuracy of data: for example, Muhleman (1897) shows Russia on depreciated paper by 1896, while the authors show it on gold. It might also be asked whether it makes sense to test credit rationing on bonds that are in actual or virtual default. The interest rates certainly tell us something, but presumably more about the probability of being paid than about a credit rationing equilibrium. Finally, credit rationing has to do with just that – rationing credit. It does not have predominantly to do with interest rates. The literature makes precisely this point: because of asymmetric information and moral hazard, interest rates are a poor rationing device.

Patrick Honohan
ESRI and CEPR

Introduction

This is a very thorough and well-reasoned paper, and it makes several important points with which I fully concur: for example, the endogeneity of central bank independence and the crucial role of gold discoveries in sustaining the gold standard during its last years. But I wonder just how much we can learn from the gold standard in looking forward to the issue of fiscal stability in EMU. For one thing, the authors shrink the heyday of the international gold standard to about a decade before the First World War – scarcely as long as the period from the signing of the Maastricht Treaty to the introduction of notes and coin. If we take this seriously, it scarcely warrants being termed a regime at all. It cannot be denied, though, that metal standards in general did last much longer: after all, the British standard, to which the others converged, boasted an unchanged gold parity for two centuries from 1717 (apart from the Napoleonic interruption).[12]

Metal standards and fiscal discipline

It is fair to ask just how important fiscal aspects are to the success of the gold standard. Was it not the collapse of silver, rather than any conversion to fiscal rectitude, that had caused so many countries to join gold in the late 1800s? At a deep level, of course, a key underlying aspect of true metal standards is that they inhibit use of the currency tax. But do they have a wider function in providing fiscal discipline? Contemporary students were less interested in fiscal aspects than in whether the automatic Humean stabilizer would work smoothly enough to ensure that enough cash remained in circulation to avoid trade crises, or in whether there was a need for activist central banking. Their preoccupation was understandable against the historical background of protracted one-way international flows of coin and bullion. Certainly, the use of paper money expansion as a public revenue source was limited in the countries that kept to a metal standard, and no evidence is provided by the authors to the contrary. Instead, they ask whether financial markets penalized heavy borrowers by demanding higher interest rates on their bonds (to which the answer has to be: yes). This question can be asked regardless of the currency regime. Although deflation certainly put pressure on indebted govern-ments, let us not forget that private debtors also felt the squeeze, as William Jennings Bryan's political career attests. Nor was it the fiscal burden that prevented the old parities being successfully restored after the First World War.

Incidentally, it is not evident that the data cast much doubt on the conventional wisdom that wars and the like are what caused major run-ups in debt during the nineteenth century. The three countries worst affected by interest rate hikes in the data – namely, Greece, Spain and Portugal – were all involved in unsuccessful, albeit relatively minor wars (Greece in 1897; Spain in 1898) or in the loss of extensive colonies (Portugal in 1890) within a few years of the hikes.

Spillovers, anchors and base drift

In the EMU context, the relevant issue is whether fiscal irresponsibility will spill over on to the functioning of the system as a whole. Will the ECB slip into a soft currency policy as a response to the fiscal difficulties of some members (or conversely, will its

[12] It is plausible that this decentralized convergence has a model, consciously or otherwise underlying the UK proposal, widely canvassed in the late 1980s, for a 'parallel ecu' route to monetary union.

toughness lead to offsetting fiscal laxity in some members)? Curiously, the authors do not really look at this question for the gold standard. At one level, the same problem does not arise with gold, which as an anchor cannot itself be undermined by policy in the way the euro could. The authors do point to some interdependencies. For one thing, the adoption of gold by so many countries contributed strongly to the gold deflation of the quarter century before 1900; a deflation which – almost as if the standard could only cope with a limited number of members – bounced some countries out of the system again. But it would have been interesting to examine whether the documented surge in debt in some countries contributed to a weakening of fiscal and monetary discipline in others. The authors do show that fiscal aberration in these European countries did not affect monetary discipline in the long run: even those that had abandoned the gold peg returned close to the old parity by 1914. They displayed no base drift: departures from the parity were reversed. This was not the case in the three major Latin American countries (Argentina, Brazil and Chile), none of which ever recovered the 50–70% depreciation they experienced during the 1880s and 1890s. Nevertheless, avoidance of base drift was the hallmark of the classical gold standard – a dogma that was all too well revered by bankers in the 1920s. The sharp distinction in this respect with the euro – where inflation rates rather than price levels are likely to be the goals, and base drift the norm – very much restricts the applicability of the gold standard to EMU analysis.

Gold bonds, local currency bonds and the EMU transition period

When looking at debt stocks, the authors do not distinguish clearly between explicitly gold-denominated debt and that denominated in local currency. The latter could be legally discharged at a devalued rate; and indeed, for countries that issued both, interest rates on gold debt were often much lower – even when the country was maintaining a gold peg. The credibility of the peg would have been a major factor in influencing the spread. Did the market differentiate between risk of devaluation or suspension of gold payments, on the one hand, and default on government debts, on the other? Yield differentials, where they existed, between gold and local currency debt suggest that the market may well have priced these risks differently.

The relevance of looking at the distinction between gold and paper interest rates derives from worries that some have expressed about the period between the 'irrevocable locking of currencies' in 1999 and the withdrawal of national notes and coin no later than the beginning of 2002. It has been suggested that this could be a vulnerable time for speculation against one or more of the participating currencies. The EU has sought to eliminate the possibility of speculation by stressing that national currencies will simply be denominations of the euro during this phase, and that a legally enforceable equivalence will operate as between the national currencies and the euro. Are these legal and political safeguards enough? For me, they certainly raise the stakes for a country that might be getting cold feet about EMU membership in this early phase. This would be of a different order of magnitude than, for example, the risk of devaluation in the ERM. To attempt to pull one's currency out of the euro at that stage and to devalue would seem to be tantamount to a debt default, and would seem also to require retrospective legislation inhibiting bank depositors, for example, from enforcing the euro value of their claims on local banks. I believe that, in the 1999–2002 interval, the risk of such actions is negligibly small – with a market price of at most a few basis points on yield. But does the market agree?

Identification

The authors agonize over the problem of why, if markets discipline borrowers, we nevertheless observe excessive debt accumulation. Presumably part of the answer would be revealed if it were possible to identify and estimate the demand curve. In other words, how sensitive were the borrowers to interest costs at different times? As things stand, we have at most a supply curve, which, even if it predicts an effective ceiling to the supply of debt, is still only half the story. It is not clear what exogenous variables other than war dummies one might include that could separately identify the demand curve. But, by the same token, it is not irrefutably clear that the authors have identified a pure supply curve.

General discussion

The correlation between wars and the ability to remain on the gold standard provoked much discussion. Olivier Blanchard was keen to find out if this correlation was strict. Wars had certainly caused the debt/GDP ratio to deteriorate for Portugal, Spain and Greece. Rudi Dornbusch pointed out that, in fact, there had been many countries with debt ratios as high as Portugal and Greece that did not abandon the gold standard. In any case, the correlation with war could not be perfect as, for some countries, the deterioration of the debt/GDP ratio had actually preceded the wars. Patrick Honohan countered that this was only because preparation for war may be as costly as the war itself. Maurice Obstfeld stressed that the connection between wars and interest rates was not automatic, and may reflect evolving market perceptions. In the initial stages of Russia's war with Japan, for instance, the market belief that Russia would win the war easily kept interest rates low. It was the changing fortunes in war that had caused interest rates to rise.

Jürgen von Hagen felt that it was difficult to draw easy lessons from the experience of the gold standard. Looking for movements in interest rates could be misleading, as the sensitivity of interest rates to changing debt/GDP ratios was a difficult issue. It was a systemic characteristic of the gold standard, and perhaps its virtue, that interest rates were not very responsive to changes in debt ratios. This was because of the inherent promise under the gold standard that high debt at any time would need to be reduced in later periods. Further, when drawing lessons for EMU, it was hard to predict how strong the market discipline is likely to be without some understanding of the behaviour of the European Central Bank. The ECB could quite legitimately bail out countries that are in trouble. And, of course, it may well be that other state governments will choose to help member countries in crisis.

Patrick Honohan argued that the events of the early 1890s could be explained by exceptional, country-specific events. For instance, 1890 was an important year in Portuguese history, with the loss of its colonies and revolution in Brazil. Similarly, Greece was in an expansionist phase at that time. If so, there might have been no real financial crisis in Europe during this period.

The details of the econometric analysis and the choice of the sample and variables also drew comment. Charles Bean suggested that the robustness of the conclusions on interest rate spreads be tested by excluding Greece from the sample. As Greece contributed to nearly all the increase in the interest rate spreads, the analysis, as such, amounted to an event study of Greece. Carlo Favero felt that some important explanatory variables had been left out of the spread equation. For instance, expected depreciation could be a decisive factor in explaining the exchange rate movements. Rudi Dornbusch wanted the level of gold reserves included in any explanation of yields, as the implied ability to service debt must clearly influence investors. He observed that the exceptionally high rates of interest observed over this period probably related to debt-in-default. Richard Portes was inclined to agree that these rates did not correctly reflect the true marginal costs of borrowing. However, given the quality and completeness of the data, he encouraged the authors to estimate a complete rationing model. Stefan Gerlach found it striking that long-term interest rates differ so much in Sweden, Denmark and Norway, given that there was a Scandinavian currency union. Georges de Ménil wanted to know how the monetary regime affected trade and capital flows within the core.

APPENDIX A. DATA

We rely on a combination of second-hand sources as well as primary material that we collected, covering the period 1880–1913.

A1. Public debts and interest service

Researchers working on nineteenth-century public finance typically rely on published sources such as Mitchell (1993) and Liesner (1989). Before the creation of the League of Nations in the interwar period, no centralized statistical office existed, so that researchers have to centralize data themselves, putting together national figures: this is the approach followed by Mitchell. The problem is that Mitchell's fiscal figures (which are very imperfect in many respects) do not include public debts. On the other hand, reliable second-hand national data on public debts exist for only a few countries, including Mitchell (1990) for Britain, Gerloff (1912) for Germany, Zamagni (1997) for Italy, and Pirard (1978) for Belgium. To complete our database we used the returns of Macmillan's *Statesman's Year Book*, as well as the publications of the *Société Internationale de Statistique*, which brought together some of the most famous statisticians of the time. Neymarck (1913) contains some interesting complementary information. Finally, we used the archives of the Crédit Lyonnais, which before the First World War had a research department that was very active and appropriately staffed. These sources helped fill the holes in existing sources for both debt figures and interest service. Debt returns are all inclusive: that is, they take into account the short-term floating debt as well as the long-term funded debt, the domestic paper debt as well as the external gold debt, evaluated in nominal terms and converted into the national unit.

A2. National product and prices

Recently, substantial efforts have been devoted to extending our knowledge of European accounts well beyond pioneering works on core countries. We were able to obtain reliable data for virtually every country in the sample. The references are as follows: Austria-Hungary: Komlos (1987) and Schulze (1997); France: Lévy-Leboyer and Bourguignon (1985); Germany: Hoffmann *et al.* (1965); Greece: Kostelenos (1995); Spain: Prados de la Escosura (1995); Portugal: Nunes *et al.* (1989) and Lains and Reis (1991); England: Mitchell (1990); Russia: Gregory (1994); Netherlands: Smits *et al.* (1997); Sweden: Johansson (1967); Denmark and Norway: Mitchell (1993). For Belgium and Switzerland, a series was reconstructed on the basis of end-of-period estimates as well as of indications for real GDP growth given in Maddison (1991). Swiss prices are found in Ritzmann (1996).

A3. Exchange rates

The exchange rates used were constructed on the basis of Schneider *et al.* (1991), except for Greece, for which we used a Lyonnais series. Data are annual averages.

A4. Exports

We relied exclusively on Mitchell (1993), except for the Netherlands, for which the figures are flawed. Dutch exports are from Smits *et al.* (1997).

A5. Population

Data in Mitchell (1993) completed by Gregory (1994) for Russia and by the Crédit Lyonnais returns for the Austro-Hungarian Empire.

A6. Long-term interest rates

The classic source for long-term interest rates on government (gold) bonds is Homer and Sylla (1991). However, the returns that these authors report cover only part of our sample.

For countries that are not documented in this source, and which typically include the continental countries for which Paris was an essential financial centre (Portugal, Spain, Greece, Russia and the Scandinavian countries for the latter part of the period under study), we used the *Cours Authentiques*. Quarterly figures were collected, on the basis of which annual interest rates were constructed. In order to select representative bonds, we used the information provided in the *Annuaire Officiel des Agents de Changes*, which describes the various bonds listed. Data availability as well as conversions, forced or not, required us in some cases to change our reference bond, or to make some simple transformations when the coupon was changed (in all cases, we checked that when they overlap, series for various bonds implied extremely close returns, as arbitrage theory predicts).

The series we use are gold consols: Austria (coupon: 4%); Denmark (1893 with a 3% coupon); Sweden (4% of 1878, 3% bond of 1888, 3.5% of 1895); Norway (3.5% of 1886, 3% of 1888); Portugal (3% coupon, reduced in 1892 and 1902); Greece (5% of 1881, 5% of 1884 reduced in 1893); Russia (5% of 1877 until 1889, then 4% of 1880 until 1914); Switzerland (3% of 1890, 3.5% of 1887 and 3% of 1897). For Spain, until 1882 we used the 3% 'extérieure', replaced in 1882 by a 4% consol (Spanish residents faced a forced conversion in 1898 into paper consols, but foreigners continued to get their coupon paid into gold). For Italy we use the rendita 5%, converted to 3.5% in 1906. The sample covers 1880–1913, except for Greece (1884–97 and 1905–13), Norway (1887–1913), Switzerland (1899–1912) and Russia (1885–1912).

APPENDIX B. ADDITIONAL ROBUSTNESS TESTS

We report here on additional tests of the results presented in Table 6.

B1. Specification tests

Various techniques were used to test the three specifications presented in panels (a), (b) and (c) against each other. The text reports tests where the specifications are nested. We also performed a test of the 'linear' versus 'punishing' specifications, using a Box–Cox transformation (Box and Cox, 1964) of the left-hand-side variables, which allows us to test a linear model versus a semi-log model. Again, the linear model was rejected.[13] On the other hand, the 'punishing' and 'rationing' specifications cannot be directly tested against each other, since they are not nested. Instead we performed pseudo-nested tests based on the artificial regression approach of Davidson and MacKinnon (1981). The basic idea is to embed competing functions in a more general form in order to discriminate between them. MacKinnon *et al.* (1983) adapt these tests to regression models estimated by instrumental variables. The pairs of J-tests and P-tests we computed (for each set of explanatory variables) were never able to distinguish between the 'rationing' and the 'punishing' specifications, and could not reject either specification.

---

[13] Pseudo-nested P-tests also pointed to the same conclusion.

In another attempt to discriminate between the two non-linear models, we computed a model selection test, known as the Schwarz Bayesian Information Criteria (SBIC), which has the asymptotic property of picking up the true model, if the true model is one of the alternatives being tested (see Geweke and Meese, 1981). We observe that in all cases the criteria favour the punishing specification. Again, we read this result as supportive of the idea of a non-linear steep supply curve facing state borrowers, irrespective of the specific functional form.

B2. Sensitivity

In Table B1 we provide results for regressions that exclude problem countries in an attempt to check for the stability of the coefficient. While removing Greece (a high-debt country) has the mechanic effect of lowering estimated rationing levels, these remain very high (180%). In Table B2, we report the results of regressions that allow for random effects (linear and punishing equations). As can be seen, parameter estimates are robust to the introduction of random effects.

Table B1. Sensitivity to possible outliers: the cases of Greece and Portugal

	Debt/GDP ratio	Rationing	Implied threshold	R^2 adj.
Regression without Portugal	1.647 (3.92)	0.357 (13.24)	280%	0.74
Regression without Greece	2.778 (7.82)	0.556 (16.83)	180%	0.63

Notes: We only report results for the rationing model with fixed effects. Regressions for the linear and punishing specifications without Greece and Portugal yield results that are initially identical to the ones obtained without omitted countries. Results when both countries were excluded are similar to the ones without Greece.

Table B2. Random effects

	Debt/GDP ratio	Constant	Export/GDP ratio	Per-capita GDP	On gold	R^2 adj.
Linear	4.744 (9.90)	−0.721 (−0.90)	0.899 (0.62)	−0.742 (−1.00)	−0.588 (−2.32)	0.31
Punishing	0.821 (5.30)	1.105 (4.28)	−1.178 (−2.47)	−1.998 (−8.29)	−0.208 (−2.63)	0.39

Notes: Random effects estimations have been computed only for punishing (in logs) and linear specifications. Random effects in the rationing model involve specific techniques that would require more space for a comprehensive presentation. Hausman tests of fixed effect (FE) versus random effects (RE) support FE for the above regressions, but RE for other regressions with less explanatory variables. In all cases, F-tests choose FE versus simple pooling.

Table B3. Different sets of instruments

	Debt/GDP ratio	Export/GDP ratio	Per-capita GDP	On gold	Rationing	Implied threshold	R^2 adj.
C, TIME, POP, IR/Rev	0.475 (0.48)	−0.295 (−0.34)	−1.049 (−1.86)	−0.727 (−4.13)	0.395 (9.24)	253%	0.62
C, POP, IR/Rev, 3 lagged explanatory variables	1.681 (3.30)	−0.485 (−0.45)	−1.960 (−2.71)	−0.535 (−3.23)	0.357 (8.75)	280%	0.69
C, TIME, POP, B/GDP(−1)	1.708 (2.97)	−1.030 (−1.02)	−1.311 (−2.54)	−0.556 (−3.30)	0.355 (10.05)	282%	0.67
All instruments	1.751 (3.39)	−0.752 (-0.75)	−1.799 (−2.53)	−0.534 (−3.22)	0.340 (8.51)	294%	0.70

Notes: The full set of possible instruments is: a constant term, a time trend, the rate of growth of countries' populations (POP), the burden of interest service for each country (IP/Rev), the lagged explanatory variables.
Source: See Appendix A.

B3. Instruments

To decide whether it is necessary to use instrumental variables, we first perform a Hausman–Wu specification test (Hausman, 1978) reported in Table 6 for each regression. The test generally rejects the equality of the two sets of estimated coefficients (instrumental variables versus non-linear least squares), indicating the need to use instrument variables techniques (Davidson and MacKinnon (1993) indicate how this test is applicable to non-linear models). Second, we test for the adequacy of our instruments by regressing the appropriate independent variables on our instruments set. In all three cases, an F-test rejects the hypothesis that the instruments are jointly insignificant (results not reported). Third, we test the validity of our choice of instruments using a Sargan test (Sargan, 1958; Mátyás and Sevestre (1996) consider the use of the Sargan test in the context of panel data econometrics, and Davidson and MacKinnon (1993) show the analogue of the test for non-linear models). The success of the test (see Table 6) implies that all of the explanatory power of the instruments is being captured in the independent variables. Finally, we have tried alternative subsets of instruments with the rationing equation, again in order to assess parameter stability. Table B3 shows that the parameter estimates and the implied rationing thresholds are stable.

REFERENCES

Alesina, A. (1994). 'Comment', in *NBER Macroeconomics Annual*, MIT Press, Cambridge, MA.
Bairoch, P. (1974). 'Geographical structure and trade balance of European foreign trade from 1800 to 1974', *Journal of European Economic History*.
—— (1993). *Economics and World History: Myths and Paradoxes*, Harvester Wheatsheaf, Hemel Hempstead.
Barsky, R. and J. Bradford De Long (1991). 'Forecasting pre WWI inflation: the Fisher effect and the gold standard', *Quarterly Journal of Economics*.
Baxter, R.D. (1871). *National Debts* (2nd edn), Robert John Bush, London.
Bayoumi, T. (1990). 'Saving–investment correlations: immobile capital, government policy, or endogenous behavior', *IMF Staff Papers*.
——, M. Goldstein and G. Woglom (1995). 'Do credit markets discipline sovereign borrowers? Evidence from the US states', *Journal of Money, Credit and Banking*.

Bishop, G., D. Damrau and M. Miller (1989). *1992 and Beyond: Market Discipline Can Work in the EC Monetary Union*, Salomon Brothers, London.

Bloomfield, A. (1959). 'Monetary policy under the international gold standard, 1880–1914', *Federal Reserve Bank of New York*.

—— (1963). 'Short-term capital movements under the pre-1914 gold standard', *Princeton Essays in International Finance*.

Bordo, M. and H. Rockoff (1996). 'The gold standard as a good housekeeping seal of approval', *Journal of Economic History*.

Bouvier, J. (1988). 'The Banque de France and the state from 1850 to the present day', in G. Toniolo (ed.), *Central Banks' Independence in Historical Perspective*, Walter de Gruyter, Berlin.

Box, G.E.P. and D.R. Cox (1964). 'An analysis of transformations', *Journal of the Royal Statistical Society*.

Capie, F. (1997). 'Central bank statutes: the historical dimension', Die Bedeutung der Unabhängigkeit der Notenbank für die Glaubwürdigkeit der Europäischen Geldpolitik/Proceedings of the 25th Conference of the Österreichische Nazionalbank.

——, C. Goodhart, S. Fischer and N. Schnadt (eds.) (1994). *The Future of Central Banking*, Cambridge University Press, Cambridge.

Cerrito, E. (1995). 'Su alcuni aspetti della crisi del 1893 in Italia', in P. Macry and A. Massafra (eds.), *Fra Storia e Storiografia: Scritti in onore di Pasquale Villani*, Il Mulino, Bologna.

Conant, C. (1915). *A History of the Banks of Issue* (2nd edn), Putnam's, New York and London.

Cukierman, A. (1992). *Central Bank Strategy, Credibility, and Independence*, MIT Press, Cambridge, MA.

Davidson, R. and J. G. MacKinnon (1981). 'Several tests for model specification in the presence of alternative hypotheses', *Econometrica*.

—— (1993). *Estimation and Inference in Econometrics*, Oxford University Press, Oxford.

Eichengreen, B. (1992). *Golden Fetters: The Gold Standard and the Great Depression, 1919–1939*, Oxford University Press, Oxford.

—— (1996). *Globalizing Capital: A Short History of the International Monetary System*, Princeton University Press, Princeton, NJ.

—— and M. Flandreau (1996). 'The geography of the gold standard', in B. Eichengreen, J. Reis and J. Braga De Macedo (eds.), *Currency Convertibility: The Gold Standard and Beyond*, Routledge, London.

—— (1997). *The Gold Standard in Theory and History* (2nd edn), Routledge, London.

Flandreau, M. (1995a). *L'Or du monde: La France et la stabilité du système monétaire international, 1848–1873*, Études d'Économie Politique, L'Harmattan, Paris.

—— (1995b). 'Was the Latin Union a franc zone?', in J. Reis (ed.), *International Monetary Systems in Historical Perspective*, Macmillan, London.

—— (1996). 'The French crime of 1873: an essay on the emergence of the international gold standard', *Journal of Economic History*.

Flood, R.P. and P.M. Garber (1984). 'Gold monetization and gold discipline', *Journal of Political Economy*.

Flora, P. *et al.* (1983). *State, Economy and Society in Western Europe, 1815–1975: A Data Handbook in Two Volumes*, Campus Verlag, Frankfurt.

Ford, A.G. (1962). *The Gold Standard 1880–1914: Britain and Argentina*, Clarendon, Oxford.

—— (1989). 'International financial policies and the gold standard, 1870–1914', in P. Mathias and S. Pollard (eds.), *The Cambridge Economic History*, vol. VIII, Cambridge University Press, Cambridge.

Foreman-Peck, J. (1991). 'The international gold standard as a European monetary lesson', in J. Driffil and M. Beder (eds.), *A Currency for Europe*, Lothian Foundation Press, London.

Gallarotti, G. (1995). *The Anatomy of an International Monetary Regime*, Oxford University Press, Oxford.

Gerloff, W. (1912). *Die Finanz und Zollpolitik des Deutschen Reiches*, Verlag von Gustav Fischer, Jena.

Geweke, J.F. and R. Meese (1981). 'Estimating regression models of finite but unknown order', *International Economic Review*.

Goodhart, C. (1988). *The Evolution of Central Banks*, MIT Press, Cambridge, MA.

Gregory, P. (1994). *Before Command*, Princeton University Press, Princeton, NJ.

Haupt, O. (1894). *Arbitrages et Parités*, Librairie Truchy, Ch. Leroy, Successeur, Paris.

Hausman, J.A. (1978). 'Specification tests in econometrics', *Econometrica*.

—— and W.E. Taylor (1982). 'A generalized specification test', *Economics Letters*.

Hoffmann, W. *et al.* (1965). *Das Wachstum der deutschen Wirtschaft seit der Mitte des 19. Jahrhunderts*, Springer, Heidelberg.

Holtfrerich, C.-L. (1988). 'The relations between monetary authorities and government institutions: the case of Germany from the nineteenth century to the present', in G. Toniolo (ed.), *Central Banks' Independence in Historical Perspective*, Walter de Gruyter, Berlin.

Homer, S. and R. Sylla (1991). *A History of Interest Rates*, Rutgers University Press, Rutgers.

James, H. (1997). 'From Bismarck to Kohl: monetary and fiscal unification in nineteenth century Germany as a model for the European Union?', *Princeton Essays in International Finance*.

Johansson, O. (1967). 'The gross domestic product of Sweden and its composition, 1861–1955', *Stockholm Economic Studies*.

Kindleberger, C.P. (1988). *Keynesianism vs Monetarism and other Essays in Financial History*, Allen and Unwin, London, Boston and Sydney.

Komlos, J. (1987). 'Financial innovation and the demand for money in Austria-Hungary, 1867–1913', *Journal of European Economic History*.

Kostelenos, G.C. (1995). *Money and Output in Modern Greece, 1858–1938*, Centre of Planning and Economic Research, Athens.

Lains, P. and J. Reis (1991). 'Portuguese economic growth, 1833–1985: some doubts', *Journal of European Economic History*.

Lévy, R.G. (1911). *Banques d'émission et Trésors publics*, Économiste Européen, Hachette, Paris.

Lévy-Leboyer, M. and F. Bourguignon (1985). *L'Économie française au XIXème siècle*, Economica, Paris.

Liesner, T. (1989). *One Hundred Years of Economic Statistics*, Economist Publications, London.

MacKinnon, J.G., H. White and R. Davidson (1983). 'Tests for model specification in the presence of alternative hypotheses: some further results', *Journal of Econometrics*.

Maddison, A. (1991). *Dynamic Forces in Capitalist Development: A Long-Run Comparative View*, Oxford University Press, Oxford.

Mátyás, L. and P. Sevestre (eds.) (1996). *The Econometrics of Panel Data: A Handbook of the Theory with Applications* (2nd revised edn), Kluwer, Dordrecht.

McCloskey, D. and R. Zecher (1984). 'The success of purchasing power parity: historical evidence and its implications for macroeconomics', in M. Bordo and A. Schwartz, *A Retrospective on the Classical Gold Standard*, University of Chicago Press, Chicago, IL.

Mélitz, J. (1997). 'Market discrimination between the debts of different sovereigns under EMU', unpublished manuscript.

Mitchell, B.R. (1990). *British Historical Statistics*, Cambridge University Press, Cambridge.

—— (1993). *International Historical Statistics: Europe 1750–1988*, Stockton Press, New York.

Morgenstern, O. (1959). *International Financial Transactions and Business Cycles*, Princeton University Press, Princeton, NJ.

Muhleman, M. (1897). *Monetary Systems of the World*, Charles Nicoll, New York.

Neisser, H. (1929, 1930). 'Der internationale Geldmarkt vor und nach dem Kriege', *Weltwirtschaftliches Archiv*.

Neymarck, A. (1913). 'La statistique internationale des valeurs mobilières' (IXème Rapport de M. Alfred Neymarck), *Bulletin de l'institut international de statistique*, Van Stockum, La Haye.

Nunes, A., E. Mata and N. Valerio (1989). 'Portuguese economic growth', *Journal of European Economic History*.

Pirard, J. (1978). 'La dette publique belge de 1830 à 1913', in 9e colloque international, *La Dette publique aux XVIIIe et XIXe siècles son développement sur le plan local, régional et national*, Spa, 12–16 September.

Plessis, A. (1985). *La Politique de la Banque de France sous le Second Empire*, Droz, Geneva.

Polanyi, K. (1944). *The Great Transformation*, Rinchard, New York.

Posen, A. (1994). 'Declarations are not enough: financial sector sources of central bank independence', *NBER Macroeconomics Annual*, MIT Press, Cambridge, MA.

Prados de la Escosura, L. (1995). 'Spain's gross domestic product: 1850–1993: quantitative conjectures' and 'Appendix', Working Papers 95–05 and 95–06, Universidad Carlos III de Madrid.

Raffalovich, A. (1900). 'Les méthodes employées par les États au XIXème Siècle pour revenir à la bonne monnaie', Congrès International des Valeurs Mobilières, Paris.

Ritzmann, H. (1996). *Historical Statistics for Switzerland*, Chronos Verlag, Zurich.

Russell, H.B (1898). *International Monetary Conferences*, Harper, London.

Sargan, J.D. (1958). 'The estimation of economic relationships using instrumental variables', *Econometrica*.

Schneider, J., O. Schwarzer and F. Zellfelder (1991). *Währungen der Welt I*, Verlag, Stuttgart.

Schulze, M.-S. (1997). 'Re-estimating Austrian GDP, 1870–1913: methods and sources', Working Papers in Economic History, no. 36/97, LSE, London.

Smits, J.P., E. Horlings and J.L. Van Zanden (1997). 'The measurement of gross national product and its components: the Netherlands, 1800–1913', research memorandum, N.W. Posthumus Insituut, Netherlands Graduate School for Economic and Social History.

Statesman's Year Book, annual, since 1866.

Stiglitz, J. and A. Weiss (1981). 'Credit rationing in markets with imperfect information', *American Economic Review*.

Taylor, A.M. (1996). 'International capital mobility in history: the saving–investment relationship', NBER Working Paper no. 5743.

Théry, E. (1894). *La Crise des changes*, Études Économiques et Financières, Économiste Européen, Paris.

Triffin, R. (1964). 'The myth and realities of the so-called gold standard', in *The Evolution of the International Monetary System: Historical Reappraisal and Future Perspectives*, Princeton University Press, Princeton, NJ.

Verley, P. (1997). *L'Échelle du monde*, Albin Michel, Paris.

Williamson, J. (1996). 'Globalization, convergence and history', *Journal of Economic History*.

Yeager, L.B. (1969). 'Fluctuating exchange rates in the 19th century: the experiences of Russia and Austria', in R. Mundell and A. Swoboda (eds.), *Monetary Problems of the International Economy*, University of Chicago Press, Chicago, IL.

Zamagni, V. (1997). 'Ricostruzione della serie del debito pubblico italiano, 1861–1946,' mimeo.

Zevin, R.B. (1992). 'Are world financial markets more open? If so, why and with what effects?', in T. Banuri and J. Schor (eds.), *Financial Openness and National Autonomy*, Oxford University Press, Oxford.

Redistribution vs insurance

Does Europe need a fiscal federation?

SUMMARY

The stabilization provided by the US federal budget has been used as an example of the adjustment mechanisms that are lacking in Europe and which are needed to make a currency area viable. This paper presents four sets of findings that suggest that the benefits of a European fiscal federation would be modest. First, we show that some of the previous estimates of the benefits of the US federal budget overestimate the amount of interstate insurance by a factor of 3. Second, Europe already has national tax systems which, according to our estimates, can insure more than 50% of a European fiscal federation. Third, we find evidence that the potential insurance benefits of a European fiscal federation have decreased over time. Fourth, there are large cross-country differences in the benefits provided by federation. We conclude that the potential to provide interregional insurance by creating a European fiscal federation is too small to compensate for the many problems associated with its design and implementation.

— Antonio Fatás

Does EMU need a fiscal federation?

Antonio Fatás

INSEAD and CEPR

1. INTRODUCTION

The future adoption of a single currency among some of the members of the European Union has raised many concerns regarding its ability to deal with shocks that are asymmetric (i.e., idiosyncratic to either regions or countries). The main concern arises from the lack of tools that countries will possess to mitigate the effects of asymmetric shocks once they join EMU. As prices and wages are not flexible enough to compensate for the loss of exchange rates and the degree of labour mobility in Europe is very limited, there is a fear that asymmetric shocks will lead to deep regional recessions and large increases in unemployment, which could create a social burden that is politically unacceptable to many governments.[1]

In a currency union, in the absence of monetary policy, the burden of adjustment lies on fiscal policy. Governments are able to use countercyclical budgets to stabilize economic fluctuations (within the limits on deficits and debt/GDP ratios of the Stability Pact). This is not, however, the only possible stabilizing mechanism associated with fiscal policy. For the regions that form part of a country, the fiscal system provides automatic transfers from fast-growing regions to depressed regions, which contribute to interregional risk sharing.

I wish to thank Jürgen von Hagen, Torben M. Andersen, Philippe Martin and Panel participants for their helpful comments and suggestions.
[1] See Eichengreen (1990), Feldstein (1992), Krugman (1993), Blanchard and Katz (1992), Decressin and Fatás (1995), Sachs and Sala-i-Martín (1992) and von Hagen and Neumann (1994) for a general discussion of some of these issues.

The USA, where automatic interregional transfers take place through the federal budget, has been presented as an example of a tax system that helps alleviate the costs associated with a single currency.[2] These transfers play an insurance role that compensates for the lack of internal exchange rates. In the case of EMU, as there is no equivalent system of insurance, countries will have to suffer the full consequences of asymmetric shocks. The estimates of the benefits of interregional transfers in the USA are large. Sachs and Sala-i-Martín (1992) estimate that a fall in state income causes transfers (or reductions in taxes) that amount to between 30 and 40% of the original fall in income, and Bayoumi and Masson (1996a) estimate a net effect of around 30%.

In this paper we argue that these estimates can only be interpreted as a measure of the stabilizing effect of interstate transfers and that they overestimate the amount of interstate risk sharing by a factor of 3. The logic is simple. The methodology used in these studies is to estimate the response of taxes and transfers to income fluctuations, ignoring the impact that these transfers have on the overall federal budget balance. If a state's income falls, total tax revenues will decrease unless other regions' tax revenues exactly offset the initial fall (which would occur only if there were no aggregate risk). The fall in tax revenues will create a deficit that will have to be paid through future taxes by all states, including the depressed state. Therefore, the amount of insurance that the depressed state receives is less than what the change in this period's state disposable income indicates. This effect, ignored in the work of Sachs and Sala-i-Martín (1992) and Bayoumi and Masson (1996a), is significant given the high correlation of income across US states.[3] We replicate our analysis for the countries of the European Union and find estimates for the insurance potential of a hypothetical European fiscal federation similar to those of the USA.

The distinction between intertemporal transfers and interregional insurance is critical because, while intertemporal transfers can be provided by countercyclical budgets at the national level (an option that will be available to EMU participants), interregional insurance can be provided only through a common federal budget.

We also apply our analysis to data on European regions (subunits of countries). Our estimates show that the amount of interregional insurance provided by the current national systems is more than half of a hypothetical European fiscal federation. This figure is estimated under the unrealistic assumption that the European system is a replica of the national systems (which has implications for its size and progressivity of taxes). Under more realistic assumptions about the European fiscal federation, the additional benefits of adding a fiscal federation to

---

[2] See Sachs and Sala-i-Martín (1992).

[3] Indeed, von Hagen (1992), who controls for the effect that a fall in a state's income has on the federal budget, obtains estimates of the benefits of the US federal budget around 10%, close to our estimates of interstate insurance.

the current layer of national systems would be even smaller. We also find some evidence that these benefits have been decreasing over time. Within our sample, we find that in the second part (1979–95) the benefits of a European federation relative to national systems are lower. If this reflects a trend caused by the process of European integration and co-ordination of economic policies, the creation of EMU might further decrease these benefits. Overall, the results of the analysis at the regional level provide a picture of interregional transfers in Europe very different from that of Sachs and Sala-i-Martín (1992), where it is argued that the current amount of European interregional insurance is practically zero.

Finally, we find large cross-country differences regarding the potential insurance benefits of a European fiscal federation. While countries like France and Austria would benefit very little from the system, the benefits for the UK and Ireland would be substantial. This asymmetry would make the implementation of a European-wide fiscal system very complicated as some countries might not be interested in joining. A possible solution to this asymmetry is to set different risk premia for different countries. However, the political viability of this option remains doubtful.

Before concluding, we review some of the problems associated with the design and implementation of a European-wide insurance system. More specifically, we show that any fiscal system designed to provide cross-country insurance is very likely to generate permanent transfers across countries that will be viewed as redistributive. These problems lead us to conclude that the costs of implementing the system exceed the modest insurance that a European fiscal federation could provide.

Section 2 presents the main theoretical arguments in the debate on the role of fiscal policy in a monetary union. Section 3 reviews previous empirical estimates in the literature and presents a simple theoretical framework that leads to our estimates. Section 4 estimates the interstate insurance provided by the US federal budget. Section 5 applies the same methodology to European countries. Section 6 estimates the insurance benefits provided by the current national systems. Section 7 presents empirical evidence about the difficulties involved in designing an insurance system that avoids redistribution. Section 8 concludes.

2. FISCAL POLICY IN A CURRENCY AREA

In this section we discuss the role that fiscal policy can play in a currency area. Our unit of analysis is a group of regions that form part of a fiscal federation. We are interested in analysing how regional governments and the federal government can stabilize asymmetric cyclical fluctuations using fiscal policy. This analysis can be applied to regions that form part of a country or to future country members of a European fiscal federation.

Fiscal policy can be active at two levels. First, governments can use countercyclical budgets to smooth disposable income. This stabilization takes place through *intertemporal transfers*. Second, by sharing tax receipts among several regions, the federal budget can help to alleviate the effects of regional fluctuations through automatic *interregional transfers*, which help to share interregional risk.[4]

2.1. Intertemporal transfers

When income fluctuates, consumers can isolate themselves from transitory fluctuations using savings as a buffer. In the absence of market imperfections, there is no role for the government to stabilize consumers' income. If consumers are unable to use financial markets to borrow against their future income, the government could help consumers to smooth consumption by running countercyclical budgets.

On the revenue side, progressive taxation and procyclical transfers make disposable income less volatile than pre-tax income. This allows credit-constrained individuals to smooth their consumption. These policies are, in many cases, the result of automatic stabilizers and not the result of active discretionary policies.[5]

What is the reaction of consumers to automatic stabilizers through tax and transfer schemes? In a Ricardian world, such policies have no effects on output or welfare as consumers foresee the implications in terms of future tax payments.[6] There is no effect on consumers' wealth and saving offsets the changes in disposable income. The welfare effects (assuming no distortionary taxes) are zero. In the case where Ricardian equivalence fails, the previous statement does not hold. In the presence of liquidity constraints, consumption depends on disposable income and the welfare effects depend on the ability of fiscal policy to smooth consumption to an extent that consumers are willing but unable to. If Ricardian equivalence fails because consumers do not internalize the future tax implications of current deficits ('future generations will pay for them'), then intertemporal transfers can be considered a form of insurance across generations.

There is some empirical evidence in favour of the stabilizing effects of government's fiscal policies. Galí (1994) shows that the size of the government budget is inversely related to the amplitude of business cycles in a sample of OECD countries. Bayoumi and Masson (1996a) present estimates of the smoothing of disposable income achieved by this type of policy in European countries.

---

[4] See Bayoumi and Masson (1996b) for a similar analysis of some of the issues analysed here and estimates of the relative impact of each of these transfers.

[5] One could also consider the effects of government expenditures. There could be an active policy to increase spending during periods of weak private aggregate demand. In this way, fiscal policy could contribute to aggregate demand and could have beneficial effects on overall income. We ignore this possibility to simplify our analysis and concentrate on the debate on interregional insurance through tax and transfer mechanisms.

[6] This assumes that government expenditures are unaltered by cyclical fluctuations. We will make this assumption throughout our analysis.

2.2. Interregional transfers

The same fiscal system that allows individuals to stabilize consumption through intertemporal transfers can also provide interindividual or interregional transfers. The nature of these transfers can be very different from those generated by countercyclical budgets because they are designed to reduce not only the volatility of disposable income, but also the volatility of permanent income. As a result, interindividual or interregional transfers can not only help credit-constrained consumers to smooth consumption, but also isolate permanent income from fluctuations. In other words, they provide insurance.[7] If a region goes into a recession, it receives transfers from other regions that are booming. Consumers are not concerned with higher future taxes because transfers from fast-growing regions offset their decline in income. Because these transfers provide insurance to consumers, they can be considered as a more efficient tool to stabilize consumption than intertemporal transfers. They have direct implications for consumers' wealth without relying on the failure of Ricardian equivalence. Indeed, Bayoumi and Masson (1996b) present some favourable evidence in this direction. They estimate the impact on consumption of interregional and intertemporal transfers, and conclude that the stabilizing effects of interregional transfers are larger.

Clearly, as suggested above, the distinction between stabilization and insurance is not evident if consumers do not internalize future tax payments. For example, if consumers' horizons are finite, intertemporal transfers also provide insurance. This insurance, across generations, is equivalent to that provided by interindividual or interregional transfers. For most of our analysis we abstract from this type of insurance and consider that the main role of intertemporal transfers is stabilization, while interregional transfers are intended to provide insurance. This distinction is not relevant when we consider the benefits of a European fiscal federation. What matters is that intertemporal transfers, regardless of their welfare effects and insurance properties, will still be available to national governments in EMU, while automatic interregional transfers will not, unless a fiscal federation is created.

2.3. The role of a federal budget: interregional insurance or intertemporal stabilization?

For the federal budget to be able to generate any amount of interregional insurance, regional incomes must not be perfectly correlated. Otherwise, all the risk would be aggregate risk, which cannot be insured by interregional transfers. If a region went

---

[7] This insurance could also be provided by the private sector. See Atkeson and Bayoumi (1993) and Asdrubali *et al.* (1996) for estimates of the role that private markets play in insuring region-specific risks.

into a recession, there would be no booming regions from which to transfer resources. In general, any fiscal federation will have some amount of idiosyncratic risk, and transfers will be a combination of interregional insurance and intertemporal stabilization.

To see the interaction between insurance and stabilization, we can think about a region that goes into a recession. Let us assume that income in other regions of the fiscal federation is not affected. Aggregate output and, consequently, federal tax revenues will decrease in response to the shock, the federal budget will go into a deficit and all regions will foresee an increase in taxes to pay for the current deficit. Note that the region in recession still benefits from the policy because it will only pay its share of the future tax payments, which is clearly lower than the amount of taxes that the region is foregoing this period. In other words, there is some insurance built into the system. But, in addition, that region also receives the benefit of the intertemporal stabilization provided by the budget deficit, as the government postpones the tax payments required to balance the budget today. Of course, the government could avoid the budget deficit by raising taxes in all regions to compensate for the fall in revenue during this period. In this case, all the transfers occur within the same period and the system is one where there is interregional risk sharing but no intertemporal stabilization.[8]

A second way of understanding the connection between stabilization and insurance is to look at the effects of regional shocks on other regions' tax liabilities. By being in a fiscal federation, a region is also responsible for the taxes generated by cyclical fluctuations in other parts of the federation. As a result, other regions' volatility influences the insurance benefits of being a member of the federation. A negative shock to the income of a region reduces the permanent income of all the other regions because of the future taxes to cover this year's deficit. In the extreme case of a region with no income volatility, if it decides to join a fiscal federation, the region will always see its volatility increase due to income fluctuations in other members of the federation.

The difference between intertemporal transfers and interregional insurance is key to understanding the benefits of creating a fiscal federation in EMU. The reason is that intertemporal stabilization will still be available to countries that belong to EMU through their national budgets. Therefore, the relevant question is how large the potential for *interregional insurance* is in a European fiscal federation. Before addressing this issue, we review the empirical literature on the estimates of the benefits of the US federal budget to assess the extent to which these estimates are measures of intertemporal stabilization or interregional insurance.

---

[8] Under Ricardian equivalence, and assuming that the tax payments are shared equally among all regions in both cases, both of these scenarios are equivalent. In the first case, a transitory deficit will have to be compensated by higher taxes in the future and consumers will anticipate those higher taxes today.

3. PREVIOUS EMPIRICAL LITERATURE

The majority of studies on the benefits of automatic transfers in a fiscal federation use data on US states to understand the economic importance of those transfers in a currency area of similar size to the future EMU.[9] The general methodology is to measure the reaction of regional taxes and transfers to income fluctuations. The question addressed by all these studies is: if income in a region goes down by 1% relative to the national average, what is the change in that region's taxes and transfers?

One of the first studies was Sachs and Sala-i-Martín (1992). They used data on taxes and transfers from US states to measure the stabilizing effects associated with the federal budget. Their empirical methodology consisted of measuring the effects of changes in state income on state taxes and transfers.[10] Their conclusion was that the US federal fiscal system provides a significant stabilizing role. Quoting from their article, 'the fraction of the initial shock that is absorbed by the federal budget is between one third and one half' or 'a one dollar reduction in state personal income reduces final disposable income by only 56 to 65 cents'.

Bayoumi and Masson (1996a) reached similar results by running regressions in growth rates. The reason for using growth rates is that the methodology of Sachs and Sala-i-Martín (1992) captured two very distinct effects of the federal budget: redistribution and insurance. The mechanisms associated with income taxes that create stabilizing transfers are also responsible for any redistribution built into the fiscal system. Indeed, Sachs and Sala-i-Martín, by estimating their regressions in levels, were mainly capturing interregional transfers in response to differences in income per capita (redistribution) and not in response to asymmetric business cycles (insurance). Despite the difference in methodology, the estimates of Bayoumi and Masson for the USA are very close to those of Sachs and Sala-i-Martín, as they conclude that the stabilization effects of the US federal system are around 30%.

To what extent are the estimates of Sachs and Sala-i-Martín (1992) or Bayoumi and Masson (1996a) a measure of interregional insurance? Despite the differences in the methodology used, both studies measure the volatility of state disposable income relative to state current income by estimating either the response of taxes and transfers to income changes or the response of disposable income to income changes. In both cases, the main finding is that the volatility of disposable income is significantly smaller than the volatility of income.[11] Following our arguments in the

---

[9] There is also a more theoretical literature on this subject that deals with the design and political implementation of fiscal federations. See, for example, Persson and Tabellini (1996), von Hagen and Hammond (1997) and Mélitz (1994). We will refer to some of these issues in section 7.

[10] Both of the variables are measured relative to their national counterparts.

[11] Bayoumi and Masson (1996a) present specific estimates of the source of this stabilization, distinguishing between the effects of taxes, transfers and government expenditures. In general, government expenditures do not seem to react and most of the automatic stabilization takes place through unresponsive transfers.

previous section, this estimated stabilizing effect on disposable income could only be an upper bound to the amount of interregional insurance provided by the system. Only in the extreme case, where a change in state taxes did not have any impact on the overall government budget, would they be equivalent. This can occur only in the special case where there is no aggregate risk.

A simple example can highlight the importance of this issue. Suppose there are two regions with incomes that are perfectly correlated and, moreover, the volatility of their incomes is the same. Suppose taxes are proportional to income and transfers are unresponsive to output fluctuations. If we regressed state disposable income on state income, we would find a coefficient less than 1, which could be misinterpreted as interregional risk sharing, but which is only a measure of the stabilizing of disposable income done by countercyclical budget balances. Indeed, in this special case, there is absolutely no interregional insurance. This issue is already recognized in Sachs and Sala-i-Martín (1992) when they argue that all the variables in their analysis should be thought of as present discounted values. However, their empirical analysis ignores this and makes use only of contemporaneous values.

Von Hagen (1992) presents estimates of the benefits of the US federal budget that are much smaller than those of Sachs and Sala-i-Martín or Bayoumi and Masson. According to his estimates, the federal budget absorbs only 10% of a change in state income. His empirical specification takes into account the effect that changes in state income have on the overall federal budget by controlling for aggregate time effects. Because of this correction, this estimate (three times smaller than the previous ones) can be considered a more accurate measure of the interstate insurance provided by the US federal budget.[12] In fact, in the next section, using a different methodology, we calculate the interregional insurance benefits of the US federal budget, and our estimates are almost identical to those of von Hagen (1992).

3.1. From stabilization to insurance

From the previous analysis, it is clear that to obtain an estimate of the interregional insurance provided by a fiscal federation, one cannot simply measure the response of taxes and transfers to changes in income. One also needs to consider the impact that this has on the overall federal budget. This is indeed equivalent to looking at the amount of idiosyncratic risk relative to aggregate risk present in the federation. In this section we use a simple theoretical argument to unveil the relationship between stabilization and insurance. Our goal is to understand how the ratio of idiosyncratic

[12] Von Hagen's estimates are very close to those of Asdrubali *et al.* (1996). They measure the relative contribution of three different channels of interstate risk sharing in the USA. The three channels analysed are capital markets, federal government and credit market. Their estimates show that the federal government absorbs around 13% of the fluctuations in gross state product.

to aggregate risk, or, equivalently, the correlation between regional risks, affects the insurance potential of a fiscal federation.

For simplicity, we look at a federation with two regions (i and j) of equal size. In any period, income in each of the regions is a random variable with the same mean Y, possibly different volatility σ_i and σ_j, and a correlation equal to ρ.

We assume that the government needs to finance a given amount of government expenditures, which is constant and does not respond to shocks.[13] The government initially sets a tax rate in order to keep a balanced budget. As the government needs to satisfy its budget constraint, the deficit or surplus in any period determines future changes in the tax rate.

The deficit or surplus in this period's government balance measures the intertemporal stabilization built into the tax system (its ability to stabilize disposable income). In this simple model where income is stationary, the simplest way of generating any type of stabilization is to assume a proportional tax. If the tax rate is τ, then it follows that the volatility of disposable income (defined as its standard deviation) is equal to

$$\sigma_{i,d} = (1 - \tau)\sigma_i$$

We define *intertemporal stabilization* as the decrease in volatility of disposable income relative to pre-tax income. This is equal to

$$\text{Intertemporal stabilization} = (\sigma_{i,d}/\sigma_i) - 1 = \tau \tag{1}$$

One should therefore interpret the parameter τ as the overall stabilizing effect of taxes and transfers on disposable income. In this simple example it coincides with the tax rate, but in a more complicated set-up, the tax rate might be unrelated to the magnitude of stabilization.[14]

As we argued before, the previous estimate of stabilization is not a good measure of interregional insurance because it does not consider future tax payments generated by the current imbalance of the federal budget. In general, from the perspective of region i, there will be future tax payments associated with the current government balance. These payments will be a function of this year's deficit, which is equal to

$$\tau(Y - Y_i) + \tau(Y - Y_j)$$

Internalizing these payments to calculate all current changes affecting permanent

[13] This assumption seems to be supported by the evidence presented in von Hagen (1992) about state government expenditures.
[14] For example, if we measured the volatility of disposable income as the percentage deviation from its mean, then a proportional tax rate would not have any stabilizing effect on disposable income as the elasticity of taxes with respect to income would always be 1. A progressive tax rate could generate stabilization, and in that case the parameter τ would represent the progressivity of the tax system and not the average tax rate.

income, one obtains

$$Y_{i,p} = (1 - \tau)Y_i - 0.5[\tau(\mathbf{Y} - Y_i) + \tau(\mathbf{Y} - Y_j)]$$

where we assume that taxes are equally divided between both regions. This expression includes all changes in today's environment that have an effect on permanent income.[15] The variance of this expression is simply

$$\sigma_{i,p}^2 = (1 - 0.5\tau)^2\sigma_i^2 + (0.5\tau)^2\sigma_j^2 + \tau(1 - 0.5\tau)\sigma_i\sigma_j\rho$$

Volatility is therefore a function of three variables: first, the parameter τ which determines the stabilization effect on disposable income; second, the variance of region j relative to region i (if the volatility of region j is very high, then the insurance for region i might be small or even negative); and third, the correlation between regional incomes (if this correlation is very high, the overall insurance potential of the system is low). We can define interregional insurance as the reduction in the volatility (standard deviation) of $Y_{i,p}$ relative to pre-tax income. That is,

Interregional insurance $= (\sigma_{i,p}/\sigma_i) - 1$ (2)

Two extreme examples illustrate the connections between insurance and intertemporal stabilization. If the two regions' incomes are perfectly correlated ($\rho = 1$) and their risks are identical ($\sigma_i = \sigma_j$), then the amount of insurance is zero as the volatility of $Y_{i,p}$ is equal to the volatility of pre-tax income ($\sigma_{i,p} = \sigma_i$). The logic is clear: if income is below its average today, the tax rate absorbs part of this fall, providing some stabilization, but the government is running a deficit that needs to be financed by an increase in future period taxes. Given the symmetry of the model, the increase will exactly offset the stabilizing effect of the first period.

Suppose now that the correlation is equal to -1, so that there is no aggregate risk. Assuming symmetry in risk ($\sigma_i = \sigma_j$), the insurance effect is exactly equal to the stabilization effect. In other words, the volatility of $Y_{i,p}$ is equal to the volatility of disposable income ($\sigma_{i,p} = (1 - \tau)\sigma_i$). In this special case, where there is no aggregate risk, the government can achieve as much insurance as needed by setting a very high τ. For example, if income is completely shared ($\tau = 100\%$) and the excess of tax revenues over government expenditures is split between the two regions, the variability of $Y_{i,p}$ will be zero. Therefore, we conclude that, in a two-country symmetric federation (same average income and volatility), the stabilization effect sets an upper bound for the amount of insurance that the system can provide.[16]

In the next section, we use equation (2) to estimate the interregional insurance benefits provided by the US fiscal federation.

---

[15] Clearly, this expression is not equal to permanent income, as future periods are not included. To simplify our analysis we are bringing to the present all future implications of current changes in the government balance. We also take the shortcut of ignoring the possibility that the interest rate faced by the government is different from the one faced by consumers. Taking into consideration these additional elements would not affect our reasoning.

[16] If the volatility of income is different for different regions, then the amount of insurance that the most volatile region gets can be larger than the stabilization effect.

4. INSURANCE AND STABILIZATION: THE USA

We now apply the logic of the previous model to data from US states. The question is: how much of the stabilization of state disposable income achieved through the federal budget can be identified as interstate insurance? Our starting point is to take as given previous estimates of the elasticity of taxes and transfers to income. We use these estimates to calibrate the 'stabilization' parameter (τ) of the model in section 3. We set $\tau = 30\%$, a value which is close to the estimates of Sachs and Sala-i-Martín (1992) and Bayoumi and Masson (1996a). We then combine this value with estimates of the distribution of state risks (using volatility and correlation) to assess the amount of interregional insurance generated by the federal budget for each of the US states.

4.1. Measuring volatility

The first question in our empirical analysis is the measure of volatility or risk to be used. We choose the standard deviation of the growth rate of state income.[17] The advantages of using the growth rate of state income are that it is a simple measure of volatility and that is likely to be stationary. Simplicity might be an important argument when it comes to implementing a system of transfers. As an example, the recent Stability Pact in the EU takes growth rates of GDP as reference values. Stationariness is crucial if one wants to avoid redistribution. At the same time, we recognize the limitations of income growth as a measure of volatility. First, by using growth rates, we might be capturing permanent shocks to income that one might want to leave outside the insurance system. One way to avoid this problem is to distinguish between permanent and transitory shocks, but any decomposition between permanent and transitory shocks is going to be very dependent on the method used to decompose them. Also, the short length of the available time series makes the separation between the long-term and short-term components even more arbitrary. We have performed some robustness tests and looked at alternative measures of volatility, such as detrended state income and the residuals of an autoregressive process, but the results are practically unchanged. The second difficulty in identifying the standard deviation of the growth rate with volatility is that it does not take into consideration the dynamic properties of a shock. If a state-specific shock might be propagated across several periods, we might be capturing only the impact of the shock, but not the propagation effects.[18]

[17] In our later analysis, when we look at European regions, because of data availability we will use employment growth.
[18] This issue is not critical in our analysis, given that we are only interested in separating intertemporal stabilization from interregional insurance. As long as our correction applies also to future periods, the ratio of insurance to stabilization will not be affected.

4.2. Volatility and correlation

Table 1 presents basic statistics of the series.[19] The table calculates the volatility of state income, its ratio to the volatility of the aggregate and the correlation coefficient between the region and the aggregate. When calculating the last two variables we remove from the aggregate the state in question.

Columns (2) and (3) provide a first estimate of the insurance potential of the federation. The state-to-aggregate volatility ratio suggests that the amount of idiosyncratic variability is small. Indeed, the numbers in column (2) may be interpreted as the maximum amount of insurance that can be provided to each of the states. Using the average of all states (1.36), we conclude that even if all the idiosyncratic risk is insured, the volatility of state income (or employment) growth will be reduced by only about one-quarter. This result is caused by the high correlation between state and aggregate variables. The weighted average of the correlation is 0.72.

Table 1. Volatility and correlation: state income growth rates, USA, 1969–90

State	(1)	(2)	(3)	State	(1)	(2)	(3)
ME	2.23	1.40	0.65	NC	2.20	1.39	0.92
NH	2.28	1.43	0.75	SC	2.11	1.33	0.91
VT	2.23	1.40	0.80	GA	2.16	1.36	0.89
MA	1.86	1.16	0.66	FL	2.31	1.45	0.75
RI	1.95	1.22	0.75	KY	2.17	1.36	0.77
CT	2.09	1.31	0.71	TN	2.20	1.38	0.93
NY	1.84	1.11	0.53	AL	1.85	1.16	0.82
NJ	1.64	1.02	0.71	MS	2.66	1.67	0.69
PA	1.55	0.96	0.86	AR	2.70	1.70	0.75
OH	2.31	1.48	0.93	LA	2.59	1.61	0.29
IN	2.96	1.89	0.90	OK	2.55	1.59	0.20
IL	2.01	1.27	0.91	TX	2.02	1.22	0.29
MI	3.54	2.32	0.86	MT	4.05	2.54	0.46
WI	2.07	1.30	0.90	ID	3.54	2.22	0.50
MN	2.64	1.67	0.82	WY	4.55	2.85	0.13
IA	4.07	2.58	0.70	CO	2.05	1.28	0.37
MO	1.84	1.16	0.88	NM	1.61	1.01	0.29
ND	10.36	6.53	0.39	AZ	2.97	1.87	0.66
SD	6.06	3.81	0.51	UT	1.89	1.18	0.42
NE	3.34	2.09	0.55	NV	3.58	2.25	0.51
KS	2.13	1.34	0.73	WA	2.48	1.55	0.60
DE	2.24	1.41	0.72	OR	2.62	1.65	0.77
MD	2.01	1.26	0.82	CA	1.65	1.01	0.78
VA	1.64	1.03	0.88				
WV	2.08	1.30	0.32	**Average**	**2.17**	**1.36**	**0.72**

Note: (1) Standard deviation; (2) standard deviation relative to aggregate; (3) correlation with aggregate.

[19] See the appendix for an explanation of the state codes.

An important additional finding in this table is the large differences across states. Some states have a volatility that is almost as low as the aggregate. This low volatility, combined with very high correlations, leaves very little room for insurance. Although this asymmetry might not be very important for the US states, where the federation already exists, it could become a key issue in Europe if countries can decide whether or not to join a newly created federation.

4.3. Insurance

Using the methodology described in section 3, we estimate the insurance benefits of the federal budget. We use the expression for *interregional insurance* (equation (2)) modified to take into account the different sizes of states.[20] We assume that the tax system reduces volatility of regional disposable income by 30% (in line with the estimates of Sachs and Sala-i-Martín (1992) or Bayoumi and Masson (1996a)). We match this estimate to the parameter τ of our model, and by using equation (2) we can calculate the amount of volatility that is being insured. Note that insurance is defined as the reduction (%) of volatility, measured by the standard deviation, of state permanent income.

Table 2 presents the results. It is clear that the estimate of insurance is much lower than the estimate implied by the static analysis, which focuses on the stabilization of disposable income and ignores the implications of the intertemporal budget constraint of the federal budget. The amount of insurance is around one-third of the estimates of the static analysis. In other words, the static analysis overestimates insurance by a factor of 3.[21]

Table 2 also confirms that not all states benefit in the same magnitude from the system. While some states see their permanent income variability reduced by almost the value of τ, others do not see the benefits of the system at all.

What can Europe learn from the US experience? Our results show that some previous estimates in the literature of the benefits of the federal budget overestimate (by a factor of 3) the amount of interregional insurance in the US system. Interregional insurance is only one-third of the overall stabilizing effect and the other two-thirds can be attributed to intertemporal transfers. Given that the possibility of generating intertemporal transfers through countercyclical government balances will still be available to European national governments after the introduction of the single currency, our estimates indicate that the possible benefits for Europe of a system like the US fiscal federation are modest. It remains to be

---

[20] To adjust for differences in sizes, we replace the coefficient 0.5 in equation (2) by the share that a state's income represents in aggregate income. This is equivalent to assuming that a state is responsible for a fraction of federal taxes that is equal to its relative size.

[21] Interestingly, this estimate is very close to that of von Hagen (1992), who appropriately controls for the effects of state shocks on the federal budget. It can be shown that the empirical specification of von Hagen (1992) leads to estimates almost equivalent to our calculations.

Table 2. Insurance: state income growth rates, USA, 1960–90

State		State	
ME	14.49	NC	9.58
NH	13.06	SC	8.85
VT	11.85	GA	9.65
MA	10.51	FL	12.86
RI	10.11	KY	11.79
CT	12.02	TN	9.40
NY	11.82	AL	7.44
NJ	6.64	MS	16.51
PA	1.82	AR	15.87
OH	10.29	LA	22.16
IN	15.05	OK	23.63
IL	7.54	TX	18.40
MI	17.90	MT	23.80
WI	8.51	ID	22.29
MN	14.34	WY	27.87
IA	21.18	CO	18.07
MO	6.28	NM	16.30
ND	28.01	AZ	18.34
SD	25.63	UT	15.94
NE	21.08	NV	22.28
KS	12.22	WA	16.76
DE	13.24	OR	15.08
MD	9.35	CA	4.53
VA	3.25		
WV	19.48	**Average**	**11.13**

Notes: Interstate insurance assuming $\tau = 30\%$. See text for details on calculations.

seen whether the European situation is different. If we find that there is more idiosyncratic risk among European countries than among US states, the insurance potential of a European federation could still be much larger than the one estimated for the USA.

Before estimating the insurance potential of a hypothetical European fiscal federation, it is worth discussing two caveats about our methodology. First, we have calibrated the parameter τ to match the estimates of Sachs and Sala-i-Martín (1992) and Bayoumi and Masson (1996a). The empirical specification of both papers is very different (regressions in levels versus regressions in growth rates) and neither of them makes a clear distinction between insurance and stabilization. Therefore, it is very difficult to find a perfect map between their estimates and any theoretical model. We believe that our calibration is a good approximation because the intuition behind the parameter τ is almost identical to the spirit of their empirical estimates. In both cases, the key concept is the response of state taxes and transfers to changes in state income.

A second important issue is the connection between insurance and redistribution. The approach taken by von Hagen (1992) and Bayoumi and Masson (1996a), of separating the effects by running regressions in levels or growth rates, is just an approximation. If output shocks are persistent and output has a unit root, then a shock to state income will reduce the relative income of that state for ever. If transfers take place as a result of this shock, it is unclear whether these should be classified as insurance or redistribution. The design of a tax system that can distinguish between the two functions is an extremely complicated task that is certainly beyond the scope of this paper. For the sake of simplicity, in Table 2 we have abstracted from this issue. We will return to it in section 7.

5. EMU AND FISCAL FEDERALISM

In a currency area, in the absence of monetary policy, governments have to use fiscal policy to deal with asymmetric shocks. European countries that join EMU will be able to use fiscal policy as a stabilizing tool, but they will lack the automatic interregional transfers that are normally present in currency areas (because currencies are usually associated with autonomous national fiscal systems). Therefore, the question of how important these transfers can be is crucial for European countries.

   In the case of the European Union, given that a fiscal federation does not currently exist, we can only estimate the potential effects of a hypothetical system. Our strategy is to assume that the hypothetical European fiscal federation achieves the same degree of stabilization (of disposable income) as the current US fiscal system. Then, using the methodology that we applied to the USA, we use data for volatility and correlation of national business cycles to calculate how much of this stabilization can be translated into cross-country insurance. The benefits of a European fiscal federation will depend on how important insurance is. If only a small part of the stabilization of disposable income is considered insurance, then there would be no need for a European-wide system, since the intertemporal stabilization could be done by fiscal policy at the level of national governments.[22]

5.1. Volatility and correlations

Table 3 shows some basic statistics about the series used in the analysis. As we did in the case of the USA, we perform all our calculations for GDP growth.[23] We consider the current composition of the European Union (fifteen countries) as our

[22] There is also the question of whether it will be easier to implement stabilization policies at the national level or the European level. One could argue that the limits imposed on budget deficits and debt by the Stability Pact make stabilizing policies at the national level very difficult to implement. This argument would favour a European fiscal federation, even if it can only perform the role of stabilizing disposable income. On the other hand, for political economy reasons it might be argued that it would be harder for a European-wide budget to run large deficits or surpluses. We abstract from these issues in this paper and leave them for further research.
[23] Given that we want to make comparisons at different levels of aggregation, we use PPP estimates of GDP, which allow us to aggregate output across countries to obtain aggregate GDP.

unit of analysis. The table reports the standard deviation of the variables, the standard deviation relative to the aggregate, and the correlation between the country and the aggregate. We always exclude the country in question from the aggregate.

In the first three columns, we can see that the correlations between the country and the European aggregate are generally quite high. The (weighted) average is 0.66. The ratio of country to European volatility is 1.31 for the case of GDP. Although not directly comparable because of differences in the level of disaggregation, these figures are close to those of the US states. Correlations are generally lower, but the ratio of volatility is practically identical. Both the ratio and the correlation are indications of the insurance potential of a European fiscal federation. For example, the average ratio of volatility is 1.31, which implies that the maximum potential for insurance is (on average) around one-quarter (if all idiosyncratic risk is eliminated, the volatility of countries will be reduced by approximately 25%).

As was the case for the USA, the figures in columns (2) and (3) show large differences across countries. Income is between two and three times more volatile in countries like Greece than in countries like France and Austria.

An interesting question is how these correlations have changed over time. The second set of columns in Table 3 presents estimates for correlation and volatility during the second part of the sample. We break the sample in 1979 (the starting point of the EMS) to test for the effects of European integration and increased coordination of economic policies. These results have to be handled with great care, given the short period involved and the fact that German unification seems to have a significant effect on these figures. There seems to be a fall in the overall correlation and an increase in the volatility ratio. Absolute country volatility falls, but by less than the volatility of the aggregate. In some countries, such as Italy and the Netherlands, the correlation with the aggregate has increased and the ratio of national to aggregate volatility has fallen. Other countries, like the United Kingdom, display opposite trends: stable or falling correlation with the aggregate and an increase in idiosyncratic volatility relative to the aggregate.[24]

5.2. Insurance

We now use the previous estimates of volatility and cross-country correlations to measure the insurance potential of a European fiscal federation. As mentioned before, our goal is to estimate the insurance that could be provided by a European fiscal federation under the assumptions that the tax structure resulted in a certain

---

[24] Artis and Zhang (1995) estimate in more detail the synchronization of European countries' business cycles with Germany. Their results show a larger increase in the degree of synchronization than is presented in Table 3. The use of a different series for GDP, a different frequency and a different detrending method might be responsible for the apparent contradiction with some of our results.

Table 3. Volatility and correlation: GDP growth rates, 1961–96

Country	1961–96			1979–96		
	(1)	(2)	(3)	(1)	(2)	(3)
Germany	2.11	1.28	0.67	1.80	1.46	0.43
France	1.92	1.18	0.85	1.31	1.07	0.75
Italy	2.34	1.46	0.68	1.57	1.33	0.74
Netherlands	2.10	1.28	0.74	1.48	1.23	0.71
Belgium	2.10	1.29	0.85	1.53	1.29	0.68
Luxembourg	2.79	1.71	0.67	1.85	1.56	0.76
UK	2.06	1.16	0.43	2.16	1.72	0.25
Ireland	2.08	1.26	0.13	2.07	1.74	0.31
Denmark	2.40	1.47	0.60	1.61	1.34	0.33
Spain	2.98	1.82	0.73	1.74	1.46	0.68
Greece	3.47	2.14	0.64	1.58	1.33	0.60
Portugal	3.17	1.95	0.76	2.29	1.93	0.62
Sweden	2.08	1.26	0.66	1.76	1.49	0.75
Finland	3.12	1.91	0.54	3.40	2.88	0.49
Austria	1.81	1.10	0.76	1.32	1.11	0.77
Average EU	**2.15**	**1.31**	**0.66**	**1.71**	**1.41**	**0.56**

Note: (1) Standard deviation; (2) standard deviation relative to aggregate; (3) correlation with aggregate.

amount of disposable income stabilization. As we did for the case of the US states, we set the parameter τ equal to 30%. Table 4 reports the results.[25]

As was the case for the USA, the average insurance is approximately one-third of the parameter that measures the smoothing of disposable income. As mentioned before, there are important differences across countries. Countries with low volatility, such as France and Austria, benefit very little compared to countries like Greece, Finland and Luxembourg, whose benefits are three times as large.

We also estimate these figures for the post-1979 sample. The estimates confirm the results of Table 3 regarding the evolution over time of the correlations between regions and the aggregate. The average insurance potential slightly increases over time. This evolution is greatly influenced by the United Kingdom and Germany, which have a large weight in the average.

6. THE ROLE OF NATIONAL SYSTEMS

The current European situation, with a small EU budget unrelated to cyclical stabilization, has led people to conclude that interregional insurance is absent in the European Union. For example, Sachs and Sala-i-Martín state that 'if a European region or country suffers a one dollar adverse shock, its tax payments to the

[25] These estimates are, once again, measuring interregional insurance using equation (2) from section 3.

Table 4. Insurance: GDP growth rates

Country	1961-96	1979-96
Germany	10.00	14.99
France	6.20	5.99
Italy	12.20	10.03
Netherlands	10.84	10.63
Belgium	9.08	12.15
Luxembourg	17.21	14.36
UK	13.36	19.72
Ireland	22.99	22.79
Denmark	15.88	19.54
Spain	17.20	14.81
Greece	19.89	14.32
Portugal	17.43	19.17
Sweden	12.16	13.41
Finland	20.13	23.99
Austria	7.41	7.28
Average EU	**10.94**	**13.01**

Notes: Intercountry insurance $\tau = 30\%$. See text for details on calculations.

European Community will be reduced by half a cent. This contrasts with the 34 cents we found for the United States.' This conclusion might be true for countries, but not for European regions – subunits of countries. European regions receive transfers from the current fifteen national systems that are much larger than the 'half a cent' received from the EU budget.

This section applies the previous methodology to study the insurance benefits that national fiscal systems provide, and compares them to the benefits that these regions would obtain from a European-wide system. Of course, studying subunits of countries will not modify our previous results about the amount of national risk that can be insured at the European level. In that sense, it could be argued that a European fiscal federation is a complement to national systems. National systems insure regional risks within countries, while the European federation can insure country risk. Our approach is to analyse the current national systems to gain additional perspective on the debate about the need for a fiscal federation. By providing estimates of the insurance potential of national fiscal systems, we can better assess the benefits that a European-wide system would bring to European regions.[26]

In this case we do not use GDP growth, as the available data series for regional income and GDP are too short. Instead, we use the standard deviation of

[26] This is indeed related to the general debate on EMU. By studying subunits of countries, one can gain perspective on the issue of Europe as an optimum currency area beyond the limited comparison between the current arrangement of fifteen currencies and the alternative of a single currency.

employment growth as a measure of volatility.[27] The analysis is restricted to five countries for which sufficiently long regional time series are available. The regions analysed are 8 regions for Germany, 7 for France, 11 for Italy, 7 for Spain and 11 for the UK.

6.1. Regional, national and European volatility

Table 5 shows the basic statistics for these regions. We summarize the information by providing only the (weighted) average of regions for a given country. The appendix shows the figures for all the regions.

We calculate the relative volatility and the correlation between regional to national and regional to EU15 employment growth rates. As usual, we exclude the region in question from the aggregate. The region to country volatility is within the range found for the US states and for the European countries. The region to European volatility is much higher, except for France. The reason is that France is the only country in this sample where the volatility of national employment growth is lower than the European one.[28] The figures in columns (1) and (2) are simply another way of presenting the information contained in Table 3, where we showed that there is a certain amount of idiosyncratic national risk among European countries.

Table 5. Volatility and correlation: regional employment growth rates

Country	1961–95				1979–95			
	(1)	(2)	(3)	(4)	(1)	(2)	(3)	(4)
Germany	1.25	2.29	0.74	0.50	1.27	1.91	0.72	0.52
France	1.21	0.95	0.74	0.50	1.21	0.89	0.75	0.59
Italy	1.34	1.97	0.68	0.41	1.29	1.75	0.71	0.55
UK	1.26	2.33	0.70	0.54	1.26	2.39	0.70	0.55
Average*	**1.26**	**1.89**	**0.72**	**0.49**	**1.26**	**1.74**	**0.72**	**0.55**
Spain	–	–	–	–	0.93	2.53	0.80	0.78

* Excludes Spanish regions.
Notes: Standard deviation relative to country aggregate; (2) standard deviation relative to European aggregate; (3) correlation with country aggregate; (4) correlation with European aggregate. All numbers are weighted averages of regional data. See appendix for availability of data for different countries.

[27] To check for the implications of using employment growth instead of GDP growth, we have replicated Table 2 and Table 3 (GDP country data) using employment. All the estimates are very similar. The results are available from the author.
[28] This effect would be smaller if we were using GDP. As Table 3 showed, French to European volatility of GDP growth rates is close to, but above 1.

The regional to European volatility is larger than the state to national in the USA or the country to Europe. This implies that, from the perspective of one of these regions, the potential for European-wide insurance is larger than the potential for insurance of US states. The average, 1.89, implies that the maximum insurance is approximately 45% compared to 25% in the case of the USA.

When we compare the evolution of these coefficients over time, we see that within-country correlations have been quite stable while there has been an increase in correlations across countries (with the exception of the UK). Similarly, although the ratio of regional to national volatility has not changed, the regional to European volatility has decreased.

6.2. Insurance

In this section we estimate the insurance benefits that European regions can obtain from both national and European fiscal systems. Our estimates do not reflect the actual insurance that the current national systems provide (for that we would require detailed knowledge of the exact tax structure of each of the national systems). They do not measure either the insurance that a European system would provide, as it will be a function of the size of the budget and the design of the system. We estimate the potential for insurance of both systems based on the evidence presented in Table 5. The methodology is, as before, to set the parameter τ that measures intertemporal stabilization equal to 30%. From this value and the figures in Table 5, we can infer the insurance that such a system could provide. In that sense, our estimates will show the relative contribution of national-based and European-wide fiscal systems under the assumption that the European system is an exact replica of the national-based system.

Table 6 presents these estimates and summarizes the information by calculating the (weighted) average of regions that belong to the same country.[29] The estimates of national insurance range from 7% to 11%. On average, national insurance is close to 10%. The estimates for European insurance range from 9% to 22%, the average being 18%. Therefore, national systems can insure more than 50% of a European system. For the EMS sample, while the potential for national insurance does not significantly change except for the case of Italy, the insurance potential of a European system declines for all countries except the UK. The case of Spain shows, as expected, that countries with higher than average volatility could benefit more from the European system. Spanish regions, although they have a very high correlation with other European regions, have a volatility that is more than double

[29] Strictly speaking, the estimates of Table 6 cannot be considered a measure of insurance because we are using employment growth instead of income. One would need to specify how the system of transfers translates changes in employment to changes in taxes and transfers. As a result, the figures in Table 6 should be read as our estimate of the insurance potential under the assumption that employment growth volatility is a good proxy for income volatility.

Table 6. Insurance: regional employment growth rates

Country	1961–95		1979–95	
	(1)	(2)	(1)	(2)
Germany	8.74	21.72	8.65	19.61
France	8.23	9.10	7.12	4.53
Italy	10.75	21.48	8.87	17.37
UK	9.54	21.39	9.62	21.49
Average*	**9.31**	**18.42**	**8.57**	**15.75**
Spain			5.37	19.67

ᵃExcludes Spanish regions.

Notes: Interregional insurance assuming $\tau = 30\%$. See text for details on calculations. (1) National insurance; (2) European insurance. All the numbers are weighted averages of regional data. See appendix for availability of data for different countries.

the volatility of the aggregate. As a result, Spain's national fiscal system insures less than a third of the European insurance.

We need to emphasize that the previous estimates are constructed under the assumption that the European system is a perfect replica of the national systems in terms of the parameter τ. This parameter represents the stabilization that the tax system builds into regional disposable income. This stabilization is a function of the size of the budget and the countercyclical behaviour of taxes (net of transfers). The assumption that the European system is a replica of the national systems does not imply that the size of the budget needs to be identical to the size of the national government budgets. A very high level of insurance can be achieved with a small budget where taxes and transfers are very reactive to income changes.

6.3. An example: Italy and Germany

All the previous calculations have been done under the assumption that all countries form part of the European fiscal federation. What would happen if only a subset of them joined EMU? We analyse here a federation with only two countries: Germany and Italy. Of the five countries for which regional data were available, we have chosen these two for the availability of data (the data start in 1960) and because Italy is a country that has had frequent realignments in the EMS.

We repeat the calculations of Table 6, but now we measure the insurance provided by national systems and the insurance provided by a hypothetical federation of German and Italian regions. In this case we present the results only for the pre-EMS period (1960–79) and the post-EMS period (1979–94). Results are shown in Table 7.

Overall, the numbers are similar to those in Table 6, but now there is a more

Table 7. Insurance: regional employment growth rates

	1961–79		1979–94	
Country	(1)	(2)	(1)	(2)
Germany	7.80	19.85	8.58	13.29
Italy	12.25	26.41	8.79	12.25

Notes: Interregional insurance assuming $\tau = 30\%$. See text for details on calculations. (1) National insurance; (2) federal insurance.

pronounced change between the pre-EMS period and the post-EMS period.[30] While, in the pre-EMS period, national insurance is only 40% of the insurance provided by the federation, in the post-EMS period, national insurance is almost 70% of the insurance of the federation. Based on these estimates, if Italy and Germany were to form a currency union, the additional benefits of merging their fiscal systems into a unique federal system not only are small, but have been substantially decreasing over time. If there are reasons to believe that this trend will continue, the benefits of a fiscal federation will become even smaller in the future. This is an important result that allows us to extrapolate our estimates to a future EMU. All the estimates presented in this paper are based on historical data that can be the result of institutions, economic policies or even fundamental shocks that are likely to change with the creation of EMU. The comparison between the pre- and post-EMS period provides some information on the changes that EMU is likely to bring. Bayoumi and Eichengreen (1997), Fatás (1997) and Frankel and Rose (1997) provide additional evidence in favour of the idea that EMU will increase the synchronization of European business cycles.[31]

7. REDISTRIBUTION OR INSURANCE?

In previous sections we have studied the risk-sharing potential of a European-wide fiscal federation. In this section we review some of the problems associated with its implementation, stressing the difficulty of avoiding redistribution.

The first issue is to define and measure the risk that needs to be insured. Risk is directly related to the unexpected component of output, usually associated with what we refer to as its cyclical component. For the system to respond to cyclical

---

[30] The numbers are not directly comparable because in Table 6 we did not report the data for the pre-EMS period, given that the data available for the other countries were not long enough.
[31] The results of Table 7 can be interpreted in terms of the criteria for an optimum currency area. This evidence suggests that the benefits for Germany and Italy in forming a currency area are larger in the second part of the sample. Given that the second part of the sample coincides with the existence of the EMS, this means that the criteria for an optimum currency area are endogenous and that countries are more likely to satisfy these criteria once they enter EMU.

fluctuations, we need to specify a long-term reference value or trend for income, and transfers would be defined in response to deviations from the trend. The problem is that defining a reference value requires the identification of the long-term component of the variable in question. In order to avoid redistribution, the fitted model would need to be updated as new data were released. If there is clearly no agreement among economists about how to filter the long-term component of a time series, it seems even more problematic to design a system that would be agreed by politicians and where automatic adjustments are made as new data become available.[32]

To understand the importance of this issue, Figure 1 plots Spanish GDP relative to the aggregate of the other fourteen countries.[33] It is evident that, although there might be a pattern of convergence, the trend is anything but stable. There are large deviations from the trend around the oil crises of the 1970s and the recession of the early 1990s. How do we classify these movements and, more importantly, should a fiscal federation insure them? A possible interpretation of some of the observed changes is that a structural break in the growth rate of relative GDP has taken place. In this case, an adjustment would need to be made to the reference value (or trend) to calculate the cyclical deviations from this trend. But at which point in time could we have concluded that there was a structural break in the growth rate of GDP in

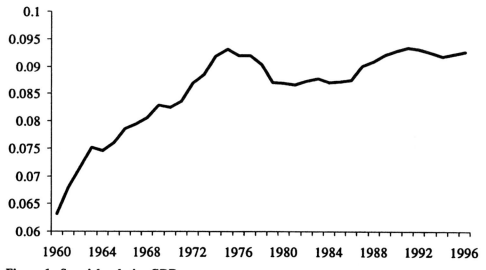

Figure 1. Spanish relative GDP

[32] Von Hagen and Hammond (1997) test alternative methods to construct an insurance system that avoids redistribution. They find that, although simple models create large errors, a fairly complex econometric model could easily avoid redistribution transfers. Their methodology ignores the problems of updating the system as new data are released.
[33] More precisely, the variable plotted is 1000 times the ratio of Spanish GDP to the aggregate GDP for the other fourteen countries.

the early 1970s? Was this an unexpected break? What would happen if, after having agreed that there has been a structural break, new data overturned our conclusion? These are questions that highlight the difficulties that any European system of insurance would have faced if it had been in place in the last three decades.

In addition to the above issue of structural breaks in the growth rate of GDP, the system would also need to manage permanent shocks to the level of GDP. In other words, even if we can agree on the existence of a long-term trend defined by an average growth rate, some of the cyclical (unexpected) movements can be quite persistent or even leave permanent effects on the level of GDP. Should these fluctuations be insured? In principle, any risk associated with income fluctuations could be part of an insurance mechanism. However, it would be natural to restrict the insurance role of a possible European fiscal federation to transitory fluctuations. The main reason is that the debate on the creation of a fiscal federation in EMU is related to the possible use of fiscal policy to 'replace' the role currently played by exchange rates. As a result, in the presence of permanent shocks to income, the system might be designed to deal with the cyclical component of these shocks, but not with its permanent consequences. If the fiscal system were to generate transfers in response to the permanent effects on output, it would be generating transfers that would look very much like redistribution.[34]

To measure the importance of permanent shocks we have performed a simple exercise, measuring the volatility of the permanent component of relative GDP for the fifteen countries in our sample. This measure provides us with a rough estimate of how well a naive system, designed around a deterministic trend, would perform. The logic of our analysis is that a system where payments are generated in response to income deviations from a trend will serve its purposes only if the size and frequency of permanent shocks (relative to transitory shocks) is small. If, on the other hand, the permanent component of income is very volatile, the system will frequently create permanent interregional transfers.

To perform our empirical exercise we look at a measure of the contribution of the permanent component of relative GDP to its overall volatility using a ratio of variances. We prefer this measure to more traditional ways of decomposing fluctuations in temporary and permanent shocks because it does not specifically rely on any time-series model to describe the variable in question. The variance ratio that we use simply looks at whether the economy tends to dampen cyclical disturbances (in which case, relative GDP returns to a deterministic trend after a shock) or, on the contrary, tends to amplify them, leading to permanent effects on

---

[34] Once we allow for cyclical shocks to be permanent, the distinction between cycle and trend disappears. We avoid some of these issues by making a clear distinction between structural changes in output growth and permanent shocks to the level of output. As becomes obvious in our discussion, these two phenomena are theoretically related and, in most cases, empirically indistinguishable. This highlights, even more, the difficulty of measuring cyclical deviations in income.

the level of GDP. The estimate we use, proposed by Cochrane (1988), is a weighted average of GDP growth autocorrelations.

$$V_{\mathcal{J}} = \frac{1}{\mathcal{J}} \frac{\mathrm{var}(y_t - y_{t-\mathcal{J}})}{\mathrm{var}(y_t - y_{t-1})} = 1 + 2 \sum_{j=1}^{\mathcal{J}-1} \frac{1-j}{\mathcal{J}} \rho_j$$

where y is the log of GDP, ρ_j is the jth autocorrelation of the growth rate of output and $\mathcal{J}$ is the 'window' for which the ratio is calculated. Taking the limit of this expression as $\mathcal{J}$ tends to infinity, we obtain a measure of long-run persistence. If a variable is trend stationary, we expect higher than normal growth to be followed by lower than normal growth (negative autocorrelations). In this case, the variance ratio will be very small. Indeed, given the construction of the ratio, if a variable is trend stationary, the ratio will be equal to zero. If the variable were a random walk with a drift, the ratio would be equal to 1.[35]

Table 8 provides the estimates of this variance ratio for each of the fifteen European countries in our sample. We have calculated the variance ratio for three 'windows': 5, 10 and 15 years. For each country, we look at the GDP relative to the aggregate of the other fourteen countries. The table shows that in all cases the ratio is much larger than zero. This result indicates that relative GDP is far from being a stationary variable and that permanent shocks are large and frequent. Indeed, in some cases (France, Spain and Greece), the ratio is very high and reflects the instability of their GDP growth rates relative to the growth rate of GDP of the aggregate.[36]

Overall, the estimates of Table 8 confirm the difficulties associated with designing and implementing any form of cyclical insurance across European regions or countries. Any simple design based on measuring deviations from a reference value or trend will certainly lead to significant permanent transfers. These transfers can, of course, go in any direction (e.g., from poor to rich regions), which will undermine the support for the system and will further create tensions among its members. More complicated mechanisms based on models that decompose output (or unemployment) changes into permanent and transitory components might correct some of these deficiencies, but will create endless debates about both the design of the model and the data that are inputted into the system. It is hard to imagine a system that will find enough support and credibility to be politically viable.

Having seen that fluctuations are long lasting and that permanent shocks are large and frequent, an interesting issue is to measure the insurance potential regarding output fluctuations at lower frequencies. In other words, we want to measure the

---

[35] Cochrane (1988) gives further details on the interpretation of this ratio.

[36] In the cases of Spain and Greece, the fact that their average growth rate has been much higher than the growth rate of the European aggregate can explain the instability. This reinforces our claims about the difficulties of separating trend and cycle.

Table 8. Variance ratio: relative GDP growth rates

Country	V_5	V_{10}	V_{15}
Germany	1.072	0.884	0.778
France	1.698	2.501	2.921
Italy	0.829	0.986	1.005
Netherlands	1.014	1.031	0.689
Belgium	1.028	0.816	0.841
Luxembourg	1.314	1.563	1.648
UK	1.460	1.530	1.853
Ireland	1.514	1.594	1.398
Denmark	0.887	0.318	0.282
Spain	2.291	2.694	2.980
Greece	1.705	2.703	3.165
Portugal	0.898	0.890	0.920
Sweden	0.930	0.613	0.440
Finland	1.288	0.907	0.619
Austria	0.940	0.698	0.425

cross-country correlation of GDP growth rates at longer horizons. Table 9 presents the correlation between national and European GDP growth rates for three different frequencies: 1, 3 and 5 years.[37] The numbers show that, as the horizon gets longer, cross-country correlations increase. The (weighted) average at a five-year horizon is 0.84, 25% higher than the correlation of one-year growth rates. This result is

Table 9. Correlation: GDP growth rates

Country	1 yr	3 yrs	5 yrs
Germany	0.67	0.69	0.82
France	0.85	0.93	0.96
Italy	0.68	0.77	0.90
Netherlands	0.74	0.89	0.94
Belgium	0.85	0.91	0.95
Luxembourg	0.67	0.62	0.68
UK	0.43	0.45	0.64
Ireland	0.13	0.32	0.52
Denmark	0.60	0.64	0.80
Spain	0.73	0.86	0.93
Greece	0.64	0.88	0.91
Portugal	0.76	0.87	0.95
Sweden	0.66	0.79	0.87
Finland	0.54	0.59	0.70
Austria	0.76	0.86	0.92
Average EU	**0.66**	**0.73**	**0.84**

Notes: Correlation of GDP growth rates with European aggregate at different horizons.

[37] As before, the country in question is removed when calculating the aggregate.

consistent with our previous findings of long-lasting fluctuations. It also suggests that, given the high correlation associated with low-frequency fluctuations, there is little room for insurance at those frequencies.

8. CONCLUSIONS AND POLICY IMPLICATIONS

The future adoption of a single currency among European countries has raised many concerns about how national governments will deal with shocks that are asymmetric (specific to regions or countries). Some of these concerns have their origin in the comparison between the USA and Europe. From this comparison, the literature has concluded that the US states are better equipped to deal with asymmetric shocks not only because of the higher level of labour mobility, but also because of the existence of automatic transfers provided by the federal budget. When a state suffers a recession, the combination of lower taxes and additional transfers absorbs a significant part of the initial decrease in income. Empirical estimates of this effect suggest that, in response to a fall in state income of 1 dollar, disposable income falls by only between 56 and 65 cents. These estimates are presented as evidence that the US federal budget provides significant interregional insurance not present in EMU.

This paper presents four sets of findings that suggest that the benefits associated with the creation of a European fiscal federation are much smaller than previously thought. First, we show that some of the previous estimates of the amount of interstate insurance provided by the US federal budget overestimate the true amount of insurance by a factor of 3. The reason is that the original estimates simply measured the stabilization effect of the tax system on disposable state income. This can be identified as insurance only under the assumption that there is no aggregate risk in the federation. Otherwise, when a state suffers a recession, and the fall in its tax revenues is not compensated by revenue increases coming from other states, then the federal budget will run a deficit that will need to be paid in the future by all states. As a result, the state in a recession does not benefit as much as indicated by the smoothed disposable income and, moreover, the other states suffer because of the future tax payments. We apply the same reasoning to data from countries of the European Union and find estimates of insurance potential that are very close to those for the USA. Even if a European-wide fiscal system managed to reduce the volatility of disposable income by 30%, it would be providing less than 10% insurance. The other two-thirds would be inter-temporal stabilization through countercyclical budgets – a tool that is already available to European countries and will be available to future member countries of EMU.

This result highlights the importance of maintaining future flexibility in conducting fiscal policy at the national level, and signals the possible costs of the Stability Pact. If government deficits are constrained by the limits of the Stability

Pact, the ability of the current national systems to adjust to shocks through intertemporal transfers will disappear.[38] Under this scenario, there will be a much greater need for a European fiscal federation. In the absence of national fiscal policies, the benefits of a European fiscal federation will also include the intertemporal stabilization role that the national systems, constrained by the Stability Pact, will not be able play.

Second, Europe already has national tax systems that partially insure regions from idiosyncratic risk. We estimate the importance of these systems by comparing the current system with a hypothetical European-wide system that would replicate the stabilizing properties of the national systems. We find that the current national systems insure more than 50% of a European fiscal federation.

Third, we find some evidence that the potential insurance benefits of a European fiscal federation have decreased over time. When we break the sample in 1979, we find that in the post-EMS period, because of increased correlations across countries, the potential for insurance of a European fiscal federation has been reduced. If, as a consequence of EMU, this trend persists in the future, the insurance possibilities of a fiscal federation will continue to fall.

Fourth, we look at cross-country differences with respect to the insurance benefits that a European fiscal federation would provide. These benefits are a function of the amount of risk that different countries have and the correlation with the European aggregate. Some countries, such as the UK and Ireland, could greatly benefit from the system, but others, such as France and Austria, could benefit much less. This implies that if these countries are offered the possibility of joining the federation, they may decline it, which will in turn reduce the overall insurance possibilities of the federation. If all countries are forced into the system, the only solution to this tension is to have a different risk premium for each country depending on its volatility. This asymmetry adds to the already complicated design of the system and would make its implementation even more problematic.

In the last part of the paper, we review some of the practical difficulties associated with the implementation of interregional risk sharing through a fiscal federation. We show that there is a very high probability that any system designed to share risk across regions or countries will generate permanent transfers. The nature of these transfers, which might go in any direction (for example, from poor to rich regions), will probably conflict with the redistribution goals of structural funds.

Overall, we conclude from our analysis that the potential to provide additional interregional insurance by creating a European fiscal federation is modest. We find it difficult to argue that these benefits can compensate for the many problems associated with the design and implementation of a European fiscal federation.

---

[38] This is especially true if governments start with deficits close to the upper limit of 3%.

Discussion

Torben M. Andersen

University of Aarhus

Antonio Fatás' paper analyses whether the establishment of EMU creates a need for a federal fiscal system. Based on a simple model and empirical evidence from the USA, an assessment is made of the gains from interregional risk sharing. It is concluded that the potential gains from interregional insurance via a European fiscal federation are too small to compensate for the many problems associated with its design and implementation. The paper raises an important issue and provides an interesting attempt to quantify the gains from interregional risk-sharing arrangements.

Whether EMU creates a need for a fiscal federation depends on the extent to which the room and need for active fiscal policy are affected. Based on the optimal currency area literature, it might be argued that abandoning the exchange rate instrument in a situation with insufficient labour market flexibility raises the importance of fiscal policy as a stabilization instrument, and the more so, the more the common monetary policy will be geared at fighting inflation rather than at stabilization. Moreover, it may be argued that the restrictions that EMU imposes on the fiscal policy of member states (in particular, the deficit norm) create a need for a common fiscal policy. That the fiscal norms are constraining fiscal policy is witnessed by the difficulties that a number of countries have in meeting these requirements.

Hence, this raises the question of the appropriate role for fiscal policy in its capacity as a stabilizer of economic activity in EMU. However, this is not the question addressed in this paper, which explicitly assumes that the fiscal norms associated with EMU and the Stability Pact do not put binding constraints on fiscal policy in the member states. Rather, the paper considers only whether there are gains from pooling permanent-income risk.

A distinction is made between 'intertemporal' transfers within a member state and 'interregional' transfers (insurance). The former are disregarded, while insurance is defined as the ability to share risk between regions to lower the variance of permanent income. This raises the question of why EMU would affect the incentive to enter such a scheme. An incentive to insure permanent income is present with or without EMU. This incentive may be strengthened due to EMU, if one assumes that the latter would increase the volatility of permanent income. If so, this takes us back to the question of stabilization policy. Of course, it could be argued that EMU provides an institutional arrangement within which it is easier to establish such a risk-sharing institution. However, to the extent that common fiscal arrangements already exist in the EU, which could have been extended if there had been sufficient political will to do so, the strength of this argument is not obvious. Moreover, the gains from entering risk-sharing arrangements with countries outside the EMU would be even larger.

Sharing permanent-income risk raises difficult questions concerning incentive effects, as discussed by the author, but also concerning the implementation and credibility of such a scheme. Even though there is an *ex ante* incentive to enter such an arrangement, it will inevitably evolve into a mechanism for permanent redistribution from lucky to unlucky regions. How is it possible to implement such a scheme while avoiding this, and to make it credible?

As noted, the distinction between intertemporal and interregional transfers is important to the analysis in the paper. Strictly speaking, the paper's definition of insurance, as reducing the volatility of permanent income, is valid only under Ricardian equivalence. However, even under Ricardian equivalence, there is a need for interregional risk sharing to the extent that available instruments in international capital markets are incomplete. The measure of insurance provided in the paper (section 3) is, however, very special in that it does not really address the problem of measuring permanent income and its volatility. Moreover, the metric implicitly relies on a one-period transitory shock. It seems very special to assume that shocks of this type are driving the volatility of permanent income. Furthermore, cyclical measures for the standard deviation and cross-correlations of output are used. Hence, we are not sure about how to interpret the empirical findings.

To assess the potential gains from interregional risk sharing, the author uses empirical findings from the USA. It is not quite clear whether it makes sense to use these findings as a basis for evaluating the gains from interregional risk sharing in Europe (especially under the assumptions made by the author). First, whereas most US states effectively operate under a balanced budget rule, this is not the case in Europe. Secondly, it is not clear that the gains from interregional risk sharing are independent of the underlying risk-sharing arrangements in society. Finally, the structure of the economy, especially in terms of labour market flexibility and mobility, affects the need for and gains from insurance critically.

There is a relatively large literature on fiscal federalism in the USA, and the author draws on this and discusses whether there is an upward bias in the measured interregional risk sharing. The argument is that these estimates do not take into account future budgetary consequences. This is surely a relevant problem. However, there is also another problem, which runs the other way. The benefits of stability cannot be judged directly from the tax rates (and their progressivity), as the underlying variability of income is dependent on this – the better stabilizers work, the lower the variance of output. Similarly, the correlation of economic activity under fiscal federation will automatically be upward biased – this is one of the transmission mechanisms. To assess the stability gains via fiscal arrangements, we need a structural model to evaluate the quantitative importance of automatic stabilizers for output volatility. Moreover, it is not clear that an overestimation of the risk-sharing parameter leads to an overestimation of the gains from insurance, as the metric used is not monotone in the risk-sharing parameter. This points to another problem with interpreting the findings in the paper. No attempt is made to assess the gains from optimal interregional risk sharing. Rather, we are told what the effects would be of having the same interregional sharing in Europe as in the USA. But what do we learn from being told that the gains from a non-optimal risk-sharing arrangement are small?

Finally, it is difficult to conclude that the assessed scope for risk sharing is of modest importance, as the welfare consequences of this depend critically on the aversion to risk. Moreover, it seems dangerous to base conclusions about the need for insurance on historical data. *Ex post*, there will always be winners and losers – the lucky would regret entering the risk-sharing arrangements, while the unlucky would be pleased that they did join. The author's finding that certain countries have only a weak incentive to enter an interregional risk-sharing arrangement is thus not necessarily well founded.

Philippe Martin

Graduate Institute of International Studies, Geneva; CERAS, Paris; and CEPR

The paper by Antonio Fatás has three main points. The first point is that in the USA, interstate insurance provided by the federal budget is small. The second is that the potential insurance provided by a fiscal federation in Europe would be limited compared to the existing system of national fiscal budgets. The third is that such a fiscal federation would be very difficult and costly to implement. I do not have any specific qualm on the first result, especially as it is consistent with the results of previous papers by von Hagen (1992) and Asdrubali *et al.* (1996) on the USA. I find Fatás' paper very convincing on the cost and difficulty of a fiscal federation in Europe. My comments will concentrate on his second argument, which I find more controversial.

One way to put Fatás' first argument is that, because the USA represents quite a good monetary union – in particular, because the correlation of shocks across states is relatively high – the USA cannot be a good candidate for an interstate federal insurance system. We know from the basics of insurance theory that such a system does indeed require its members to have a low or, even better, a negative correlation of shocks. In some sense, Fatás tells us that you cannot have the cake and eat it: a country or a group of countries cannot be a good monetary union and a good candidate for a federal fiscal insurance system at the same time. Other criteria for an optimum currency area, such as the amount of volatility of production, the extent of labour mobility and the level of price and wage flexibility, would bring the same message. This makes me think that an almost perfect mapping exists between the optimal currency area theory and a theory of optimal federal insurance areas. For example, low wage and price flexibility certainly increases the benefits of federal fiscal insurance, as shocks will be longer lasting and pure market mechanisms of adjustment will work less well. If, for a given correlation of shocks, a region has a high volatility of output, it will be a bad candidate for a monetary union, but it will also gain a lot from fiscal insurance.

This interpretation of the message of the paper leads me to be cautious on its main policy implication. Why does the author find that EMU would not be such a good candidate for federal insurance? The result arises because he uses data that tell us EMU is a good candidate for monetary union. Indeed, the correlations of growth rates across countries that he finds for Europe are not very different from those across states in the USA. My reading of the existing empirical literature on whether EMU is a good currency area or not is more agnostic, even on the issue of the correlation of shocks. We know that the answer depends very much on how the shocks are identified. Moreover, there are other dimensions beyond the correlation and volatility of shocks, which are necessary to judge the benefits of a currency area and federal fiscal insurance, and which are missing in Fatás' analysis. If one believes, based on existing empirical work, that Europe is not such a good currency area, then one is bound to believe also that federal fiscal insurance would have greater benefits in Europe than Fatás asserts.

The amount of potential insurance that Fatás calculates for Europe is based on European data for a period (1961–96) during which monetary policies and exchange rate realignments still had a quite important role in the adjustment to asymmetric shocks. This may imply that the potential insurance that he predicts for a situation where no realignments will be allowed is biased downwards because the observed volatilities and correlations take into account the role of exchange rate adjustments. This can actually be seen in the data presented in Table 3, which shows that the average national standard deviation of growth rates relative to the European aggregate was 1.31 during the period 1961–96 and 1.41 during the period 1979–96. The average correlation of growth rates was 0.66 and 0.56 during these two periods. This means that the potential for insurance increased between the two periods as relative national volatility increased and correlation decreased. There are many ways to explain this, but the creation of the EMS and its hardening, by removing some of the smoothing mechanism allowed by exchange rates, would be strong possibilities. If so, EMU itself should increase the potential for federal insurance compared to the period analysed here.

The USA is a natural benchmark to compare to the future euro zone. However, there are some important differences that could once again lead to underestimating the potential role of a federal fiscal system in Europe. In the USA, the federal government smoothes around 10% of state shocks. Why so little? Fatás argues convincingly that high correlation of shocks is one reason. The results of Asdrubali *et al.* (1996) suggest further that the role of private insurance is essential in the USA: they find that 39% of shocks are smoothed by capital markets, 23% by credit markets and 13% (an estimate close to Fatás) by the federal government. Can we expect private insurance to play such an important role in Europe? Although there is evidence (Canova and Ravn, 1996) that international risk sharing is higher in Europe than elsewhere, it is still far from risk sharing at the national level, such as in the USA. The integration of financial markets in Europe will be strengthened by EMU, which should itself help private markets to take a more important role in insurance. However, at least at the beginning of the process, private markets will not be as efficient as in the USA. Moreover, the holding of stocks by private agents is still much less important in Europe than in the USA.

The separation between interregional and intertemporal transfers is analytically useful, but I do not fully agree with the normative interpretation of the results. Because the stabilization of state disposable income in the USA is due one-third to interregional insurance and two-thirds to intertemporal transfers, and because these intertemporal transfers will still be available to national governments, Fatás concludes that most of the stabilization can still be performed by national governments in Europe and that a fiscal federation would not add much. This is true only if intertemporal transfers can be performed as efficiently at the regional or state level as at the federal level. This assumes implicitly that there are no gains in managing the smoothing of disposable incomes for a larger zone, or, putting it differently, that there are no economies of scale in this respect. If a liquidity effect exists on public debt markets, however, this will not be true. For example, the interest rate on the debt of the region Île de France (the largest region in France) is 10–20 basis points higher than the rate on the French state debt, even though both have the same rating. Market participants attribute this difference solely to a liquidity effect. This is absent from Fatás' calculations, as he assumes the same interest rate for regions and for the federation, and this therefore underestimates the benefit of a federal budget. Certainly, future research should analyse whether this liquidity effect could be quantitatively important when going from a national to a federal budget.

Another related issue is whether Ricardian equivalence is as strong at the local and at the aggregate level. If Ricardian equivalence is more prevalent at the local level than at the federal level (perhaps because private agents have a better understanding of the dynamics of debt at the local level), then the intertemporal smoothing may be more effective at the federal level. A final issue is that Fatás does not take into account the limits to national intertemporal transfers that the Stability Pact will impose. In fact, Fatás' results suggest that the Stability Pact is a really bad idea, as he convincingly shows that the possibility of resorting to national deficits will be more crucial in Europe than in the USA, which has a federal budget.

There are, then, two ways to interpret Fatás' interesting results. The one he gives is refreshingly optimistic: there is no need for a fiscal federation in Europe, which anyway would be too complicated and costly to put in place. The other one is more agnostic or pessimistic: for the reasons given above, the need for fiscal insurance may be more than he claims. If the complexity and the cost of implementing such a system are even higher, this leaves Europe in an uncomfortable position, in which the question of how asymmetric shocks will be dealt with is left unanswered.

General discussion

Charles Bean felt that the paper had overstated the distinction between stabilization and insurance. These were both forms of insurance, differing primarily in whom the insurance contract was drawn with. Insurance, narrowly defined, is a contract with others at a moment in time; stabilization is an insurance contract with future generations. To push the point further, even a redistributive scheme could be viewed as a form of insurance, say, against the risk of being born in a poor state. More importantly, while stabilization may insure against temporary disturbances, it was of little use against permanent disturbances. It is the latter that make a case for interregional insurance. However, he was not convinced that monetary union *per se* makes a case for more interregional assistance. The loss of independent monetary control affects, in the first instance, the speed of adjustment to disturbances, and thus increases only the volatility of temporary disturbances. This alone was not a case for fiscal federalism.

Olivier Blanchard reiterated that stabilization was, in essence, risk sharing with future generations. To him, a proposal for federal insurance that doubles the amount of insurance currently provided by national systems spelt a large increase, even though the increase appears to be small in absolute terms. He outlined an interregional assistance scheme that achieves full insurance across regions but avoids current redistribution. The current distribution could be fixed by making appropriate per-capita transfers and still insure all regions against all future transitory and permanent shocks. While it was conceptually easy to design such schemes, there were practical difficulties in implementing them. If income levels diverge over time due to permanent shocks, what was insurance *ex ante* would, *ex post*, look redistributive in character. He concluded with the prediction that, as private capital and credit markets become more integrated across countries, they will increasingly take the lead in providing insurance against regional disturbances.

Andrew Rose too felt that the need for public insurance was somewhat overstated. First, with rising international mobility of capital, and the increased role of private banks, markets will partially take over the task of insuring against regional shocks. Second, with monetary union, demand shocks are likely to be more correlated across regions, thereby reducing the scope of such insurance. Third, fiscal systems seem to be the focus of universal public dissent in recent years, making fiscal federalism a potentially unpopular project. In his opinion, Europe could do without stoking such dissent.

Paul De Grauwe agreed with the Panel that the scope for federal insurance through risk pooling was somewhat limited, especially as common shocks tend to dominate idiosyncratic shocks in the EU. However, the central question was: how should Europe handle the really large shocks? These, at the very least, will strain the system and, at worst, may even create secessionist dynamics.

Jürgen von Hagen argued that national insurance is not a substitute for aggregate EU-wide insurance. If national shocks are uncorrelated with aggregate shocks, the latter will complement rather than substitute for national insurance systems. Patrick Honohan wondered if it was possible to estimate the amount of insurance that could be achieved with income pooling.

Lucrezia Reichlin was critical of measures of risk based on aggregate variance alone, as they ignored its concentration across frequencies. She proposed an alternative approach to the problem: to estimate a dynamic model and look at the variance at some cyclical band. Such dynamic analysis could change the comparison between Europe and the USA. For instance, the US business cycle was predominantly national in character, in contrast to the European ones, which tended to be more localized.

APPENDIX

Data sources. USA: *real state income*, state income at current prices deflated by the US GDP deflator. 1960–90. European countries: *real GDP*, GDP converted at PPP rates, source: OECD *Economic Outlook*, 1960–96; *employment*, total employment, source: OECD *Economic Outlook*, 1960–95 (except France, 1966–95). European regions: *employment*, France 1970–90, Italy 1960–94, Germany 1960–94, UK 1965–94, Spain 1981–95, source: Eurostat and different national sources.

Table A1 (a). Regional codes: USA

Code	State	Code	State
ME	Maine	WV	West Virginia
NH	New Hampshire	NC	North Carolina
VT	Vermont	SC	South Carolina
MA	Massachusetts	GA	Georgia
RI	Rhode Island	FL	Florida
CT	Connecticut	KY	Kentucky
NY	New York	TN	Tennessee
NJ	New Jersey	AL	Alabama
PA	Philadelphia	MS	Mississippi
OH	Ohio	AR	Arkansas
IN	Indiana	LA	Louisiana
IL	Illinois	OK	Oklahoma
MI	Michigan	TX	Texas
WI	Wisconsin	MT	Montana
MN	Minnesota	ID	Idaho
IA	Iowa	WY	Wyoming
MO	Missouri	CO	Colorado
ND	North Dakota	NM	New Mexico
SD	South Dakota	AZ	Arizona
NE	Nebraska	UT	Utah
KS	Kansas	NV	Nevada
DE	Delaware	WA	Washington
MD	Maryland	OR	Oregon
VA	Virginia	CA	California

Table A1(b). Regional codes: Europe

Country	Code	Region	Country	Code	Region	Country	Code	Region
Germany	G1	Schleswig-Holst./Hamburg	**France**	F1	Île de France	**Spain**	S1	Noroeste
	G2	Niedersachsen/Bremen		F2	Bassin Parisien		S2	Noreste
	G3	Nordrhein-Westfalen		F3	Nord/P. de Calais		S3	Madrid
	G4	Hessen		F4	Est		S4	Centro
	G5	Rheinland-Platz/Saarland		F5	Ouest		S5	Este
	G6	Baden-Württemberg		F6	Sud-Ouest		S6	Sur
	G7	Bayern		F7	Centre-Est		S7	Canarias
	G8	Berlin		F8	Méditerranée			
Italy	I1	Nord-Ovest	**UK**	U1	North			
	I2	Lombardia		U2	Yorks and Humberside			
	I3	Nord-Est		U3	East Midlands			
	I4	Emilia Romagna		U4	East Anglia			
	I5	Centro		U5	South-East			
	I6	Lazio		U6	South-West			
	I7	Campania		U7	West Midlands			
	I8	Abruzzi-Molise		U8	North-West			
	I9	Sud		U9	Wales			
	I10	Sicilia		U10	Scotland			
	I11	Sardegna		U11	Northern Ireland			

Table A2. Volatility and correlation: regional employment growth rates

Region	Full sample				EMS sample			
	(1)	(2)	(3)	(4)	(1)	(2)	(3)	(4)
G1	1.16	2.15	0.70	0.41	1.11	1.70	0.61	0.41
G2	1.06	1.99	0.69	0.43	1.06	1.61	0.79	0.48
G3	1.32	2.35	0.85	0.50	1.39	2.00	0.79	0.46
G4	1.00	1.86	0.86	0.61	1.02	1.55	0.95	0.69
G5	0.98	1.84	0.71	0.56	0.88	1.36	0.83	0.68
G6	1.35	2.44	0.88	0.57	1.13	1.69	0.91	0.58
G7	1.27	2.46	0.47	0.44	1.53	2.42	0.36	0.41
G8	1.85	3.42	0.53	0.61	1.86	2.86	0.38	0.74
F1	1.32	1.04	0.63	0.73	1.48	1.08	0.62	0.84
F2	1.24	0.95	0.84	0.54	0.98	0.73	0.90	0.79
F3	1.32	1.03	0.80	0.22	1.10	0.82	0.84	0.42
F4	1.16	0.90	0.90	0.47	1.09	0.81	0.87	0.62
F5	1.28	1.02	0.58	0.17	1.39	1.04	0.53	0.11
F6	0.74	0.60	0.72	0.59	0.69	0.53	0.85	0.67
F7	1.39	1.08	0.71	0.36	1.51	1.09	0.69	0.27
F8	1.12	0.88	0.87	0.62	1.19	0.88	0.86	0.71
I1	1.06	1.57	0.78	0.49	0.95	1.32	0.78	0.76
I2	1.00	1.52	0.75	0.46	1.06	1.47	0.76	0.63
I3	1.03	1.58	0.61	0.47	0.89	1.26	0.63	0.67
I4	1.00	1.51	0.65	0.56	0.83	1.15	0.70	0.67
I5	1.20	1.78	0.69	0.26	0.95	1.32	0.71	0.41
I6	1.64	2.38	0.62	0.32	1.67	2.23	0.60	0.29
I7	2.19	3.07	0.65	0.23	2.25	2.91	0.66	0.37
I8	1.68	2.47	0.60	0.54	1.35	1.82	0.68	0.65
I9	1.61	2.34	0.62	0.33	1.62	2.14	0.70	0.48
I10	1.76	2.54	0.69	0.37	1.97	2.55	0.84	0.50
I11	1.94	2.84	0.67	0.63	1.95	2.61	0.82	0.66
U1	1.34	2.48	0.66	0.52	1.29	2.43	0.66	0.54
U2	1.28	2.37	0.71	0.66	1.25	2.39	0.67	0.66
U3	1.24	2.28	0.74	0.49	1.23	2.31	0.74	0.51
U4	1.44	2.68	0.47	0.41	1.38	2.62	0.41	0.37
U5	1.09	2.09	0.67	0.50	1.15	2.23	0.67	0.51
U6	1.29	2.36	0.90	0.67	1.26	2.35	0.93	0.70
U7	1.26	2.33	0.78	0.66	1.20	2.27	0.77	0.64
U8	1.48	2.68	0.80	0.56	1.54	2.83	0.79	0.56
U9	1.92	3.47	0.75	0.47	1.99	3.67	0.76	0.48
U10	0.91	1.74	0.65	0.57	0.84	1.63	0.61	0.55
U11	1.95	3.61	0.30	0.29	1.97	3.72	0.30	0.27
S1	–	–	–	–	1.67	1.42	0.57	0.66
S2	–	–	–	–	1.06	2.09	0.95	0.88
S3	–	–	–	–	0.82	2.68	0.72	0.63
S4	–	–	–	–	1.04	2.16	0.77	0.72
S5	–	–	–	–	0.69	2.96	0.90	0.87
S6	–	–	–	–	0.70	3.05	0.85	0.80
S7	–	–	–	–	0.75	2.92	0.65	0.46

Note: (1) Standard deviation relative to country aggregate; (2) standard deviation relative to European aggregate; (3) correlation with country aggregate; (4) correlation with European aggregate.

Table A3. Insurance: regional employment growth rates

Region	1961–79		1979–94	
	(1)	(2)	(1)	(2)
G1	9.38	22.92	10.22	20.91
G2	7.38	21.88	5.35	19.06
G3	7.17	21.64	8.68	20.82
G4	2.80	18.76	1.69	15.14
G5	5.47	19.42	0.16	13.25
G6	8.50	21.65	4.53	17.86
G7	13.99	23.09	17.75	23.30
G8	19.32	24.15	21.49	21.81
F1	11.05	6.60	12.66	5.26
F2	7.22	8.65	1.39	−5.05
F3	10.25	18.22	5.62	8.45
F4	5.73	9.47	4.59	2.58
F5	12.73	19.25	14.70	21.07
F6	−2.51	−6.73	−8.20	−15.28
F7	11.99	15.58	13.43	17.87
F8	5.39	4.94	6.73	2.73
I1	5.49	18.65	3.23	11.34
I2	4.78	18.61	5.71	15.27
I3	8.54	19.00	4.87	12.12
I4	7.35	16.96	1.36	10.39
I5	9.92	23.56	4.85	17.75
I6	16.02	24.68	16.63	24.74
I7	18.77	26.84	18.97	25.26
I8	17.51	22.67	12.93	18.31
I9	15.54	24.46	14.42	22.00
I10	16.23	24.60	15.58	23.25
I11	18.44	22.82	16.61	21.87
U1	13.03	22.80	12.23	22.42
U2	10.94	20.78	11.27	20.78
U3	9.94	22.42	9.73	22.35
U4	17.60	24.56	18.15	24.81
U5	6.71	20.62	7.51	20.98
U6	7.95	20.61	6.95	20.27
U7	9.37	20.57	8.60	20.58
U8	11.60	22.72	12.37	23.13
U9	16.90	25.38	17.21	25.55
U10	5.20	18.54	3.78	18.12
U11	3.52	27.08	23.57	27.27
S1	–	–	−5.16	14.41
S2	–	–	−0.50	16.92
S3	–	–	9.36	22.19
S4	–	–	3.52	19.26
S5	–	–	7.92	20.49
S6	–	–	9.80	21.55
S7	–	–	13.40	24.62

Notes: Interregional insurance assuming $\tau = 30\%$. See text for details on calculations. (1) National insurance; (2) European insurance.

REFERENCES

Artis, M. and W. Zhang (1995). 'International business cycles and the ERM: is there a European business cycle?', CEPR Discussion Paper no. 1191.

Asdrubali, P., B.E. Sorensen and O. Yosha (1996). 'Channels of interstate risk sharing: United States 1963–1990', *Quarterly Journal of Economics*.

Atkeson, A. and T. Bayoumi (1993). 'Do private capital markets insure regional risk? Evidence from the United States and Europe', *Open Economies Review*.

Bayoumi, T. and B. Eichengreen (1997). 'Ever closer to heaven? An optimum-currency-area index for European countries', *European Economic Review*.

Bayoumi, T. and P.R. Masson (1996a). 'Fiscal flows in the United States and Canada: lessons for monetary union in Europe', *European Economic Review*.

—— (1996b). 'Debt-creating versus non-debt-creating fiscal stabilization policies: Ricardian equivalence, fiscal stabilization and EMU', unpublished manuscript, IMF.

Blanchard, O. and L. Katz (1992). 'Regional evolutions', *Brookings Papers in Economic Activity*.

Canova, F. and M. Ravn (1996). 'International risk sharing', *International Economic Review*.

Cochrane, J.H. (1988). 'How big is the random walk in GNP?', *Journal of Political Economy*.

Decressin, J. and A. Fatás (1995). 'Regional labor market dynamics in Europe', *European Economic Review*.

Eichengreen, B. (1990). 'One money for Europe? Lessons of the US currency union', *Economic Policy*.

Fatás, A. (1997). 'Europe: countries or regions? Lessons from the EMS experience', *European Economic Review*.

Feldstein, M. (1992). 'Europe's monetary union: the case against EMU', *The Economist*, 13 June.

Frankel, J. and A.K. Rose (1997). 'The endogeneity of the optimum currency area criteria', NBER Working Paper no. 5700.

Gali, J. (1994). 'Government size and macroeconomic stability', *European Economic Review*.

Krugman, P. (1993). 'Lessons of Massachusetts for EMU', in F. Torres and F. Giavazzi (eds.), *Adjustment and Growth in the European Monetary Union*, Cambridge University Press, Cambridge.

Mélitz, J. (1994). 'Is there a need for community-wide insurance against cyclical disparities?' *Economie et Statistique*, special issue.

Persson, T. and G. Tabellini (1996). 'Federal fiscal constitutions: risk sharing and redistribution', *Journal of Political Economy*.

Sachs, J. and X. Sala-i-Martin (1992). 'Fiscal federalism and optimum currency areas: evidence from Europe and the United States', in M. Canzoneri, V. Grilli and P. Masson (eds.), *Establishing a Central Bank: Issues in Europe and Lessons from the US*, Cambridge University Press, Cambridge.

von Hagen, J. (1992). 'Fiscal arrangements in a monetary union: evidence from the US', in D. Fair and C. de Boissieux (eds.), *Fiscal Policy, Taxes, and the Financial System in an Increasingly Integrated Europe*, Kluwer, London.

—— and George W. Hammond (1997). 'Insurance against asymmetric shocks in a European monetary union', in J.-O. Hairault, P.-Y. Henin and F. Portier (eds.), *Business Cycles and Macroeconomic Stability*, Kluwer, London.

von Hagen, J. and M.J.M. Neumann (1994). 'Real exchange rates within and between currency areas: how far away is EMU?, *Review of Economics and Statistics*.

Asymmetric shocks
Regional non-adjustment and fiscal policy

SUMMARY

How will countries handle idiosyncratic macroeconomic shocks under the single currency? Since the regional adjustment patterns currently prevailing within European currency unions are likely to prevail at the national level under the single currency, looking at the ways in which European countries react to internally asymmetric shocks today provides a good preview for the answer to that question. In this paper, we compare the USA with Germany, Italy and the UK, and with Canada, which is closer to Europe than the USA in its labour market and fiscal institutions.

Europe's (and to some extent Canada's) model of regional response differs from that of the USA. Changes in regional real exchange rates are small in all countries. Outside of the USA, however, there is more reliance on interregional transfer payments, less on labour migration, and the pace of regional adjustment appears to be slower. If EMU aims at the same degree of economic and social cohesion that its constituent nations enjoy today, this suggests that its members may find it hard to resist the eventual extension of existing EU mechanisms of income redistribution − a transfer union. We propose an alternative strategy based on a relaxed Stability Pact, further strictures against central EU borrowing, labour market and fiscal reform, and the issuance by individual member states of debt indexed to nominal GDP.

— *Maurice Obstfeld and Giovanni Peri*

Regional non-adjustment and fiscal policy

Maurice Obstfeld and Giovanni Peri

University of California, Berkeley, CEPR and NBER; University of California, Berkeley

1. INTRODUCTION

How will members of Europe's economic and monetary union (EMU) adjust to asymmetric macroeconomic shocks after the single currency is in place? On the eve of the third and final stage of EMU, considerable uncertainty over the answer remains, despite nearly three decades of research.[1] Much of that research has tried to distil lessons for Europe by studying the performance of existing currency unions. In this paper we extend this evidence and review some of its main findings, in the process identifying key areas in which definitive conclusions remain elusive. On the basis of our interpretation, we advance some conjectural scenarios for macro-economic adjustment patterns in the euro zone.

Given its overall satisfactory economic performance and political stability, the USA has been the natural starting point for research into intranational adjustment

We thank Reza Baqir, Ryan Edwards and Stefan Palmqvist for excellent research assistance. Tamim Bayoumi, Giovanni Favara, Ingo Fender, Larry Katz, Paul Masson, Chris Salmon and Till von Wachter offered valuable help in locating and organizing data. Olivier Blanchard, David Card, Barry Eichengreen, Antonio Fatás, Peter Kenen, Barry McCormick, Jacques Mélitz, Andrew Oswald, Frédéric Zumer and especially Jürgen von Hagen made many very helpful suggestions, as did participants in the October 1997 Panel meeting in Bonn and the Berkeley Labor Lunch. All errors and opinions are our own. Research support was provided by the National Science Foundation (through a grant to the National Bureau of Economic Research), the Alfred P. Sloan Foundation, and the Center for German and European Studies at the University of California, Berkeley.
[1] One of the early academic discussions is Corden (1972), which was inspired by the Werner Report and sets out many of the themes that the subsequent literature explores. Ingram (1973) is another notable early contribution. A recent comprehensive review of issues is contained in Kenen (1995).

mechanisms. Sometimes the USA is taken as a model for predicting integrated Europe's evolution. More often, it serves as an example of regional adjustment or insurance mechanisms that at present appear largely absent among prospective EMU members, but may need to evolve to ensure the union's success. The key regional adjustment mechanisms are labour mobility and local relative price responses, whereas the main insurance mechanism, alongside private capital markets, is based on interregional transfer payments mediated by the central government.

In this paper the focus is instead to compare the internal adjustment patterns that European countries display with those of the USA. We also look at Canada, which is closer to Europe in its labour market and fiscal institutions than is the USA. A direct comparison of the USA with other currency unions is revealing. It suggests that Europe's (and to some extent Canada's) model of regional response to idiosyncratic shocks differs from that in the USA. Changes in relative regional real exchange rates are generally small. Outside of the USA, however, there is more reliance on interregional transfer payments, less on interregional labour migration, and the overall pace of regional adjustment appears slower. The large and continuing transfers from western to eastern Germany, where open unemployment still runs at around 18%, represent a notably pathological example of this tendency.

Ultimately, EMU may lead to changes in the institutions governing economic relations within and between European Union member states. Given those institutions, however, the subnational economic adjustment patterns of European countries offer a better guide than the USA to how the euro currency area is likely to evolve. One goal of the paper is to ask whether regional response patterns typical of individual European economies are likely to emerge at the EMU level. Another goal is to judge the past performance of the European countries themselves as currency unions. The implication for EMU of this assessment is immediate. Because country-specific shocks often affect subnational regions differently, sluggish regional adjustment, if uncorrected by policy reforms, will worsen the pain they inflict, and thereby complicate life under the single currency.

The plan of the paper is as follows. Section 2 reviews the main mechanisms of adjustment and insurance available to a region or country hit by an idiosyncratic economic shock. An overview of data for the USA, Canada and some EU members is suggestive of national differences in the primary modes of response to shocks. In section 3 we look more closely at regional unemployment data, observing that local unemployment persistence is higher outside the USA and that interregional migration plays a much smaller role in adjustment in Europe than in the USA. Section 4 takes up regional relative price adjustment as an element in the return to full employment after a shock. In none of the countries we examine does regional relative price adjustment play a large role when compared with the long-term changes in international relative prices that one commonly observes. The reasons for this contrast are uncertain and surely differ across countries. But the slow adjustment of regional labour markets in European countries suggests that the low variability of their interregional real exchange rates partly reflects price rigidities that impede adjustment, rather than the efficient operation of natural currency areas. By preventing large relative price changes, such price rigidities may support the political viability of free trade within currency unions.

The extent of regional risk sharing through capital markets and especially through government transfer payments has received considerable attention in research on currency unions, starting with the estimates on fiscal redistribution and stabilization in the influential MacDougall Report (Commission of the European Communities, 1977). In section 5 we review this literature and conclude that fiscal transfers play a central role in supporting existing currency unions, albeit less in the USA, where labour is more mobile than in Canada and Europe. A main point of our discussion is that transfers tend to be quite persistent and sometimes respond to shocks with lags. Indeed, through various mechanisms, transfer programmes intended to provide social insurance may lengthen the adjustment process and, in extreme cases, induce regional dependence on fiscal inflows. Thus, we argue that the sharp distinction that the literature has made between the redistribution and stabilization functions of fiscal transfers, while conceptually valid, is overdrawn in practice. Given the central role of fiscal transfer systems in other currency unions, we are led to ask, in section 6, whether the EMU countries will inevitably see a need to augment substantially current EU transfer programmes. Our conclusion is that it will become hard to resist pressures for a more extensive 'transfer union', especially if the EU wishes to pursue deeper and broader political or economic integration in the face of existing national income disparities. This conclusion leads us to propose a set of alternative measures that could reproduce the benefits of an extended transfer mechanism while avoiding many of its pitfalls.

2. ADJUSTMENT AND INSURANCE: QUESTIONS AND TRENDS

2.1. Mechanisms of adjustment and stabilization

A country suffering an unexpected adverse real economic shock has several options for response when domestic market rigidities generate higher unemployment. Options that are attractive in the face of a transitory shock may be less so when the shock is permanent, or highly persistent. In the latter case, the country faces a problem of long-run *adjustment* to a permanently lower standard of living. In the former, it faces a less severe financing problem, that of cushioning employment and output in the face of transitory bad luck.

National fiscal stabilizers, either discretionary or automatic, can be helpful in riding out temporary real shocks. So can private external borrowing. A country with a flexible exchange rate may gain from currency depreciation. However, a temporary disturbance generally warrants a relatively small (and short-lived) depreciation, and a currency participating in an adjustable peg system would not normally realign. For this reason, the prospect of temporary disturbances is of secondary relevance in comparing the merits of outright currency union with those of an adjustable peg regime such as the European Monetary System.[2]

When a negative real shock is permanent, however, there are no options for cushioning its impact over the long term, simply because a country cannot live outside its long-run budget constraint. Solvency constraints rule out using permanently higher fiscal or external deficits to maintain public or private spending (Corden, 1972; Krugman, 1993).

Thus, there is no choice but adjustment, and adjustment can occur in one of two ways (in the absence of significant international labour mobility). The first option is to do nothing and rely on deflation and falling real wages to restore full employment, possibly a long and agonizing process marked by persistently high joblessness. The second is to devalue the domestic currency. If there is some nominal stickiness in prices and wages, and room for real wage adjustment as well, a country can devalue its currency, thereby making its goods more competitive internationally and restoring full employment quickly. Importantly, devaluation does not enable a country to escape a long-run real income loss. But although the country's terms of trade worsen permanently and immediately, this loss is widely shared by residents and is widely viewed as preferable to the fiscal drain and social tensions that protracted unemployment causes. Moreover, and quite fundamentally, the currency realignment leads to a more efficient national and international allocation of resources.

As noted, the existence of a devaluation option depends not only on some nominal wage or price stickiness, but also on some willingness of domestic price setters to accept an exchange-rate-induced reduction in their real incomes as a *fait accompli*. Without this prerequisite, devaluation will have only short-lived relative price effects that are quickly offset by higher domestic inflation (Hinshaw, 1951; McKinnon, 1963). After this surge of inflation, the price level and real wages will fall as the economy gradually adjusts to its worsened terms of trade. In the case of substantial real wage resistance, there is therefore no short-cut through devaluation: only a lengthy period of high unemployment will bring about the necessary fall in real wages. The real effects of devaluation tend to be weaker in smaller and more open economies.

A country that can enter private insurance arrangements with foreigners (equity contracts, for example) can partially guard against permanent and transitory shocks

---

[2] In the specific context of EMU, however, the prospect that the Stability Pact will hamstring national fiscal policies brings more urgency to the question of temporary shocks. See Eichengreen and Wyplosz (in this issue) for analysis of the Stability Pact's possible effects.

alike. In the case of a temporary shock, protection through insurance contracts may be more effective than borrowing, which must be repaid irrespective of the economy's future performance. Even when a permanent adverse national shock occurs, a permanently lower level of real net dividend outflows affords some offset. In practice, however, labour income is vastly less insurable than capital income, so the benefits from cross-border insurance arrangements accrue disproportionately to those who own internationally diversified financial wealth. At best, the resulting dividend payments affect labour incomes and employment indirectly. Exchange rate adjustments thus remain potentially useful as a way of regaining full employment and redistributing domestically the pain of adjustment to permanent adverse shocks.

Regions within a currency union plainly lack the devaluation option after a permanent region-specific setback, but they may be able to obtain persistent and even permanent streams of inward net transfer payments from more fortunate regions. To some degree these transfers represent private intranational insurance payments, but in modern economies government-intermediated redistributions from other regions also bulk large. Public transfers support the incomes of the unemployed and enhance local demand, in theory substituting for outward migration, which is a major adjustment mechanism within national units, if not always between them. Short-lived inward transfers, like local fiscal expansion, can play a stabilization role by cushioning the initial impacts of adverse shocks. Open-ended transfers also stabilize, but they are not a mode of regional adjustment to permanent shocks. Instead they finance regional *non-adjustment* indefinitely.

2.2. Regional unemployment, inflation and fiscal flows

An overview of regional unemployment trends in some existing currency unions provides a backdrop for the closer analyses of regional economic adjustment described in the following sections. The data provide hints about both the speed of adjustment and international differences in intranational adjustment patterns.

Several authors have looked at the dispersion of regional unemployment rates to assess both the incidence of regionally asymmetric shocks and the speed of adjustment to them (Eichengreen, 1990, 1991; Emerson *et al.*, 1992; De Grauwe and Vanhaverbeke, 1993; Masson and Taylor, 1993; Viñals and Jimeno, 1996). An initial fact important in comparing the behaviours of different currency unions is that the regional divergence in unemployment rates is relatively low in the USA, with little tendency to increase secularly. Figures 1 and 2 plot, respectively, standard deviations and coefficients of variation (standard deviations divided by means) for regional unemployment rates.

Shown for comparison are data from Canada, Germany, Italy, the UK and the 'EU11' – the signatories of the Maastricht Treaty except Luxembourg. Italy stands out for its sharply increasing regional unemployment rate disparities, which are

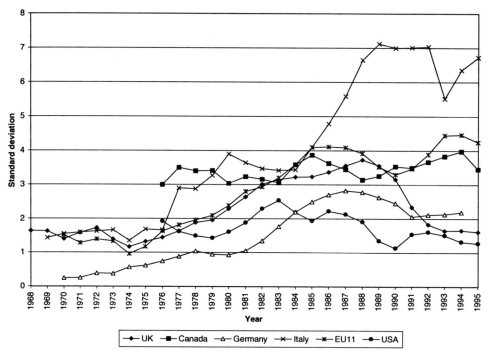

Figure 1. Standard deviations of regional unemployment rates, 1968–95

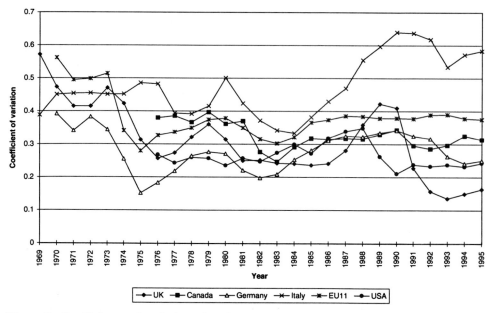

Figure 2. Coefficients of variation of regional unemployment rates, 1969–95

much more severe even than those among the EU11. Dispersion in the UK was also relatively high until the mid-1980s, and its drop afterwards, notwithstanding the recession of the early 1990s, is remarkable.[3] In Canada, unemployment dispersion has been relatively high but steady for many years. In Germany, it has been relatively low among the western *Länder* included in Figures 1 and 2, but has risen over time on a simple standard deviation measure, and would appear higher still were eastern Germany included. The coefficient of variation for western *Länder* has remained fairly constant in recent years because overall western unemployment has risen sharply. Overall, Germany's unemployment dispersion seems intermediate between those of the USA and the EU11, and in recent years it looks quite similar to that of the EU11 minus Spain.[4]

Patterns of unemployment dispersion have been *persistent* outside the USA, in the sense that the regions of relatively high unemployment have tended to remain the same over time. This feature is evident in Figures 3–6, which show the evolution of regional unemployment rates for Canada and the three European countries.

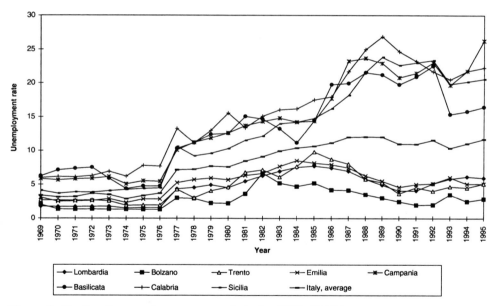

Figure 3. Regional unemployment rates in Italy, 1969–95 (%)

[3] McCormick (1997) discusses UK regional employment trends.
[4] A quick look at two other large European countries confirms the trend towards regional unemployment divergence on the continent. The standard deviation of regional unemployment rates in nineteen French *départements* increased from 1.1% in 1980 to 3.7% in 1993 (compare with Figure 1), while the average national unemployment rate increased from 6 to 11%. For Spain the evolution seems even more unbalanced, as the standard deviation of seventeen regional unemployment rates has increased from 3% in 1985 to 5.2% in 1993 with little net change in national average unemployment (Spain's unemployment rate stood near 21% in both years; see Eurostat, various years).

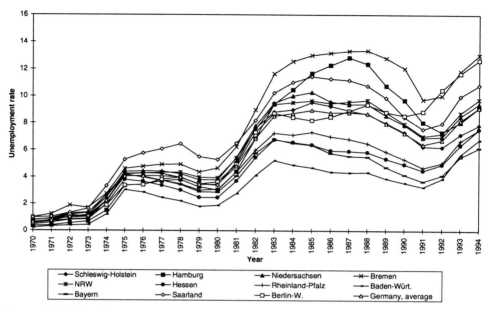

Figure 4. Regional unemployment rates in Germany, 1970–94 (%)

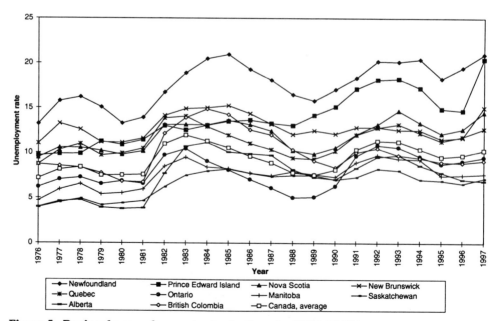

Figure 5. Regional unemployment rates in Canada, 1976–97 (%)

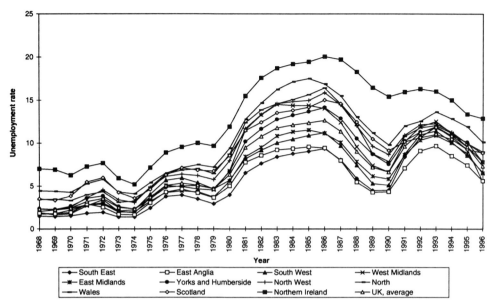

Figure 6. Regional unemployment rates in the UK, 1968–96 (%)

To document the contrast with US regional unemployment behaviour, Figures 7–11 show scatter plots of regional relative unemployment rates in 1995 against 1985 rates. (For Germany the years compared are 1994 and 1984.) The plots in Figures 7–10 show significantly positively correlated unemployment rates in the two periods. For the case of American states illustrated in Figure 11, there is a less strongly significant positive relationship with a much lower R^2 statistic, suggesting less history-dependence in US regional unemployment rates.[5]

The estimated intertemporal correlations in these figures do not allow us, however, to distinguish between two explanations with somewhat different implications for evaluating regional macroeconomic adjustment speeds. A region may have a persistently high 'natural' rate of unemployment, resulting from differences in industrial mix, urbanization, unemployment benefit administration and so on. On the other hand, slow adjustment to regional shocks is reflected in the persistence of unemployment deviations from these regional means. The econometric identification of such deviations, however, requires a specific statistical model. We will argue in the next section that, particularly in Europe, regional

---

[5] The results are: Canada, slope = 0.78, t-statistic = 5.20, R^2 = 0.75; Germany, slope = 0.77, t-statistic = 3.65, R^2 = 0.58; Italy, slope = 1.35, t-statistic = 6.42, R^2 = 0.68; UK, slope = 0.60, t-statistic = 8.77, R^2 = 0.79; USA, slope = 0.26, t-statistic = 2.50, R^2 = 0.15. Eichengreen (1990) finds that unemployment rates in US regions are less serially correlated than the aggregate unemployment rates of European countries. He interprets the finding as evidence of slower labour market adjustment in Europe. Here, we have shown that the empirical result carries over to regional unemployment rates outside the USA.

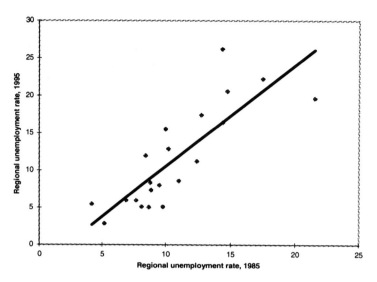

Figure 7. Persistence of regional unemployment rates in Italy, 1985–95

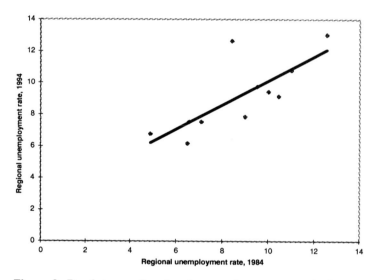

Figure 8. Persistence of regional unemployment rates in Germany, 1984–94

shocks with persistent effects play an important role, and that persistence is in part due to a low propensity of workers to migrate away from regions where unemployment exceeds the local natural rate.[6]

---

[6] The distinction between means and deviations cannot always be drawn sharply, as benefits administration may respond endogenously to local unemployment, with further feedback effects on unemployment duration. In Canada, for example, the duration of unemployment benefits in a province and the minimum prior work requirement to qualify for benefits depend on the level of the provincial unemployment rate. See Green and Riddell (1997).

According to the model of adjustment sketched at the start of this section, an unemployment rate persistently above the local natural rate should be associated with downward pressure on regional prices. Eventually, increasing local competitiveness will feed through positively to local labour demand. For Canada and Italy, Figures 12 and 13 show some negative long-run cross-sectional association between average regional relative inflation (measured by the GDP deflator) and average regional relative unemployment. For Germany, Figure 14 shows a positive correlation. Thus, although ongoing unemployment should in theory

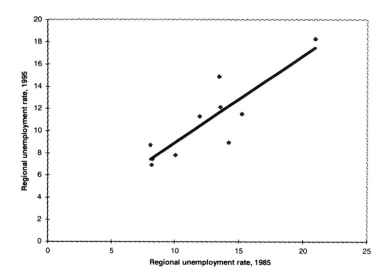

Figure 9. Persistence of regional unemployment rates in Canada, 1985–95

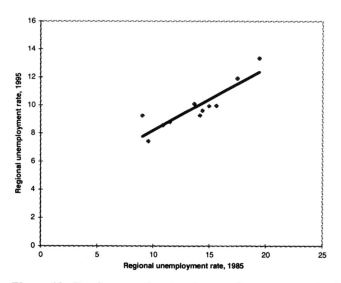

Figure 10. Persistence of regional unemployment rates in the UK, 1985–95

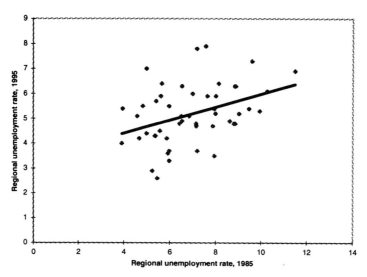

Figure 11. Persistence of regional unemployment rates in the USA, 1985–95

lead to a regional terms of trade loss over time, the tendency for this to occur in practice is tenuous. (For the UK and USA, regional/state price indices are not available.)[7]

Government fiscal stabilizers deliver transfers to depressed regions; furthermore, national fiscal systems typically redistribute revenue from richer to poorer jurisdictions. Figures 15 and 16 document, for Canada and Italy alike, a significant positive correlation between average regional unemployment and average transfer inflows. Figure 17, for the USA, shows a positive but only marginally significant correlation.[8] These diagrams suggest a potentially important role for fiscal transfers in providing insurance against regional recession.

The persistence of transfers mirrors that of unemployment rates. In both Canada and Italy, the ranking of high-unemployment regions is remarkably stable over time and correlates well with ranking by net transfer inflow per population member. Clearly, intranational fiscal flows to Canada's Atlantic provinces and Italy's *Mezzogiorno* play a significant redistributive role, and are not merely responding as

[7] The left-hand variable in the regression is the difference between average annual regional inflation and average annual national inflation (% per year). The right-hand variable is the average regional unemployment rate less the national average (%). Results are: Canada (1976–95), slope = −0.07, t-statistic = −0.62, $R^2 = 0.06$; Germany (1976–95), slope = 0.01, t-statistic = 0.35, $R^2 = 0.01$; Italy (1977–94), slope = −0.03, t-statistic = −2.46, $R^2 = 0.27$.

[8] The left-hand variable in the regression is the per-capita net transfer inflow in thousands of 1991 ecu. The right-hand variable is the average regional unemployment rate less the national average (%). Results are: Canada (1976–95), slope = 0.03, t-statistic = 3.12, $R^2 = 0.54$; USA (1976–85), slope = 0.10, t-statistic = 2.01, $R^2 = 0.05$; Italy (1977–94), slope = 0.05, t-statistic = 3.57, $R^2 = 0.42$. The transfer data for Canada, the USA and Italy, which we also use in econometric analysis in section 5, are not comparable, as those for Italy include social insurance payments only, and exclude, for example, flows related to tax payments. See the data appendix for details. We do not graph our German data, which are also severely limited.

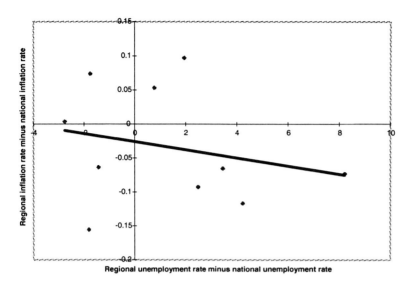

Figure 12. Average regional inflation – average regional unemployment, Canada (1976–96)

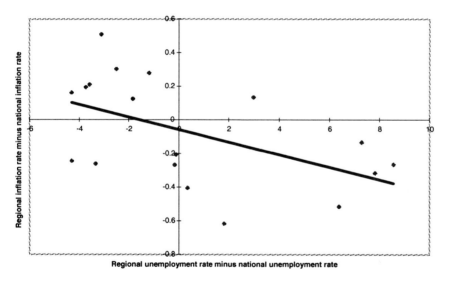

Figure 13. Average regional inflation – average regional unemployment, Italy (1977–94)

short-term automatic stabilizers to temporary regional shocks.[9] Their availability facilitates delayed regional adjustment. An entire national economy could postpone

[9] In Italy the official data on unemployment underestimate its true extent because of the *Casa Integrazione Guadagni* (CIG) programme, which covers part of the wages of workers who might otherwise be laid off (see, for example, Bertola and Ichino, 1995). Since CIG payments are quite persistent, classifying workers on CIG as unemployed would raise the correlation between social insurance inflows and true unemployment. Of course, many who are officially unemployed work in the underground economy. Notice that by entering the underground economy and evading taxes, officially unemployed workers automatically generate a net fiscal transfer into the region where they operate.

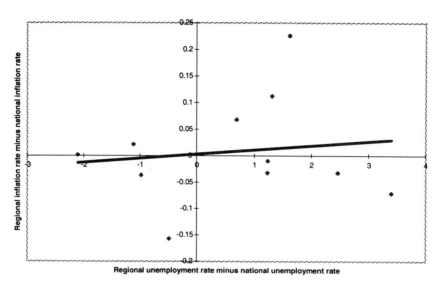

Figure 14. Average regional inflation – average regional unemployment, Germany (1974–94)

adjustment in the same way only if it could arrange for persistent streams of unrequited transfers from foreigners.

2.3. Barriers to regional adjustment

The balance of this paper contains a critical review and synthesis of earlier studies relevant to a study of regional adjustment within existing currency unions. On the basis of this review and some new evidence, we argue that in Europe and to some

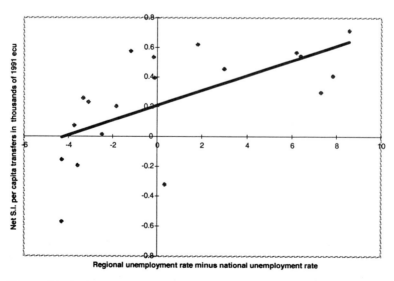

Figure 15. Average regional net transfers – average regional unemployment, Italy (1977–94)

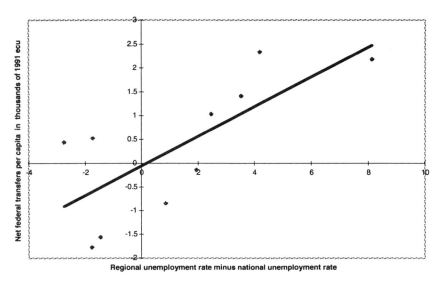

Figure 16. Average regional net transfers – average regional unemployment, Canada (1976–96)

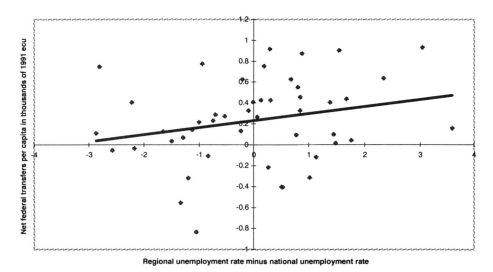

Figure 17. Average regional net transfers – average regional unemployment, USA (1976–85)

extent in Canada, adjustment to local employment shocks via domestic migration is more limited than in the USA.

In addition, relative regional price adjustment also appears to play a limited role. It could be that interregional real exchange rates are potentially quite flexible, but that in existing currency unions, labour mobility, high interregional trade elasticities and a paucity of asymmetric real shocks all make for regional relative price stability. To some degree the USA fits this picture. We argue that in existing European currency unions, however, interregional real exchange rates are actually rather rigid, and hypothesize that political imperatives underlie the rigidity.

Interregional fiscal transfers, especially long-term redistributive transfers, seem to be used quite heavily in Europe and Canada. Given the absence of prompt and strong internal adjustment mechanisms, fiscal flows therefore appear to play a prominent role – sometimes an uneasy one – in the non-American currency unions.

Two related conclusions for EMU follow. First, limited market flexibility within EMU countries will make it harder for them to cope with nation-specific shocks, as the latter generally have heterogeneous regional impacts. Second, if EMU aims to attain the degree of economic cohesion of its constituent nations, limitations on national fiscal policies will eventually make it hard to resist the extension of existing EU mechanisms of income redistribution.

3. ADJUSTMENT THROUGH MIGRATION

3.1. Data on migration

A comparison of labour mobility in the USA, Canada and Europe begins with the raw data on interregional labour movements. The OECD reports that, in 1986, 1.1% of Britons and Germans changed their region of residence, as opposed to only 0.6% of Italians but 1.5% of Canadians and 3% of Americans (OECD, 1990).[10] These numbers probably understate the Canadian economy's capacity to reallocate labour interregionally, as they do not account for foreign migration, which is substantial for Canada. Canada thus would appear to occupy an intermediate position between the European countries and the USA. De Grauwe and Vanhaver-beke (1993) report similar magnitudes for a larger sample of EU countries in 1987, defining a country's mobility index by the regional average of immigration plus emigration as a percentage of regional population. Their results indicate lower intranational labour mobility in southern than in northern Europe. While *intra*national migration is lower in most of Europe than in the USA or Canada, *inter*national movements of people within Europe are, at present, smaller still.

If the goal is to assess the role of migration in reducing large regional employment differentials, net rather than gross migration numbers might be more revealing. Table 1 reports such numbers for Canada, the USA, Germany, Italy and the UK. Here we approximate net inward or outward migration for a region as the average absolute value of the percentage change in regional working-age population

---

[10] A problem with such measurements – indeed, the problem applies to all the subnational evidence discussed in this paper – is that constitutionally recognized regional units are based on politicohistoric rather than economic boundaries, so that the definition of 'region' has a substantive effect on one's conclusions. Since the available data correspond to these units, however, not much can be done except to control for obviously anomalous cases. The numbers reported in this paragraph refer to Canadian provinces and territories, Italian *regioni*, eleven west German *Länder*, ten UK regions (excluding Northern Ireland), and 51 US states (including Washington DC as a 'state').

Table 1. Average net interregional migration (% of regional population)

Period	Canada	USA	Germany	Italy	UK
1970–9	0.62	1.20	0.27	0.37	0.47
1980–9	0.63	0.84	0.34	0.33	0.26
1990–5	0.52	0.87	0.31	0.40	0.20

Notes: National figures are population-weighted averages over regions. For the period indicated, each regional figure is calculated as the average absolute value of the change in regional working-age population (measured net of national working-age population growth). German numbers are for western *Länder* only, leaving out Berlin.

(measured net of the rate of national working-age population growth). National averages are population-weighted averages of the regional growth rates. For Germany our sample consists of ten western *Länder*, Berlin being the omission.

Subject to the caveat that average regional sizes differ across countries, the general impression that emerges is that net migration is substantially higher in North America than in Europe. If these numbers can be taken as a rough indicator of labour mobility, mobility is higher in Canada than in Europe, and higher still in the USA. Mobility, as measured by net flows, seems on the whole to be similar in Germany, Italy and the UK. However, a comparison of these figures with those reported by De Grauwe and Vanhaverbeke (1993) suggests that 'gross' or two-way labour flows are more important in Germany and the UK than in Italy.

3.2. Interpreting migration data: low barriers or regionally balanced shocks?

There is a major conceptual problem in accepting migration data as evidence on mobility. Observed net flows reflect the push of asymmetrical shocks as well as the resistance due to migration barriers. Thus, if idiosyncratic regional shocks have not been prominent, then little migration will be observed even with low barriers. As Eichengreen (1991) notes in discussing similar data, 'simple tabulations still do not distinguish the disturbance from the response'. Indeed, because our basic data are mostly endogenous economic variables, this identification problem is the central one in reliably assessing regional adjustment patterns. In the present context of migration, the identification problem surfaces in the possibility that labour mobility is (potentially) really quite high even though labour movements are small.

The wide and variable regional unemployment differentials in Europe might be viewed as prima-facie evidence of asymmetric localized shocks that should create migratory pressures. Also supportive of the prevalence of such shocks is the finding of De Grauwe and Vanhaverbeke (1993) that, over the period 1976–90, the variability in long-run average regional employment growth rates *within* European countries tends to exceed that *among* European countries (with less regional divergence in northern than in southern Europe). But, as these authors point out, employment levels and unemployment rates are endogenous variables that respond to policies and may convey little information about the incentives to migrate. For example, more liberal administration of unemployment benefits in a region may not only increase unemployment there, but even lead to migration of workers *into* high-unemployment areas, a phenomenon seen in Canada (Courchene, 1993). It is important to correct for idiosyncrasies in regional institutions or structure in assessing the typical migratory response to a regional shock within a country.

One way to accomplish this end is to postulate a specific statistical model of regional shocks, and to gauge their prevalence econometrically. There have been several attempts along these lines. On balance, they point to a potentially important role for asymmetric region-specific disturbances within EU economies. Viñals and Jimeno (1996) estimate a dynamic model of annual regional unemployment in which a region's unemployment rate can be decomposed into a region-specific constant (the region's 'natural' rate) and regional, national and EU-wide random components. These components are identified by the assumption that region-specific shocks do not influence the national data-generating process for unemployment and that nation-specific shocks do not influence the EU-wide unemployment process. Thus, the EU unemployment rate is strongly exogenous with respect to individual EU members' unemployment rates, and both EU and national unemployment are strongly exogenous with respect to regional unemployment. Viñals and Jimeno find that, for forecast horizons of up to five years, almost two-thirds of the conditional variance of European subnational unemployment rates can be explained by region-specific factors.[11]

Forni and Reichlin (1997) use a dynamic unobserved-index model to separate fluctuations in annual regional growth rates of real output into parts due to EU, national and regional factors. They find that the decomposition for EU regions is quite similar to that for US states. Although regional shocks are found to play a significant role in Europe, they do not appear as important as in the Viñals–Jimeno analysis of unemployment rates. However, the statistical method of Forni and Reichlin allows the EU-wide component of growth and the national components to have divergent regional effects. They also search for a European 'core', defined as a group of regions in which at least 70% of the variance of output growth comes from the common Europe-wide shock component. The resulting set of regions does not

---

[11] The authors also impose the constraint that the national and EU components of unemployment have identical effects across the regions of a country – an assumption that is necessary to conserve degrees of freedom in estimation, but which also makes it impossible to distinguish econometrically between truly idiosyncratic regional shocks and national or EU shocks that have divergent regional effects. For the purpose of thinking about regional adjustment problems the two are not that different, as we shall argue later, so the figures that Viñals and Jimeno report are probably a reasonable guide to the frequency of regional shocks that warrant long-run labour reallocation. (They find that country-specific shocks explain roughly 75% of the variance of EU unemployment rates when EU shocks are restricted to act symmetrically upon different countries.)

coincide with a group of EU member states, and all major countries are, to some degree, out of the core. Conversely, Spain and Italy, which are usually identified as 'peripheral' in studies of EMU as an optimum currency area, have important regions that belong to the core. These findings again suggest the presence of regional asymmetries within EU countries.

3.3. Structural models of migration response

The studies just summarized contradict the view that migration barriers within European countries are low and that the low degree of observed migration reflects a scarcity of regionally asymmetric shocks. But even if one accepts that asymmetric shocks have occurred, an international comparison of their effects still requires some quantitative standardization of the shocks.

A fairly direct way to compare regional labour mobility across countries is to look at the responsiveness of domestic labour flows to interregional wage differences. Taking this route, Eichengreen (1993a) finds that interregional migration is much more sensitive to lagged changes in wage differentials in the USA (1962–88) than in the UK (1961–82) or Italy (1962–85). Lagged unemployment also has the largest estimated effect in the USA. [12]

Eichengreen's (1993a) estimates constitute strong evidence of relatively limited labour mobility in Europe. However, the current wage difference alone may be an imperfect indicator of the expected lifetime income difference associated with a job change. Furthermore, given the nation-wide wage determination process that prevails throughout much of Europe, regional unemployment differences may find little reflection in regional wage differences. Thus, an alternative framework capturing the dynamic response of regional labour markets to local shocks is a useful complement to Eichengreen's findings.

Such an empirical framework was originated and applied to US states by Blanchard and Katz (1992). Decressin and Fatás (1995) have explored the implications for regions within Europe. Blanchard and Katz proceed by estimating a three-equation vector-autoregressive (VAR) system in which the variables of interest are the change in the log level of regional employment, the log employment rate (ratio of employment to labour force) and the log participation rate (ratio of labour force to working-age population) – all variables being expressed as deviations from respective national means. The motivation for focusing on the *change* in the employment level is that the variable appears to have a unit root component: that is, a random component subject to permanent changes. This result for the USA, which generalizes to European countries as Decressin and Fatás (1995) illustrate, is itself

---

[12] Eichengreen (1993a) also documents that energy prices and national real exchange rates, which may be viewed as largely exogenous to regions, have asymmetrical effects on regional labour markets within the USA, the UK and Italy.

suggestive that permanent (or at least highly persistent) regional shocks are regular occurrences in industrial countries.

In each of Blanchard and Katz's three regression equations, the left-hand variable depends on its own lags and those of the other two variables, as well as a random disturbance. In addition, while the change in employment depends only on lagged variables, the employment and participation rates depend on the current change in employment. This feature reflects Blanchard and Katz's critical identifying assumption that innovations in the employment-change equation are exogenous labour demand shocks, which affect the other two variables contemporaneously with no immediate reverse feedback. If one buys the identifying assumption, the estimated dynamic system allows one to trace through time the responses of all three variables to an asymmetric regional labour demand shock.[13] One can also track the effect on migration from the region. Note the identity that regional employment, N, equals the product of the employment rate, E (1 minus the unemployment rate), the participation rate, P, and working-age population, Pop:

$$N = (E)(P)(Pop)$$

In terms of logarithmic changes (which approximate percentage changes), the preceding relationship equates the percentage change in total employment to the sum of the corresponding percentage changes in the employment rate, the participation rate and population:

$$\frac{\Delta N}{N} = \frac{\Delta E}{E} + \frac{\Delta P}{P} + \frac{\Delta Pop}{Pop}$$

Since our variables are expressed as deviations from national averages, $\Delta Pop/Pop$ can be interpreted as inward migration provided regional demographic trends are shared by the entire nation, or if those trends evolve independently of labour demand shocks. Migration can be inferred from the behaviour of employment, the employment rate and the participation rate.

The other key assumption that Blanchard and Katz make is that region-specific characteristics creating mean differentials in labour market variables can be modelled as region-specific constants in the regression equations. To estimate, they pool their data over all US states, thus allowing regional fixed effects to differ, but imposing uniform dynamics. Blanchard and Katz thus address the econometric identification problem by identifying regional labour demand shocks as the

---

[13] Davis *et al.* (1997) and Blanchard and Katz (1992) provide alternative estimates for the USA based on observable exogenous determinants of regional labour demand, e.g. defence contracts. These results are broadly consistent with those for the USA that we discuss below. Davis *et al.* find, however, some sensitivity of the adjustment pattern to the measure of employment used in estimation, and suggest a somewhat slower response of migration in response to some shocks.

estimated residuals from relative employment growth equations that assume fixed
but possibly distinct unconditional regional mean growth rates.[14]

Table 2 shows the reactions of the key regional labour market variables to a 1%
positive shock to relative labour demand. The impulse response profiles are based on
estimation and simulation of Blanchard–Katz VARs, assuming two lags of each
variable. (A variable's impulse response profile simply tracks through time the
dynamic effect on the variable of the 1% shock to employment.) We have updated
the original Blanchard–Katz US data sample to extend it over 1976–95 (their data
ended in 1990). We also report estimates for Canada (1976–96), Italy (1969–95),
Germany (1970–93) and the UK (1969–94). For Germany we omit West Berlin:
only partial data are available and the city appears to be an outlier in terms of its
labour market behaviour.

Table 2. Impulse response profiles for a Blanchard–Katz regional labour demand shock

Country	Variable	First year	Five years	Ten years	Fifteen years
Italy	Employment	1.00	0.69	0.55	0.45
	Employment rate	0.23	0.12	0.07	0.04
	Participation rate	0.56	0.36	0.24	0.15
	Migration	0.22	0.21	0.24	0.27
Germany	Employment	1.00	1.03	0.57	0.17
	Employment rate	0.28	0.49	0.10	−0.02
	Participation rate	0.61	0.23	0.34	0.20
	Migration	0.11	0.31	0.13	−0.01
UK	Employment	1.00	0.63	0.37	0.36
	Employment	0.11	0.04	−0.04	−0.02
	Participation rate	0.85	0.42	0.14	0.04
	Migration	0.04	0.17	0.28	0.33
Canada	Employment	1.00	0.63	0.37	0.34
	Employment rate	0.46	−0.05	−0.12	−0.08
	Participation rate	0.43	0.25	0.12	0.09
	Migration	0.11	0.43	0.37	0.32
USA	Employment	1.00	0.74	0.44	0.48
	Employment rate	0.24	−0.01	−0.03	0.00
	Participation rate	0.43	0.16	−0.02	−0.01
	Migration	0.33	0.59	0.49	0.49

Notes: Units are percentage points. The German estimates are based on western Germany, excluding
Berlin. Migration, participation rate and employment rate may not sum to employment because of
rounding.

---

[14] Because of trends in technology or preferences, agglomeration economies, externalities, better local institutions, or
for social and cultural reasons, some regions tend to attract more workers and firms over the long run, while others
have a secular tendency to decline in scale. Thus, employment trends may arise. (See Peri (1997) for an empirical
study relating long-run employment growth in Italian cities and provinces to local sociocultural characteristics.)

While the table offers a rich diversity in responses, a few regularities stand out. Perhaps the most salient feature is the much lower persistence of the employment rate effect in the USA and Canada compared with the three EU countries. Five years out, the employment rate has returned to its initial level in the USA and Canada, while in Europe the half-life of the employment rate response is about 4–7 years. Part of the reason can be found in migration. In the USA, there is a substantial initial migratory inflow to the region, which grows, peaks and then reverses, but remains substantial in the long run. In Canada, initial migration is smaller, but it then follows a pattern similar to that in the USA (albeit with consistently lower migratory flows). In Italy, in contrast, the adjustment pattern suggests that worker mobility is on average fairly low, but that there is a part of the labour force (young, skilled, educated workers, and those who live within commuting distance of other 'regions') that is rather mobile and thus in a position to respond rapidly to shocks. After these workers have reacted, others find it more difficult to move, even if they experience a long unemployment spell or ultimately move out of the labour force. The very persistent participation changes for Italy (and some other countries) could reflect changes in disability status, early retirements, and movement between the legitimate and underground economies. In 1993, only 32.9% of Italian men aged 55 to 64 were officially participating in the labour force. (The comparable participation rates were about twice as high in the USA and UK, and roughly 85% in Japan and Switzerland.)

Like Italy, Germany displays a small initial migration response and a large initial participation response. Migration subsequently grows but then reverses direction, because the long-run permanent component of the labour demand shock is small. In the UK, the participation response is an even more dominant equilibration mechanism, with migration appearing to gain in importance only in the very long run.

Two caveats are important in interpreting these long-run results. First, by modelling the participation and employment rates as stationary or mean-reverting rather than unit root processes, the statistical model forces migration to accommodate in full permanent changes in the level of employment. Second, the data series are too short to provide any reliable information about long-run responses. Thus, no long-run predictions of the model can be taken too seriously. The question, really, is whether the modelling assumptions we have made seriously distort estimates of short- and medium-term responses. We therefore estimated a version of the model in which relative employment is stationary, experiencing exclusively temporary fluctuations around a deterministic time trend. Necessarily in this alternative model, the long-run effects of labour demand shocks on migration are zero. However, the first year effects and the response five years out are very close to those reported in Table 2.

Decressin and Fatás (1995) apply the Blanchard–Katz methodology (over the years 1975–87) to European countries and to a pooled sample of European subnational regions and small countries. As above, they find large initial participation effects. They also find that migration, while quite low in the short run, rises in the long run to accommodate a fairly large estimated permanent component of the typical employment shock. Most importantly, their results differ from ours in finding that European employment rate responses are not noticeably more persistent than in the USA. We have already described why the long-run implications of these models should be discounted. We are less certain why Decressin and Fatás find such low employment rate persistence. The discrepancy seems to result from their identification of region-specific variables not as simple differences from national averages, but as residuals from a regression of the log regional variable on the log national average. Blanchard and Katz (1992) found that using this approach instead of simple differences matters little for the USA. We have found that the choice has only minor effects on the Canadian and UK results. But when one applies the 'residual' approach to Germany and Italy, the employment rate response does indeed appear much less persistent.

We are unpersuaded that the method used by Decressin and Fatás yields an economically meaningful representation of the region-specific component of shocks. The justification for using their method to identify idiosyncratic regional shocks is, presumably, that for each region, the estimated time series of shocks is uncorrelated with the time series of the corresponding national-average variable. But this property is not clearly desirable or reasonable. As the study by Eichengreen (1993a) illustrates, region-specific shocks may be correlated with aggregate unemployment because they are generated by events – real exchange rate shifts, oil shocks, increased competition from low-wage countries – with divergent impacts on different regions (see also Davis *et al.*, 1997). Furthermore, common shocks may feed into unemployment through distinct regional persistence mechanisms, as in the statistical model of Forni and Reichlin (1997). Our analysis, instead, embodies the simple hypothesis that any gap between the regional unemployment rate and its natural level should set in train pressures for migration. On this assumption, regional labour demand shocks would seem to have much more persistent effects in Europe than in North America. This finding, consistent with the other evidence, suggests that there is indeed substantially lower labour mobility not just among, but within the existing currency unions of Europe.

It is tempting to relate the different unemployment adjustment patterns to differing labour market institutions, but this is not straightforward. Germany has more open-ended unemployment benefits than Canada or the USA, and a higher benefit replacement rate than either of those countries or the UK (Nickell (1997) presents a convenient OECD comparison; see also Bertola and Ichino, 1995). However, Italy's official unemployment entitlement is very modest, and Canada's system can easily be 'worked' to allow a high level of income support punctuated only by a short spell of employment each year (Courchene, 1993; Green and Riddell, 1997). Although unemployment benefits may be paid in disguised forms in Italy (e.g., medical benefits), generous jobless provisions seem at best only part of the reason for persistent regional unemployment. Other factors relevant particularly to continental Europe may be the very high coverage of wages by union contracts, a factor inhibiting regional wage flexibility, and relatively high tax rates, which discourage job creation, increase 'wait' unemployment and make underground activities more attractive. A definitive explanation of sluggish labour reallocation must rest on further microeconometric evidence.

Housing markets are very likely to be part of the story, however. Hughes and McCormick (1987) explain how rent controls, publicly allocated rental housing and subsidized owner occupation restricted the stock of private rental housing in the UK, reducing mobility and raising aggregate unemployment. Oswald (1996) demonstrates a negative relationship between the private rental housing stock and unemployment for OECD countries. The USA has low unemployment despite a high rate of home ownership, but US markets for long-term mortgages are relatively efficient and overall transaction costs low.

4. REGIONAL RELATIVE PRICE ADJUSTMENT

Research on the developed currency unions of North America and Europe suggests that, on almost any measure, relative regional prices tend to fluctuate less than international relative prices (Vaubel, 1976, 1978; Eichengreen, 1991; De Grauwe and Vanhaverbeke, 1993; von Hagen and Neumann, 1994). This fall in relative price variability is often viewed as one of the advantages of a currency union. At the same time, it raises questions about how the intranational mechanism of adjustment to permanent shocks differs from the international mechanism.[15] For Canada, Germany and Italy, Table 3 shows standard deviations of (log) regional GDP deflators relative to national GDP deflators. Table 4 does an analogous calculation of the standard deviation of annual first differences in such real exchange rates. Table 3 is meant to illustrate the long-run range of variation in real exchange rates that these currency unions have experienced over a quarter-century, while Table 4 is meant to illustrate the degree of short-run (year-to-year) variability in real exchange rates around their trends (which are small in these regional data).[16]

[15] In contrast to the general tendency in the literature, Poloz (1990) found relatively high variability in the relative GDP deflators of some Canadian provinces – higher, in some cases, than that between European countries. However, these findings applied mainly to Alberta and Saskatchewan, which are extremely open to trade and are heavy exporters of primary commodities. In such cases, regional real exchange rate movements themselves are largely exogenous shocks, in that they strongly reflect global movements in primary commodity prices. The change in the regional real exchange rate is not a response primarily to some region-specific shock. Also, Poloz's method of normalizing real exchange rate levels over 1980–7 gives an exaggerated appearance of variability for several provinces, since the variability measure he calculates is apparently the standard deviation in the level (not logarithm) of relative price. (Poloz chooses a 1971 base year despite the run-up in commodity prices and especially energy prices since the early 1970s.) Thus, Poloz's volatility figures for the Alberta/Ontario real exchange rate over 1980–7, say, are not readily comparable to those he calculates for the France/Germany rate.

[16] The choice of GDP deflators is meant to capture regional export competitiveness. Vaubel (1976, 1978), Eichengreen (1991), and von Hagen and Neumann (1994) study regional CPI-based real exchange rates. De Grauwe and Vanhaverbeke (1993) use data on regional unit labour costs.

Table 3. Intranational relative price variability: annual levels (%)

Country	Period	Average	High region	Low region
Canada	1970–95	1.4	2.1	0.6
Germany	1970–95	1.2	3.0	0.3
Italy	1970–96	2.5	5.0	1.0

Notes: Regional standard deviations of the log regional GDP deflator less the log national GDP deflator. Regional figures are averaged (with equal weights) to obtain each country's aggregate regional variability measure.

Table 4. Intranational relative price variability: annual changes (%)

Country	Period	Average	High region	Low region
Canada	1970–95	0.8	1.1	0.3
Germany	1970–95	0.9	1.2	0.3
Italy	1970–96	0.8	1.2	0.6

Notes: Regional standard deviations of regional GDP deflator inflation rate less national GDP deflator inflation rate. Regional figures are averaged (with equal weights) to obtain each country's aggregate regional variability measure.

Table 5 (on 1988–96 national real exchange rate levels *vis-à-vis* Germany) and Table 6 (on changes over that same period) allow a comparison of intranational with international variability in relative prices. Real exchange rate variation within currency unions is often quite low compared to that between countries, as previous research has shown. With more of the European exchange rate mechanism's (ERM) track record available, however, it is clear that fixed exchange rates can induce international real exchange rate volatility levels matching those seen across regions of low-inflation countries. Of Germany's five 'ERM core' partners – those that have not realigned against Germany in the last ten years – all with the possible exceptions of Denmark and France show real exchange rate variability that is closely consistent with that within the three currency unions. Austria, indeed, shows less variability on either measure than the average German *Land*.

Table 5. International price variability relative to Germany, 1988–96: annual levels (%)

ERM core		Other current ERM		Non-ERM Europe		Non-Europe	
Country	%	Country	%	Country	%	Country	%
Austria	0.6	Finland	17.2	Greece	3.5	Australia	12.4
Belgium	1.1	Ireland	9.1	Norway	10.1	Canada	16.6
Denmark	3.9	Italy	12.6	Sweden	13.3	Japan	8.4
France	3.4	Portugal	6.8	UK	9.6	New Zealand	11.3
Netherlands	3.2	Spain	9.4			USA	8.1

Note: Standard deviation of the log national GDP deflator less Germany's log national GDP deflator, in national currency.

Table 6. International price variability relative to Germany, 1988–96: annual changes (%)

ERM core		Other current ERM		Non-ERM Europe		Non-Europe	
Country	%	Country	%	Country	%	Country	%
Austria	0.7	Finland	10.7	Greece	3.7	Australia	11.4
Belgium	1.2	Ireland	4.2	Norway	4.9	Canada	10.1
Denmark	2.0	Italy	8.8	Sweden	9.8	Japan	10.7
France	1.7	Portugal	5.2	UK	6.9	New Zealand	10.1
Netherlands	1.0	Spain	7.3			USA	7.7

Note: Standard deviation of national GDP deflator inflation less inflation in Germany's national GDP deflator, measured in national currency.

Outside the ERM core, real exchange rate volatility is much higher, but to differing degrees. In this respect there is little difference, on the whole, between the non-core ERM members, which have realigned or floated against Germany in the 1990s, and European countries outside the ERM, which have at times shadowed the DM or ecu. Finland and Sweden, both reliant on primary product exports, stand out for their wide real exchange rate swings. Greece's low real-rate volatility is remarkable; evidently changes in the drachma's nominal rate have largely offset differential inflation. Real exchange rate variability against Germany tends to rise outside Europe, but in this respect the US record differs little from that of most other countries likely to enter EMU in 1999.

For Vaubel (1976, 1978), the amplitude and frequency of real exchange rate movements between two regions is almost a sufficient statistic of their suitability to form a currency union. An absence of asymmetric real shocks, interregional factor mobility, regional proximity and a high extent of mutual trade should all promote stability in the real exchange rate. Vaubel and the authors who have followed him all recognize that the observed volatility of international real exchange rates may well overstate the macroeconomic disadvantages of forming a currency union. Particularly under floating nominal exchange rates, monetary and portfolio shocks that would be absent in a currency union contribute powerfully to real exchange rate volatility. [17]

The opposite possibility has received less recognition, however. Market distortions and government policies may allow *too little* real exchange rate variation in a currency union, given the asymmetric shocks that occur. On this reading, the

---

[17] Using a data sample that includes locations in Europe and an econometric specification that controls for distance and trade barriers, Engel and Rogers (1995) find that higher nominal exchange rate volatility between two markets systematically raises inter-market variability in relative prices. See Obstfeld (1998) for a survey. It is not correct, however, to assert that monetary factors have no effect on interregional real exchange rate volatility within currency unions. The evidence is that interregional relative price variability is higher when mean national inflation is higher. Debelle and Lamont (1997) offer a useful capsule review of the evidence, as well as new evidence that the dispersion of prices within US cities is positively related to the city-wide inflation rate.

stability of interregional real exchange rates could reflect systematic interference with the workings of markets, motivated by distributional or political ends, and reveal little about a currency union's innate desirability.

For Europe, the latter possibility derives credence from the existence of nation-wide wage norms and the practice of administered pricing in many sectors, including housing. Thus, the authors of *One Market, One Money* express the hope that under the single currency, competition and wage discipline will enhance price and wage flexibility, facilitating intra-EMU real exchange rate adjustment in the absence of significant international labour mobility (Emerson *et al.*, 1992). On this view, EMU optimists should wish to see *more* real exchange rate flexibility between the ERM core and Germany than among German regions (see Tables 3–6), but there is scant evidence of this. The effect should be all the more pronounced because an internationally asymmetric permanent shock gives rise to a permanent real exchange rate change, whereas the corresponding disturbance should have only a temporary real exchange rate effect within an area of free factor mobility. The counter-argument, that there have been no asymmetric shocks, rings rather hollow given that the sample underlying Tables 5 and 6 includes German reunification. (More formal evidence on the existence of asymmetric national shocks is discussed by Bayoumi and Eichengreen (1996), Forni and Reichlin (1997), Viñals and Jimeno (1996) and Weber (1997).)

For the USA, Blanchard and Katz (1992) find that regional relative wage and price movements play at best a small supporting role in the adjustment to permanent labour demand shocks. They ascribe this finding to the predominance of migration as a regional adjustment mechanism in the USA. In light of the previous section's finding that interregional migration is of more limited importance in Canada and especially in Europe, one might expect to find regional prices playing a bigger role in offsetting regional shocks. Figures 12–14 suggest that any such tendencies may be small, but these figures do not indicate whether high regional unemployment rates are due to shocks that might warrant price adjustment.[18] To focus on this issue, we attempt to estimate local price responses conditional on asymmetric shocks to employment.

We do this by estimating bivariate VARs in relative regional employment growth and the (log) relative regional GDP deflator. This specification imposes the

---

[18] The relative price decline within Italy shown in Figure 13 probably does not represent the operation of market forces as described in textbook accounts of regional adjustment. Attanasio and Padoa Schioppa (1991) explain why southern Italian CPIs tend to be relatively low, and most of the reasons carry over to GDP deflators: 'The reasons for their low cost of living can probably be found partly in subsidies provided by the Central Government in some services (highways, for instance, are free in the South and not in the North-Centre), partly by cheaper labour in the underground and criminal economy, partly by cheaper rents which are publicly regulated (both for residential and business dwellings) and finally by the lower weight the Southern regions assign to non-agricultural consumption which is everywhere the most expensive and the one whose cost rises more rapidly.' Given the convergence between southern and north-centre nominal wages over the last couple of decades or so (a result of the *scala mobile* along with other features of Italian wage setting), the implication is that relative real wages in the south have actually *risen*.

assumption that relative regional employment is subject to permanent shocks, while relative regional prices are not. Eventually, factor inflows within a national economy should eliminate regional price discrepancies due to relative labour demand shocks, even when those shocks have permanent components.

As in the previous section, we impose a common propagation mechanism on all regions in a country, but allow for region-specific unconditional mean levels of employment growth and the price of GDP. Our estimated impulse responses incorporate the maintained identifying assumption that employment growth shocks are labour demand shifts that can affect local prices within a year, but which themselves respond to local prices only after a year has passed. Again, the German results are based on the ten western German *Länder* excluding Berlin.

Table 7 reports our findings. Only in Germany is there a noticeable short-run local price increase in response to a positive labour demand shock, and the effect disappears (indeed, becomes slightly negative) immediately after the period of the shock. This pattern provides very weak support for the idea that in Germany local prices help in regional adjustment, since in that country the employment rate remains high long after the initial year of a labour demand shock (recall Table 2). In Canada, local prices eventually show a small tendency to rise after the first period, whereas in Italy they do not seem to move at all. The results for Canada change very little when Alberta and Saskatchewan, both big primary commodity producers, are excluded.

The estimates in Table 7 imply larger permanent effects of employment shocks than those in Table 2, which are based on a VAR including the participation and employment rates. This discrepancy is puzzling. When we add prices to the larger VAR system underlying Table 2, however, the implications for regional real exchange rates are close to those of Table 7.[19]

Table 7. Impulse response of local price level to a labour demand shock

Country	Variable	First year	Five years	Ten years	Fifteen years
Italy	Employment	1.00	0.80	0.79	0.79
	GDP deflator	0.02	0.00	0.00	0.00
Germany	Employment	1.00	1.50	1.53	1.53
	GDP deflator	0.30	0.08	0.00	0.00
Canada	Employment	1.00	1.25	1.22	1.22
	GDP deflator	0.06	0.21	0.07	0.02

Notes: Units are percentage points. The German estimates are based on western Germany, excluding Berlin.

[19] We also estimated VARs involving relative per-capita GDP as well as relative prices, with results broadly similar to those in Table 7.

While the low responsiveness of prices could in principle reflect rapid migratory responses or high interregional trade integration, neither explanation seems plausible for Europe in view of the low migration responses and persistent employment rate effects documented in section 3.

The analysis thus does not contradict the view that interregional real exchange rate variability is relatively low in Europe in part because of price rigidities and government policies that slow the pace of adjustment. This conclusion is neither surprising nor novel. Governments routinely interfere with the income redistributions that relative price changes would otherwise cause – the common agricultural policy and the contorted compensation devices that have supported it being one extreme example. Continental European wage-setting institutions by and large also reflect a philosophy of regional equalization in earnings. It is often argued that intra-EU exchange flexibility is incompatible with the survival of the Single Market, since currency-induced real exchange rate movements would induce strong pressures for protection (see, for example, Eichengreen, 1993b). The same argument suggests, however, that large swings in relative regional prices could be politically problematic for economic integration at the national level. Even when domestic labour mobility is low, sharp regional price swings are therefore unlikely to be allowed a big role in adjustment. When interpreted in this light, the low extent of interregional price movement tells us little about the ease with which resources are reallocated in currency unions, or about the need for reallocation.

5. INTERREGIONAL INSURANCE AND FISCAL TRANSFERS

Private insurance markets and government interregional transfer schemes can cushion the effects of temporary and permanent economic shocks. In the case of temporary shocks, they provide more complete protection than borrowing would. In the case of permanent shocks, they reduce the need for a long-run adjustment in regional consumption levels. A key facet of a currency union's performance is how well private or public insurance can fulfil these roles. In this section we compare the roles of private insurance for US states and for EU countries, and then examine the operation of public interregional transfer systems in the USA, Canada and Europe. A major finding is that transfers are quite persistent, reflecting the persistence of unemployment, and thus facilitate slower regional adjustment.

5.1. Evidence on private insurance

Some basic evidence on the mechanism of private insurance within currency unions has been developed by Atkeson and Bayoumi (1993), who compare the extent of private risk sharing across US census regions with that across European countries. A starting point for comparison is the relation of gross regional product to personal income, the difference between the two consisting of external capital income, remittances of labour earnings and government transfers. Even excluding government and labour transfers, the percentage by which GDP differs from personal income in US census regions is one to two orders of magnitude above the percentage difference between French, German or Italian GDP and GNP. Thus, New England's personal income exceeded its GDP by around 9% on average over 1963–86, whereas the corresponding figure for Germany or France is only one-fifth of a per cent.

Atkeson and Bayoumi also found (in 1966–86 data) that US national capital income is the preponderant determinant of US regional capital income, and that US regional capital income is slightly (but significantly) negatively correlated with regional labour income, suggesting some role of financial wealth in insuring human wealth, albeit a small one. The situation appeared to be quite different in the European Community on 1970–87 data. Capital incomes in Belgium, France, Greece, the Netherlands and the UK appeared more weakly correlated with the aggregate capital income of those countries plus Germany. In a more recent study covering the years 1981–90, Sørensen and Yosha (1996) conclude that cross-border asset ownership contributes much more towards smoothing the cross-sectional variability of annual consumption in the USA than in the EU.

The dismantling of EU capital account restrictions under the Single European Act has probably gone some way to diminish the contrast between the USA and Europe. Furthermore, the introduction of the euro will greatly enhance the integration and efficiency of the European capital market. But fully catching up to the USA will take time, and depends on the further opening of domestic European financial markets. In the meantime, an important private insurance mechanism of the US currency union seems to be less developed in the future EMU. As long as Europe's capital markets lag behind those of the USA, the need for the government to provide substitute insurance is correspondingly greater.

5.2. Fiscal transfers in existing currency unions

Since at least the work of Ingram (1959), economists have recognized the role of interregional fiscal transfers in equilibrating regional balances of payments within currency unions. The question was placed squarely on the European agenda by the MacDougall Report (Commission of the European Communities, 1977), although the issue had been raised years earlier in the Werner Report. MacDougall and his colleagues argued that in existing industrialized currency unions, both fiscal *redistribution* to offset long-run regional income differentials, and *stabilizing* fiscal transfers aimed at providing a short-term cushion against cyclical shocks, are substantial. Their report suggested that on average roughly 40% of any long-run regional per-capita income disparity is eliminated by equalization policies. They also contended that in the UK and France, 'as much as one-half to two-thirds of a short-term loss of primary income due to, for example, a fall in a region's external sales may be offset through the public finance system, and much the same may be true of regions in other modern integrated economies'.

Although the MacDougall Report regarded international fiscal flows at that level as impracticable for the near term, it suggested that a European Community budget of about 5–7% of Community GNP, providing for net transfers between member states for both equalization and stabilization purposes, might provide sufficient support to allow Europe to proceed to monetary unification: 'A federation with these special characteristics would facilitate creation of a monetary union. Existing national federations enjoy such union internally, and its maintenance is powerfully assisted by the largely automatic equalising and stabilising inter-regional flows through the channels of federal finance.' Importantly for the argument we shall make below, the MacDougall Report regarded both redistribution and stabilization as vital elements in sustaining a currency union. In the authors' view, a country giving up substantial fiscal as well as monetary autonomy within a single market served by a single money might be running a greater risk of permanent economic decline.

The study of US fiscal federalism by Sala-i-Martín and Sachs (1992) moved the discussion to a more rigorously quantitative level. They regressed log-levels of US census regions' relative transfers and taxes on the log-level of relative personal income in the region. The bottom-line finding is that on average across regions during the years 1970–88, federal taxes and transfers together offset fully 40% of a one-dollar shock to local personal income. Taken at face value, the result would imply that even the US currency union, with its relatively footloose labour force, relies heavily on fiscal transfers to offset regional shocks (though not as heavily as a credulous reader of the MacDougall Report might have predicted).

Von Hagen (1992) argues that the Sala-i-Martín and Sachs (1992) regression of relative tax and transfer levels on relative income levels confounds the stabilization role of transfers with their redistributive role. He proposes to regress year-to-year tax and transfer changes on income changes to get at the stabilization effect, and to regress yearly levels of taxes and transfers on yearly levels of incomes to get at the redistributive effect. Von Hagen's estimates over a 1981–6 sample of US states look at the response of net fiscal inflows to gross state product rather than personal income before taxes (the two differing primarily because of asset income from other states). Thus the results are not immediately comparable to those of Sala-i-Martín and Sachs. He finds that the short-run stabilizing role of net transfers – their response to a one-year change in GSP – amounts to only 10 cents on the dollar. Long-run redistribution in the USA is, however, estimated to be very large, roughly 47 cents on the dollar.

Subsequent researchers have continued to reconsider the US experience, but also have added data on other countries. Goodhart and Smith (1993) apply von Hagen's (1992) specifications to US, Canadian and UK data, finding stabilization effects similar to his for the USA and Canada, but somewhat larger (21 cents on the dollar) for the UK. They find, however, that the estimated redistributive effects are quite close to the stabilization effects. They argue that these estimates are likely to understate the true effects, since von Hagen's measure of taxes omits social security contributions. Pisani-Ferry *et al.* (1993) revisit the USA and introduce France and Germany, using a simulation methodology based on the characteristics of national fiscal systems, rather than regression analysis. They find a 17 cents on the dollar offset to a decline in gross regional product in the USA, and offsets roughly twice that size for France and Germany. The huge difference compared with the USA stems in large part from the operation of the French and German unemployment insurance and social security systems, together with the system of interregional grants (*Länderfinanzausgleich*) in Germany.

Returning to econometrics, Bayoumi and Masson (1995) analyse the USA and Canada. (In Canada, as in Germany, interregional equalization is a constitutional principle.) Using a specification somewhat different from von Hagen's, and pursuing estimation of stabilization via yearly differences but of redistribution via long-run averages of levels, they find a 31% stabilization effect and a 22% redistribution effect for the USA. These effects refer to percentages of shocks to personal income, not GSP. For Canada, where federal taxes are less important and provinces exercise considerable discretion in fiscal policy, the stabilizing effect of fiscal flows is only 17%. However, the extensive Canadian equalization system results in a redistributive effect of 39%.[20]

Mélitz and Zumer (1997) try to reconcile these conflicting conclusions by applying uniform accounting procedures and a common econometric methodology to the USA, Canada, the UK and France. Their estimated stabilization coefficients with respect to personal income are around 20% for the USA, UK and France, but only 10–14% for Canada. They estimate a 38% long-run equalization of personal incomes in France, an equalization of 26% in the UK, and equalizations of around 17% in Canada and the USA. Their estimate of Canadian redistribution is much lower than the 39% 'headline' estimate of Bayoumi–Masson. The explanation is their exclusion of federal grants to provincial governments from their estimate of personal income stabilization. Mélitz and Zumer argue that such grants belong only

---

[20] While the modern system of Canadian equalization grants dates from 1957, its current incarnation originates in the Constitution Act of 1982 (section 36[2]), which committed the national government to 'the principle of making equalization payments to ensure that provincial governments have sufficient revenues to provide reasonably comparable levels of public services at reasonably comparable levels of taxation'. Under the present system, five provinces – British Columbia, Manitoba, Ontario, Quebec and Saskatchewan – define a 'standard' level of per-capita revenues from 33 specified revenue sources. The standard refers not to actual revenues, but to their hypothetical level at national average tax rates. Provinces with per-capita revenues (at national average tax rates) above the standard receive no equalization payments, but make none either. Payments to provinces below the five-province standard (again, at national average tax rates) come from the federal government, which is supposed to bring the poorer provinces up to par. (See Boadway and Hobson, 1993.) While this system might be thought to complicate econometric analysis, it is only part of the total tax and transfer system, which also includes federal taxes, social assistance payments and unemployment insurance. Indeed, the overall long-run relationship between personal income before and after taxes and transfers appears quite linear for Canada, as Figure 2 of Bayoumi and Masson (1995) shows.

in estimates of output stabilization. One might justify the Bayoumi–Masson procedure, however, if direct grants from the centre or from other localities allowed local governments to lower taxes or provide more public goods and services valued by consumers.

Thus, a considerable range of estimates remains for some countries. Does any consistent pattern emerge? Returning to the USA, a stabilization coefficient with respect to personal income of 20% – a figure not inconsistent with von Hagen's (1992) estimate of 10% with respect to GSP – seems to emerge from the literature as a rough consensus figure. Interestingly, Asdrubali *et al.* (1996), who explain empirically the cross-sectional correlation of per-capita GSP and per-capita state consumption, present estimates that imply a US stabilization coefficient of 21% with respect to personal income. The extent of redistribution among US states appears to be close to that figure as well, although there is less convergence in the literature. For Canada, redistribution seems to be higher and stabilization lower than in the USA, though the latter result is explained by Canada's more decentralized fiscal system. Such evidence as is available for France, Germany and the UK indicates a higher degree of stabilization and/or redistribution compared with the 'twenty-twenty' standard of the USA, especially in the two continental countries.[21] The continuing transfer flow from western to eastern Germany is a conspicuous example of interregional redistribution.

In assessing the role of transfers, it is important to remember that their importance in stabilizing labour incomes might be disproportionately large, due to the limited access to the capital market of those with little financial wealth. Atkeson and Bayoumi (1993) confirm that in the USA, fiscal transfers play a larger role than asset income in insuring labour income. A related point is that continental European financial markets have provided more limited opportunities for diversification in general than those of the USA, making fiscal transfers more valuable at the margin.

5.3. Stabilization, redistribution and transfer dynamics

The textbook case of complete contingent securities markets – in which all risks can be marketed – provides a useful benchmark from which to assess the roles of government transfers in the realistic case where asset markets are far from complete. In complete markets, any uncertain contingency, whether it has a permanent or temporary effect, can be insured against. Events that are perfectly predictable cannot be insured, although borrowing and lending will be available to smooth their effects over time.

In the absence of complete markets, an omniscient government planner might facilitate regional risk sharing by making the contingent interregional transfers that

---

[21] On redistribution in Germany, see Costello (1993).

might otherwise have been effected privately. In this case we would view the government as providing insurance services. The government might also make non-contingent transfers based on known structural features of regions – for example, an exogenously fixed payment from an oil-producing region to one without natural resources. These are pure redistributions.

The notion of *stabilization* used in the empirical fiscal federalism literature does not correspond perfectly to that of insurance, because elements of the tax-and-transfer system that provide insurance against permanent (or highly persistent) shocks may induce fiscal flows that are indistinguishable from redistributions once a shock has occurred. One might instead view the proper stabilizing function of fiscal transfers as that of partially compensating for missing interregional insurance markets.[22] In that case, however, the redistributive effects as estimated in the literature will also tend to capture the stabilization function in its response to permanent or long-lived shocks. Estimated redistributive coefficients would not be irrelevant to the question of stabilization, although it might be hard to distinguish their stabilization and true redistributive components. At the same time, the stabilization coefficients estimated by standard approaches might fail to capture lags in stabilizing fiscal flows (see, e.g., Eichengreen's (1991) case study of Michigan in the early 1980s).

These factors motivate the search for a dynamic fiscal flow model in which pure redistribution can be separated empirically from transfers that provide insurance against idiosyncratic shocks.[23] To that end we propose a bivariate VAR specification based on the same variables that Bayoumi and Masson (1995) and Mélitz and Zumer (1997) analyse. Denote by $y_{i,t}$ region i's relative per-capita personal income in period t: that is, the log of regional per-capita personal income less that of national per-capita personal income. Let $y_{i,t}^a$ denote relative *available* per-capita income, defined in terms of per-capita personal income less tax outflows from the region, plus transfer inflows.[24] The VAR specification we propose is

$$y_{i,t}^a = \alpha_i + (1-\gamma)y_{i,t} + b_{11}(L)y_{i,t-1} + b_{12}(L)y_{i,t-1}^a + \varepsilon_{1i,t} \tag{1}$$

$$y_{i,t} = \beta_i + b_{21}(L)y_{i,t-1} + b_{22}(L)y_{i,t-1}^a + \varepsilon_{2i,t} \tag{2}$$

where the lag polynomials $b_{ij}(L)$ imply two lags: that is, are all linear functions of the lag operator L (which assigns to any variable its value the period before). In this set-up, we assume that the innovation in the second equation is an exogenous change in

[22] This is the approach taken by Persson and Tabellini (1996), who study the endogenous determination of risk sharing and redistribution within a federal union. Their simplified model is not immediately applicable to making positive predictions about EMU because it omits certain elements, notably potential labour mobility, that are likely to be important in practice.

[23] Goodhart and Smith (1993) and Mélitz and Zumer (1997) also stress fiscal dynamics.

[24] We focus on personal income, rather than regional product, to evaluate the extra stabilization transfers provided after private portfolio diversification. In terms of the econometrics, regional personal income will be 'more exogenous' than regional product if financial income comes from nationally diversified sources – and simultaneity bias is a potential problem notwithstanding the identifying assumption that we make below. For Italy we have no personal income data, so we us regional product instead.

regional relative income per head, which affects net transfers, and hence available income, but is not itself affected by the change in transfers in the same period.

We take the ordinary least squares estimate of γ in equation (1) as measuring the contemporaneous stabilizing effect of the transfer. Here, this coefficient measures the response of fiscal flows to an *unanticipated* relative income shock, whereas the coefficient usually associated with stabilization in the literature applies to any relative income change, expected or not. The VAR setting allows also us to trace the entire dynamic response of income and available income, and hence of transfers (which can be approximated as $y_{i,t}^a - y_{i,t}$). Notice we are assuming that, once correction is made for region-specific means, relative per-capita income is a stationary or mean-reverting variable: we do not contemplate long-run regional divergence.

The estimated VAR also allows us to estimate long-run redistribution. In this setting the estimate does not depend on random realizations of per-capita regional income. Equations (1) and (2) allow one to calculate the steady-state (unconditional mean) values $\overline{y_i^a}$ and $\overline{y_i}$ for each region, as functions of the region-specific constants α_i and β_i and the other equation coefficients. A regression of $\overline{y_i^a}$ on $\overline{y_i}$ across regions i yields the coefficient $1 - \delta$ where δ denotes the coefficient of long-run redistribution.

Table 8 reports our estimates of the redistribution and stabilization coefficients for Canada (1971–95), Italy (1979–93) and the USA (1969–85), where for the USA we have simply used the same data as Bayoumi and Masson (1995).

For Canada, our stabilization effect is quite similar to the estimates of Mélitz and Zumer (1997), and slightly below that of Bayoumi and Masson (1995). But the redistributive effect that our method indicates is much higher than those in the literature. For the USA, we find only about half the stabilization effect suggested by recent studies making the assumption that personal income, rather than regional product, is the variable that people care about insuring. (However, the stabilization effect rises from 10 to 12% in the period after the shock occurs.) The US redistribution coefficient is, however, close to the canonical 20% figure. Finally, for Italy the redistribution coefficient is significant but very small (although the extent of regional income inequality is large). The estimated first-year stabilization effect, at only 3%,

Table 8. Redistributive and stabilizing effects of transfers: Canada, USA and Italy

Country	δ: Long-run redistribution	γ: First-year stabilization
Canada (federal taxes, transfers, grants)	0.53 (0.03)	0.13 (0.02)
USA (federal taxes, transfers, grants)	0.19 (0.03)	0.10 (0.01)
Italy (social insurance system)	0.08 (0.02)	0.03 (0.03)

Note: Standard errors are given in parentheses.

is insignificant both statistically and economically. However, as we have noted, our Italian data give a very partial picture of total fiscal flows.

Table 9 provides a more complete picture of the dynamic response of relative transfers to a relative regional income shock. The main point to notice is that the transfer effect of the income shock is quite persistent, taking in all cases over five years to be reduced by half. In Canada transfers fall back to their baseline more quickly than output does, while the reverse is true in Italy and the USA. Thus, in Canada the stabilizing role of transfers declines over time for a typically persistent output shock.[25]

The high persistence of stabilizing transfers, even in the USA, suggests that their role goes beyond that of temporarily cushioning cyclical shocks. They appear to represent rather long-lived inflows to regions that have suffered macroeconomic reversals, and, as such, facilitate postponement of any necessary adjustment in labour force and relative prices.

6. LESSONS FOR EMU AND A PROPOSAL

The preceding comparative analysis of North American and European currency unions yields several regularities and contrasts that might be useful in evaluating the future performance and evolution of EMU.

- Labour mobility is a weaker aid to regional adjustment in Europe than in the USA or even in Canada. We see a glacial pace of regional labour market adjustment accompanied by high and persistent regional employment differentials.

Table 9. Dynamic response of transfers to a regional income shock

Country	Variable	First year	Five years	Ten years	Fifteen years
Canada	Δy	1.00	0.68	0.21	0.05
	$\Delta trans$	−0.13	−0.07	0.00	0.00
USA	Δy	1.00	0.27	0.07	0.02
	$\Delta trans$	−0.10	−0.07	−0.02	0.00
Italy	Δy	1.00	0.17	0.01	0.00
	$\Delta trans$	−0.03	−0.03	−0.01	0.00

Notes: The variable *trans* is defined as the log of available relative regional income per capita less the log of relative regional income per capita. The operator Δ denotes a first difference.

[25] We also tried to apply our method to the German fiscal system, but data limitations were particularly severe. The following results, based on total taxes paid by the *Länder* to the federal government (after correction for *Länderfinanzausgleich* redistributions), omit transfers and therefore should be interpreted with caution. (See the appendix for more detail on these data.) The tendency emerging was a rather large redistributive role for taxes (a 36% coefficient of redistribution). We found a delayed and rather persistent reaction of tax payments to a relative income shock (negligible in the first period, 12% in the second, 4% in the fifth).

- Despite relatively low interregional labour mobility and despite the absence of independent macro policy options for subnational European regions, regional real exchange rate flexibility is not greater than in currency unions with higher labour mobility.
- Fiscal transfers from booming to depressed regions, for both redistributive and stabilization purposes, play a significant role in all the currency unions we have examined, although their role seems most modest in the USA. Transfer flows and the economic shocks to which they respond appear to be quite persistent, making it difficult to draw a sharp line between the long-run redistributive and short-run stabilizing roles of transfers. By providing long-lived fiscal inflows from the rest of the country, existing systems of fiscal federalism in Europe ensure that regions experiencing permanent negative idiosyncratic shocks will be relieved of some of the pressure to adjust.

EMU is an entirely novel experiment in full monetary unification among major political powers without full political unification or an overarching fiscal authority. This feature makes it difficult to predict how EMU might evolve. If EMU develops national adjustment mechanisms similar to those driving regional adjustment within existing currency unions, the preceding list of regularities offers several alternative templates.

At least in the foreseeable future, EMU is unlikely to rely on international labour mobility to any great extent. In post-Schengen Europe as within its constituent states, workers theoretically have full freedom of movement. But the factors that nonetheless limit intranational migration curb international migration even more, and there is the additional barrier of language and custom. Not only are workers in potential source countries reluctant to migrate; in addition, workers in potential host countries are reluctant to welcome foreign competitors. As *One Market, One Money* puts it, 'large-scale labour mobility in the Community is neither feasible, at least not across language barriers, nor perhaps desirable' (Emerson *et al.*, 1992). Because intra-European migration on a large scale would be perceived as socially disruptive, EMU is likely to put in place incentives to remain at home – a point we elaborate below.

Does this mean that national price and wage levels in EMU will become more flexible to accommodate needed national adjustments in real exchange rates? The experiences of existing continental currency unions provide no supporting evidence, nor do those of countries that have long pegged to the DM. The heightened perception of a single market that the euro will bring could even promote a greater tendency towards EMU-wide wage bargaining or coverage. As Eichengreen (1992) notes, desires to limit cross-border migration might also contribute to this outcome. The labour market experience of eastern Germany after unification is an extreme one that does not fully apply across different European countries, but it carries a relevant warning.

From a political viewpoint, sharp movements in intra-EMU wages or competitiveness levels would undermine support for the single market as surely as sharp exchange rate movements between member states. Workers in countries that had lost competitiveness would allege unfair competition, especially in the face of plant closures and shifts of capital to low-wage EMU countries. Relatively immobile firms might call for protection. Such developments, like the threat of migration, would sharpen EMU leaders' interest in promoting wage convergence – even at the cost of economic efficiency. For all of these reasons, we doubt that EMU will display substantially greater flexibility in internal real exchange rates than its constituent members currently do.

Labouring under these constraints on adjustment, the EU will eventually face strong pressures to expand its centralized fiscal functions in the direction of inter-country stabilization transfers. Given the generally high persistence of macro-economic shocks in Europe, especially shocks at the national level, stabilization payments are likely to play a substantial *ex post* redistributive role as well. There are several reasons to expect this development.

A country that joins a currency union provides its partners with a public good by expanding the domain over which the single currency is used. Correspondingly, its claim on community protection against persistent or even permanent shocks can be legitimized. The Werner Report took it for granted that 'an increase in financial intervention effected at Community level' would be a necessary adjunct to monetary union, and the MacDougall Report argued the point in detail seven years later.[26] Van Rompuy *et al.* (1991) contend that 'States agree on the centralization of competences and on the discipline implied by the adherence to the EMU in exchange for redistributive mechanisms.'

Indeed, this has been the pattern already: the Maastricht Treaty's Protocol on Economic and Social Cohesion, which set up the Cohesion Fund, and the consequent 1992 increase in Structural Funds, were essential components in sealing the final agreement on EMU. Countries that run into severe economic difficulties under EMU may well be able to lobby successfully for additional side-payments. To the extent that the Stability Pact limits national fiscal responses and social safety nets, pressures on Brussels will be heightened further, as argued by von Hagen and Eichengreen (1996). Attempts to extend EU political or economic integration will provide ample further opportunities for bargaining over transfers.

Large intra-EMU unemployment and income differentials, coupled with some scale-back of existing support systems for the unemployed and indigent, would create incentives for substantial migrations – migrations which, as we have argued, EMU leaders could perceive as politically unacceptable. Incipient migratory pressures, and the consequent fear of social strife, would in practice be the most

---

[26] The Werner Report is reproduced in Steinherr (1994, p. 25).

compelling reason for EU leaders to extend the transfer system. Examples from existing currency unions abound. Courchene (1993) describes the role of the Canadian transfer system in keeping unemployed workers in the poorer Atlantic provinces. Within Italy, northward migration flows out of the *Mezzogiorno* have declined sharply since the early 1970s as a result of higher transfers to the south (as well as enforced real wage convergence and housing shortages due to rent controls; see Attanasio and Padoa Schioppa, 1991). In the USA, welfare programmes starting in the Depression have slowed migration out of Appalachia. In Germany, wage and fiscal policies have discouraged east-to-west movements of workers. (The prospect that the EU will be enlarged towards the labour-abundant east has already brought into contention the question of redirecting versus enlarging existing transfer facilities.)

There would naturally be serious political resistance to the enlargement of EU transfer programmes. As von Hagen (1993) observes, an enhanced international transfer facility would not draw political support from sentiments of national solidarity. Indeed, the existing regional support programmes of Belgium, Canada, Italy and other countries plainly strain the national solidarity that remains. Even if a pure insurance system could be designed, the persistence of shocks and transfers might leave the current payers unclear as to their expected future benefits from continuing the arrangement. Such tensions would make an enlarged transfer programme politically destabilizing *ex post*, but might well fail to prevent its creation.

Would an expanded 'European transfer union' (ETU) be good or bad for Europe? Obviously the development would be advantageous to the extent that it provided otherwise unavailable risk pooling among EMU countries. Van der Ploeg (1991), Wyplosz (1991) and Goodhart and Smith (1993), among many others, have spelled out that advantage, but also draw attention to the considerable moral hazards such inter-country insurance would involve. Workers might view an ETU as a backstop for high wage demands (as occurred in eastern Germany after unification). Governments might give in more easily to demands for anti-competitive labour market measures. (Courchene (1993) relates how Quebec during the 1970s maintained a higher minimum wage than other provinces, successfully shifting the costs of its policy on to the federal budget.) In addition, individual incentives for job search at the EU level would be curbed (as intended by some of those who would support setting up an ETU).

The scope for moral hazard could be reduced in several ways, but probably not eliminated. Goodhart and Smith (1993) suggest that adverse incentive effects could be minimized by ensuring that the transfers were temporary.[27] Since shocks in Europe tend to have persistent effects, however, such transfers would provide only a small degree of risk sharing. If the goal is to provide a meaningful amount of

---

[27] Von Hagen and Hammond (1997) illustrate some of the perils in trying to follow this route.

additional insurance against asymmetric shocks, it will be difficult in practice to avoid transfer payments that look, *ex post*, like long-term redistributions. Even if inward transfers are initially motivated by factors that are believed to be transitory, they will inherit persistence from the persistence of unemployment, and are likely themselves to induce even greater persistence in unemployment, with further positive feedback to transfers (Lindbeck (1995) discusses some plausible mechanisms).

Further dangers come with an ETU. To the extent that financing and administering the plan concentrate greater fiscal authority in Brussels, an ETU would create a more effective political counterweight to the European Central Bank (von Hagen and Eichengreen, 1996; McKinnon, 1997). That evolution could make the ECB more accountable, as the French hope, but in the process could lead to accommodation and other inflationary errors, as the Germans fear.

If one views the prospect of a European transfer union with alarm, what measures might make it less attractive to its proponents? We see four complementary avenues of approach, all subject to some political or technical difficulties, but none unsurmountably problematic.

The first option is to rethink and relax the excessive deficits procedure and the Stability Pact as soon as possible after EMU starts. Since these provisions of the EMU constitution reduce local fiscal powers while providing no substitute at the centre, countries encountering difficulties have a natural opening to press for a central fiscal institution. Greater fiscal latitude at the national level would equip countries only to cushion temporary asymmetric shocks, but that in itself would reduce the pressure for an ETU.

Do the costs of giving up the fiscal restraints outweigh these advantages? A positive side-effect of the Maastricht Treaty's fiscal norms is that they may in the long run promote internal economic reform. However, there is scant evidence that such reforms will go beyond the limited extent they have attained in 1997–8; Eichengreen and Wyplosz (in this issue) argue that the constant threat of excessive deficit sanctions could even retard reforms. Might not public deficit biases re-emerge if there are no fiscal restraints? This is a possibility, but deficit bias would be even less constrained by the capital market if practised at the EU level. On other issues, the rationale for the fiscal criteria is weak, as argued by Buiter *et al.* (1993), von Hagen and Eichengreen (1996), and many others. Once an EMU of eleven countries is a *fait accompli*, much of the original political motivation for the criteria will be gone, and the prospect of amending the pertinent sections of the Maastricht Treaty may appear less daunting.

As a second measure, the EU's total borrowing power could be limited – a guarantee against fiscal pulls on the centre, in the manner of Canada. If EMU member states can borrow, there is little justification, for example, for giving the European Investment Bank an expanded role, along the lines feared by von Hagen and Eichengreen (1996).

A third and very essential task is vigorous internal restructuring – including further reductions in the generosity of pension and other support programmes, lower taxes on employment, more hiring and firing flexibility, vigilant financial liberalization and housing market reform. Such measures would increase each member state's capacity to adjust rapidly to shocks and to deploy fiscal policy when necessary. They would also reduce moral hazards at the individual level. As always, this part of the agenda remains the most difficult to implement in view of the political realities on the ground. In Europe there is extra resistance because policies that open labour markets to domestic 'outsiders' also allow foreign workers in. However, any resulting migratory pressures would be less problematic in the environment of growth and job creation that these policies would bring about, especially if reform is pursued throughout the EU.

A fourth suggestion comes from the observation that the missing markets for human capital insurance provide much of the theoretical basis for believing that an ETU might be beneficial. In principle, each individual national government could act as a capital market intermediary for its residents, making insurance payouts to them in the form of higher transfers or lower taxes. To accomplish this end, governments would issue perpetual euro-denominated liabilities indexed to domestic nominal per-capita GDP growth.[28] The proceeds would be invested in an internationally diversified portfolio of assets. In this way each government could lay off some of its GDP risk; its net cash flow would tend to go up when GDP growth was unexpectedly low, just as under an ETU. Permanent and transitory shocks alike could be handled. But no central EU institution is needed to carry out the plan.

An advantage of this set-up is that each country would need to strive for good macroeconomic performance to maintain favourable terms for marketing its GDP-linked securities. The price of the securities would plummet if a country ever tried to issue enough to make deliberate macroeconomic policy failure attractive. Given its independence, it is unlikely that the ECB would ever be tempted in that direction either. Some technicalities would need to be worked out – for example, safeguards against deliberate misreporting of GDP. Finally, the plan's feasibility would probably require a weakening of the Maastricht deficit norms, since the government deficit might become more vulnerable to wide temporary fluctuations.

The alternative scenario we have outlined raises significant challenges for the European Union. EMU is about to be born, however, only because Europe has shown the creativity and determination to meet such challenges in the past. The same qualities will now be needed in abundance to make EMU work.

---

[28] Closely related securities have been proposed and studied by Shiller (1993). Nominal rather than real GDP indexing would protect buyers of the securities against inflation.

Discussion

Olivier Jean Blanchard
MIT and NBER

On the eve of the start of EMU, this report summarizes, extends and clarifies what we know and do not know about the functioning of existing common currency areas. It draws the implications of these findings for the EMU. After reading the paper, one is likely to reach two conclusions: we know a lot; and the news for EMU is not good. As I find myself in agreement with both the analysis and the conclusions, I shall focus my comments on what I see as the main conclusions of the paper.

EMU: a bad common currency area

Many years ago, Mundell identified the conditions for a well-functioning common currency area. If a group of regions or states wants to adopt a common currency, he said, they had better be exposed to similar shocks, so that a common monetary policy can manage the adjustment. If that were not the case, they had better have strong alternative adjustment mechanisms, so that regions or states affected by adverse, idiosyncratic shocks can recover quickly. Mundell identified three such mechanisms:

- *Factor mobility*, especially labour mobility, so that, after an adverse shock, people move out of the region until things are back to normal for those who stay.
- *Relative price flexibility*, so that regions or states affected by adverse shocks can recover by cutting wages, reducing relative prices and taking market shares away from the others.
- *Fiscal transfers*, so that regions or states that are doing badly receive help from those that are doing well.

These three mechanisms are often listed as substitutes. In fact they are not. While the first two *solve* the adjustment problem, the third, to a large extent, only *hides* it. One of the contributions of the paper is indeed to highlight this difference and to point out the dangers of relying too strongly on the third adjustment mechanism alone.

How do existing currency unions fare in regard to these alternatives? In the USA, states are exposed to large idiosyncratic shocks, but labour mobility acts as a strong adjustment mechanism. The results are steady flows of workers across states, both trend flows and flows in response to shocks. On a macroeconomic scale, the other two potential adjustment mechanisms are quite small. Indeed, because labour mobility leads to a rapid return of personal income per capita to its mean state level following an asymmetric shock, and because fiscal transfers depend largely on income per capita, fiscal transfers responding to such shocks are limited in magnitude and in duration.

Interpreting countries in Europe as individual 'common' currency areas, each composed of a set of regions, a very different picture emerges. Idiosyncratic shocks to regions within European countries are large. Labour mobility is low, as is relative price adjustment. The degree to which fiscal policy responds to differences in personal income across regions is roughly similar to that in the USA. But because of low labour mobility and relative price adjustment, the effects of shocks on personal income are long lasting, giving rise to large and long-lasting fiscal transfers across regions.

This conclusion follows from the twin facts that shocks have longer-lasting effects on employment rates in Europe than in the USA, and that the internal transfer mechanisms are similar to that of the USA. It is, however, at odds with the results in Table 9, where the transfers appear to die at roughly the same rate in the USA and in Italy. But the methodology used to derive the results of Table 9 may be flawed. As elsewhere in the paper, we want to know the dynamic effects of employment shocks on personal income and transfers, not the dynamic effects of shocks to personal income on itself and transfers.

One of the largest discrepancies in the literature is between the dynamic effects of idiosyncratic shocks on the employment rate in the Decressin–Fatás study and those in the present one. I agree with Obstfeld and Peri that their estimation strategy – the use of simple differences rather than beta-differences between regional and aggregate employment – is the right one. For the purposes at hand, we are interested in the dynamic forces that are put into play when unemployment in a region is higher than the national average, not when the residual in a regression of regional unemployment on overall unemployment is positive.

That European countries are themselves lousy 'common' currency areas is not news. For many years, Herbert Giersch advocated that Germany should introduce two currencies, one for the north and one for the south; in the event, the outcome was the adoption of the same currency for the west and the new east. Similarly, proposals have been made to give the south of Italy its own currency and to let it float to make the south more competitive.

What are the implications of these findings for EMU? One can argue – and many have – that all this evidence is irrelevant. There will be no idiosyncratic shocks, the argument goes. Or, because there had better be, there will be labour mobility, or relative price flexibility. And, if everything else fails, fiscal transfers will do the trick. Anything can happen, and perhaps more so in economics than elsewhere. But the evidence summarized in the paper gives a number of reasons to be doubtful.

It is true that high transaction costs in housing in Europe lead to lower mobility. But low labour mobility in Europe is a question not just of housing markets, but also of culture. It will not reach US levels in the near future.

It is true that regional relative price rigidity in European countries must to a large extent reflect national wage bargaining. But the – quite striking – evidence given by the authors that relative price rigidity is roughly the same across core ERM countries as across regions within these countries (Tables 3 to 6) should make those who believe that relative price flexibility will play an important role within the EMU think again.

One may also argue that, in the brand new EMU world, workers will understand the new rules of the game, and wage flexibility will prevail. The argument is not implausible a priori. But, from Reagan to Thatcher to Trichet, the evidence is that changes in regime rarely lead to dramatic changes in wage flexibility.

The role and limits of fiscal transfers

This leaves fiscal transfers. Ever since the Werner Report, there has been much emphasis on the need for fiscal transfers within a European monetary union. Obstfeld and Peri make it clear that fiscal transfers are a double-edged sword. If shocks are transitory, no action on the part of firms and workers is needed, and transfers that cushion the fall in personal income are fine. If shocks are permanent, however, transfers stand squarely in the way of adjustment. They slow down and may even stop the required adjustment of prices and factors. And the more they do so, the slower the adjustment, the larger and the longer the transfers. The distinction between redistribution and stabilization can become fuzzy. In the limit, where transfers fully protect disposable income, stabilization simply leads to larger and larger redistribution.

Based on the experience with Structural Funds, Obstfeld and Peri worry that EMU is going to create a monster, a transfer machine that will soon overwhelm European public finances. They go on to indicate ways in which to limit the growth of such a system. Issuing GDP-linked bonds is a good idea, and one that should be explored further. But I suspect that Obstfeld and Peri worry about an unlikely danger. It is true that much of the money spent at this point on Structural Funds is wasted. But this, I believe, is largely possible because voters have not caught up to it. If, as I hope, the European budget becomes subject to sharper voter scrutiny, the political economy of European integration will force transfers to remain limited in scope and size: the generosity of the French for the Portuguese or the Greek is surely much smaller than that of the Parisians for their less fortunate compatriots.

To state the obvious: There may be many reasons to favour EMU, some of them purely political, some of them microeconomic. It may lead to a new and more efficient Europe. But from a macroeconomic point of view, research to date suggests that EMU carries very serious risks. The best forecast is that individual EMU countries will go through long periods of recession or overheating, with few tools to affect the outcome.

Antonio Fatás

INSEAD

Within a currency area, adjustment to asymmetric shocks must take place through changes in relative prices rather than exchange rates. When prices and wages are not sufficiently flexible, asymmetric shocks might lead to regional recessions and persistent differences in regional unemployment rates. If the labour force is mobile, workers will migrate to booming regions, making the adjustment less costly (at least in terms of unemployment). In the absence of migration, interregional fiscal transfers can help smooth the negative effects of these shocks.

Obstfeld and Peri study these various adjustment mechanisms using regional data from a sample of European countries, the USA and Canada. The paper nicely integrates previous results in the literature with new evidence to understand the likely consequences of asymmetric shocks in the future European Monetary Union.

I will comment separately on the findings of the authors for each of the adjustment mechanisms before I review the lessons for EMU.

Adjustment through migration

It is difficult to disagree with the conclusion that migration will play only a limited role in the adjustment to asymmetric shocks under EMU. The results from the VAR analysis show that there is little migration (in the first years) in response to asymmetric shocks within European countries. International migration in EMU will surely be even lower as culture and language impose additional barriers to migration. The comparison with the USA illustrates how a mobile labour force can help the functioning of a currency area. I have, however, two small caveats about these results. In most European countries, there are persistent differences in regional unemployment rates and, in cases such as Italy, these differences have increased over time. What does this say about migration and asymmetric shocks? These differences can be the result (as the authors argue) of regional shocks causing persistent differences in unemployment rates because of insufficient migration, or of diverging upward trends in regional unemployment rates.[29] The econometric work does not allow us to distinguish between these two hypotheses. Furthermore, one has to be careful about the long-term responses produced by the VAR analysis. Because of the econometric specification and the short time series, there is a lot of uncertainty about the long-term effects of shocks.

---

[29] As a result, if one wants to study the persistence of unemployment rates, allowing for different regional trends (as the procedure of Decressin and Fatás (1995) does) produces less persistence than restricting the trend in the unemployment rate to be the same for all regions (as this paper does).

Adjustment through prices

The paper adds new results to the known fact that relative regional prices tend to fluctuate less than relative international prices. The authors admit the difficulties associated with interpreting their results because the volatility of relative regional prices is an endogenous variable. I would like to add one more caveat to their list. Under fixed but adjustable exchange rates, real exchange rate variability might be the result of infrequent and large nominal exchange rate realignments. Indeed, some of the European countries in their sample that show a very high variability relative to Germany are countries that belonged to the ERM system and went through several large realignments. In the ERM, countries with higher inflation experienced real exchange rate appreciations until a crisis took place with the associated large real depreciation. This is totally unrelated to asymmetric shocks and relative price adjustment. The fact that Greece, which never belonged to the ERM and saw its exchange rate constantly depreciate because of higher inflation, has a low real exchange rate variability supports this explanation.

Adjustment through fiscal transfers

The authors present new evidence about the size and timing of fiscal transfers in response to fluctuations, using regional data from Italy, Canada and the USA. Their results are, in most cases, in agreement with previous estimates. Their dynamic estimation shows that transfers are very persistent and, as a result, the distinction between stabilization and insurance is very difficult to establish. Moreover, the persistence of transfers raises serious questions about the moral hazard effects of those transfers. Although it is hard to find definite empirical evidence in this direction, the evidence presented suggests that fiscal transfers to regions with low income per capita have perverse effects. Because of these difficulties, the authors present an interesting suggestion, to create a system where governments issue debt denominated in euros indexed to nominal per-capita GDP growth. If the arguments in favour of the creation of a fiscal federation are based on risk sharing, this proposal, or a variant of it, should be seriously considered.

It is also interesting to see from the results for the Italian federation that the system of transfers plays only a small stabilizing role. A tentative conclusion from these estimates could be that the true benefits of the current national systems are related more to the cohesion that results from redistribution than to their insurance benefits. Or, alternatively, one could say that the current systems are responsive more to larger shocks (e.g., German unification) than to small year-to-year changes in relative income. Because of their long-term nature, some of these issues go beyond the debate on exchange rates and the adoption of a single currency.

What do we learn about regional adjustment in EMU?

A possible reading of the above results is that, given the rigidity of prices, the lack of labour mobility and the absence of a European system of fiscal transfers, EMU members are not well equipped to deal with asymmetric shocks. There is, however, a more optimistic reading. First, I have doubts about the very favourable picture portrayed by the authors about the benefits of exchange rate policy. When thinking about the implications of EMU, one has to take into consideration the way in which European countries (both ERM and non-ERM members) have dealt with asymmetric shocks in the past. I do not think that there is enough empirical evidence to support the claim that changes in nominal exchange rates have offset asymmetric shocks and allowed a quick adjustment to the new equilibrium. Second, all the evidence presented in this paper relates to regional adjustment within European countries. If the negative conclusion about the possible effects of asymmetric shocks under EMU is true, a puzzle remains. Given that Germany, Italy and France are currency areas with rigid prices and wages and little labour mobility, why is it that they have survived the presence of asymmetric shocks? One could argue that asymmetric shocks are more prevalent at the national than at the regional level. This paper does not address this issue, but recent results in the literature on optimum currency areas do not seem to support this claim. Furthermore, we might observe fewer asymmetries under EMU at the national level as a result of deeper trade integration and co-ordination of economic policies. An alternative explanation of the puzzle is that the national systems of fiscal transfers have provided enough support to regions going through recessions. Given the results presented in this paper, this answer is not fully convincing, as the stabilization provided by national systems seems to be small (especially in the case of Italy). Furthermore, some of the results suggest that the benefits are coming not from stabilization *per se*, but from the fact that the fiscal systems provide redistribution and, perhaps, transfers responding to large and infrequent shocks (not captured by annual changes in regional GDP or income). Such transfers provide the political cohesion needed for the currency area to be successful. Indeed, this view is supported by the fact that current debates on fiscal transfers, at both the national and the European level, rarely discuss risk-sharing arrangements. Finally, as argued in the paper, the economic benefits of some of these transfers are reduced, or even outweighed, by the perverse moral hazard effects that they cause in the receiving regions.

To conclude, the results presented in this paper are certainly bad news for the ability of European regions to adjust to asymmetric shocks through labour mobility and relative price changes. However, they might also be considered less bad news for EMU. A more positive view emerges if one reads the paper as showing that existing currency areas (countries) formed by European regions are sustainable even though regional prices are not flexible, interregional labour mobility is practically absent and fiscal transfers stabilize asymmetric fluctuations only to a limited extent.

General discussion

Georges de Ménil argued that labour immobility in Europe may be due, in part, to the manner in which unemployment benefits are administered. Having to report to the local agency for claiming benefits, for instance, made it more difficult for unemployed workers to search for jobs in other jurisdictions.

Hans Genberg pointed out that regional policies and interregional transfers in Europe tend to increase the persistence of unemployment. In Sweden, transfers to northern regions certainly prevented adjustment in the labour market. Further, adjustment to shocks might occur not only through the movement of labour, but also through capital mobility. When regions were hit by asymmetric shocks, local governments often changed taxes on capital in order to attract firms.

Axel Weber felt the analysis had imposed considerable restrictions on some related variables: namely, employment levels, the size of the labour force and migration. It would be useful in this context to carry out a sensitivity analysis. Furthermore, the historical lessons of German unification could be usefully incorporated when studying the effects of a currency union. In particular, the last seven years since German unification can provide information on how monetary union affects migratory flows and the adjustments in labour markets.

Charles Wyplosz stressed the desirability of transfers in some circumstances. Countercyclical fiscal policy might be needed to correct temporary shocks even when the negative incentive effects are costly in terms of slowing down the adjustment process. Olivier Blanchard reiterated that in the face of persistent shocks – say, if a country becomes uncompetitive – such fiscal intervention may interfere with the necessary wage–price adjustment.

Jürgen von Hagen pointed out that the analysis had missed the intricacies of the Canadian transfer system. The Canadian transfer scheme guaranteed the average tax revenue level of medium provinces in the poor provinces. Hence, whatever their tax revenue was, the five poorest provinces obtained a fully stabilizing transfer. The five medium provinces that were used to calculate the average received transfers or made net payments depending on whether they were above or below this average. Finally, the three richest provinces never received a transfer, but paid taxes to finance the transfer to the poor provinces. Von Hagen also stressed that the advantages and disadvantages of simple versus beta differences could not be determined without a theoretical model of the sources and the nature of regional shocks. He laid out a simple model of regional labour market shocks in which, depending on the size of the region-specific shock, beta differences would yield exactly the information that Obstfeld and Peri were looking for.

Carlo Favero wanted to know why, within each country, only a single common stochastic trend drives the data. The technical reason for doing so was obviously to allow pooling of different regions. However, looking, for instance, at the Italian data showed that there were two common trends which could change the results significantly.

APPENDIX. DATA

All data are at the annual frequency.

A1. Italy

The regional division adopted for Italy is the standard classification into *regioni* adopted by the Italian government and the EU. This definition divides the Italian territory into twenty regions: Piemonte, Valle d'Aosta, Lombardia, Trentino, Veneto, Friuli, Liguria, Emilia, Toscana, Umbria, Lazio, Marche, Abruzzo, Molise, Campania, Puglia, Basilicata, Calabria, Sicilia and Sardegna. We have divided the region 'Trentino' into its two provinces (Trento and Bolzano), given that the province of Bolzano, being a bilingual province (*provincia autonoma*), enjoys somewhat greater autonomy.

Labour markets. The regional data on employment, unemployment, total population, and population of working age for the period 1969–95 were collected from the Italian statistical yearbooks (ISTAT, *Annuario Statistico Italiano*, yearly issues), from ISTAT, *Bollettino Mensile di Statistica*, various issues, and from ISTAT, *Annuali di Statistiche del Lavoro*, yearly issues. Data on CIG, available only for the period 1984–94, were collected from ISTAT, *Annuario Statistico Italiano*.

Prices and GDP. Data on regional prices are the GDP deflators reported in *Annuario Statistico Italiano* (1969–95). Data on regional GDP (1977–92) were collected from the ISTAT publication *Le Regioni in Cifre* (1994).

Social insurance. Data on transfers to persons and on contributions to the social insurance system are taken from the *Annuario Statistico*. For the period 1977–94, the variable is defined as the value in billions of 1991 lire of the *contributi e prestazioni degli enti previdenziali*, covering all social welfare spending (pensions, unemployment insurance, health care). The definition of the variable 'net transfers' is the value (in million 1991 lire per capita) of the transfers received by a region for social insurance minus the contributions paid by the region to the central government.

A2. Germany

The regional unit for the analysis of German data is the *Land*. As we have considered only the western *Länder*, our analysis includes the following eleven regions: Schleswig-Holstein, Hamburg, Niedersachsen, Bremen, Nordrhein-Westfalen, Hessen, Rheinland-Pfalz, Baden-Württemberg, Bayern, Saarland and West Berlin.

Labour market. Data on employment and unemployment over 1970–94 for each *Land* were collected from the *Bundesanstalt für Arbeit*, data on working-age population (1970–93) come from the *Statistisches Jahrbuch*, various issues, and from the *Statistisches Bundesamt*.

Prices and GDP. GDP deflators and nominal GDP at the *Land* level for 1970–94 were provided by the Finanzamt Baden-Württemberg. Total population data also come from this source.

Fiscal variables. The data on total direct and indirect taxes collected by the federal government in each *Land* are from the *Statistisches Jahrbuch*, various issues. The data on net transfers occurring across *Länder* under the *Länderfinanzausgleich* (LFA or 'round of tax redistribution') are used to calculate the net tax 'payments' from each *Land* to the federal government. In particular, we subtracted from the taxes any net amount that the *Land* receives from other *Länder* during the LFA, while we add any negative amount. These data were taken from the *Statistisches Bundesamt*, various issues.

A3. Canada

The ten provinces constituting the Canadian Federation are the geographical units of our regional analysis. They are: Newfoundland, Prince Edward Island, Nova Scotia, New Brunswick, Quebec, Ontario, Manitoba, Saskatchewan, Alberta and British Columbia.

All data for the Canadian provinces as well as for the entire country were obtained from the 'Cansim' data base at the following world wide web address: http://www.statcan.ca/cpi-bin/Cansim.

Labour market. Data on employment and the labour force were taken from the directory Socio-Economic Statistics. We used the yearly series for total population, 'population older than 15', 'labour force older than 15' and 'employment older than 15'. These series are available for 1976–96 for each province and for the country as a whole.

Prices and personal income. Data on prices are the yearly implicit GDP deflator for each province, available for 1971–96. The data on personal income for the period 1971–96 were also purchased from the 'Cansim' website. Tamim Bayoumi and Paul Masson kindly made available to us the data set that they used in their 1995 paper. Data on personal income, personal transfers, taxes and federal grants to local government are available in this data set for the period 1965–85. For a more detailed description of these data, see the data appendix of Bayoumi and Masson (1995).

Fiscal variables. Total federal taxes for each province have been calculated as the total of direct federal taxes from persons. The total federal transfers are the sum of the transfer payments to persons and to local government. These, valued in thousands of 1991 Canadian dollars per capita, have been used to calculate the 'net transfers' to a province as the difference between the transfers received from the federal government and the taxes paid.

A4. United Kingdom

The eight regions into which England is divided plus Wales, Scotland and Northern Ireland are the geographical regional units considered for the UK. The following is the complete list: South East, East Anglia, South West, West Midlands, East Midlands, Yorks and Humberside, North West, North, Wales, Scotland and Northern Ireland.

Labour market. Data on employment, unemployment and working-age population for each region for the period 1969–94 come from the *Yearly Statistical Abstract* (yearly issues) and from the *Employment Gazette* (various issues) and *Historical Supplement of the Employment Gazette* (various issues), Department for Education and Employment, London.

A5. United States

The geographical regional units for the analysis of US labour markets are the 50 states plus the District of Columbia.

Labour market. Data on employment, unemployment and working-age population for the period 1976–90 have been taken from the data set used by Olivier Blanchard and Larry Katz in their 1992 paper. We thank them for providing these data, which we have updated for 1991–5 using information from the Geographic Profile Data Set.

Personal income and transfers. Total taxes paid to the federal government are defined as the sum of personal taxes and social insurance payments. Total transfers from the federal government are the sum of personal transfers and transfers to local governments. The data on personal income, taxes and transfers for the period 1969–85 were taken from the data set provided by Tamim Bayoumi and Paul Masson. For a more detailed description of these data, see the appendix to Bayoumi and Masson (1995).

A6. International GDP deflator and exchange rate data

Year-average figures from OECD, *Fiscal Positions and Business Cycles on Diskette, 77/1.* European cross rates were derived from dollar exchange rates using triangular arbitrage.

REFERENCES

Asdrubali, P., B.E. Sørensen and O. Yosha (1996). 'Channels of interstate risk sharing: United States 1963–1990', *Quarterly Journal of Economics.*

Atkeson, A. and T. Bayoumi (1993). 'Do private capital markets insure regional risk? Evidence from the United States and Europe', *Open Economies Review.*

Attanasio, O.P. and F. Padoa Schioppa (1991). 'Regional inequalities, migration and mismatch in Italy, 1960–86', in F. Padoa Schioppa (ed.), *Mismatch and Labour Mobility*, Cambridge University Press, Cambridge.

Bayoumi, T. and B. Eichengreen (1996). 'Operationalizing the theory of optimum currency areas', CEPR Discussion Paper no. 1484.

Bayoumi, T. and P.R. Masson (1995). 'Fiscal flows in the United States and Canada: lessons for monetary union in Europe', *European Economic Review.*

Bertola, G. and A. Ichino (1995). 'Crossing the river', *Economic Policy.*

Blanchard, O.J. and L.F. Katz (1992). 'Regional evolutions', *Brookings Papers on Economic Activity.*

Boadway, R.W. and P.A.R. Hobson (1993). *Intergovernmental Fiscal Relations in Canada*, Canadian Tax Foundation/L'Association Canadienne d'Études Fiscales.

Buiter, W., G. Corsetti and N. Roubini (1993). 'Excessive deficits: sense and nonsense in the Treaty of Maastricht', *Economic Policy.*

Commission of the European Communities (1977). 'Report of the Study Group on the Role of Public Finance in European Integration', Economic and Financial Series no. A13, Brussels (April).

Corden, W.M. (1972). 'Monetary integration', Princeton Essays in International Finance no. 93.

Costello, D. (1993). 'The redistributive effects of interregional transfers: a comparison of the European Community and Germany', *European Economy, Reports and Studies.*

Courchene, T.J. (1993). 'Reflections on Canadian federalism: are there implications for the European economic and monetary union?', *European Economy, Reports and Studies.*

Davis, S.J., P. Loungani and R. Mahidhara (1997). 'Regional labor fluctuations: oil shocks, military spending, and other driving forces', International Finance Discussion Paper no. 578, Board of Governors of the Federal Reserve System.

Debelle, G. and O. Lamont (1997). 'Relative price variability and inflation: evidence from US cities', *Journal of Political Economy*.

Decressin, J. and A. Fatás (1995). 'Regional labour market dynamics in Europe', *European Economic Review*.

De Grauwe, P. and W. Vanhaverbeke (1993). 'Is Europe an optimum currency area? Evidence from regional data', in P.R. Masson and M.P. Taylor (eds.), *Policy Issues in the Operation of Currency Unions*, Cambridge University Press, Cambridge.

Eichengreen, B. (1990). 'One money for Europe? Lessons from the US currency union', *Economic Policy*.

—— (1991). 'Is Europe an optimum currency area?', NBER Working Paper no. 3579.

—— (1992). 'Comment', *Brookings Papers on Economic Activity*.

—— (1993a). 'Labor markets and European monetary unification', in P.R. Masson and M.P. Taylor (eds.), *Policy Issues in the Operation of Currency Unions*, Cambridge University Press, Cambridge.

—— (1993b). 'European monetary unification', *Journal of Economic Literature*.

Emerson, M. *et al.* (1992). *One Market, One Money: An Evaluation of the Potential Benefits and Costs of Forming an Economic and Monetary Union*, Oxford University Press, Oxford.

Engel, C. and J.H. Rogers (1995). 'Regional patterns in the law of one price: the roles of geography vs currencies', NBER Working Paper no. 5395.

Eurostat (various years). *Regional Statistical Handbook*.

Forni, M. and L. Reichlin (1997). 'National forces and local economies: Europe and the United States', CEPR Discussion Paper no. 1632.

Goodhart, C.A.E. and S. Smith (1993). 'Stabilization', *European Economy, Reports and Studies*.

Green, D.A. and W.C. Riddell (1997). 'Qualifying for unemployment insurance: an empirical analysis', *Economic Journal*.

Hinshaw, R. (1951). 'Currency appreciation as an anti-inflationary device', *Quarterly Journal of Economics*.

Hughes, G. and B. McCormick (1987). 'Housing markets, unemployment and labour market flexibility', *European Economic Review*.

Ingram, J.C. (1959). 'State and regional payments mechanisms', *Quarterly Journal of Economics*.

—— (1973). 'The case for European monetary integration', Princeton Essays in International Finance no. 98.

Kenen, P.B. (1995). *Economic and Monetary Union in Europe: Moving beyond Maastricht*, Cambridge University Press, Cambridge.

Krugman, P. (1993). 'Lessons of Massachusetts for EMU', in F. Torres and F. Giavazzi (eds.), *Adjustment and Growth in the European Monetary Union*, Cambridge University Press, Cambridge.

Lindbeck, A. (1995). 'Hazardous welfare-state dynamics', *American Economic Review, Papers and Proceedings*.

McCormick, B. (1997). 'Regional unemployment and labour mobility in the UK', *European Economic Review*.

McKinnon, R.I. (1963). 'Optimum currency areas', *American Economic Review*.

—— (1997). 'Market-preserving fiscal federalism in the American monetary union', in M.I. Blejer and T. Ter-Minassian (eds.), *Macroeconomic Dimensions of Public Finance: Essays in Honour of Vito Tanzi*, Routledge, London.

Masson, P.R. and M.P. Taylor (1993). 'Currency unions: a survey of the issues', in P.R. Masson and M.P. Taylor (eds.), *Policy Issues in the Operation of Currency Unions*, Cambridge University Press, Cambridge.

Mélitz, J. and F. Zumer (1997). 'Regional redistribution and stabilization by the center in Canada, France, the UK and the US', mimeo., CREST-INSEE and OFCE.

Nickell, S. (1997). 'Unemployment and labor market rigidities: Europe versus North America', *Journal of Economic Perspectives*.

Obstfeld, M. (1998). 'Open-economy macroeconomics: developments in theory and policy', *Scandinavian Journal of Economics*.

OECD (1990). *Employment Outlook*, Paris.

Oswald, A. (1996). 'A conjecture on the explanation for high unemployment in industrialised nations: part I', mimeo., University of Warwick.

Peri, G. (1997). 'Do civic spirit and economic diversity help growth? Evidence from Italian cities and provinces, 1961–1991', mimeo., University of California, Berkeley.

Persson, T. and G. Tabellini (1996). 'Federal fiscal constitutions: risk sharing and redistribution', *Journal of Political Economy*.

Pisani-Ferry, J., A. Italianer and R. Lescure (1993). 'Stabilization properties of budgetary systems: a simulation analysis', *European Economy, Reports and Studies*.

Poloz, S. (1990). 'Real exchange rate adjustment between regions in a common currency area', mimeo., Bank of Canada.

Sala-i-Martín, X. and J. Sachs (1992). 'Fiscal federalism and optimum currency areas: evidence for Europe from the United States', in M.B. Canzoneri, V. Grilli and P.R. Masson (eds.), *Establishing a Central Bank: Issues in Europe and Lessons from the US*, Cambridge University Press, Cambridge.

Shiller, R.J. (1993). *Macro Markets: Creating Institutions for Managing Society's Largest Economic Risks*, Oxford University Press, Oxford.

Sørensen, B.E. and O. Yosha (1996). 'International risk sharing and European monetary unification', Foerder Institute Working Paper no. 40–96, Tel Aviv University.

Steinherr, A. (ed.) (1994). *30 Years of European Monetary Integration from the Werner Plan to EMU*, Longman, Harlow.

van der Ploeg, F. (1991). 'Macroeconomic policy coordination issues during the various phases of economic and monetary integration in Europe', *European Economy*, Special Edition no. 1.

van Rompuy, P., F. Abraham and D. Heremans (1991). 'Economic federalism and the EMU', *European Economy*, Special Edition no. 1.

Vaubel, R. (1976). 'Real exchange-rate changes in the European Community: the empirical evidence and its implications for European currency unification', *Weltwirtschaftliches Archiv*.

——— (1978). 'Real exchange-rate changes in the European Community: a new approach to the determination of optimum currency areas', *Journal of International Economics*.

Viñals, J. and J.F. Jimeno (1996). 'Monetary union and European unemployment', Banco de España, Servicio de Estudios, Documento de Trabajo no. 9624.

von Hagen, J. (1992). 'Fiscal arrangements in a monetary union: evidence from the US', in D.E. Fair and C. de Boissieu (eds.), *Fiscal Policy, Taxes, and the Financial System in an Increasingly Integrated Europe*, Kluwer, Dordrecht.

——— (1993). 'Monetary union and fiscal union: a perspective from fiscal federalism', in P.R. Masson and M.P. Taylor (eds.), *Policy Issues in the Operation of Currency Unions*, Cambridge University Press, Cambridge.

——— and B. Eichengreen (1996). 'Federalism, fiscal constraints, and European monetary union', *American Economic Review, Papers and Proceedings*.

von Hagen, J. and G.W. Hammond (1997). 'Insurance against asymmetric shocks in a European monetary union', in J.-O. Hairault, P.-Y. Hénin and F. Portier (eds.), *Business Cycles and Macroeconomic Stability: Should We Rebuild Built-in Stabilizers?*, Kluwer, Dordrecht.

von Hagen, J. and M.J.M. Neumann (1994). 'Real exchange rates within and between currency areas: how far away is EMU?', *Review of Economics and Statistics*.

Weber, A. (1997). 'Sources of purchasing power parity disparities: Europe versus the United States', mimeo., University of Bonn.

Wyplosz, C. (1991). 'Monetary union and fiscal policy discipline', *European Economy*, Special Edition no. 1.

Large banknotes

Will the euro go underground?

SUMMARY

Developing countries may hold as much as 25–30% of the $1.3 trillion OECD currency supply. Although dollar holdings appear to exceed DM holdings by a factor of four, the advent of the euro may change this balance. Indeed, by issuing large-denomination notes of 100, 200 and 500, the European Central Bank appears to be well poised to challenge the dominance of the ubiquitous US $100 note. However, large-denomination notes are also extremely popular in the OECD underground economy, which appears to hold at least 50% of the currency supply. As a result, the seigniorage revenues obtained by issuing large-denomination notes may be an accounting illusion, substantially or fully offset by losses due to increased tax evasion. Hence, the new European Central Bank may wish to consider policies that discourage underground use of currency, even at the expense of losing out on foreign demand.

— Kenneth Rogoff

Blessing or curse? Foreign and underground demand for euro notes

Kenneth Rogoff

Princeton University

1. INTRODUCTION

There has been much discussion of whether the introduction of the euro will diminish the global dominance of the dollar in trade invoicing and in global bond portfolios. But there has been surprisingly little discussion of whether the euro will help Europe capture a larger share of another dollar-dominated market: the global market for a safe, reliable vehicle currency. Dollars are in wide use in Latin America (especially Argentina, where official shipments of dollar notes during the 1990s have exceeded $40 billion) and in the former Soviet bloc (especially Russia, where official shipments during the 1990s have exceeded $60 billion). Dollar currency is also dominant in the Middle East (where dollars are typically used to pay guest workers), in parts of Asia and, of course, in the global illegal drugs trade.

On paper, the euro should be an extremely attractive alternative to the dollar. The combined nations of the European Union (EU) are slightly larger than the USA both in terms of gross domestic product (GDP) and in population. Europe is closer geographically to the profitable currency markets of the former Soviet bloc and the Middle East. If the new European Central Bank proves to be as inflation

The author is grateful to his discussants, the responsible managing editor, Klaus F. Zimmermann, and other members of the Economic Policy Panel (especially Rudiger Dornbusch) for helpful comments on earlier drafts. The author received research support from National Science Foundation grant SBR-9709083, and research assistance from Andrew Tiffin and Giovanni Olivei.

averse as its designers intend, the euro inflation rate should be at least as low as that of the dollar. The new euro notes are to be printed using sophisticated modern techniques aimed at discouraging counterfeiting. Last, but not least, the euro is to be issued in large denominations, including 100, 200 and 500 euro notes ($110, $220 and $550 at a dollar/ecu exchange rate of 1.10). Given the apparently overwhelming preference of foreign and underground users for large-denomination bills, the European Monetary Institute's decision to issue large notes constitutes an aggressive step towards grabbing a large share of developing country demand for safe foreign currencies, which we estimate here to be in the range of $300–400 billion.

Is this a game Europe should want to play? Is this a business in which the USA should seek to preserve its dominance? This paper looks at some of the evidence on world currency demand, and points out some of the policy issues facing monetary authorities in the USA, Europe and Japan. A major question is whether, in attempting to exploit the global demand for large-denomination euro notes, Europe will be facilitating tax evasion and illegal activities at home. If so, the indirect revenue costs of having large quantities of high-denomination notes in circulation might outweigh the seigniorage benefits.

The next section of the paper assesses the murky empirical evidence on who holds the world's currency supply. Legal transactions appear to account for only a small portion of total currency holdings in most countries, but it is difficult to divide the remainder decisively into domestic underground and foreign demand. This is especially the case for the USA, Germany, Japan and Switzerland. We reject the recent assertion by Sprenkle (1993) that up to 80% of all OECD currency is held outside the OECD. Quite the contrary, the evidence suggests that a very large fraction of the OECD currency supply is held domestically, in the OECD underground economy. One of the many pieces of evidence consistent with this hypothesis is the fact that tax levels appear to have a significant positive effect on currency demand. The remaining sections discuss the main policy questions that arise due to currency's mixed usages. What policies might discourage the use of currency in the underground economy without interfering with its value in the legal economy? And if such policies are successful, will they lead to precarious deflation of central banks' balance sheets, weakening their independence and their potential to serve as lenders of last resort? Is it possible that currency's role in helping to shield the underground economy from tax and regulatory authorities is actually helping to provide an essential safety valve? The concluding section summarizes the paper's main findings, and offers some tentative policy conclusions.

Appendices A and B extend the standard transactions-based intertemporal model of money demand to allow for the possibility that high cash balances might help facilitate tax evasion, and illustrate the economics of phasing out large-denomination notes. The resulting model turns out to yield similar positive conclusions to conventional models that ignore the predominance of the underground economy. Not surprisingly, however, it offers a very different perspective on the net revenue gains from seigniorage and on classic normative questions such as the optimal rate of inflation.

2. EXTERNAL AND UNDERGROUND DEMAND FOR OECD CURRENCIES

To try to understand the potential external and underground demand for the euro, it is helpful to begin by looking at the sources of demand for today's most popular international currencies. The conventional wisdom among central bankers is that the only currencies held abroad in significant quantities are the US dollar, the DM, the yen and the Swiss franc. (For example, Boeschoten (1992) estimates that less than 1% of Dutch currency is circulating abroad.) Of course, there are no hard figures on foreign holdings for any of these currencies. Indeed, except for a small number of consumer surveys, there are no hard numbers on domestic sources of demand, either. True, the central banks know exactly how much currency they have issued, subject to the minor complication that a small, unknown percentage of the currency supply has been lost or destroyed. (We ignore the implications of counterfeiting.) Each central bank also has reasonably hard data on the currency holdings of its domestic banks. While business transactions holdings are more difficult to measure, most estimates suggest that these account for only a very small percentage of total currency holdings; businesses are relatively efficient at cash management. Nor are the holdings of the general public very large, at least according to the limited survey evidence available. The bulk of the OECD currency supply – as we shall see, perhaps 70–80% – must therefore be held either by the domestic underground economy or by developing countries. Unfortunately, it is very difficult to ascertain how much to ascribe to each group. To illustrate the problems, we look first at the case of the USA, which supplies what is almost certainly the world's most widely held currency.

2.1. What can we infer about foreign demand for US dollars?

The supply of US currency outside banks is $390 billion (8/96). Divided by a population of 263 million, this implies that there is $1481 in US currency circulating for every man, woman and child in the USA. Put differently, the currency supply is almost $6000 per four-person family. A survey commissioned by the Federal Reserve Board suggested that, as of 1986, cash holdings by individuals accounted for only 11–12% of the total currency supply. A similar survey in 1995 indicated that this share had dropped to 5%, or $20 billion: that is, roughly $300 per four-person family. (See Avery et al., 1987; Porter and Judson, 1996a.) Business holdings do not appear to account for much of the currency supply, either. Sumner (1990) estimates business holdings to be only $5 billion, while Porter and Judson arrive at a similar estimate and argue that $23 billion would be an upper bound.[1] Thus $350 billion of currency held outside banks is unaccounted for. A small part of this might be explained by systematic underreporting of household holdings in the surveys (though a survey carried out by the Dutch central bank arrived at a similar 10% figure for households' share of total currency holdings: see Boeschoten and Fase (1992)). Some small portion of the currency stock may have been destroyed. Otherwise it seems hard to explain how there can be 96 $1 bills and $280 in coin for every four-person family. But these qualifications do not substantially mitigate the basic puzzle.

Figure 1 divides the US currency supply into two components, $100 bills (the largest denomination now issued) and all other denominations, with both expressed as a ratio to GDP. Overall, despite a decade and a half of rapid financial innovation, the ratio of total currency to GDP has actually risen from 4% in 1981 to 5.3% in 1995. At the same time, $100 bills now account for over 60% of the total value of the currency supply, up from 39% in 1980. A good part of this rise may be explained by inflation (the CPI, the Consumer Price Index, over this period rose 85%), but the large share of $100 bills is still remarkable given that they are used only rarely in non-underground US domestic transactions. According to the 1995

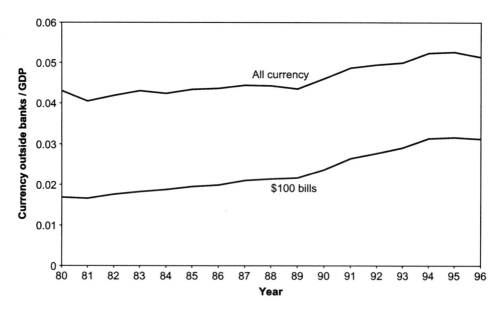

Figure 1. US currency/GDP

Source: US Treasury Department.

[1]If the roughly 3 million retail establishments in the USA each held $200 in cash for giving change, this would account for only $6 billion. If all sales were for cash, then adding one day's worth of consumption would bring the total to over $20 billion, but this is clearly an overestimate, since many transactions are by check or credit card.

Fed survey cited above, consumers average less than one-quarter of a $100 bill per family. But the outstanding stock is closer to $36 per family. The growing, but unexplained, appetite for large-denomination bills has become especially striking during the 1990s, with $100 bills accounting for well over 80% of the total increase in the US currency supply.

Flow data on US currency issuance strongly suggest that a sizeable fraction of all new currency issued in recent years has gone abroad, at least initially. The New York Federal Reserve District, which is the primary supplier of cash to foreign users, has kept records on currency shipments abroad since 1988, by country of destination. These data are still not public, but some characteristics have been published in a *Federal Reserve Bulletin* article by Porter and Judson (1996a). They report that well over $100 billion in currency has been shipped overseas, with roughly half going to Europe (especially Russia and the former Soviet bloc), 30% to the Middle East and the remainder to Latin America. Kamin and Ericsson (1993) report that shipments of US currency to Argentina from all sources appear to have exceeded $30 billion. (There is some debate as to whether Argentina has merely served as a transhipment point, though Kamin and Ericsson show that the rise in dollar holdings is consistent with a concomitant fall in real holdings of Argentinian currency.) Shipments to Russia in 1994 and 1995 alone exceeded $20 billion per year, and the total amount circulating in the former Soviet Union is now thought to exceed $60 billion. These are, of course, only *reported* outflows, and do not take into account either reflows back into the USA (which are believed to be significant) or unreported outflows.

More insight can be gained by looking at where demand for net new currency originates within the USA. Table 1 provides net currency issuance by Federal Reserve District. The table illustrates two key points. First, the New York Federal Reserve District, despite accounting for only 12% of total personal income, accounted for over 80% of net new cash issued for the years 1974–95 inclusive. Since New York appears to be the primary point of origin for foreign shipments, and since there is no reason to believe that domestic currency demand is an order of

Table 1. Share of currency issued nationally by Federal Reserve District, 1974–95

Federal Reserve	Personal income[a] (%)	$100 bills issued (%)	All currency issued (%)
New York	12.1	82.8	80.5
Chicago	12.4	13.8	29.0
Atlanta	11.2	−15.9	−34.8
San Francisco	19.6	−9.1	−13.4
All others	54.3	29.4	38.7
Total	100	100	100

[a] 1989.

Source: Porter and Judson (1996a).

magnitude higher in New York, this evidence supports the view that a considerable fraction of US currency has been shipped abroad. This phenomenon has become even more acute in recent years. Since 1988 the cash office serving New York City has accounted for 97% of net new issuance of $100 bills. Second, the table indicates that the Atlanta and San Francisco Federal Reserve Districts, in contrast to those in the rest of the nation, have had huge net redemptions of currency. Presumably, this is due in no small part to money laundering by the drugs trade, whose locus has been shifting from Miami and Atlanta to California and Texas in recent years.[2] These reflows, as Feige (1996) emphasizes, greatly complicate interpretation of the outflow data. Money shipped to Argentina, for example, may be transported to other destinations and then reshipped to the USA. A second implication of the reflow data is that it is somewhat misleading to cite New York's 80% net share as evidence that domestic underground demand is minor compared to foreign demand. Because the Atlanta and San Francisco Feds have large negative shares, the remaining Federal Reserve Districts (excluding New York, Atlanta and San Francisco) actually account for 68% of net issuance.

The above evidence suggests that foreign purchases of currency account for a substantial portion of net new currency purchases, but it is not sufficient to tell us what percentage of the *stock* of US currency is held abroad. A number of recent studies have attempted to tackle this problem, including Sprenkle (1993), Sumner (1994), Feige (1996) and Porter and Judson (1996a, b), with estimates ranging from 30% to 40% at the low end (Feige) to 79% at the high end (Sprenkle). Porter and Judson, whose point estimate is 60%, adopt perhaps the most comprehensive approach. We review their analysis briefly below, since it also helps illustrate how difficult it is to separate out foreign and domestic underground currency demand.

One method considered by Porter and Judson is to compare the changing seasonal patterns of currency demand in the USA and Canada.[3] During the 1960s, the estimated currency demand seasonals in the two countries were fairly similar, which seems plausible given that they share similar national holidays and school vacations. Also, Canada and the USA have fairly similar economies and financial service sectors, and issue notes in similar denominations (although Canada also issues a $1000 bill that today accounts for more than 8% of its currency supply). In recent years, however, the seasonal in US currency demand appears to have sharply dampened, while the Canadian seasonal has remained fairly stable. The seasonal approach assumes that, in the absence of foreign currency holdings, demand for US currency would mirror demand for Canadian currency.

Assuming (1) no foreign demand for Canadian currency and (2) no seasonal

---

[2] The Dallas Federal Reserve District (included in 'All others') had net redemptions of −3.6% of total currency issuance over this period, although it was a net issuer of $100 bills.
[3] The approach of using the changing seasonal to decompose the components of money demand was suggested by Sumner (1990).

component to the foreign demand for US currency, this implies that an ever-growing share of US currency is held abroad. (Lack of seasonality in foreign currency demand is plausible due to the transactions costs of importing US currency and the fact that a large share of foreign holdings are for hoarding.) Using the seasonal approach, Porter and Judson estimate that the share of US currency held abroad began at 40% in 1960 and rose to 70% by 1995. One difficult technical problem that complicates interpretation of these results is that it is not easy to decompose the changing trends and seasonals across the two countries. A second related approach, which yields similar results, is to take the changing ratio of currency to coin in the two countries (under the assumption that virtually all coins are held domestically).

Approaches that use Canada as a control have drawbacks that may bias the results. For example, it is quite possible that the US dollar has become more popular in the Canadian underground economy since the 1960s, especially given the chronic weakness of the Canadian dollar over the floating rate era. If so, then by treating Canada as a control, one may tend to understate the component of US currency demand that is accounted for by underground demand.

A third approach is the 'biometric method', which takes advantage of the fact that the Federal Reserve maintains separate inflow and outflow data for $100 bills issued before 1990 versus those issued during or after 1990; beginning in 1990, $100 notes began to contain an embedded security thread. The approach assumes that all 'marked' (post-1989) notes issued outside the New York office remain in the domestic pool and all marked notes issued in New York go into the foreign pool. Then, by looking at what share of notes recirculating into the non-New York Fed offices are marked, one can form an estimate of what share of the pre-1990s notes have gone abroad. This approach finds that between 66 and 75% of all $100 bills are in circulation abroad, as are 40−9% of all $50 bills.

Feige (1996) looks at both direct and indirect evidence. His direct evidence consists of confidential Federal Reserve data (of the type underlying the data in Table 1) together with data filed under the Currency and Foreign Transactions Reporting Act. Under this Act, individuals carrying more than $10 000 into or out of the country must file declarations (commonly known as 'CMIRs'). CMIR data for 1994 indicate a $32 billion inflow and a $39 billion outflow. In all likelihood, both figures are understated, especially outflows, since outbound travellers are not required to pass through customs. Regardless, it is clear that reflows of currency into the USA are quite substantial, so one cannot necessarily assume that virgin currency shipped abroad remains there. Feige also considers some indirect methods similar to those employed by Porter and Judson, but obtains somewhat lower estimates than they do for foreign currency holdings. Overall, his evidence appears to suggest an estimate of foreign holdings of US currency in the region of 35%.

The preceding discussion gives some flavour of the difficulties involved in trying to guess the component of the US currency stock that is held abroad. Some of the very characteristics of currency that make it so popular in the underground economy and abroad – portability and concealability – make it very difficult to track. In light of the potential estimation biases discussed above, and in light of evidence presented below on other OECD economies, it would seem that the middle-range estimates – implying that 45–50% of USA currency is held abroad – are more plausible than high-end estimates of 60–75%. This would imply that roughly $200 billion are held by non-residents. As we shall see, such an estimate would still imply a very high underground currency velocity in comparison to most other OECD countries. Even though agents in the USA may well have access to superior transactions technologies,[4] it seems unlikely that US currency velocity is an order of magnitude greater than in other OECD countries.

2.2. Foreign holdings of yen and DM

However difficult it is to ascertain foreign holdings of dollars, even less information is available for estimating foreign holdings of yen and DM. We look first at the yen, simply because its currency supply forms such a large fraction of the OECD total (at current exchange rates).

2.2.1. Yen. Japan, despite having a population only half that of the USA, has a similar total quantity of currency circulating outside banks, ¥41 720 billion (1 August 1996) or $382 billion at the August 1996 yen/dollar exchange rate. Moreover, 89% of the total yen money supply is in the form of the ¥10 000, the largest note (source: *International Financial Statistics* and Bank of Japan (BOJ)). The Bank of Japan (1994), however, claims that only a very small share of the total yen currency supply is circulating abroad. Assuming that roughly half the US currency supply is abroad, this claim implies that Japanese citizens hold four times as much currency per capita as US citizens. Although it is notoriously difficult to explain cross-country differences in currency holdings, several arguments for this differential can be given: (1) Low crime allows Japanese to carry around large amounts of currency without risk. (If cash is used heavily by criminals, the overall effect of crime on currency demand is ambiguous; we revisit this question later.) (2) According to Japanese custom, cash is widely used for presents and in many transactions. (3) Japanese inflation has been very low. (4) Credit cards are relatively unpopular in Japan. (5) Automated transactions machines (ATMs) and financial institutions are extremely densely scattered throughout the country. (6) The BOJ substitutes new bills for old ones at a very high rate, maintaining an exceptionally 'clean' money supply. This facilitates use in ATMs and ticket machines, and enhances general public acceptance. (7) The

[4] Quirk (1996) argues persuasively that large drug traders have become extremely sophisticated in their money-laundering operations, but this is likely to be much less true for small cash businesses.

BOJ claims that Japanese bills are technically more difficult to counterfeit and, because there are only a relatively small number of denominations, the public is quite familiar with all of them. This also makes counterfeiting more difficult.

According to the BOJ, it has not made massive official currency shipments abroad. International migration of the yen appears to occur mainly via outgoing Japanese tourists and businessmen. There are reports of widespread use of the yen in the Soviet Far East (Bank of Japan, 1994), but there is no hard quantitative evidence. Indeed, there is very little quantitative evidence in general on the issue of foreign holdings of yen.

Should one subscribe to the official view that yen currency holdings abroad are negligible? While detailed micro data are not available, there are reasons to be sceptical. As Figure 2 shows, the ratio of currency to GDP has been rising in Japan, from 7.3% in 1980 to 9.7% in 1995, an even sharper increase than for the USA. The currency/GDP ratio has continued to rise in Japan in recent years even as it has been falling in most other OECD countries, as we shall later confirm. If one were to attribute the entire post-1980 rise in Japan's currency/GDP ratio to foreign holdings, this would suggest that close to 25% of all Japanese currency is held abroad, or $80 billion at a yen/dollar exchange rate of 127. (Wilson (1992) similarly suggests that the extraordinary rate of currency growth in Japan may be evidence of significant outflows abroad.) This estimate may be treated as a plausible upper bound. However, in the absence of official currency shipment data or detailed surveys on business and consumer holdings, efforts to account for the whereabouts of the yen currency supply remain highly speculative.

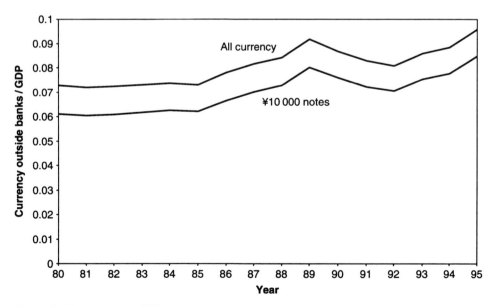

Figure 2. Yen currency/GDP

Source: Bank of Japan.

2.2.2. DM. As Figure 3 shows, Germany has also experienced a rise in its currency/ GDP ratio, from 5.7% in 1980 to 6.9% in 1996, again despite rapid evolution of alternative payment mechanisms. As with the USA, the share of the largest bills (DM500 and 1000) in the total money supply has been steadily rising, from 24% to 44%. (Again, this rise is partly explained by cumulative CPI inflation of 54%, though one might have expected it to fall given the relative advantage of modern payments mechanisms in large transactions.) As of 1 August 1996, the total German currency supply amounted to $1983 per person in value. If all currency outside banks were held by domestic residents, each would have an average of 30 notes including one DM1000 note ($581 at a DM/dollar rate of 1.72). Although cash is somewhat more common in transactions in Germany than in the USA, the idea that a typical family of four is holding nearly $8000 in DM seems rather implausible.

Thanks to an important recent study released by the Bundesbank (Seitz, 1995), a great deal more is now known about foreign holdings of DM than was the case a short while ago. Whereas Seitz does not have access to either the kind of household survey data or the international shipment data available for the USA, he is able to apply many of the various indirect methods of Porter and Judson (1996a, b) and Feige (1996) to the German case. For example, Seitz uses Austria as a control in studying the changing seasonality of DM currency demand, in much the same way that Porter and Judson use Canada as a control for the USA. He also compares trend velocity in Germany and Austria. Finally, Seitz takes advantage of the advent of German reunification as a 'natural experiment', and studies the impact on

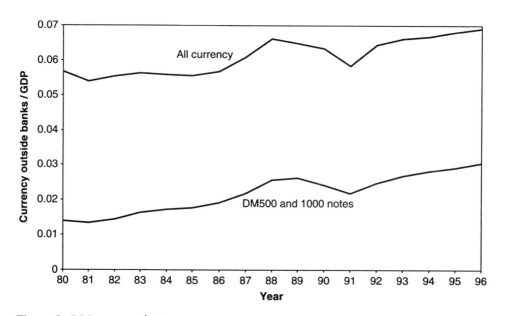

Figure 3. DM currency/GDP

Source: Deutsche Bundesbank.

currency demand. Overall, Seitz concludes that roughly 40% of the German money supply is held abroad, or $56 billion at a DM/dollar exchange rate of 1.72.

2.3. Currency demand across the OECD countries

How different are the experiences of the USA, Japan and Germany from the experiences of other OECD members? Table 2 gives currency outside banks as a percentage of GDP for the various OECD countries. Remarkably, although Japan, Germany and Switzerland have among the highest currency/GDP ratios, the USA is only about average. However, rising international demand for the dollar, DM and yen may help explain why currency velocity has recently been falling in the USA, Germany and Japan, while it has been stable or rising in other OECD countries. Figures 4a and 4b illustrate this phenomenon over the period 1980–95.

Table 3 ranks the OECD countries in terms of currency per capita. As the bottom entry on the table indicates, average currency holdings in the OECD are $1571 per capita ($1293 trillion divided by 823 million people). Suppose that 80% of all OECD currency is indeed co-circulating in developing countries alongside domestic currencies. This would imply that developing countries hold $1034 trillion of

Table 2. Currency[a] to GDP ratio

Country	1995 (%)	1990–5 average (%)
Spain	11.0	10.0
Japan	9.6	8.7
Switzerland	9.1	9.4
Greece	7.2	7.8
Germany	6.9	6.5
Austria	6.1	6.0
Netherlands	5.9	6.4
Portugal[b]	5.8	6.0
Italy	5.5	5.6
Belgium	5.4	5.8
USA	5.3	5.0
Ireland	4.9	4.8
Norway	4.2	4.2
Sweden	4.2	4.5
Australia	4.1	4.0
France	3.4[•]	3.6
UK	3.0	3.0
Canada	3.2	3.2
Denmark	3.2	3.0
Finland	2.3	2.0
New Zealand	1.7	1.5
Iceland	1.1	1.0

[a] Currency outside banks.
[b] 1994.

Sources: International Financial Statistics; central bank bulletins.

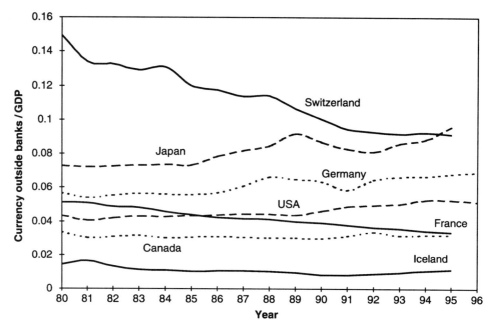

Figure 4a. Currency/GDP

Sources: International Financial Statistics; central bank bulletins.

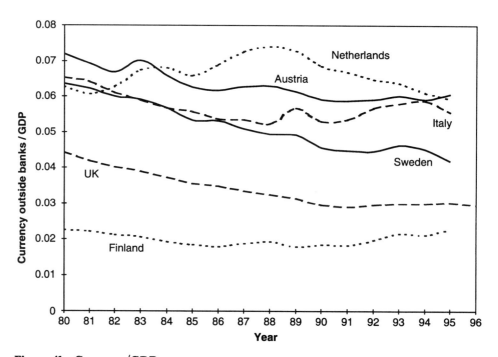

Figure 4b. Currency/GDP

Sources: International Financial Statistics; central bank bulletins.

OECD currency. Dividing this figure by the non-OECD population of 4893 billion people, one would conclude that per-capita holdings of OECD currencies are $211 per person throughout the developing world. It seems utterly implausible that the average four-person family in India and China is holding $844 in hard currency, or that the difference could be made up by vast per-capita holdings in Russia and the Middle East. Even if one assumes that all yen are held in Japan, and that developing countries hold 25% of the remainder, one comes up with an estimate of $184 per four-person family, which still seems unlikely. (Haughton (1995) makes a similar argument.) Thus, the conventional wisdom that only three or four currencies are held in any significant quantity abroad seems quite reasonable. The implication is that for most OECD countries – and therefore for most countries in the European Union – the bulk of the currency supply is held domestically.

Presumably the underground economy is a significant factor in why per-capita OECD currency holdings are so high. Unfortunately, for most OECD countries, there have been fairly few studies aimed at exploring this conjecture. An exception is Boeschoten and Fase (1992), who conclude that internal hoarding explains a large fraction of currency holdings in the Netherlands, particularly of large-denomination notes. They attribute this problem in part to the Netherlands' high tax rates. Indeed, large-denomination notes constitute a large share of the currency supply in most

Table 3. Currency per capita outside banks

Country	US dollars (August 1996)
Switzerland	3584
Japan	3048
Belgium	2059
Germany	1983
Austria	1617
Spain	1544
USA	1481
Netherlands	1468
Norway	1283
Sweden	1114
Italy	1066
Denmark	1030
France	850
Australia	821
Ireland	811
Greece	738
Canada	611
UK	575
Finland	565
Portugal	556
Iceland	281
New Zealand	266
OECD average	**1571**

Source: International Financial Statistics.

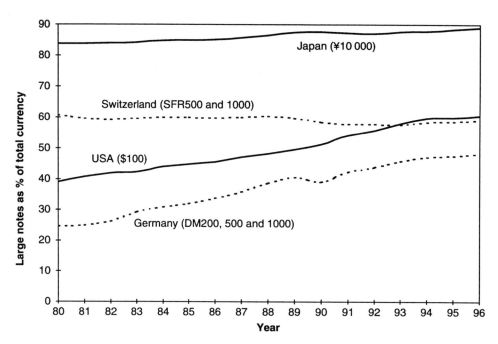

Figure 5a. Share of largest notes in total currency (%)

Source: Central bank bulletins.

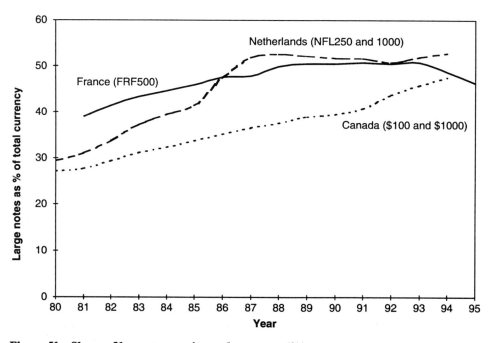

Figure 5b. Share of largest notes in total currency (%)

Source: Central bank bulletins.

countries, as Figures 5a and 5b illustrate. The share of large-denomination notes for France, Switzerland and the Netherlands has been rather flat in recent years, but their levels are still above Germany's. The Swiss franc, of course, is the fourth international currency and, as Figure 5a indicates, a very large share of its total supply is held in large-denomination notes. (There is speculation that many of these notes are held by foreigners in safety deposit boxes in Swiss banks.)

Aside from the high share of large-denomination notes, is there any other evidence consistent with the hypothesis that underground holdings of currency are high throughout most of the OECD? Table 4 looks at the determinants of currency velocity for sixteen OECD countries across annual data for the period 1980–94. The dependent variable is the ratio of nominal GDP to currency (all variables are measured in logs). Consistent with the model of underground currency demand developed in Appendix A, the variables on the right-hand side include the nominal interest rate (an overnight deposit rate) and the ratio of total central government taxes to GDP. Also included is a measure of violent crime based on cross-country United Nations (UN) survey data (see table notes).

Demand equations are notoriously unreliable for any measure of money. Nevertheless, the results are remarkably consistent across countries. The ratio of taxes to GDP, intended as a measure of the incentive to evade taxes, enters with the anticipated negative sign in fourteen of the sixteen countries (in Japan it is negative, but insignificant). (It is well known from the literature on estimating the size of the underground economy that tax levels tend to enter as significant positive variables in currency demand equations: see, for example, Tanzi's (1983) study of the USA.) Crime, on the other hand, enters with a positive (and generally significant) coefficient for fourteen of the sixteen countries. This implies that higher crime rates lower the demand for cash. As we noted earlier, the theoretical effect of a rise in crime on currency demand is ambiguous, since criminals use cash heavily. These results are at least consistent with the view that domestic tax evasion constitutes a major motivation for holding currency.[5] Of course, direct taxes are only one motivation for evading official detection of transactions. Schneider (1997), in his study of the Austrian underground economy, finds that while direct tax burden is by far the biggest influence on the size of the underground economy, other factors such as regulatory complexity have become more important in recent years.

The possibility of large-scale currency hoarding to evade taxes (especially by small businesses) has long been a concern of tax authorities. According to the US Internal Revenue Service, cash skimming, to reduce reported profits and also to avoid sales

---

[5] Cross-country panel velocity regressions on the variables in Table 4 do not appear to yield robust results. Institutional and regulatory differences across countries, not captured in the taxes and crime variables, may be too large. Also, although the UN crime data are intended to be comparable across countries, cross-country differences in reporting standards may nevertheless be significant.

Table 4. Tax levels and crime rates as determinants of currency velocity, 1980–94

Dependent variable: nominal GDP/currency (all variables measured in logs)[a]

Country	Explanatory variables (standard errors in parentheses)		
	Nominal interest rate	Taxes/GDP	Violent crime
Australia	2.91	−1.84	−0.08
	(0.49)	(0.16)	(0.05)
Austria	1.3	−1.16	0.13
	(1.03)	(0.31)	(0.16)
Canada	2.00	−1.28	0.33
	(0.54)	(0.20)	(0.05)
Denmark	1.69	−1.55	0.32
	(1.31)	(0.58)	(0.12)
Finland	1.28	−0.86	0.50
	(0.77)	(0.38)	(0.14)
France	−0.71	−1.82	0.31
	(0.54)	(0.52)	(0.09)
Germany	1.65	−0.76	0.23
	(1.23)	(0.68)	(0.28)
Greece	−0.37	0.35	1.06
	(1.61)	(0.12)	(0.10)
Italy	1.01	−0.32	0.45
	(0.63)	(0.19)	(0.08)
Japan	1.76	0.08	0.72
	(1.09)	(0.11)	(0.09)
Netherlands	0.71	−0.011	0.58
	(1.05)	(0.24)	(0.07)
Norway	0.70	−1.52	0.26
	(0.76)	(0.20)	(0.06)
Sweden	0.78	−0.48	0.48
	(0.53)	−(0.28)	(0.10)
Switzerland	0.35	−0.24	0.27
	(0.52)	(0.09)	(0.05)
UK	1.99	−0.81	−0.40
	(0.39)	(0.19)	(0.06)
USA	2.03	−0.68	0.28
	(0.56)	(0.26)	(0.08)

[a] All regressions are performed allowing for AR(1) serial correlation using Prais–Whinston transformation.

Sources: Annual data. All variables except crime measures are from *International Financial Statistics*. GDP (line 99a; or if not available, GNP line 99b), nominal interest rates are overnight money market rates (line 60b), currency holdings (line 14a) and government revenue (line 81). Violent crime includes intentional homicide, rape, major assault and robbery (theft with threatened or actual physical harm). Annual data are compiled from the Third, Fourth and Fifth *UN Surveys of Crime Trends and Operations of Criminal Justice Systems*, published online by the UN Crime and Justice Information Network at www.ifs.univie.ac.at/uncjin/mosiac/wcs.html.

taxes, is a very large source of revenue loss (see Gutmann, 1983). A zero rate of return may be attractive if, by holding profits in cash for prolonged periods, an agent has a good chance of sheltering income from detection by tax authorities. The same is obviously true of profits on illegal activities. The problem of tax evasion by small businesses appears to be universal. Indeed, one of the major arguments in favour of value added taxes is that they make it easier to force small businesses to absorb a larger share of the total tax burden.

If, indeed, more than half the OECD currency supply is being held domestically in the underground economy, then the velocity of currency circulation in the underground economy must be substantially lower than in the reported economy. Otherwise, underground OECD output would have to be at least as large as reported OECD GDP. This seems implausible, even for countries such as Italy and Sweden where the underground economy appears to be particularly large, approaching 25% of reported GDP (see Schneider, 1997).

2.4. How much OECD currency is held in non-OECD countries?

Based on the evidence considered so far, can we speculate on the likely order of magnitude for non-OECD holdings of OECD currency? Estimates for the DM suggest that roughly $50 billion in DM are held abroad, and it seems plausible that a similar quantity of yen is held outside Japan. A middle-range and plausible estimate for US dollars held abroad is $200 billion. Switzerland has an extraordinarily high currency/GDP ratio, twice the OECD average. However, Switzerland is small so that even if half of Switzerland's currency supply were held abroad, this would account only for another $12 billion. It seems unlikely that foreign shares of the remaining OECD currencies are terribly large, certainly not larger than 10–15%, or another $30–45 billion. Thus, a plausible (if admittedly quite speculative) estimate is that developing countries hold roughly 25–30% of all OECD currency – $300–400 billion – with the US dollar accounting for more than half of the total.

3. SHOULD THE EUROPEAN CENTRAL BANK CATER TO UNDERGROUND AND FOREIGN DEMAND FOR EURO CURRENCY?

At first blush, the large world demand for dollars would seem like a tempting target for promoters of the euro. Today, developing countries appear to hold only about 30% as much in European currencies as they hold in dollars. If the advent of the euro can bring Europe parity, it might imply a one-off shift into euro of $50–100 billion. Over time, as world demand for all hard currencies grew, Europe would enjoy a higher share of the flow of seigniorage revenues as well. Is this something Europe should be courting aggressively? The USA has taken a very active role in promoting, or at least trying to stabilize, foreign demand for its currency. When the new 'counterfeit-proof' $100 bill was introduced in 1996, the

Federal Reserve took pains to send auditors to Russia to reassure their 'clients' that no major change was taking place and that old bills would continue to be honoured.

In one important sense, Europe has already fired the first volley. The European Monetary Institute (EMI) has already announced that euro notes will be issued in denominations including 100, 200 and 500 euro. At a euro/dollar exchange rate of 1.10, these correspond to notes of $110, $220 and $550. Given the evidence that US $100 notes are extremely popular abroad, these large-denomination notes would seem to give Europe an important advantage in competing for the substantial revenues – and perhaps prestige – of the global market for hard currency. $1 million in $100 notes fits in a briefcase; $1 million worth of 500 euro notes could be packed in a purse.

The empirical evidence that we have presented in the preceding section suggests that there may be an important drawback to courting foreign currency demand. The same features that make OECD currencies such as the dollar, mark and yen attractive to foreign underground economies make them attractive to the domestic underground economies as well. If, as we have argued, demand in developing countries accounts for only 25–30% of all OECD currency then, given per-capita OECD currency outstanding of $1600 per person, it seems likely that the OECD underground economy accounts for as much as 40–50% of the total. The finding that tax burden seems to be an important explanatory variable in currency demand equations tends to support this view.

Here we take up three issues. First, should the new European Central Bank (ECB) be concerned if it knows that 80% of the demand for its product comes from underground and foreign sources? Is facilitating exchange in the underground economy necessarily a bad thing? Second, suppose the ECB (or the US Federal Reserve) were to take measures to inhibit either underground or foreign demand for currency. How much seigniorage revenue would be lost? Are there any important indirect costs? That is, would a sharply reduced currency supply inhibit the central bank's ability to stabilize prices or to serve as a lender of last resort? Third, suppose one accepts the view that the ECB should aim to reduce currency usage by the underground economy, even at the possible cost of reduced supply to foreigners. What concrete steps can be taken to inhibit underground currency usage without significantly inconveniencing legitimate domestic users?

3.1. Is fuelling the underground economy necessarily a bad thing?

If a Colombian drug lord offered a medium-term, zero-interest loan to the US Treasury in return for access to a superior smuggling and hoarding technology, presumably the offer would be refused. Yet such an agreement is implicitly entered when criminals are offered the convenience and anonymity of large-denomination bills. As Feige (1996) points out, currency smuggling is one of the major costs of drug smugglers, costing them perhaps an amount equivalent to the resources involved in smuggling the product itself. If foreign and domestic criminal activity accounted for the bulk of all currency holdings, then there would be a strong moral case at least to consider ways to restrict currency usage.

However, given the increasing sophistication of criminal laundering operations (see Quirk, 1996), it seems likely that most underground demand for currency comes from agents engaged in otherwise socially productive activities: small businesses, street vendors, moonlighting workers, tradespeople, etc. One might argue that, in circumventing burdensome tax rates and regulations, these agents are helping to make their economies more productive and more efficient. Thus, if currency helps fuel the 'shadow' economy, it is perhaps doing more good than harm. Greasing the wheels of underground commerce can be thought of as an 'nth-best' policy in a world where political constraints make it difficult to address directly the underlying source of government-induced inefficiencies.

This sympathetic, libertarian view of the underground economy is certainly a legitimate one. But it overlooks some important drawbacks to having a large underground economy. First and foremost, if agents working in the underground economy can evade taxes, it raises the tax burden in the above-ground economy, thereby exacerbating distortions. Standard public finance considerations suggest that efficiency would be promoted by spreading tax burdens more evenly. Second, not all regulation is ill-considered. If a moonlighting worker is avoiding regulations on the handling and disposal of toxic waste, it is not necessarily in the public interest. If apartments being renovated by moonlighting workers do not meet fire and other safety standards, the public may well end up bearing some of the long-run costs. Overall, currency is a dangerously blunt instrument with which to try to mitigate the distortions caused by big government.

Promoting currency usage by foreigners would seem to be a clearer issue. Legal and tax systems in many developing countries are an order of magnitude more oppressive than in most OECD countries. The efficiency gains from promoting the parallel dollar economy may greatly outweigh other considerations. Dollarization may also be efficiency enhancing because many developing countries lack the institutional and legal infrastructure to achieve any measure of price stability. On the other hand, one can also argue that this policy is paternalistic, and that dollarization greatly exacerbates the problems of authorities in regularizing economic activity. Seigniorage is an important source of tax revenue in many developing countries, and its loss (perhaps) forces the authorities to resort to even more distortionary taxes. Moreover, not all foreign underground activity is productive; the Russian Mafia and Latin America's drug kings also appear to be heavy users of dollars.

In the ensuing discussion, we will take an agnostic view, and assume that the OECD central banks care about foreigner currency holders only because they provide an important source of seigniorage.

3.2. Direct and indirect costs of allowing a sharp decrease in the currency supply

Assuming for the moment that the ECB can indeed find effective measures to reduce sharply the underground use of its currency, what would the likely consequences be?

3.2.1. Lost seigniorage versus lost direct tax revenue. The most obvious costs are fiscal. With a lower currency base, the ECB would enjoy much lower seigniorage profits. In this section, I argue that by fuelling the underground economy, currency has negative effects on the collection of direct taxes, and these indirect revenue losses may substantially offset the loss that the government suffers by giving up the underground economy's seigniorage business.

Table 5 contains recent figures for OECD countries for Cagan's (1956) measure of seigniorage, the real value of money creation:

$$\text{Seigniorage} = \frac{M_t - M_{t-1}}{P_t} \tag{1}$$

Here, M is the stock of money, P is a price index and t refers to a time index. As

Table 5. Real revenues from currency creation

Country	1995 (% of GNP)	1990–5 average (% of GNP)
Japan	0.80	0.34
Greece	0.73	0.82
Spain	0.53	1.07
Ireland	0.49	0.28
Belgium	0.40	0.01
Austria	0.37	0.32
Germany	0.33	0.48
Portugal	0.31	0.34[a]
Finland	0.29	0.12
USA	0.26	0.41
New Zealand	0.18	0.06
UK	0.18	0.13
Denmark	0.17	0.15
Australia	0.16	0.25
Iceland	0.12	0.09
Italy	0.12	0.34
Norway	0.12	0.22
Switzerland	0.11	0.10
Canada	0.09	0.12
France	0.05	0.03
Netherlands	0.01	0.06
Sweden	−0.02	0.09

[a] 1990–4.

Sources: International Financial Statistics.

one can see, seigniorage is not trivial by any means. During the first half of the 1990s, it averaged 0.48% of GDP for Germany and 0.41% of GDP (or more than $30 billion per year) for the USA.

Arguably, a more appropriate definition of seigniorage in the present context is the 'central banker's' definition, which is the annual savings from being able to float interest-free debt. For most countries, similar orders of magnitude for the 1995 seigniorage are obtained using either approach.[6] For example, if the average interest rate on US debt is 7% then, with currency supply of $400 billion, one obtains a seigniorage estimate of $28 billion. If half of the US currency is held abroad, this means that the USA is earning $15 billion per year from foreigners.

Suppose that, by accident or by design, the USA were to lose its domestic and underground foreign currency business. Its seigniorage profits would drop precipitously by perhaps 75% or more. Suppose further that the underground economy is 5–10% of GDP (in line with estimates for the USA by Tanzi (1983) and Feige (1996)), and that forgone taxes (including taxes for old-age retirement programmes) amounted to 4% of GDP. This estimate is consistent with official Internal Revenue Service estimates of forgone tax revenue due to the underground economy (see Gutmann, 1983). If eliminating currency use by the underground economy brought 5% of the underground economy 'above ground', the revenue gain would substantially offset the drop in seigniorage. This estimate is not implausible, since presumably some spectrum of the underground economy must be close to indifference between reporting and not reporting income (due to the deadweight evasion costs to non-reporting). Of course, if making currency less attractive to the underground economy also leads to even a marginal drop in unproductive criminal activity, the savings on law enforcement costs could also be quite significant. Since the underground economy in the USA is generally considered small relative to Europe's (see Schneider, 1997), the potential tax gains in Europe are relatively larger.

In the appendices to this paper, the idea that currency may be useful in transactions, especially large-denomination bills, is formalized. The analysis shows that, even if underground transactions constitute a large share of total demand for currency, standard positive results on demand for money and price level determinacy go through (except that tax rates become an important explanatory variable in money demand). Normative conclusions, however, may be sharply altered. For example, the literature on the optimal quantity of money stemming from Friedman (1969) is completely oblivious to the fact that most currency is held by agents either

---

[6] The present value of the 'central banker's' definition of seigniorage is the same as what one gets using equation (1), except that it is smaller by an initial term, M_{t-1}/P_t. (This equivalence is demonstrated on p. 537, fn. 26 of Obstfeld and Rogoff, 1996). The difference, of course, is that the central banker's definition assumes that the principal of the 'loan' will be paid back someday, whereas the academic's preferred version is more cynical (since the government can default by inflating).

evading taxes or engaged in unproductive illegal activities (for a recent survey, see Mulligan and Sala-i-Martín (1997)).

3.2.2. Will a sharp reduction in real balances compromise the ability of the central bank to stabilize prices or to serve as a lender of last resort? If

dispensing with large-denomination notes leads to a precipitous drop in real currency balances, will this complicate the tasks of the central bank? This question has relevance beyond the scope of issues considered here. Regardless of how currency is restructured, central banks are likely to face ever-increasing difficulty in maintaining their monopoly on currency-like devices as electronic alternatives proliferate. Eventually, even the OECD central banks' most solid customers, the home and foreign underground economies, are going to find alternatives.

It is well known that a central bank can stabilize prices even if the non-bank public ceases to use currency entirely (e.g., Wallace, 1983). As long as banks use central bank money (in electronic form) for liquid reserves, and as long as there is a well-defined demand for bank liabilities, then the central bank can use its control of aggregate liquidity to stabilize prices. Indeed, this is essentially how central banking is practised today in the industrialized countries.

If the OECD governments were forced to buy back the entire supply of currency held by the public, it *would* be expensive. Germany would have to issue new interest-bearing debt equal to almost 7% of GDP, while Japan would have to issue debt of almost 10% of GDP, assuming they wished to keep prices stable. (Under the Maastricht Treaty, Germany would have to bear the cost of buying back its original currency share even after the European Central Bank was established. Implicitly, the sharing provisions for negative seigniorage are different from the sharing provisions for positive seigniorage. The latter is divided up according to a treaty-determined revenue-sharing formula; the former is divided up according to each country's share of the initial pre-conversion money stock.)

Having to buy back the currency supply would certainly take the shine off many central bank balance sheets, as Table 6 indicates. Should the effect on central banks' balance sheets of mass currency repurchases be of any great concern? One issue is that, if its operating profits (from government bond interest) are reduced too sharply, the central bank may no longer have enough revenues to cover its operating expenses (note that Table 6 includes non-interest-bearing gold reserves). [7] This seems like a rather mundane issue, but if the central bank had to request funds for operating revenues each year from the government, its independence might be

---

[7] The Bank for International Settlements (1996) calculates the percentage decline in seigniorage that can be tolerated by major central banks before revenues will no longer be sufficient to cover operating costs. According to their calculations, the Bundesbank can absorb an 86% decline in operating revenues, but the Bank of France can absorb only a 54% decline. For related calculations, see Boeschoten and Hebbkink (1996).

seriously compromised. Based on the figures in Table 6, this does not appear to be a decisive problem for Europe.

A more vexing question is whether a sharp drop in currency demand might compromise a central bank's ability to serve as a lender of last resort. Ultimately, the central bank's capacity to sterilize emergency lending is limited by its assets. For example, if the Federal Reserve wants to serve as a lender of last resort to IBM, it will open its discount window to banks lending to IBM. But it will also sterilize these loans using open market operations, to the extent that IBM's financial troubles did not lead to an aggregate rise in demand for base money. The central bank does not have to sterilize, of course, and can allow some inflation. But if the currency base shrinks, this option becomes less attractive. Loosely speaking, the smaller the base of real base money demand, the more inflation that any given level of increase in central bank money will cause.

The problem of sharply reduced central bank balance sheets is a serious one, but as Table 6 indicates, most OECD central banks would still have substantial resources even after buying back their entire currency supply. This would clearly be the case for the ECB.

Table 6. Currency as a fraction of market value of total central bank assets [a]

Country	End-1995
Japan [b]	0.83
Canada	0.76
USA	0.65
Germany [b]	0.57
Spain	0.48
Australia	0.46
Belgium	0.46
Austria	0.42
Netherlands [b]	0.40
UK	0.35
Switzerland	0.33
Ireland [b]	0.32
France	0.30
Italy	0.27
Sweden	0.26
Norway	0.22
Denmark	0.19
Finland	0.19
Portugal	0.18
Greece	0.15
New Zealand	0.14
Iceland	0.09

[a] Gold reserves are measured at market value.
[b] End-1994.

Source: Central bank annual reports.

3.3. Private substitutes for currency

If the government were to withdraw large-denomination notes, would private substitutes not fully supplant the functions of currency? The modern case for retaining public monopoly of currency is that the government is a very efficient provider. Currency costs governments very little to produce and, in principle, the taxpayer benefits from the revenues generated. If private competitors are allowed to compete with the government, they will be willing to bear large costs in setting up their payments systems, provided they can gather a share of the government's profits. From a social point of view, these set-up and maintenance expenditures are wasteful unless the private money is superior in some dimensions to the public money.[8] This argument has some force, but it should not be decisive. If facilitating the use of private money speeds up the rate of innovation in transactions technologies, the long-run efficiency gains may more than compensate for the initial costs involved in setting up new private currency substitutes.

Government currency has an anonymity feature that differentiates it sharply from media such as ATMs and credit cards. It is this anonymity that makes large-denomination notes so useful to the underground economy. Government regulation of private currency substitutes may be needed to limit their use in illegal activities. Such regulation has costs, but these are not likely to be as important as the benefits. Humphrey *et al.* (1996) put the cost of the current payments system of the USA at 2–3% of GDP. Increased efficiency in this sector is therefore valuable, but probably less important than controlling the size of the underground economy, including illegal activities.

3.4. Exchange rate stability

If the euro and the dollar do co-circulate in many countries, will the resulting instabilities from currency substitution not lead to instability in the euro/dollar exchange rate? If, indeed, half of all demand for these two currencies comes from abroad, international substitution between them may lead to massive swings in money demand for the euro and the dollar. In principle, this will not be a problem if the ECB uses the interest rate as its instrument, but it could be a very serious problem if the ECB targets money. Even using an interest rate target, it is still possible for massive money demand shifts to create major technical problems in interpreting data. This is one possible reason why Europe might prefer to be cautious, at least initially, in promoting use of the euro abroad.

Even if Europe actively courts foreign demand, it is not obvious that the euro can break the dollar's strong position in developing countries. The literature on

---

[8] See Lacker (1996) for a model of this issue and a survey of the literature.

co-circulating currencies suggests that there are likely to be multiple equilibria (e.g., Matsuyama *et al.*, 1993), in some of which both the euro and the dollar co-circulate in developing countries, and in some of which one currency is dominant. In such situations, history and initial conditions can be important determinants of the equilibrium. The euro may also suffer because the physical currency will initially be new and unfamiliar. The foreign public may not be able easily to distinguish counterfeits and, if so, this will reduce acceptance for an extended period.

4. REDUCING THE USEFULNESS OF CURRENCY TO THE UNDERGROUND ECONOMY

Though the arguments are complex, it would appear that on balance the new ECB, and indeed all OECD central banks, should strongly consider policies aimed at reducing currency's usefulness in underground transactions. This may be an uphill battle, especially considering that the strict anti-inflationary statutes of the ECB will otherwise make currency more attractive.

There are many institutional ways to try to tackle the problem of underground currency use, and it may take considerable study and experimentation to determine the best one. Our contention, however, is that a simple and relatively unobtrusive first step would be to remove large-denomination notes from circulation. Large-denomination notes are increasingly rare in legal transactions, having generally been replaced by credit and debit cards, cheques, and other more modern transaction media. The demand for large-denomination notes comes mainly from agents interested in storing or transporting very large sums of currency; such agents tend to be involved in the underground economy.[9] The idea of withdrawing large-denomination notes from circulation is hardly novel. In the early 1980s, the US Internal Revenue Service placed the removal of $100 and $50 bills on its 'wish list' of the most desirable tax enforcement measures (see Gutmann, 1983).

One cannot guarantee that this policy will have even a marginal effect on tax evasion (though as we have argued, tax evasion is so rampant that only a marginal effect would be needed to justify the policy from a revenue standpoint). One cannot even guarantee that underground currency use would drop dramatically. If it did not, the policy would not have any significant direct revenue cost, save for the small extra cost of printing ten 50 euro notes in place of every 500 euro note. Even this cost might be mitigated by reduced counterfeiting, since the economics of counterfeiting give a considerable incentive to focus mainly on the largest-denomination note.

---

[9] Van Hove and Vuchelen (1996) also emphasize that large-denomination notes are really needed only by agents planning to store or physically transport large sums of cash.

There is the possibility that the underground economy will find a private substitute for large-denomination notes, and that the only effect will be for the government to lose seigniorage revenue. This extreme outcome seems unlikely, since any private alternative will probably carry much greater credit risk. It will also be difficult to replace the complete anonymity of cash.

There are certainly alternative policies that one might consider, aimed at achieving the same end. One can, for example, make it more difficult to launder cash by prohibiting the payment of cash in large transactions – an idea that has already been implemented in some countries in Europe.

Many other imaginative policies are also possible. For example, the central bank can periodically require that people trade in all their large-denomination notes for new ones, and force any individuals turning exceptionally large cash holdings to register with the authorities. The US Treasury could have – perhaps should have – done this when it issued the new off-centre $100 bill in 1996. India implemented such a policy in 1978, when ultimately 13% of its notes were never redeemed (see Thomas, 1992). Current plans are to begin switching new euro notes for existing national currency notes three years after the start of EMU. This switch provides a golden opportunity for Europe simultaneously to eliminate large-denomination notes, and to force hoarders of large amounts of currency to identify themselves to the authorities. The idea should at least receive serious consideration.

5. CONCLUSIONS

Over the past two decades, despite major innovations in transactions technology, the supply of OECD currency has actually grown as a share of OECD GDP. There is strong evidence that a major reason for this surprising trend is that a large and growing share of OECD currency – probably well over 50% – is held in the domestic OECD underground economy. A wide range of evidence appears to support this conclusion, including the fact that currency demand seems to be positively related to tax burdens in most OECD countries. Another piece of evidence is the high demand for the largest-denomination notes. Despite the increasing convenience of modern technologies for large transactions, and despite some survey evidence indicating that businesses and consumers do not report significant holdings of large-denomination notes, over 60% of the OECD money supply is held in the form of notes equivalent to $100 or more. A good fraction of the remainder is held in notes equivalent to $50 or more.

There seems little question that underground demand greatly inflates OECD central bank balance sheets, and that without underground demand seigniorage revenues would be dramatically lower. This paper argues, however, that the revenue benefits obtained by catering to the currency needs of the underground economy may well be an accounting illusion. When one takes lost tax revenue into account, the net benefits to governments' balance sheets are likely to be quite small and perhaps negative. If removing the convenience of large-denomination notes helps induce even a small percentage of underground activities to be reported, the revenue gains could easily outweigh any seigniorage costs. This is likely to be true even if developing country holdings of OECD currency, which presently constitute perhaps 25% of the total, dropped dramatically as well. (Changes that discourage the use of the domestic underground economy are likely to discourage its use in the foreign underground economy as well.) Note that our revenue calculation would be strengthened if one took into account potential savings on law and tax enforcement costs. The best way to reduce underground currency usage is not entirely clear. Eliminating large-denomination notes, or placing reporting requirements on them, seems like a good place to start.

By all appearances, the decision to issue large-denomination euro notes was aimed at accommodating the DM bloc countries (Germany, the Netherlands, Austria and Belgium). At the end of 1996, these were the only European Union countries issuing notes equivalent to 200 euro or higher. It is surely no co-incidence that the fifteen planned denominations of the euro closely match the fifteen existing denominations of the DM. Issuing large-denomination notes certainly makes sense from the point of view of maximizing demand for the new currency. After all, the large-denomination countries in Europe tend to have the highest currency/GDP ratios. As we have just argued, however, this logic is ill-considered.

True, it is possible that the elimination of 100, 200 and 500 euro notes would have little effect on the overall demand for euro currency, with agents simply substituting into smaller bills. This seems unlikely, however, given that $1 million worth of 500 euro notes can be stored in a large purse, while £1 million in 50 euro notes would take a large suitcase. The ECB might also seriously consider urging national authorities to require identification and reporting of agents attempting to convert quantities of national currencies into euro.

An important contrary viewpoint must be acknowledged. Some may view the ability of agents to shift economic activities underground as an important safety valve in a region where taxes and regulation are high. According to this viewpoint, the underground economy is basically an important resource. If large-denomination notes drastically facilitate production in the tax-evading sector, the contrary viewpoint is that this is a good thing. Providing large-denomination notes may be thought of as an nth-best policy that mitigates other distortions. Indeed, the ECB's strict anti-inflation statutes should be applauded because they reduce the one tax that governments can currently levy on the underground economy.

The above contrary viewpoint is a legitimate one, and it has undeniable libertarian appeal. But, on balance, it is difficult to agree with it. First and foremost, the inability of the government to tax the underground economy increases taxes and distortions in the legal economy. Second, promoting the tax-favoured status of currency-intensive businesses is an extremely arbitrary way to reduce taxes. Surely a policy of free trade and factor mobility within Europe provides a more sensible and efficient safety valve against high taxes. Moreover, the low-inflation policies of the new ECB already make currency use by the underground economy relatively attractive. It is not wise or necessary to enhance this attractiveness any further by issuing large-denomination notes.

Perhaps an ideal policy is one that allows the ECB to expand foreign demand for its currency while discouraging its use in the underground economy. There may be clever devices for achieving this. But the benefits of curtailing the convenience of currency for the underground economy may be sufficient to justify such a policy, regardless of its implications for foreign demand.

Finally, we note that the logic of this paper probably applies to the US dollar as well, even if over half of all dollars are held by foreigners. The popularity of the $100 bill, which Europe appears to want to emulate, may well be a mixed blessing.

▬▬▬
Discussion

Francesco Giavazzi
Università Bocconi, Milan

Why did the European Monetary Institute (EMI) decide that the new European Central Bank (ECB) will issue 500 ecu notes? The simple answer is that we have DM1000 notes and the EMI followed the example of the Bundesbank. Ken Rogoff's paper has the merit of showing that the decision on which size notes to issue is not irrelevant. But should we agree with his conclusion that the ECB should not issue 500 ecu notes because the availability of banknotes of this size facilitates tax evasion and other illegal transactions?

As Rudi Dornbusch pointed out during the Panel discussion, people who use cash for illegal transactions look for a balance between value (a DM1000 note takes up very little space) and anonymity (if only drug dealers use DM1000 notes then the anonymity is gone). This suggests that, if there is a discontinuity in the size of banknotes issued (say 5, 10, 20 and 500), pooling becomes more difficult and only those individuals who use large banknotes for legal purposes (e.g., travellers who wish to travel light) will use them. This may be better than not issuing large-denomination banknotes at all. The ECB instead plans to issue a continuum of banknotes: 5, 10, 20, 50, 100, 200, etc.

When large-denomination banknotes are not available, people find other ways to carry out underground transactions: not providing large denominations may cause only a small inconvenience to the underground economy. Italy offers an interesting experiment. A large-denomination banknote has been issued by the Banca d'Italia since the early 1970s: the ITL100 000 note. However, because of inflation, the purchasing power of this banknote has fallen by a factor of ten between 1970 and today. Therefore, it is as if a large-denomination banknote had been withdrawn by the Banca d'Italia, which never issued denominations in excess of ITL100 000 lire. Estimating a simple money demand function for the ITL100 000 note, one discovers that in the early part of the sample, the 1970s, the only variable on the right-hand side that appears to be significant in the regression is 'crime' – an estimate of the yearly value of crime-related transactions. This variable, however, drops out of the regression in the second part of the sample, the 1980s and early 1990s. This finding is consistent with the view that, as long as the purchasing power of the ITL100 000 note was relatively high, it was indeed used by the underground economy. But when its value fell, the Italian underground economy found other ways to carry out its transactions: for example, bearer treasury bills became a common instrument. Eliminating large-denomination banknotes may cause only a minor nuisance to the underground economy.

The fact that the European Commission has already chosen the drawings for the new ecu banknotes does not mean that in four years' time they will all need to be issued. This paper suggests that it may be a good idea to think through the issues once more.

Friedrich Schneider

Johannes-Kepler-Universität Linz

Kenneth Rogoff argues that, by issuing large-denomination euro notes of 100, 200 and 500, the European Central Bank will challenge the US Federal Reserve as the leading purveyor of currency to unstable developing countries, to tax-evaders (or to people working in the underground economy) and to criminals throughout the world. Rogoff concludes that it is not a good policy for the European Central Bank to issue large-denomination notes because this helps (or stimulates) the underground economy, including criminal activities such as drug dealing. Moreover, the euro will be vastly used outside its currency domain, and it will be a real competitor to US dollar notes. He therefore suggests that it might be a better idea *not* to bring out large-denomination notes with the potential results that the shadow economy will shrink (perhaps by 10%), that fewer euro currency notes may be held abroad, and that less currency may be used for criminal activities. Furthermore, he argues that the use of cash is 'out' for normal (legal) transactions. Against these findings I have the following four objections:

1. A theoretical approach to using the elimination of large-denomination notes as an efficient instrument to fight crimes and/or to reduce the shadow economy is missing. The author's main argument is that, if large-denomination notes are not printed, this will have a considerable negative effect on underground and criminal activities: that is, it will reduce the underground economy (and possibly other criminal activities) because the use of cash is much less attractive. In my opinion this conclusion is not convincing because the author does not analyse the reasons why people evade taxes or work in the underground economy. Research in Europe and North America shows that the major reasons for working in the underground economy are the high direct and indirect tax burden (including social security payments, which, at least in Europe, are treated as an additional tax due to the insecurity of getting a pension in the future) and overregulation of the economy (at least in most European countries). Most transactions in the underground economy are undertaken with cash because cash transactions do not leave traces for the tax authorities. (See, e.g., Frey and Pommerehne, 1984; Frey and Weck-Hannemann, 1984; Feige, 1989; Schneider, 1994a, 1997.)

The abolition of large-denomination notes will hardly reduce the incentives to work in the underground economy (or to evade taxes) because the major causes are not tackled at all by this policy measure. The only effect will be that the transaction costs of working in the underground economy or evading tax will rise because people will have to use smaller-denomination notes. This might 'drive out' a few people at the margin of the underground economy, but the effect will be rather small. Hence, Rogoff should develop a more convincing theoretical approach or a more decisive argument, such that an increase in transaction costs is really an efficient means to fight tax evasion or to substantially reduce the underground economy.

2. The review of the empirical analysis of using cash for various purposes is incomplete. There exists a large literature on estimating the size and development of the shadow economy in Europe and in the USA (see, e.g., Frey and Pommerehne, 1984; Frey and Weck-Hannemann, 1984; Feige, 1989; Schneider, 1994a, 1997; Aigner et al., 1988; Clovland, 1984.) The latest empirical results on the size of the shadow economy using the currency demand approach are shown in Table 7. Taking the results on the size of the underground economy for the latest available year, 1994, it can be seen that Italy (25.8%), Spain (22.3%), Belgium (21.4%) and Sweden (18.3%) have the largest shadow economies. In the mid-group are Norway (17.9%), Denmark (17.6%), Ireland (15.3%), Canada (14.6%) and France (14.3%). At the lower end are the Netherlands (13.6%), Germany (13.1%), the UK (12.4%), the USA (9.4%), Austria (6.8%) and Switzerland (6.6%). From Table 7 it can also be seen that the increase in size of the shadow economy over time is quite remarkable. Whereas in 1960 the shadow economy accounted for less than 5% of GNP in the investigated countries, in 1994 (excluding the USA, Austria and Switzerland) it accounted for over 10% of GNP.

By definition, an advantage of the currency demand approach is that one is able to calculate roughly how much currency will be used for activities in the underground economy. Furthermore, there is some knowledge of how much currency is used for legal cash transactions and how much currency is used abroad. So Rogoff could have calculated how much currency is used in the underground economy and

Table 7. Size of the shadow economy applying the currency demand

Country	Author(s)	\multicolumn{8}{c}{Size of the shadow economy (% of official GNP)}							
		1960	1965	1970	1975	1978	1980	1990	1994
Austria	Schneider (1997)	0.4	1.2	1.8	1.9	2.6	3.0	5.1	6.8
Belgium	Hove and Vuchelen (1994)	–	7.8	10.4	15.2	–	16.4	19.6	21.4
Canada	Karoleff et al. (1993)	–	–	–	5.8–7.2	–	10.1–11.2	–	14.6
Denmark	Schneider (1986)	3.8–4.8	5.0–6.3	5.3–7.4	6.4–7.8	6.7–8.0	6.9–10.2	9.0–13.4	17.6
France	Barthelemy (1989)	–	–	3.9	–	6.7	6.9	9.4	14.3
Germany	Kirchgässner (1983)	2.0–2.1	3.6–4.3	2.7–3.0	5.5–6.0	8.1–9.2	10.3–11.2	11.4–12.0	13.1
Ireland	Boyle (1982)	–	–	4.3	6.9	–	8.0	11.7	15.3
Italy	Contini (1989)	–	8.4	10.7	–	–	16.7	23.4	25.8
Netherlands	Broesterhuizen (1989)	–	–	4.8	–	–	9.1	12.9	13.6
Norway	Lundager and Schneider (1986)	1.3–1.7	3.2–4.1	6.2–6.9	7.8–8.2	9.6–10.0	10.2–10.9	14.5–16.0	17.9
Spain	Lafuente (1989)	–	–	–	–	18.0	–	21.0	22.3
Sweden	Lundager and Schneider (1986)	1.5–1.8	3.7–4.6	6.8–7.8	10.2–11.2	12.5–13.6	11.9–12.4	15.8–16.7	18.3
Switzerland	Weck-Hannemann et al. (1986)	1.2	1.6	4.1	6.1	6.2	6.5	6.9	6.6
UK	Matthews and Rostagi (1985)	–	–	2.0	6.5	7.8	8.4	10.2	12.4
USA	Tanzi (1983)	2.6–4.1	2.5–3.8	2.6–4.6	3.5–5.2	3.7–5.3	3.9–6.1	5.1–8.6	9.4

Notes: A dash means that no value exists for this period for this country. Only a crude comparison of the size of the shadow economy between the different countries can be done because of (1) different tax variables; (2) different specifications of the dependent variable and estimation equation; and (3) different assumptions about the velocity of currency.

Sources: For the currency demand approach, see references in the text. The values for the years 1990 and 1994 for Austria, Belgium, Canada, Denmark, France, Germany, Ireland, Italy, Netherlands, Norway, Spain, Sweden, Switzerland, UK and USA are calculated by Schneider (1997).

the residual of the currency for other criminal activities, such as drug dealing. Such a calculation could be done for both the US dollar and the German mark. This would shed some light on whether the abolition of large-denomination bills would reduce the size of the underground economy.

3. There is a missing link between the underground and the official economy. Various studies have shown that there is a strong interaction between the underground and the official economy. (Compare, e.g., Neck *et al.*, 1989; Schneider and Neck, 1993; Schneider, 1994b.) First, people work in the underground economy only because the official economy is overburdened with regulation. A trader working in the official economy is too expensive. On the other hand, at least 70% of all income earned in the underground economy is spent again in the official economy, so that this additional purchasing power is a strongly stabilizing factor in the official economy.

For example, it has been estimated that the underground economy in Austria was worth roughly 200 billion Austrian Schillings in 1994, of which 140 billion are spent again in the official Austrian economy. Hence, if the Austrian underground economy were considerably reduced (assuming that the author's suggestion not to print large-denomination notes works efficiently) then Austria would suffer from a considerable recession. People would not work more in the official economy because the reasons for their working in the underground economy would not have been tackled at all. People would either work even more in the underground economy or take more leisure.

4. The use of 'hard' currencies abroad. It is difficult to evaluate what domestic and foreign effects the dollar (or, in the future, the euro) really has if it is widely used outside the own currency domain. I am not aware of any study that estimates the costs and benefits for the US dollar of its being used as a 'hard currency' in Argentina or Russia. What effect does this have on the US economy, what costs and benefits are involved, and will these costs and benefits change if large-denomination notes are reduced? There might be a trade-off between using hard currencies (like the dollar or the German mark) in developing or other countries, which have severe problems in stabilizing their own currency, and the illegal activities that might also result. One could argue that this is a kind of development aid from hard currency countries to soft currency countries because individuals in the latter will learn to use hard currencies, and that eventually soft currency countries will turn into hard currency countries when they see the advantages. As long as it has not been convincingly shown that the use of money abroad has severe disadvantages for the home country, it can be argued that large-denomination notes should be allowed.

General discussion

In Rudi Dornbusch's opinion, the analysis of the interaction between crime and demand for cash was reminiscent of the Chicago tradition of the 1960s and 1970s. He was also reminded of Mundell's monetary theory of empires, which postulated that the potential for seigniorage may have been a crucial incentive for holding on to large empires. Moving on to the specifics, he thought that even though the cash holdings of the Japanese yen seem stunningly large, these may well be domestic rather than foreign. Given the high price stability, the low return on bank deposits and the relative absence of street crime in Japan, households prefer to hold cash rather than bank deposits. Second, eliminating large-denomination notes was futile, and likely to inconvenience only honest people, as long as the private sector could supply perfect substitutes for illegal purposes. For instance, large-denomination unsigned travellers' cheques had been common currency in Hollywood in the past. Third, large-denomination banknotes are convenient to store and transport, but are relatively illiquid. This trade-off must be incorporated in the analysis.

He went on to propose methods for estimating the different components of the demand for dollars. Foreign demand that is induced by hyperinflations could be estimated, for instance, by assuming that the entire reduction in the demand for real balances in hyperinflationary countries is substitution towards the dollar. The countries concerned, namely Argentina, Russia and Israel, and the timing of their hyperinflationary episodes, were well known. This would provide an upper estimate for such a demand. When it came to the domestic demand, he wondered if there was a seasonal pattern in the use of large-denomination notes. If so, one could further improve the estimates of foreign versus domestic holding of such notes. Finally, he speculated that modern technology, in particular the ability to 'bug' and then monitor the flow of large-denomination notes, might provide new ways to check illegal activity.

Robert McCauley felt that the paper was written from a somewhat parochial American perspective, and had missed some significant differences between Europe and the USA. First, large cash holdings in Europe could be a consequence of the relatively safe environment in European cities, rather than large-denomination notes being a contributory cause of criminal activity. Second, in the European case, seigniorage will be lower as the launch of the new European currency will involve a call-in of existing currency notes. The USA was careful to avoid a call-in of old notes when new $100 bills were launched. He too speculated on the possibilities afforded by new technology. The advent of the electronic purse and the growing ability of the private sector to generate close substitutes for cash meant that governments may soon lose their monopoly of issuing large-denomination banknotes.

Olivier de Bandt added that money is increasingly laundered through credit cards and other sophisticated methods rather than banknotes. Furthermore, when it comes to choosing denominations, removing large denominations is unlikely to reduce black market activity as substitution to smaller denominations is almost costless. Rudi Dornbusch felt that, instead of abolishing large-denomination notes, one could restrict their use by imposing reporting requirements for large cash transactions.

Hans Genberg wondered if counterfeiting of banknotes was sensitive to the denomination in which they were issued. Stefan Gerlach pointed out that counterfeiting costs would vary systematically across denominations and, moreover, these costs would be borne by the public at large. He thought that pooled data on currency demand – pooled across countries and time periods – would yield additional information about the incentives to hold money.

Hélène Rey argued that large-denomination euro notes are unlikely to be perfect substitutes for dollar notes. Criminals' demand for currency may be quite heterogeneous and, further, currency substitution models indicate that there is considerable hysteresis in currency holdings. Richard Portes felt that the possibility of currency substitution introduces complications for monetary policy and, therefore, merited greater attention. Olivier Blanchard wondered if criminals with European currency holdings will convert to the dollar before the euro is launched. If so, would this affect the demand for money in the run-up to the launch?

Georges de Ménil stressed that it was important to appreciate the reasons for large unofficial sectors in some countries. For instance, one has to ask why half the Ukrainian GDP is generated in the unofficial sector. In his opinion, it was the enormous amount of regulatory intervention and bureaucratic red tape that generated and supported illegal transactions. If so, law enforcement and the correction of these economy-wide imperfections were better approaches than focusing on the choice of currency denominations.

APPENDIX A. THE THEORY OF CURRENCY DEMAND AND TAX EVASION

Although the empirical literature on currency demand has long recognized the importance of currency use in the underground economy (e.g., Feige, 1979; Tanzi, 1983), standard theoretical treatments of money demand and optimal inflation taxation have remained curiously oblivious to this possibility.[10] For positive results, the distinction between legal and illegal or tax-avoiding transactions may be secondary, but this is certainly not the case for normative questions such as the optimal level of money growth and inflation. This appendix presents a simple modification of a standard transactions cost model that accounts for the potential role of currency in tax evasion.

A1. A transactions-based model of currency demand with tax evasion

Consider a small, open economy in which the domestic currency is the sole legal tender. The representative individual is endowed each period with y units of output and can borrow and

[10] E.g., Sidrauski (1967) (money in the utility function), Lucas and Stokey (1987) (cash-in-advance constraint), Kiyotaki and Wright (1989) (matching model), or Sims (1994) (transactions costs).

lend at the world real interest rate r. The agent has a utility function given by

$$U = \sum_{s=t}^{\infty} \beta^{s-t} u(c_s) \tag{A1}$$

where c is consumption in period s, $\beta < 1$ is the time discount factor, and $u' > 0$, $u'' < 0$. The individual is endowed each period with gross real income y. However, due to trading frictions, a portion of this income dissipates in production so that net pre-tax income in period t is given by

$$y[1 - v(M_t^i/P_t y)] \tag{A2}$$

where M_t^i denotes the individual's holdings of currency at time t (for now we will ignore the distinction between notes of differing denominations), and P_t is the money price level. The function $v(M/Py)$ has the properties that $v'(.) < 0$, $v''(.) > 0$, $\lim_{M/Py \to \infty} v(M/Py) = 0$, and $v(0) < 1$. Thus currency is helpful in reducing the transactions costs associated with exchange, but it is not absolutely essential. This is, of course, a variant of the well-known money-in-the-utility-function approach, in which demand for money is rationalized as being derived from an underlying transactions technology.[11] In interpreting this model, it is not necessary to view currency as being the sole mechanism for effecting payments, provided there is no perfect substitute in all transactions. For example, the individual may use cheque accounts on which bank intermediaries hold currency reserves, so that the demand for currency is a derived one.

In addition to receiving income, the agent also faces a proportional tax on earned income (y) at notional rate τ. (For simplicity, we assume that interest income is not taxed.) The tax rate is notional in that the agent can reduce his or her effective tax rate by holding a higher level of real balances M/P. The idea is that using currency helps avoid detection of income by the tax authorities.[12] Thus the net real taxes paid by the individual are

$$\tau g(M_t^i/P_t y) \tag{A3}$$

where $g(0) = 1$, $g'(.) < 0$, $g''(.) > 0$, and $\lim_{M/Py \to \infty} g(M/Py) \geqslant 0$. (Obviously, we do not need to think of every individual as engaging in tax evasion, but thinking of the representative agent as wearing two hats is a useful shortcut to analysing a more heterogenous economy.) In addition to paying a tax proportional to income, the individual receives a lump-sum nominal transfer of $\Delta M_t \equiv M_t - M_{t-1}$, where ΔM_t is the increase in the per-capita money supply. Thus holding currency facilitates avoiding income taxes, but does not affect the individual's ability to accept lump-sum transfers from the government.

Our assumptions on the transactions and tax evasion technology imply that the individual's budget constraint can be written in money terms as

$$P_t b_{t+1}^i + M_t^i = P_t(1 + r) b_t^i + M_{t-1}^i + P_t y[1 - v(M_t^i/P_t y) - \tau g(M_t^i/P_t y)] - P_t c_t + \Delta M_t \tag{A4}$$

---

[11] The formulation is the same as Sims (1994), except that he posits the transactions savings as being proportional to consumption rather than income. Since income and consumption are proportional here, this distinction is not important for present purposes. Taken literally, one can think of cash here as being needed in production (for stocking cash registers, for giving change, for purchasing intermediate goods and for paying wages).

[12] A more sophisticated approach would be to have the individual's income y be private information, with currency a mechanism for concealment.

where b^i_{t+1} denotes the individual's holding of real bonds, and M^i_t his or her money holdings at the end of period t.

The first-order conditions for individual utility maximization (of (A1) subject to (A4)) imply

$$u'(c_t) = \beta(1 + r) u'(c_{t+1}) \tag{A5}$$

and

$$\frac{1}{P_t} u'(c_t)\left[1 + v'\left(\frac{M_t}{P_t y}\right) + \tau g'\left(\frac{M_t}{P_t y}\right)\right] = \frac{1}{P_{t+1}} \beta u'(c_{t+1}) \tag{A6}$$

where we have dropped i superscripts. Equation (A5) is the standard consumption/Euler equation,[13] while equation (A6) determines the allocation of income between money and consumption. Combining (A5) and (A6) yields

$$-v'\left(\frac{M_t}{P_t y}\right) - \tau g'\left(\frac{M_t}{P_t y}\right) = 1 - \frac{P_t}{P_{t+1}(1 + r)} = \frac{i}{1 + i} \tag{A7}$$

which, given our assumptions on v' and g', implies a standard demand function for real balances, increasing in y, and decreasing in the nominal interest rate i.[14] The one important difference, however, is that money demand also depends positively on the marginal tax rate.

To see the implications of the model more clearly, it is helpful to consider the specific functional forms

$$g(M/Py) = \exp - \frac{1}{\eta} (M/Py) \text{ and } v(M/Py) = a \exp - \frac{1}{\eta} (M/Py),$$

where $0 < a < 1$. In this case, (A7) reduces to

$$\frac{M_t}{P_t} = \eta y\left\{\log \frac{1}{\eta} (a + \tau) - \log\left(\frac{i}{1 + i}\right)\right\} \tag{A8}$$

A2. A digression on price-level determinacy

Before proceeding, it is important to pause to ask about price-level determinacy in this model. If τ is exogenous and M grows at a constant exogenous rate, then an analysis of price-level determinacy parallels that for a standard money-in-the-utility-function model.[15]

---

[13] A nuance here, however, is that although the individual's gross income is constant, his or her income net of taxes and transactions costs fluctuates depending on his or her holding of real balances.
[14] The nominal interest rate i is defined as

$$1 + i = \frac{P_{t+1}}{P_t} (1 + r)$$

[15] See also Obstfeld and Rogoff (1983) and Obstfeld and Rogoff (1996), chapter 8.

Specifically, equation (A7) can be rewritten

$$m_{t+1} = (1 + \theta)(1 + r)m_t\left\{1 + v'\left(\frac{m_t}{y}\right) + \tau g'\left(\frac{m_t}{y}\right)\right\} \tag{A9}$$

where $m \equiv M/P$ and $\theta = (M_{t+1} - M_t)/M_t$. Our assumptions on the transactions and tax evasion technologies imply that this difference equation has a single stationary state with $m > 0$, but the equation also admits speculative bubble paths. Paths where real money balances grow without bound can be ruled out by a transversality argument. Hyperinflationary paths where real balances fall to zero, however, cannot be ruled out without making an assumption that the government offers to back the currency fractionally with real resources (although the fractional backing can be arbitrarily small and need not be certain). Implicit in this analysis is the assumption that the government endogenously varies government spending to maintain a constant notional tax rate τ and a constant money growth rate θ. Otherwise, if τ varies endogenously, the analysis becomes more complicated, though the price level is still determinate under plausible conditions.

A3. Optimal rate of steady-state money growth

Assume that when the notional tax rate is τ, real revenues to the government are $\tau y f(M_t/P_t y)$, where $f(M/Py) \leqslant g(M/Py)$. The two functions are equal in the case where tax evasion does not consume any real resources so that the public's cost of paying taxes equals the government's revenue. In general, even if $f(M/Py) = g(M/Py)$, Ricardian equivalence does not hold here. The notional tax rate affects the demand for money, which in turn affects the real resources dissipated in transactions. Correspondingly, raising the steady-state rate of money growth will raise receipts from direct taxes, since, in general, steady-state real balances fall as inflation rises: that is, denoting steady-state real balance as $\bar{m}(\theta)$, $\bar{m}'(\theta) < 0$.

These observations have implications for the two standard exercises in the analysis of money demand. First, the usual optimal rate of money growth arguments suggest that the higher are real balances, the lower are transactions costs and the higher is welfare. If, however, there is a wedge between government tax revenue and the private cost of paying taxes $[f(M/Py) < g(M/Py)]$ then this may no longer be the case. The optimal level of inflation will then also depend on the properties of the function $g(M/Py) - f(M/Py)$, since higher real balances may increase the deadweight costs of tax evasion.

Second, standard calculations of the optimal seigniorage revenue-maximizing rate of inflation (as in Cagan, 1956) ignore the fact that net revenues to the government from direct taxation may be decreasing in M/P and, therefore, *rising* in the rate of inflation.[16] In the present model, total steady-state government revenues are given by

$$\theta \bar{m}(\theta) + \tau y f\left[\frac{\bar{m}(\theta)}{y}\right] \tag{A10}$$

---

[16] This is the opposite of Tanzi's (1977) result. Tanzi emphasizes that tax levels are often nominally sticky, and therefore a rise in inflation may curtail the real value of government tax revenues. Dixit (1991) argues that the Tanzi effect disappears if tax rates are appropriately indexed. The same is true here, but only if there are no deadweight costs to tax evasion.

Differentiating with respect to θ yields the first-order condition

$$\bar{m}(\theta) + \theta\bar{m}'(\theta) + \tau f'\left[\frac{\bar{m}(\theta)}{y}\right]\bar{m}'(\theta) = 0 \tag{A11}$$

or

$$\theta = -\frac{\bar{m}(\theta)}{m'(\theta)} - \tau f'\left[\frac{\bar{m}(\theta)}{y}\right] \tag{A12}$$

Standard analyses (e.g., Obstfeld and Rogoff, 1996, ch. 8) focus only on the first term on the right-hand side of (A12). However, since the second term is unambiguously positive (recall $f' < 0$), allowing for tax evasion as in this model unambiguously raises the revenue-maximizing rate of inflation at any given level of τ). The potential empirical significance of this effect is discussed in the text.

APPENDIX B. EXTENSION TO MULTIPLE DENOMINATIONS OF CURRENCY

The preceding analysis treated currency as homogeneous, but the empirical evidence suggests that for most countries, large-denomination notes are used disproportionately in the underground economy. An extension of the model to allow for multiple currency denominations illustrates a natural way that net direct tax revenues might be raised without necessarily raising either steady-state inflation or prices.

In this appendix, we extend our model to allow for two different denominations of currency, 1 and 2. Think of currency 1 as $20 bills and currency 2 as $100 bills. The numeraire currency is 1, and the exchange rate of currency 1 for currency 2 is S (units of currency 1 required to purchase a unit of currency 2). We will initially assume that the government fixes the exchange rate at $\bar{S}$ by trading the currencies in unlimited quantities as necessary. (Obviously, in the example of $100 and $20 bills, the official exchange rate is 5.) As we shall see, the unofficial exchange rate can deviate from the official exchange rate if the government ceases to print new $100 bills in an effort to remove them gradually from circulation.

If the denominations were perfect substitutes in all uses then, of course, the public would willingly accept them in whatever ratio the government chose. If, however, the two currencies are not perfect substitutes (say, because denomination 1 is a more suitable size for most transactions or because smugglers find denomination 2 lighter and more convenient for making bulk currency shipments) then the central bank must allow the relative supplies of the two currencies to be demand determined if it wishes to fix S at the face-value exchange rate. For convenience, we model this imperfect substitutability in an extreme way, so that currency 1 alone is useful for reducing transactions costs in legal transactions, and currency 2 alone is useful in tax evasion.[17] Nothing important in the analysis below would be changed by

---

[17] In the traditional currency denomination literature (e.g., Manski and Goldin, 1987), the demand for different-denomination notes depends on the distribution of transaction sizes in the economy. Here we abstract from this issue.

modifying these assumptions so that either currency could be used for either purpose, provided that tax evasion was relatively currency-intensive. Denote $P_{1,t}$ as the price level at time t in terms of currency 1, and $P_{2,t}$ as the price level in terms of currency 2. Because both currencies are legal tender, purchasing power parity must hold so that

$$P_{1,t} = S_t P_{2,t} \qquad (B1)$$

or, as long as S_t is fixed at $\bar{S}$,

$$P_{1,t} = \bar{S} P_{2,t} \qquad (B2)$$

Given our assumptions, the individual's period budget constraint (A3) is replaced by

$$P_{1,t} b_{t+1}^i + M_{1,t}^i + S_t M_{2,t}^i - P_{1,t}(1+r) b_t^i - (M_{1,t-1}^i + S_t M_{2,t-1}^i)$$
$$= P_{1,t} y[1 - v(M_{1,t}^i / P_{1,t} y) - \tau g(M_{2,t}^i / P_{2,t} y)] - P_{1,t} c_t + \Delta M_{1,t} + S_t \Delta M_{2,t} \qquad (B3)$$

where the numeraire is currency 1. The first-order consumption/Euler condition (A5) remains the same, but the other first-order condition (A6) is replaced by the two conditions

$$\frac{1}{P_{1,t}} u'(c_t) \left[1 + v'\left(\frac{M_{1,t}}{P_{1,t} y} \right) \right] = \frac{1}{P_{1,t+1}} \beta u'(c_{t+1}) \qquad (B4)$$

and

$$\frac{1}{P_{2,t}} u'(c_t) \left[1 + \tau g'\left(\frac{M_{2,t}}{P_{2,t} y} \right) \right] = \frac{1}{P_{2,t+1}} \beta u'(c_{t+1}) \qquad (B5)$$

Combining the three first-order conditions, (B4), (B5) and (A5), with the purchasing power parity relationship (B1) implies

$$1 = \frac{v'\left(\dfrac{M_{1,t}}{P_{1,t} y} \right)}{\tau g'\left(\dfrac{M_{2,t}}{S_t P_{1,t} y} \right)} \qquad (B6)$$

Given τ, (B6) determines the relative supplies of the two moneys needed to fix the exchange rate at face value $\bar{S}$. Then, given a path for M_1, one can think of the currency-1 price level P_1 being determined by (A5) and (B4) in the usual way, with (B6) determining the requisite supply of M_2. Of course, the analysis is more complex if the government does not adjust spending to achieve budget balance (as we assume for simplicity here), since tax revenues, money growth and expenditures are all related through the government budget constraint. We will not attempt an analysis of the general case here.

What happens when, as suggested in the text, the government phases out currency 2 by ceasing any printing of new notes, offering to redeem any old ones for currency 1 at the face-value exchange rate? The official exchange rate $\bar{S}$ now provides a floor for the value of currency 2 in terms of currency 1, but (since there is only one-way exchange), it does not provide a ceiling. There can be an appreciation, since currency 2 is more efficient for tax evasion and its supply is now limited. Thus, initially, there is the possibility that phasing out the large-denomination currency will actually raise the value of existing notes, perversely giving hoarders a capital gain. This effect is probably small, however, compared to the long-term revenue gain. It can also be mitigated by adopting a more elaborate phase-out scheme (e.g., specifying that after a certain interval all redemptions of $100 bills will have to be registered with the government).

REFERENCES

Aigner, D.J., F. Schneider and D. Gosh (1989). 'Me and my shadow: estimating the size of the US underground economy from time series data', in W. Barnett *et al.* (eds.), *Economic Theory and Econometrics*, Cambridge University Press, Cambridge.

Avery, R., G. Elliehausen, A. Kennickell and P. Spindt (1987). 'Changes in the use of transactions accounts and cash from 1984–1986', *Federal Reserve Bulletin*.

Bank for International Settlements (1996). 'Implications for central banks of the development of electronic money', Geneva.

Bank of Japan (1994). 'The circulation of Bank of Japan notes', *Quarterly Bulletin*.

Barthelemy, Ph. (1989). 'The underground economy in France', in E.L. Feige (ed.), *The Underground Economy: Tax Evasion and Information Distortion*, Cambridge University Press, Cambridge.

Boeschoten, W. (1992). *Currency Use and Payments Patterns*, DNB, Dordrecht.

———and M. Fase (1992). 'The demand for large bank notes', *Journal of Money, Credit and Banking*.

———and G. Hebbkink (1996). 'Electronic money, currency demand and seigniorage loss in the G10 countries', De Nederlandshe Bank NV, *Staff Report*.

Boyle, G. E. (1982). 'Glimpse at the non-accounted economy: the case of Ireland', paper presented at the International Conference on the Unobserved Economy, NIAS WASSENAAR.

Broesterhuizen, G.A.A.M. (1989). 'The unrecorded economy and the national income accounts in the Netherlands: a sensitivity analysis', in E.L. Feige (ed.), *The Underground Economy: Tax Evasion and Information Distortion*, Cambridge University Press, Cambridge.

Cagan, P. (1956). 'The monetary dynamics of hyperinflation', in M. Friedman (ed.), *Studies in the Quantity Theory of Money*, University of Chicago Press, Chicago, IL.

Clovland, J. (1984). 'Tax evasion and the demand for currency in Norway and Sweden: is there a hidden relationship?', *Scandinavian Journal of Economics*.

Contini, W. (1989). 'The irregular economy of Italy: a survey of contributions', in E.L. Feige (ed.), *The Underground Economies: Tax Evasion and Information Distortion*, Cambridge University Press, Cambridge.

Dixit, A. (1991). 'The optimal mix of inflationary finance and commodity taxation with collection lags', *IMF Staff Papers*.

Feige, E.L. (1979). 'How big is the irregular economy?', *Challenge*.

———(1989). *The Underground Economy: Tax Evasion and Information Distortion*, Cambridge University Press, Cambridge.

———(1996). 'Where is America's currency? Examining the world dollarization hypothesis', mimeo., University of Wisconsin.

Frey, B.S. and W.W. Pommerehne (1984). 'The hidden economy: state and prospects for measurement', *Review of Income and Wealth*.

——— and H. Weck-Hannemann (1984). 'The hidden economy as an "unobserved" variable', *European Economic Review*.

Friedman, M.(1969). *The Optimum Quantity of Money and Other Essays*, Aldine, Chicago, IL.

Gutmann, P. (1983). 'The subterranean economy five years later', *Across the Board*.

Haughton, J. (1995). 'Adding mystery to the case of the missing currency', *Quarterly Review of Economics and Finance*.

Hove, L.V. and J. Vuchelen (1994). 'The demand for currency and the underground economy: two amendments on the Tanzi-method', University of Brussels Discussion Paper.

Humphrey, D., L. Pulley and J. Vesala (1996). 'Cash, paper and electronic payments', *Journal of Money, Credit and Banking*.

Kamin, S. and N. Ericsson (1993). 'Dollarization in Argentina', Federal Reserve Board, *International Finance Discussion Paper*.

Karoleff, V., R. Mirus and R.S. Smith (1993). 'Canada's underground economy revisited: update and critic', paper presented at the IIPF meeting, Berlin.

Kirchgässner, G. (1983). 'Size and development of the West German shadow economy 1955–1980', *Zeitschrift für die gesamte Staatswissenschaft*.

Kiyotaki, N. and R. Wright (1989). 'On money as a medium of exchange', *Journal of Political Economy*.

Lacker, J. (1996). 'Stored value cards: costly private substitutes for government currency', Federal Reserve Bank of Richmond, *Economic Quarterly*.

Lafuente, A. (1989). 'The unobserved economy in Spain', in E.L. Feige (ed.), *The Underground Economy: Tax Evasion and Information Distortion*, Cambridge University Press, Cambridge .

Lucas, R.E. and N. Stokey (1987). 'Money and interest in a cash-in-advance society', *Econometrica*.

Lundager, J. and F. Schneider (1986). 'The development of the shadow economies for Denmark, Norway and Sweden: a comparison', *Nationaloekonomisk Tidskrift*.

Manski, C. and E. Goldin (1987). 'The denomination-specific demand for currency in a high-inflation setting: the Israeli experience', in R.D.H. Heijmans and H. Neudecker (eds.), *The Practice of Econometrics*, Martinus Nijhoff, Dordrecht.

Matsuyama, K., N. Kiyotaki and A. Matsui (1993). 'Toward a theory of international currency', *Review of Economic Studies*.

Matthews, K. and A. Rastogi (1985). 'Little Mo and the moon lighters: another look at the black economy', Liverpool Research Group in Macroeconomics, *Quarterly Economic Policy*.

Mulligan, C. and X. Sala-i-Martin (1997). 'The optimum quantity of money: theory and evidence', NBER Working Paper no. 5954.

Neck, R., F. Schneider and M. Hofreither (1989). 'The consequences of progressive income taxation for the shadow economy: some theoretical considerations', in D. Bös and B. Felderer (eds.), *The Political Economy of Progressive Taxation*, Springer, Heidelberg.

Obstfeld, M. and K. Rogoff (1983). 'Speculative hyperinflations in maximizing models: can we rule them out?', *Journal of Political Economy*.

—— (1996). *Foundations of International Macroeconomics*, MIT Press, Cambridge, MA.

Porter, R. and R. Judson (1996a). 'The location of US currency: how much is abroad?', *Federal Reserve Bulletin*.

—— (1996b). 'The location of US currency: how much is abroad?', mimeo. (unpublished technical version).

Quirk, P. (1996). 'Macroeconomic implications of money laundering', IMF Working Paper.

Schneider, F. (1986). 'Estimating the size of the Danish shadow economy using the currency demand approach: an attempt', *Scandinavian Journal of Economics*.

—— (1994a). 'Measuring the size and development of the shadow economy: can the causes be found and the obstacles be overcome?', in H. Brandstätter and W. Güth (eds.), *Essays on Economic Psychology*, Springer, Heidelberg.

—— (1994b). 'Can the shadow economy be reduced with major tax reforms? An empirical investigation for Austria', *Public Finance*, Supplement 'Public Finance and Irregular Activities', edited by W.W. Pommerehne.

—— (1997). 'Empirical results of the size of the shadow economy for 15 OECD countries', mimeo., University of Linz.

—— and R. Neck (1993). 'The development of the shadow economy under changing tax systems and structures: some theoretical and empirical results for Austria', *Finanzarchiv*.

Seitz, F. (1995). 'The circulation of the Deutsche Mark abroad', Deutsche Bundesbank Discussion Paper.

Sidrauski, M. (1967). 'Rational choice and patterns of growth in a monetary economy', *American Economic Review*.

Sims, C. (1994). 'A simple model of the determination of the price level and the interaction of monetary and fiscal policy', *Economic Theory*.

Sprenkle, C. (1993). 'The case of the missing money', *Journal of Economic Perspectives*.

Sumner, S. (1990). 'The transactions and hoarding demand for currency', *Review of Business and Economics*.

—— (1994). 'The case of the missing currency, correspondence', *Journal of Economic Perspectives*.

Tanzi, V. (1977). 'Inflation, lags in collection, and the real value of tax revenue', *IMF Staff Papers*.

—— (1983). 'The underground economy in the United States: annual estimates, 1930–1980', *IMF Staff Papers*.

Thomas, J.J. (1992). *Informal Economic Activity*, Harvester Wheatsheaf, London.

Van Hove, L. and J. Vuchelen (1996). 'Who needs high-denomination euro banknotes?', *Rivista Internazionale di Scienze Economiche e Commercial*.

Wallace, N. (1983). 'A legal restrictions theory of the demand for money', Federal Reserve Bank of Minneapolis, *Quarterly Review*.

Weck-Hannemann, H., W.W. Pommerehne and B.S. Frey (1986). *Die heimliche Wirtschaft: Die Entwicklung der Schattenwirtschaft in der Schweiz*, Respublica helvetica, Bern.

Wilson, J. (1992). 'Physical currency movements and capital flows', Background Paper to IMF Report on the Measurement of International Capital Flows.

Euro vs dollar
Will the euro replace the dollar as the world currency?

SUMMARY

Will and should the euro become an international currency? Previous work has noted that measuring size by GDP, role in international trade or even financial markets, Europe matches the USA. On these grounds, the euro is expected to challenge the dollar's supremacy. Cost−benefit analyses have looked at seigniorage, benefits for home financial institutions, relaxation of the external constraint, influence on international institutions, effects on macroeconomic policy co-ordination, and the wider consequences of exercising or sharing 'currency hegemony'. This paper revisits these issues with a new framework that stresses the role of financial asset markets and uses new data to evaluate scenarios. As euro securities markets become deeper and more liquid and transaction costs fall, euro assets will become more attractive, and the use of the euro as a vehicle currency in trade will expand; the asset and trade effects interact. A welfare analysis reveals potential benefits for the euro area of the same order of magnitude as international seigniorage − at the cost of the USA and the 'Asian bloc'. If policy-makers wish to promote the international role of the euro, they should focus their efforts on integrating the European capital markets: increasing their liquidity, breadth and depth. Here both (de)regulation and various aspects of policy harmonization across Europe will be important; so too will private market initiatives (e.g., in establishing benchmark interest rates and securities).

— Richard Portes and Hélène Rey

The emergence of the euro as an international currency

Richard Portes and Hélène Rey

London Business School and CEPR; London School of Economics

1. INTRODUCTION

After nearly a century of domination in world monetary affairs, the dollar is about to face stiff competition when the euro is created. Political calculations and national symbolism will undoubtedly play a part: they already shape current debates. The international status of the euro will have substantial implications for the international monetary system, the composition of portfolios, exchange rates and monetary policies. Economic efficiency and welfare are also at stake. The rapidly growing literature on the potential international role of the euro typically fails to specify a clear analytical framework, resorting mostly to comparing the sizes of economic areas and financial markets, and making guesses about possible changes in the use of currencies for both trade invoicing and asset denomination.

Earlier versions of this paper were presented at the CEPR Workshop, Options for the Future of the Exchange Rate Policy of the EMU, Paris, 4–5 April 1997; at the CentER Macroeconomics Workshop; at the NBER Summer Institute, 14 July 1997; and at ESI, Berlin, 12 September 1997. We are grateful for comments and help from David Begg, Michael Brennan, Creon Butler, Susan Collins, Angela Cozzini, Paul De Grauwe, Angelika Donaubauer, Sylvester Eijiffinger, Michael Fleming, Koji Fusa, Charles Goodhart, Philipp Hartmann, Seppo Honkapohja, Harry Huizinga, Fabienne Ilzkovitz, Kees Koedijk, Jan Lemmen, Richard Lyons, Robert McCauley, Jacques Mélitz, Marco Pagano, Avinash Persaud, Eli Remolona, Andrew Rose, Zoeb Sachee, Kermit Schoenholtz, Alexander Swoboda, Harald Uhlig, Charles Wyplosz and the Economic Policy Panel, as well as for comments from Peter Kenen on Alogoskoufis and Portes (1997). Salomon Brothers and Cross Border Capital gave especially valuable assistance with data. Montserrat Ferré-Carracedo and Jordi Riera provided excellent research assistance. Hélène Rey thanks the European Commission (Marie Curie Fellowship) and the Centre for Economic Performance (LSE) for financial support.

Here we offer a discussion and specific estimates based on a new and explicit analytical framework as well as on new data. The key determinant of the extent and speed of internationalization of the euro will be transaction costs in foreign exchange and securities markets. We emphasize that synergies between these markets imply the existence of different possible configurations, including the status quo and a very diminished role for the dollar. Given the euro's fundamentals – the EU's economic size, the liberalization and integration of its financial markets, and confidence in its international creditor status and stability-oriented monetary policy – we find that the most likely outcome is that the dollar will have to share the number-one position.

With few exceptions, such as Bergsten (1997), observers in the United States tend to underplay this possibility. Frankel (1995), for example, argues that 'there is little likelihood that some other currency will supplant the dollar as the world's premier reserve currency by 2020. One national currency or another must occupy the number-one position, and there is simply no plausible alternative.' Similarly, Deputy Treasury Secretary Lawrence Summers said, 'The dollar will remain the primary reserve currency for the foreseeable future ... We expect the impact of the euro on the monetary system to be quite limited initially and to occur only gradually' (speech to Euromoney Conference, New York, 30 April 1997). Perhaps the wish is father to the thought, or this assessment is influenced by scepticism about the likelihood or desirability of monetary unification in Europe. Perhaps they disregard future challenges to the dollar because they believe that the limited decline in its dominance after the break-up of the Bretton Woods exchange rate regime came mainly from relatively high US inflation, now apparently conquered. But then they should take into account another macroeconomic source of long-run dollar weakness: the US current account deficits that have led to massive accumulation of external debt. Our point, however, is that the euro will be a competitor to the dollar simply because of a size effect, which will be more than proportional to the sum of the currencies that will go into the euro.

Does it matter whether the euro achieves the status of international currency? Policy-makers and academic writers have long regarded currency hegemony as a source of political as well as economic benefits. For instance, Kunz (1995) writes: 'Geopolitical power depends on financial power, each of which supports the other. To ignore the real benefits of controlling the international currency system is [unfortunate] ... The death of the dollar order will drastically increase the price of the American dream while simultaneously shattering American global influence.' Even the recent east Asian currency crises, which led to the demise of dollar pegs, is sometimes interpreted as an alarming example of the impending decline of the 'dollar order' (e.g., *Los Angeles Times*, 22 July 1997). According to Cohen (1997), monetary supremacy 'confers substantial political benefits on the hegemon. At home, the country should be better insulated from outside influence or coercion in formulating and implementing policy. Abroad, it should be better able to pursue foreign objectives without constraint as well as to exercise a degree of influence or coercion over others. The expansion of its currency's authoritative domain, in principle, translates directly into effective political power.' Frankel (1995) also notes the 'benefits to political power and prestige', which, though 'nebulous', reflect the association between the loss of key currency status and the historical decline of great powers.

The economic advantages from currency hegemony include a comparative advantage for markets and institutions of the issuing country, the advantage for trade of having other countries peg their exchange rates to one's own (elimination of exchange rate uncertainty), and the ability to finance balance of payments deficits with liabilities denominated in the international money, which other countries will accept without effective limit. This does weaken a constraint on economic policy, although the possible resulting overhang of liquid liabilities may ultimately pose problems. De Gaulle went too far in claiming that the power of the dollar 'enabled the United States to be indebted to foreign countries free of charge' (quoted by Kunz, 1995) – if only because foreigners hold most of that debt in interest-bearing US Treasury securities – but there was some substance in his basic insight. Still, under Bretton Woods other countries had to accumulate dollars or threaten to break up the system. With a floating dollar (and flexible exchange rates, in general), the nature of the external constraint has changed (see the Introduction to Alogoskoufis *et al.*, 1991). Yet, in the short and medium run, the USA has been able to build up international liabilities in dollars at a lower interest rate than it would otherwise have had to pay (see below and Artus, 1997a). Moreover, it has the option to eliminate some of this debt with a surprise inflation. McKinnon (1993) states that 'The "privilege" of going into international debt so heavily in your own currency is one that is open only to the centre ... country.'

Some of the debt is indeed 'free of charge'. Foreign residents hold US currency in large quantities (the conventional estimate is 60% of the total stock outstanding, but elsewhere in this issue Rogoff puts it closer to 50%). This is the source of seigniorage to the issuer of the international currency: the ability to obtain real resources (net imports) in exchange for almost costless notes. The flow of this international seigniorage to the United States is around 0.1% of GDP (Alogoskoufis and Portes, 1991; Commission of the European Communities, 1990; Frankel, 1995; Rogoff, this issue). There is another, often neglected source of seigniorage accruing to the issuer of the international currency: a liquidity discount. Non-resident holdings of US government securities are 25% of the total stock, compared with 17% in other major markets (J.P. Morgan, 1997b), and the volume of transactions in US government bonds is an even more disproportionate share (relative to the size of stocks outstanding) of the global bond markets (see Table 7 below). This inter-national currency effect reduces the real yields that the United States government has to pay. From J.P. Morgan (1997a) estimates, we calculate that this is worth 25–50 basis points. Applied to non-resident holdings of US government debt of approximately $2000 billion, this $5–10 billion annual flow is of the same order of magnitude as international currency seigniorage. Furthermore, efficiency gains arise from the deepening of exchange and financial markets. We estimate that for the EU these gains are of the same order of magnitude as both sources of seigniorage (section 4). These results provide a new economic argument for policy-makers who wish to promote the international role of the euro.

We assume that the euro will be launched on 1 January 1999. Indeed, we go further and assume that, not long thereafter, the euro area will cover the entire existing EU, and in particular the United Kingdom (important because of London's financial markets), although it will take longer to bring in the countries expected to join the EU from 2002–3 onwards. We assume also that the European Central Bank (ECB) will quickly establish its credibility and reputation, and that it will conduct a neutral monetary policy relative to the initial exchange rate of the euro. Its monetary policies will have far more important international spillovers than those of any of the existing EU central banks. These spillovers will affect exchange rates and the process of international policy co-ordination. International institutions such as the G7, the IMF and the OECD will have to adapt (see Alogoskoufis and Portes, 1991; Begg *et al.*, 1997; Henning, 1997).

In section 2, we propose alternative 'steady-state' scenarios for the roles of the euro as an international means of payment and a store of value, and we discuss the process that generates each scenario. In section 3, we use foreign exchange and securities market data to assess the plausibility of these scenarios. As euro securities markets become deeper and more liquid and transaction costs fall, euro assets will become more attractive, and the use of the euro as a vehicle currency will expand; the two effects interact. The extent to which the euro may take on some of the current roles of the dollar will depend on policy decisions and on the beliefs of market participants. In section 4, we find potentially significant economic efficiency and welfare benefits for the euro area, at the cost of the USA and Japan. Section 5 focuses on the transition from the current configuration towards the new role of the euro, and the implications of that process for the exchange rate between the dollar and the euro, both in the short and in the medium run. Private asset demand shifts into the euro, supplemented by some rebalancing of official reserves, may initially outweigh the expansion of new liability issues in euros, which will also be encouraged by the development of euro financial markets. Such excess demand for euro-denominated assets would favour an appreciation of the new currency *vis-à-vis* the dollar and the yen. Finally, we consider the policy implications of these developments. If they wish to promote the emergence of the euro as an international currency, European authorities must make the domestic euro financial markets more efficient, more integrated and cheaper for participants. If pressures for euro appreciation materialize, the authorities will have to eschew rigid monetary or inflation targeting. And if the euro does challenge the dollar's hegemony, the result may be instability in the international monetary system, which appropriate policy co-ordination could mitigate.

2. SCENARIOS FOR THE INTERNATIONALIZATION OF THE EURO

Within national borders, the sole use of one currency is usually imposed by government fiat. Only in exceptional circumstances, such as very rapid inflation, is a national currency replaced in one or more of its functions by other currencies or commodities. In the international economy, demand factors play a much more important role in the determination of which currencies are used. The view that public (state) use of a currency precedes and dictates private use (Goodhart, 1996) is not valid in the international domain. Since there is no supranational authority that can impose the use of a single currency, these issues are decided in the market place, by the behaviour of private and public agents of all countries. But here the market may not function well. Because of economies of scale and externalities in the use of currencies, considerable uncertainty and asymmetric information, there is no guarantee that the world will end up with the best monetary system, let alone a single international currency.

History matters, however. Once an exchange structure is established, it will persist unless the system experiences a shock large enough to shift it from one equilibrium to another (Krugman, 1980; Rey, 1997a). Many of the institutions and modes of behaviour from previous regimes do not change overnight, or do not change at all. We observe inertia and hysteresis (Yeager, 1976; Kindleberger, 1984). The possible existence of multiple equilibria and threshold effects gives a role to history and institutions. Moreover, if the shocks are big enough to overcome inertia, expectations will be important in determining which equilibrium will prevail, and that may create considerable instability. Our framework allows us to estimate the potential for internationalization of the euro using foreign exchange and securities market data. The use of vehicle currencies and demand for financial assets denominated in different currencies are driven by, and themselves affect, the liquidity of the different bilateral foreign exchange and bond markets.

2.1. The current configuration and potential changes

2.1.1. Foreign exchange markets and trade invoicing. The dollar is currently used in 83% of two-way transactions in foreign exchange markets, while the DM is used in only 37%; other EMS currencies are used in 21% of transactions, and sterling in 10%; the yen is used in 24% of transactions (BIS, 1996). This is despite the fact that the EU accounts for a higher proportion of world trade than the USA (even netting out intra-EU trade): in 1992, the EU accounted for 17% of world exports, the USA 12% and Japan 9%. But the dollar intermediates in the financing of trade between the EU and third countries, as well as trade of third countries among themselves, partly because of lower transaction costs in the inter-bank market. The lower transaction costs in all markets involving the euro will make some substitution likely (Kenen (1996) reaches a similar conclusion). We do not believe that changes in invoicing practices are driving forces behind internationalization of currencies; rather, they are accompanying phenomena. Still, invoicing could introduce some additional inertia when we switch to the euro, but could then strengthen the externality.[1]

Whereas European firms invoice a very large proportion of their exports in their own currencies, the proportion of their imports invoiced in other currencies, and especially dollars, is significant. Japanese firms invoice mainly in dollars, while LDCs invoice overwhelmingly in dollars. The share of Japanese exports invoiced in dollars has been falling over time, while the share denominated in yen is rising; and the share of US trade denominated in foreign currencies is rising (Black, 1985, 1989). In 1992, according to the ECU Institute (1995), 48% of world exports were invoiced in dollars, 15% in DM, 18% in other major European currencies, and still only 5% in yen. Meanwhile, the Japanese and European shares of world exports have also been rising, while the share of US exports seems to have been stagnant (see Tavlas, 1991; Tavlas and Ozeki, 1992).

EMU is likely to bring almost exclusive invoicing in euros by EU firms. Economies of scale in use of the euro will induce firms from other areas that trade mainly with the EU to start invoicing in euros (e.g., central and eastern Europe, the Middle East and north Africa), as will many multinational Japanese and US firms. Some imports from the USA and Japan will remain exceptions, as will some primary commodities. But there will be an initial one-off 'arithmetic' effect, raising the share of dollar-denominated trade, when intra-EU trade becomes domestic. Hartmann (1996a) estimates that the initial post-EMU position would see 59% of world trade denominated in dollars and, on his 'euro-optimistic' scenario, 28% in euros. The euro's role will grow at a rate determined by its ability to capture more of the dollar's vehicle currency position in non-US trade. The process will also depend on the stability of exchange rates between the dollar, the yen and the euro. If the dollar were to display high volatility against the yen and the euro, while their bilateral exchange rate was relatively stable, it would boost the chances of the euro (and the yen) substituting for the dollar as an international unit of account. Tavlas (1997) argues that firms will seek to invoice in a currency that has relatively low inflation risk and real exchange rate risk.

If trade relations become concentrated in regional blocs (e.g. Europe–Africa–Middle East, Japan–south-east Asia, USA–Latin America), we might end up with at least three vehicle *cum* unit of account currencies. But in so far as trade is more uniformly distributed geographically and multilateral, there will still be powerful forces behind the use of a single dominant currency for these roles. In that case the

[1] We are grateful to Seppo Honkapohja for this insight.

change in the fundamentals will favour the euro, but history (inertia) will favour the dollar.

2.1.2. Securities markets. The share of US dollar bonds in the international bond market has fallen substantially since the early 1980s: from 62% of the stock of bonds outstanding in 1985 to only 38% at end-1996 (of a total stock amounting to $3200 billion), with a corresponding sharp rise in the share of yen-denominated bonds to 16% (BIS, 1997). According to McCauley and White (1997), the euro money market is likely to prove a very liquid market from its inception (see also European Commission, 1997a). Even a 'narrow' monetary union (essentially France and Germany) would have a market in derivative transactions larger than that for the yen, and a larger market than the dollar for futures on longer-dated government securities (Prati and Schinasi, 1997).

The domestic market in Europe for private bonds is already fairly unified, close to having a common reference yield curve (McCauley and White, 1997). With outstanding stocks of $2948 billion, it is two-thirds the size of the American market. The segmentation that one observes in this market appears to derive primarily from the effect of different currencies. In the pricing of government debt, prospects for integration in trading debt of the most creditworthy governments look brighter than is generally acknowledged (McCauley and White, 1997). Total public sector domestic debt in the EU15 amounts to $4618 billion, two-thirds of that in the USA (BIS, 1997). Moving to the euro will promote the integration of the EU15 government debt markets, so that their breadth, depth and liquidity will become comparable – if not for some time equal – to those of the United States.[2] This will be partly the consequence of policy and institutional changes in the markets (see section 6), and partly an endogenous response, arising from the inverse relation between transaction volumes and costs that is the key to our argument.

Major European institutional investors are currently very little diversified into foreign assets, except those in the UK and the Netherlands (Artus, 1996; Miles, 1996; PDFM, 1997). But they may initially prefer to diversify across countries, in the newly integrated European capital markets, without incurring exchange risks. Meanwhile US institutional investors – who also currently show very high home preference – are likely to find the new euro financial market attractive as they diversify (Artus, 1997b), especially if euro bond interest rates are less correlated with US bond yields than are current European government bond rates. We might expect this, if the ECB is a more independent actor – if only because of the size of its economy – in monetary policy.

---

[2] Robert McCauley suggests (in correspondence) that there is evidence from derivatives markets that the prices of bonds from smaller European countries should be more integrated with valuations elsewhere under a single currency. The data suggest that the purchase by non-residents of bonds denominated in 'lesser' European currencies is inhibited by the costs of managing exchange rate risk and by the greater difficulty of managing duration and volatility of the portfolio in these countries. Moving to the euro will eliminate these cost differentials.

2.1.3. The official sector. We have focused so far on private sector behaviour, because we believe that financial market use of an international currency takes the lead, that use as a vehicle currency is the main determinant of use by the monetary authorities as an intervention currency (Kenen, 1995), and that this in turn determines use as a reserve currency (Krugman, 1984). But reserve holding and currency pegging by governments deserve some attention. Pegging either follows the establishment of a currency as an international currency or is dictated by international politics (e.g., the CFA franc zone, the prospective incorporation of at least some of the 'Associated Countries' of central and eastern Europe in the Exchange Rate Mechanism, Mark 2).

The share of the US dollar in official reserves, although declining, is overwhelmingly higher than the share of any other single currency.[3] From 76.1% of total official currency reserves in 1973, the dollar fell to 63.3% in 1994. The share of major European currencies shows a steady increase, from 14.3% in 1973 to 21.9% in 1994 (the share of the DM has risen from 7.1% to 15.5%). The Japanese yen rose from almost zero in 1973 to 8.5% of the total in 1994.

Despite significant efforts (e.g., Dooley *et al.*, 1989), we do not have a satisfactory empirical account of the determinants of reserve-holding behaviour and these observed trends.[4] The trend decline in the share of dollar reserves in the portfolios of central banks is likely to be somewhat reinforced by the EMU process (McCauley (1997) carefully assesses the arguments). But this will not necessarily make the euro a major reserve currency outside the EU, unless foreign exchange intervention by non-EU countries is also in euros; that, we suggest, will follow trends in the financial markets.

The unit of account role of an international currency, in regard to the official sector, is related to whether there are countries that peg their own currency against it. Of the 47 countries that either pegged their currency or maintained limited flexibility against a single other currency in March 1994, 25 did so against the US dollar and 14 against the French franc. All these economies are small, however, and even jointly they do not amount to a significant share of the world economy. The growing integration of the central and east European economies with the EU will enhance the euro's role as an international unit of account. (Bénassy-Quéré (1996) stresses the potential anchor role for the euro, going beyond pegging strictly defined, at the regional level.)

2.2. Synergy between the medium of exchange and store of value functions

The use of the euro in financial services will depend on transaction costs: that is, how efficiently those services are provided. Transaction costs (typically measured by

---

[3] See Alogoskoufis and Portes (1991, 1992), Bénassy-Quéré (1996).
[4] Most recently, Eichengreen and Frankel (1996) find that the elasticity of a currency's share in official reserves with respect to the corresponding country's share in world output is in the range 0.5–1.33.

bid–ask spreads) in financial markets are normally very low for liquid assets, but the volumes to which they apply are huge (e.g., well over one trillion dollars daily in the foreign exchange markets), so their incentive effects are considerable. Moreover, the pattern (ranking) of transaction costs gives a qualitative differentiation among markets that drives choices in the international market place.

Whereas international transactions in goods markets are arranged between importers and exporters, eventual payment is intermediated through commercial banks. In monetary transactions, 'network' or 'thickness' externalities are very important. The more agents who use a given money, the more attractive it will be for other agents to use it. The more transactions in that currency, the easier and quicker they are, and the less resources needed to find a match for any given supply or demand. The entry of any trader into the market therefore confers a positive externality on all other traders. The 'thickness' externalities may cause dealers to prefer indirect exchange, through a vehicle currency, to direct exchange of one currency for another. If there are many dealers prepared to exchange dollars (the dollar market is 'thick'), then a dealer wishing to exchange pesetas for rupees finds it less costly to go through two exchanges, one of pesetas for dollars and one of dollars for rupees, than to go through a direct exchange of pesetas for rupees (see Hartmann (1996b) for a recent discussion with full references).

The key parameter in our analysis is the elasticity of transaction costs with respect to volumes. 'Numerous studies have related bid–ask spreads to trading activity and price volatility for a variety of financial markets. These studies generally find a negative relationship between volume and bid–ask spreads and a positive relationship between price volatility and bid–ask spreads. The volume–spread relationship probably reflects decreasing order-processing costs, decreasing inventory-carrying costs, and increasing market maker competition as volume increases' (Fleming, 1997). We assume that volatility on the different markets will remain of the same order of magnitude as before the introduction of the euro, so that liquidity is the main driving force behind change in the pattern of transaction costs.

There is a synergy between the vehicle currency role on the foreign exchange markets and trading of financial assets denominated in this currency. An efficient domestic financial system encourages capital inflows, which increase the liquidity of the bilateral foreign exchange markets involving that domestic currency, so making it more likely that the currency becomes a vehicle. Conversely, being a vehicle currency enhances foreign exchange market liquidity and lowers the cost of portfolio substitution, which feeds back into foreign exchange market turnover. These 'circular' forces leave scope for multiple equilibria, which, we believe, are a necessary feature of any convincing model of the medium of exchange function of money.

The internationalization of the euro will depend mainly on the liquidity of the euro financial markets (the analysis is made under the assumption that the ECB has established its anti-inflationary credentials and that monetary policy is 'neutral' in all the countries). The driving force towards internationalization will come from the financial market side and then will expand the vehicle currency function. If financial transactions inside the new euro zone enhance the liquidity of the euro securities markets above a critical level, then the 'old' equilibrium, where the dollar is the international currency for both financial assets and foreign exchange market transactions, becomes unsustainable. There is a shift towards a new equilibrium where the euro either replaces the dollar completely in its major international roles, or replaces it only in some dimensions. In the latter case, the economic links between the 'dollar bloc' and the 'Asian bloc' would still be dominated by the dollar. But if transaction costs on euro securities markets remain higher than on dollar securities markets, only very limited changes in the pattern of world payments will occur.

The internationalization of the euro therefore hinges critically on the speed of integration of euro financial markets, on the willingness of the ECB not to hinder internationalization, and on the number of participants in the monetary union, especially on UK participation. Since the turnover on the UK bond market is high by European standards, the participation of the UK in EMU can tilt us from one equilibrium to another.

2.3. A simplified story of the pattern of world payments

Consider a three-country world with a European, an American and an Asian bloc. The demand for a currency comes from two sources: trade in goods and trade in financial assets. Demand for financial assets denominated in a given currency derives from the pattern of cross-border bond and equity flows and from savings. We assume that sellers of goods and financial assets are paid in their own currency predominantly, but that a fraction of the denomination of the transactions depends on the international status of the currency. This assumption is in line with the evidence presented in Table 1.

Purchases and sales of financial assets as well as foreign exchange transactions involve the intervention of financial intermediaries. These financial intermediaries

Table 1. Share of exports invoiced in domestic currency (%)

	1980	1992
USA	96	92
Germany	82	77
Japan	29	40
UK	76	62
France	60	55

Source: ECU Institute (1995).

choose on which foreign exchange and bond markets to operate by minimizing transaction costs. Exchange rate and interest rate volatility are assumed to be of the same order of magnitude before and after the introduction of the euro, so that changes in transaction costs reflect only changes in the liquidity of the different markets. Thus risk–return trade-offs, which in theory also affect portfolio investment decisions, are not taken into account, so that demands for equities and for some bond transactions are invariant with the currency regime. Consequently, real returns are unaffected.

Some other bond transactions, however, such as the ones made for hedging purposes, vary with the international status of the currency. For example, a financial intermediary who carries some cash in currency j at date t and who wants some currency i at date $t+1$ has several possibilities. He can change his currency j against currency i on the spot foreign exchange market at date t and then buy bonds denominated in currency i, which will be redeemed in currency i at date $t+1$. He can also buy bonds denominated in currency j at date t and go to the spot foreign exchange market at date $t+1$. But he could also go to the spot foreign exchange market at t, exchange currency j against currency k, buy bonds denominated in currency k and change currency k against currency i at $t+1$. His choice will depend on the structure of the transaction costs on the different markets, which will depend on the strategies of all the other agents through the existence of thick market externalities. Thus turnover on the different markets is determined partly by the underlying real trade fundamentals, equity and bond trading, and savings behaviour, but also partly by history. Transaction costs reflect the liquidity of the different markets, but they also pick up other effects. In particular, more liquid markets tend to be institutionally better organized.

2.4. The present situation: the dollar as international currency

A stylized three-bloc description of the current world system of payments is shown in Figure 1. The dollar dominates in transactions linked to trade in goods and financial assets between the three blocs. (As we focus on *inter-bloc* exchanges, we ignore *intra-European* trade.) Because of a complete home portfolio bias, we consider that, inside each bloc, savings are invested in domestic financial assets. This is not too far-fetched: pension funds hold only 9.6% of foreign assets in the USA, 6.6% in Japan and 4.9% in Germany (Miles, 1996; PDFM (1997) estimates 13% for the USA, 10% for Japan). Data on foreign exchange market turnover by currency pairs are presented in Table 2. There are virtually no direct bilateral transactions between the yen and EU currencies.[5] Thus Japanese traders who may pay for imports in

---

[5] The exception is the DM/yen market, but even this market has a low turnover compared to the major markets as well as compared to the size of the trade and financial flows between Japan and Europe.

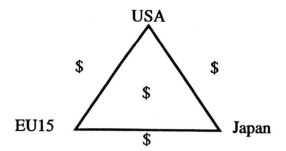

Figure 1. Present situation, status quo: dollar vehicle

Figure 2. Quasi status quo: dollar vehicle

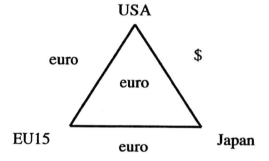

Figure 3. Big euro: euro vehicle

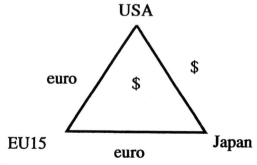

Figure 4. Medium euro: dollar vehicle

Note: The vehicle currency is shown in the middle of each triangle. The dominant currency used for financial exchanges between two blocs appears on the sides of the triangles.

Table 2. Average daily foreign exchange market turnover ($bn), 1995

	Spot, forward and swaps	Spot	Swaps
DM/$	254	143	93
$/yen	242	88	133
Yen/DM	24	19	2
DM/EU	99	82	14
Yen/all others[a]	8	2	2
DM/all others[b]	1.5	1	0.2
FF/all others[c]	5	1	2

[a] Excluding $ and DM.
[b] Excluding $, yen, EU and Swiss francs.
[c] Excluding $ and DM.
Source: BIS (1996).

DM, and who would therefore wish to exchange yen for DM, will tend to use dollar-denominated assets for intermediate financial transactions such as hedging. Some transactions that would add to the yen/DM market turnover (or the yen/FF market turnover) are actually performed on the yen/$ and $/DM or $/FF markets.

2.5. The emergence of the euro zone: alternative scenarios

Is the EMU shock big enough to induce a shift in the equilibrium structure of payments described in Figure 1? If transaction costs in euro-denominated securities remain higher than those in dollar-denominated securities, two cases may arise. One is the *status quo*, the other is the *quasi status quo* described in Figure 2. While the dollar is still the vehicle currency on the foreign exchange markets, the euro becomes the dominant currency for exchanges between Europe and the Asian bloc.

If transaction costs in euro-denominated securities fall below those in dollar-denominated securities, three other equilibria may emerge. In the *pan euro* scenario, the euro replaces the dollar as the currency used for financial asset transactions between blocs and as the vehicle currency on the foreign exchange market. The use of the euro in all financial transactions leads to its use as a vehicle on the foreign exchange markets, and there are no direct transactions between the dollar and the yen. Transaction costs are low on the euro/$ and euro/yen markets, now enhanced by the vehicle currency use of the euro. This scenario is unlikely to happen as the post-euro $/yen market should be at least as liquid as the pre-euro yen/DM market.

Figure 3 shows the *big euro* scenario: the euro takes the role of vehicle currency on the foreign exchange markets and replaces the dollar as the main international currency for financial asset transactions, but transactions between the dollar bloc and the Asian bloc are still in dollars. Transaction costs on the $/yen exchange market are high compared to transaction costs on the $/euro and euro/yen markets, where volumes have risen following the vehicle currency role of the euro. Not all transactions between the yen and the dollar are intermediated by the euro. Some are direct and some are indirect because of the 'double coincidence of wants problem' on the bilateral foreign exchange markets (see Krugman, 1980).

In the final alternative, the *medium euro* scenario, represented in Figure 4, the euro replaces the dollar as the main international currency for financial asset transactions, but transactions between the dollar bloc and the Asian bloc are still dominated by the dollar. The euro is not the vehicle currency on foreign exchange markets. As before, however, some transactions between the euro and the yen are intermediated through the dollar, others through the euro.

Which of the *big* or *medium euro* scenarios is more likely depends mostly on the degree of symmetry of the trade relations between the blocs. From the structure of transaction costs, it is apparent that the less integrated Europe and Asia are (the higher the transaction costs on the euro/yen market), the more the dollar is likely to keep its vehicle currency role. Note that we do not consider here the existence of other equilibria in which the yen could be a competitor for the dollar or the euro. Given the present data, this seems unlikely, although major institutional changes could enhance the prospects of the yen in the long run.

3. NUMERICAL ESTIMATES

In this section, we determine which equilibria are indeed possible. To do so, we use data on trade, equity and bond flows for each of the bilateral foreign exchange and bond markets to estimate the size of the relevant markets under each scenario. Using plausible estimates of the response of transaction costs to transaction volumes, we can reject some scenarios, but we find that multiple equilibria are likely.

3.1. Estimates for the foreign exchange markets

3.1.1.   The market fundamentals. Foreign exchange market turnover can be divided into inter-dealer and customer–dealer transactions. Lyons (1995, 1997a) describes inter-dealer transactions as a 'hot potato' game. Imagine ten risk-averse dealers, each of whom starts with a zero net position. A customer now wants to sell $10 million worth of DM and contacts one of the dealers. The dealer does not want to carry the full open position. He keeps his share – one-tenth of $10 million – and calls another dealer to sell the remaining $9 million worth of DM. And so on until each dealer has a $1 million position. The inter-dealer transactions will have represented 90% of all the transactions carried out throughout this process. This proportion roughly matches the actually observed shares. Table 3 shows that the shares of inter-dealer transactions are remarkably similar on all the bilateral markets. The huge predominance of inter-dealer transactions over customer–dealer

Table 3. Share of inter-dealer trading, spot foreign exchange, 1995 (%)

	DM	Yen	Pound	FF	Swiss F	Can $
$	85	81	85	80	83	79
DM		90	92	88	88	84

Source: Authors' computations based on BIS (1996).

transactions is a feature that differentiates the foreign exchange markets from all other financial markets.

The volume of customer–dealer transactions on the foreign exchange market can be decomposed into four different components:

$$v = T + E + B + I \qquad (1)$$

volume of	trade	cross-border	cross-border	international
customer–dealer	transactions	flow of	flow of	use as
transactions		equities	bonds	vehicle

Because of the inter-dealer transactions, the total volume of exchange transactions is a multiple of the volume of customer–dealer transactions:

$$V = v \times m \qquad (2)$$

total volume	volume of	multiplier
of exchange	customer–dealer	
transactions	transactions	

The size of the multiplier is inversely related to the share of customer–dealer transactions (it is 10 in our example, since each trader has a share of one-tenth of the market).

Table 4 presents data on these various components, including the direction of flows. The two first components, trade and equity flows (panels b and c), account for a small fraction of the global turnover (panel a) on each bilateral market. We assume that these are pure customer–dealer transactions, which generate a cascade of inter-dealer transactions but are invariant with the currency regime. This is why we call them 'fundamentals'. Cross-border bond flows (panel d) can be decomposed into two parts, inter-dealer and customer-dealer transactions, each of which accounts for roughly 50% of the total.[6] The customer–dealer part of the bond flows (B) is also assumed to be invariant with the currency regime, whereas the inter-dealer part will vary with the scenarios and the international currency. There is ample evidence that the most liquid bonds (such as the 5- or 10-year US Treasuries) are widely used by financial intermediaries for hedging practices. This is why the turnover ratio of these bonds is much higher than for the other securities. We

[6] We find that inter-dealer transactions represented 47% of the global transactions of both the US and UK bond markets in 1994 (another remarkable similarity). The remainder is customer–dealer transactions.

Table 4. Bilateral foreign exchange market transactions ($bn)

(a) Total foreign exchange turnover (April 1995)

	Yen	EU15
US$	1753	3966
Yen		377

Source: BIS (1996).

(b) Trade transactions (monthly average, 1993)

	USA	Japan	EU15
USA		5	11
Japan	11		6
EU15	11	4	

Source: IMF, *Direction of Trade Statistics.*

(c) Cross-border equity transactions (monthly average, 1993)

	USA	Japan	EU15
USA		8	29
Japan	3		2
EU15	25	11	

Source: Cross Border Capital.

(d) Cross-border bond transactions (monthly average, 1995)

	USA	Japan	EU15
USA		132	445
Japan	116		49
EU15	497	225	

Sources: BIS, personal communication and authors' estimates.

(e) Cross-border transactions in bonds and equities (annual, $bn)

	USA	Japan	Germany	UK
1992	6658	2674	1677	5396
1993	8440	3326	3258	6485
1994	9088	2814	3244	6777
1995	9812	3357	4142	10318

Source: BIS.
Note: Panels (b) to (d) show direction of bilateral flows, *from* country indicated in row *to* country indicated in column.

consider this to be a direct consequence of the dollar's dominance as the international currency. In our perspective, the more liquid markets are those that are the most likely to be affected by the switch to the euro.

Summarizing, we define the fundamentals of a bilateral exchange market as:

$$\text{Fundamentals} = \quad T \quad + \quad E \quad + \quad B \quad \quad (3)$$

| trade transactions | cross-border flow of equities | cross-border flow of bonds |

Note that B is only the customer–dealer part of global cross-border bond flows, set at 50% of the total. The remaining transactions $(I = V/m - T - E - B)$ are those due to the international use of a currency. Unlike the 'fundamentals', they vary with the scenario. Note that I can be positive or negative.[7] If I is positive, it means that the currency considered is used beyond what the real fundamentals would give: the currency is internationalized. For example, the turnover of the \$/DM market is likely to exceed what would have been predicted by the fundamentals of the USA and Germany. This is because some central European economies, for example, use the DM for international trade settlements. If I is negative, on the other hand, it means that the currency is less used than fundamentals would predict. For example, the major part of Japanese exports are invoiced in dollars.[8]

Our breakdown of transactions into fundamentals and customer–dealer transactions is presented in Table 5. The turnover on the yen/DM market is smaller than suggested by the fundamentals, while turnovers on the \$/DM or \$/yen markets are higher. This corresponds to the international currency role of the dollar.

3.1.2. Effects of EMU. In order to assess the effect of EMU we proceed as follows. Each scenario specifies which currency is being used on each financial market. This allows us to estimate the size of each market. Knowing how costs are related to market size, we can derive the corresponding cost structure. Then we can verify that the cost structure is compatible with the assumed scenario. Compatibility is assessed

Table 5. Decomposition of foreign exchange transactions: fundamentals versus customer–dealers (monthly averages, \$bn, 1995)

	Fundamentals			Customer–dealer transactions	
	Japan	EU15		Yen	EU15
US\$	160	570	US\$	333	595
Yen		167	Yen		38

Source: Authors' computations.

---

[7] I is likely to overstate the international use of a currency, since we have omitted some variables such as real estate transactions; but the volumes involved are small.

[8] We ignore speculation. Recent empirical papers (Lyons, 1997b; Ammer and Brunner, 1997) argue that the share of speculative profits is negligible compared to the profits generated by financial intermediation.

by considering the triangles in Figures 1–4. For example, the *big euro* scenario asserts that the euro is used when Europe deals with Japan and the USA, while the dollar remains the currency of choice for US–Japan relationships. This implies, for example, that it is cheaper to change yen into euros directly rather than via the dollar, and conversely. Does this match our new cost estimates? If so, the *big euro* scenario is a possible equilibrium; if not, we can rule it out. The appendix presents all the transaction cost restrictions implied by each scenario as well details of the calculations performed to estimate transaction volumes.

To find how changes in transaction volumes affect transaction costs, we need an estimate of the corresponding elasticity. For the foreign exchange markets, we adopt the estimate of −0.03 carefully derived by Hartmann (1996b). He stresses 'the apparent stability of [his] parameter estimates, not only between the different estimators but over time' (1997). In all cases, we start from the current transaction costs on the different foreign exchange markets, derived from Hartmann (1997), as presented in Table 6; then we apply the elasticity to the estimated change in volume to obtain new cost estimates.[9] For bond markets, we use a similar procedure (Table 8). We start from the current transaction costs on the different bond markets (Salomon Brothers dealers' survey) and apply the only estimate that we know of: Takagi (1989) finds a value of −0.11 for the Japanese government bond market. We also present a sensitivity analysis.

3.2. Bond market estimates

To decide between *status quo* (or *quasi status quo*) on the one hand and *big, pan* or *medium euro* on the other, the key criterion is the depth of the European bond market compared to the US bond market. As we see from Table 4, trading in bonds dominates trading in equities and real trade flows $(B > E > T)$. Do we believe that the financial markets of the euro bloc will be more liquid than those of the dollar bloc? Table 7 clearly shows that, relative to their underlying stocks, US government bonds

Table 6. Unit transaction costs (US cents, basis points)

Exchange market	Current	Exchange market	Quasi status quo	Medium euro	Big euro
$/DM	4.06	euro/$	4.02	4.02	4.02
DM/yen	4.37	euro/yen	4.33	4.33	3.43
$/yen	4.16	$/yen	4.17	4.17	4.27
FF/$	4.61				
£/$	4.27				

Source: Authors' calculations from Hartmann (1997).

[9] Hartmann's estimation allows transaction costs to depend on both transaction volumes and market price volatility. To obtain comparability across markets, we set the volatility level to 0.

are much more traded than others. Table 8 provides another measure of liquidity: the average bid–ask spreads on 10-year government bonds.[10] This measure can be used as a proxy for global transaction costs for each government bond market considered. These securities are used as a benchmark because they are usually the most widely traded, and they account for a very large part of the turnover.

Today's transaction costs favour the dollar as the currency of denomination for financial assets. However, turnovers and therefore transaction costs are endogenous and depend on the international status of a currency. Even if we control for this effect and bring in additional turnover in euro-denominated bonds stemming from foreign demand, the transaction costs we compute using the elasticity estimate still favour dollar financial markets. The gap is such that, in the absence of institutional changes or market participants' initiatives on the European bond markets, the dollar-denominated securities market will remain the most efficient one.

Consequently, the most likely scenarios based on bond market transaction costs seem to be either the *status quo* or *quasi status quo*. Estimates of the transaction costs on the foreign exchange market discriminate then in favour of the *quasi status quo* scenario: the euro will be more widely used than any European currencies for transactions involving Europe and the Asian bloc, but the dollar will keep its pre-eminence for all the other types of transaction, and in particular as the main vehicle currency.

Table 7. Government bond markets, 1995 ($bn)

	USA	Europe	Japan
Annual turnover domestic bonds	35843	45635	20625
Stock outstanding	2547	4618	3303
Ratio turnover/outstanding	14.0	9.9	6.2

Sources: McCauley and White (1997); Salomon Brothers, dealers' survey.

Table 8. Bid–ask spreads on the benchmark bonds (10-year) (US cents, basis points)

		Bond market	Quasi status quo	Medium euro	Big euro
USA	1.56	Dollar	1.57	1.57	1.57
Germany	4	euro	4.0	1.57	1.57
Japan	3.5	Yen	3.5	3.5	3.5
UK	3.12				
France	4				

Source: Salomon Brothers and authors' calculations.

[10] Since most of the trade in bonds is done OTC, a dealers' survey is the most reliable source for transaction costs. We are grateful to Kermit Schoenholtz and Zoeb Sachee for providing this information.

On the other hand, there are important institutional differences between US and European corporate bond markets. In the end, transaction costs on the euro market will depend also on policy decisions and regulations. US firms tend to rely much more on debt financing than their European counterparts. Of course, this is partly due to the greater liquidity of the US bond markets, and one can expect a process of financial disintermediation in Europe with the arrival of the euro.

3.3. The potential effect of institutional changes

The introduction of the euro carries with it the potential for creating the largest domestic financial market in the world, as suggested by Table 9. Current costs indicate, however, that this potential will probably require policy decisions. If, within five to ten years, financial market integration is completed within Europe, then euro transaction costs may indeed fall below dollar transaction costs. This is all the more likely if the UK joins EMU, because of the size of the UK financial market. To examine the effect of action by policy-makers to encourage the internationalization of the euro, we now assume that institutional changes, such as those discussed in section 6, lower the costs of trading in euro financial assets to the level that applies to dollar-denominated financial assets. Under these circumstances, the fundamentals support both the *medium euro* and the *big euro* scenarios, but exclude the *pan euro* scenario.

In the *medium euro* scenario, the dollar retains its vehicle currency role, but there is some additional turnover on the euro/yen foreign exchange market and less turnover on the $/yen foreign exchange market. Our estimate of the corresponding transaction costs is shown in Table 6. In the *big euro* scenario, the euro takes up the vehicle currency role. Consequently, there is much more turnover on the euro/yen foreign exchange market and much less turnover on the $/yen foreign exchange market. Again, we show the corresponding transaction costs in Table 6. In both cases, the costs on the euro/$ and euro/yen markets decline in comparison to the DM/$ and DM/yen markets, especially when the euro becomes the international

Table 9. Stock market capitalization *plus* debt securities *plus* bank assets, end-1995 ($bn)

EU15[a]	27270
EU11[b]	21084
UK	4658
USA	22865
Japan	16375
USA + Canada + Mexico	24711

[a] Austria, Belgium, Denmark, Finland, France, Germany, Greece, Ireland, Italy, Luxembourg, the Netherlands, Portugal, Spain, Sweden and the United Kingdom.
[b] Austria, Belgium, Denmark, Finland, France, Germany, Ireland, Italy, Luxembourg, the Netherlands, Portugal and Spain.
Source: Prati and Schinasi (1997).

currency. There is in both cases, however, an increase in the transaction cost on the $/yen market due to lower liquidity of that market. These results confirm that several equilibria are possible. Which one will emerge depends on the agents' beliefs.

3.4. Sensitivity analysis

The elasticity of costs to volumes plays a crucial role in our calculations.[11] The bigger the elasticity (in absolute value), the bigger the economies of scale and therefore the bigger the incentives to pool transactions. If transaction costs in euro-denominated assets fall sufficiently, the likelihood of a *big euro* or a *medium euro* scenario rises. It is necessary, therefore, to examine how sensitive our conclusions are to the value of this parameter. The frontier between *quasi status quo* and *medium* or *big euro* is independent of the foreign exchange market elasticity. It depends only on the transaction costs on bond markets. But the frontier between the *big euro* and *medium euro* scenarios varies with the elasticity parameter. For a very high elasticity (when its absolute value exceeds 0.16), the *medium euro* scenario can be ruled out, leaving the *big euro* scenario as the only possible one. For a low elasticity (absolute value less than 0.006), on the contrary, the *medium euro* scenario is the only possibility. Both scenarios are possible in the intermediate range, where the empirical estimates lie.

4. WELFARE ANALYSIS

The transaction costs on the foreign exchange and bond markets are obviously small and are expected to decline further, in particular with the introduction of the Electronic Brokerage Service (EBS). Does this mean that economic effects of cost reductions are too trivial to warrant attention? To start with, we have shown that even small changes may have powerful effects on the patterns of international monetary transactions. In this section we look at the effects on market efficiency, when small costs are applied to truly enormous flows. The European Commission's study *One Market, One Money* (1990) reports microeconomic efficiency gains ranging between 0.1% and 1% of GDP per year, depending on the size of the country under consideration. These estimates are found by simply setting to zero all the foreign exchange transaction costs within EU countries. This approach ignores the monopolistic margins (now falling) as well as the impact of EMU on foreign exchange transaction costs between EU countries and the American and Asian blocs. Our approach provides estimates for efficiency gains from forex transactions outside the euro area and on the bond markets.

---

[11] Hartmann's (1997) estimate is in the range −0.03 to −0.045 (with *t*-statistics around 1.7).

In principle, there is a direct relationship between economic welfare and global transaction costs. Because transacting involves real resource costs in terms of labour, transaction efficiency gains translate into savings in the use of labour. The bigger the share of labour in production, the more labour can be freed to perform other duties, raising aggregate consumption and welfare. Thus estimates of cost reductions can be interpreted as welfare gains. In this section we compute for each bloc and under each scenario the real resources going into financial intermediation, by multiplying transaction costs by volumes exchanged on each market and summing across markets.

Using the transaction costs and trade volumes calculated in section 3, one can rank the different possible scenarios (*quasi status quo*, *big euro* and *medium euro*).[12] The results are summarized in Table 10. From the point of view of Europe, the *big euro* scenario is the best one, ahead of *medium euro* and *quasi status quo*. For the USA the best scenario is obviously the *quasi status quo*, and welfare declines as we move to *medium euro* and *big euro*. Japan should favour the *medium euro* scenario, ahead of *quasi status quo* and *big euro*. The *medium euro* case is the best for the world as a whole, followed by *big euro* and *quasi status quo*, in that order.

The logic of these results should be clear. Efficiency gains and losses are mainly determined by bond market transactions. The dollar and euro bond markets are both very efficient in the *big* and *medium euro* cases, while in the *quasi status quo* case, the euro bond market is far less efficient than its dollar counterpart. Europe, therefore, strongly benefits from an enhanced usage of the euro. The US situation is symmetric: the more people use the euro, the less people use the dollar, and hence the welfare ranking is reversed. The USA does not suffer from higher transaction costs on the euro bond market in the *quasi status quo* case, because its residents use mainly financial assets denominated in dollars. Japan does, and this is why it is better off in the *medium euro* case. However, since Asia is more integrated with the USA than with Europe, there are increasing returns in using the dollar as a vehicle currency for exchanges involving Asia and Europe. This explains why Japan is made worse off when the euro becomes an international currency. For the world as a whole, transaction costs on the euro bond market matter less, while given the pattern of integration of the three blocs, there are increasing returns in using the dollar as the international currency. The rankings are insensitive to the elasticity used for bond market transactions for any reasonable values (between −0.0001 and −1). Takagi's (1989) estimate of −0.11 falls well within that range.

How big are the micro efficiency gains and losses? When we compare the *quasi status quo* and the *big euro* cases, our estimates indicate a (flow) gain worth 0.2% of

[12] The internationalization of the euro does not necessarily mean efficiency gains for EU countries. Indeed, depending on which of the degrees of internationalization is actually realized, the fragmentation of the currency system into different poles can decrease the efficiency of the global payments mechanism.

Table 10. Welfare rankings of the various scenarios

	Europe	USA	Japan	World
Quasi status quo	3	1	2	3
Medium euro	2	2	1	1
Big euro	1	3	3	2

Note: 1 is best outcome, followed by 2 and 3.

GDP for Europe, a loss of 0.04% of GDP for the USA, and a loss of 0.07% for Japan. The gains for Europe come mainly from decreasing costs on the bond markets. The losses for the USA and Japan come from foreign exchange market transactions: both countries are better off when the dollar is the vehicle currency. These results suggest that Europe would gain by promoting the use of the euro as a rival international currency to the dollar, but such a policy would go against the interests of both Japan and the USA.

5. THE TRANSITION: THE EURO AND THE DOLLAR

How can we characterize the transition to the plausible case where the Euro partly displaces the dollar? Such a shift will initiate a dynamic process that could affect the euro/dollar exchange rate. McCauley (1997) considers a wide variety of influences, which add up to an ambiguous conclusion. One of the important questions that arise is whether the expected higher demand for euro-denominated assets will be matched by a corresponding higher supply. Euro-denominated assets will be supplied even before the year 2002, as banks and financial intermediaries will be allowed to issue liabilities denominated in euros. No later than the first half of 2002, the stock of financial assets denominated in the existing EU currencies will be denominated in euros. Most government debt stocks are likely to be redenominated on 1 January 1999. These stocks will, of course, include assets held by the rest of the world.

The initial share of international assets denominated in euros will be much lower than the size of the EMU bloc in world GDP and trade. A private sector portfolio shift to bring the share of euro asset holdings close to parity with the economic size of the EMU bloc might involve increasing euro asset stocks by about $700 billion (McCauley and White, 1997): that is, 15–20% of the total outstanding stock of international assets. Henning (1997) estimates a private portfolio shift of $400–800 billion as well as a shift in official reserve holdings of $75–150 billion. Bond suppliers will respond endogenously to the increase in demand – liability managers will increase their offerings denominated in euros. But the likely shift in stock demand will be large relative to the flow of new issues. For illustration, *total* new dollar issues of international bonds averaged $140 billion annually during 1990–5. In the most unlikely event that *all* were to shift to euros, it would still require *five years* to absorb a stock increase in demand of $700 billion. Two cases can be fruitfully examined.

5.1. Case 1: Immediate quantity adjustment

A first scenario considers that the additional demand for euros arises slowly enough to be met by a corresponding increase in supply, through the creation of euro liabilities in sufficient quantities by commercial banks and other financial intermediaries. In such a case, the creation of the euro need have no exchange rate implications. Private financial markets, with a little help from central banks, will ensure a smooth transition to a new equilibrium, in which assets denominated in dollars and yen will be replaced by assets denominated in euros. Quantities adjust without price adjustments.

5.2. Case 2: Slow supply response

A second scenario envisions the case where demand for euro assets increases quickly, but the supply of euro liabilities initially trails behind. For equilibrium, the price of the euro against the dollar has to rise: that is, we have a real euro revaluation. How large could it be? Again for illustration, we assume a zero supply response and we consider that the $700 billion stock shift suggested above would convert about 20% of existing dollar assets into euro assets. If the initial levels of the two are about the same, and if the values of the two debt stocks and of interest rates were held constant, the dollar would have to depreciate by 40%! In due course, the effect would be a current account deficit for the euro area, so that the initial excess demand for euros would partly be met through the capital account, just as the United States has created dollar liabilities to finance its current account deficits. By supplying additional euros or disposing of dollar holdings through the capital account, the European Union would facilitate the process of establishing the euro as an international currency. Eventually, the euro will weaken (in real terms) towards its long-run equilibrium. This process may not start immediately, if a J-curve effect initially provokes a narrowing rather than a widening of the current account. In this case, the euro would overshoot its long-run equilibrium level even more, causing expectations of a future devaluation that would lead to even higher real interest rates in Europe. In the new equilibrium, the real euro/dollar rate may not differ much from its initial level. Moreover, the ECB may always choose to moderate the temporary appreciation, although this may conflict with early efforts to establish a strong anti-inflationary reputation.

6. CONCLUSIONS

The scenario in which the euro shares international currency status more or less equally with the dollar is plausible. This outcome would generate substantial increases in European Union real incomes (welfare). Are there countervailing arguments that might dissuade policy-makers from pursuing this actively as a policy objective? In the past, central banks outside the United States have sought to avoid internationalization of their currencies. Henning (1994) underlines that 'both Germany and Japan vigorously and systematically resisted the international use of their currencies – particularly as a currency for private assets and official reserves – during most of the post-war period ... Both governments ... wanted to avoid the conflict between the provision of liquidity and the preservation of confidence that had plagued the dollar, and in a different sense, the pound sterling. Because the Bundesbank and Bank of Japan might have to adjust monetary policy in response to capital movements, monetary control would be impaired under both fixed and flexible exchange rate regimes ... The Bundesbank remains acutely concerned that the volume of outstanding foreign D-Mark assets and liabilities could destabilise exchange markets.' To these considerations one might add a reluctance to act as lender of last resort in international financial crises, as indicated in European resistance to the US-led bailout of Mexico.

Suppose, however, that the ECB agrees – with other EU and national authorities – to promote the internationalization of the euro, recognizing the welfare gains, some extra seigniorage revenue and the other 'nebulous' benefits that international currency status provides. It may have first to mitigate some undesired pressures for exchange rate appreciation. Section 5 has highlighted the uncertainties regarding the supply of and demand for euro-denominated *assets*. From the viewpoint of monetary and exchange rate policy, one must distinguish between euros as money and as interest-yielding assets. Kenen (1995) argues that the 'introduction of the ECU [euro] may reduce the demand for the ECU [euro] as money. By helping to unify capital markets within the EC, however, EMU may produce a long-lasting increase in the demand for ECU-denominated claims. That is why the ECU [euro] is likely to appreciate after Stage Three begins ... The ECB can readily offset a once-and-for-all reduction in the demand for ECU [euro] balances by reducing the supply. It will be harder to offset the exchange-rate effects of an ongoing capital flow.'

Next, we have shown that, to move beyond the *quasi status quo*, European authorities will have to introduce structural reforms. The prime objective must be to integrate the European capital markets. Our analysis highlights the key role of transaction costs and hence of the liquidity, breadth and depth of financial markets. The extent to which transaction costs in euro financial markets may be reduced will depend in part on the success of financial deregulation in bringing down the cost of banking in the EU (Giovannini and Mayer, 1991) as well as on the effects of the heightened banking competition that currency unification is likely to bring (McCauley and White, 1997). It will also depend on central bank and regulatory policies determining the costs of using the euro payments mechanism (Folkerts-Landau and Garber, 1992). A working group under the auspices of the European

Commission has investigated in detail policies for 'creating a euro securities market as broad, liquid, deep and transparent as possible'. European Commission (1997b) stresses: (1) redenomination of all existing debt; (2) harmonized market rules and conventions; (3) continuity in price sources (e.g., benchmark interest rates); (4) informal co-ordination of government debt-issuing procedures. To these we might add unifying payments systems in the most efficient manner and not imposing unnecessary taxes or other burdens that would make European financial institutions less competitive (e.g., unremunerated reserve requirements). Private market initiatives are already under way in several of these areas: the co-ordination efforts of ISDA and ISMA; the decision by DTB and MATIF to bring some aspects of derivatives trading under one roof (which is partly intended to enhance their competitive position *vis-à-vis* LIFFE); and co-ordination to establish a common benchmark rate to replace LIBOR (although there are currently two separate competing efforts). On the other hand, we cannot expect that within the foreseeable future there will be a large 'federal' EU budget, with major EU borrowing, and hence an EU benchmark security; the markets will have to accord this role to one or more of the individual government bonds.

If the ECB does actively promote the international use of the euro, one cannot discount the possibility of an overt tug of war between the euro, the incumbent (the dollar) and the major other contender (the yen) for international monetary supremacy. Some of the recent language of European political leaders suggests that they look forward to this prospect and that they believe the United States – despite its official pro-EMU position – in fact opposes the single European currency precisely because it regards the euro as a threat, in this sense. The interwar experience of rivalry between sterling and the dollar, with the French franc on the sidelines (Eichengreen, 1987), suggests that such an attitude could be dangerous. Even without rivalry, if EMU were to result in large-scale substitution of euro for dollar balances and a quick appreciation of the euro against the dollar (and the yen), there is room for concern. This would justify better monetary policy co-ordination at the international level, as noted by Alogoskoufis and Portes (1991, 1992, 1997), Bergsten (1997) and Begg *et al.* (1997).

We have contrasted the influences of history, hysteresis and inertia in the international monetary system with the instability associated with multiple equilibria and threshold effects. Continuity and instability are not necessarily contradictory. Whenever a system is on the border between two equilibria, it may exhibit instability, which may be brief or prolonged. The issue here is the magnitude of the shock that EMU will bring to the international monetary system. We believe it is likely to be substantial and relatively sudden. Market participants as well as the authorities appear now to be taking this possibility more seriously – and the degree of global integration of financial markets may make the transition to a new equilibrium much faster than in our historical examples.

Discussion

Paul De Grauwe

Catholic University of Leuven

This paper provides the ideal framework to analyse issues relating to the future role of the euro. In order to comment on the paper, it is useful first to summarize it. The two main conclusions are as follows. First, the euro is likely to become a major currency in the world. It may even challenge the dollar as the other major international currency, creating significant welfare gains. Second, during the transition to becoming a (or the) major international currency, the euro is likely to appreciate. I discuss these two points consecutively.

It is clear that the euro will become an important currency in the world. Will it become a serious challenger of the dollar? The authors provide a deep analysis of the factors that affect the emergence of an international currency. They use quite an attractive framework to study the problem. The basic idea behind their theoretical framework is that increasing size reduces transaction costs, thereby creating new possibilities for currencies to emerge as international currencies. Since the euro area will suddenly merge national financial markets into one, it may well become the largest financial market in the world, reducing transaction costs sufficiently to allow the euro to become the major currency in the world. This story sounds plausible and it certainly belongs to the possible future outcomes. Let me, however, play the devil's advocate, and argue that there exist compensating forces that may prevent this from happening. The basic equation that the authors use in their analysis is as follows:

$$V = m(T + E + B + I) \qquad (4)$$

where V is the volume of euro in the foreign exchange markets transaction, T is trade, E are the cross-border equity flows in euro, B are the customer–dealer cross-border bond flows in euro, and I is the international use. The authors concentrate on the bond market and stress that, by merging the national bond markets, one obtains a market that will rival the US bond market. Although it will still be smaller than the US market, the competitive pressures that exist in EMU are likely to lead to further disintermediation from banks. These, in turn, will give a further boost to the euro bond markets, creating the conditions of increasing size that, by reducing transaction costs, may give the euro a competitive edge. Fair enough. We must, however, also consider E and T. Let's consider E first. Different national regulations will continue to prevent a full integration of the stock markets in Europe. In addition, low capitalization of European business will have to be overcome to make the European stock markets equal in size to the American market. Thus, in this area, the USA is likely to maintain its preponderance in providing a sophisticated and large stock market for world-wide investment. When one adds up bond and equity markets, it seems clear that the USA will maintain its lead for a while. As a result, in the logic of the paper, transaction costs in dollar financial markets will continue to be lower for a while, preventing the euro from overtaking the dollar in financial transactions. What about T? The authors recognize that the US dollar is likely to maintain its dominant role in international trade. One of the reasons may be that the area of largest trade growth in the world is Asia, where the dollar is relatively well established.

I see two more reasons why the euro may fall short in taking over or even approaching the dollar as the major international currency, so that the most likely scenario will be that the euro, like the yen, will be restricted to a regional (European) role without acquiring the status of a global currency. First comes the importance of growth: the dollar overtook the pound sterling because of a sustained higher growth rate of the USA relative to the UK. This led to a US economy that became much larger than the UK economy, leading also to larger financial markets in the USA than in the UK. To the extent that Europe remains a low growth area of the world (as it was in the 1990s), it will have a handicap. Its financial markets may be relatively large in 1999, but they will become progressively smaller in relative terms afterwards. Put differently, it is difficult to see how Europe can provide for a leading international currency when its relative size in the world continues to shrink. Typically, currencies became world currencies in the past because the nations supplying them increased their relative economic importance in the world. The second reason for scepticism is the authors' assumption that the ECB will be able to conduct stable and predictable monetary policies, producing low inflation and low nominal interest rates. There exists an equally plausible alternative scenario. Due to the heterogeneity of the euro area, there will be frequent asymmetric shocks. These will produce chronic conflicts in the ECB about the desirable monetary policy. Shifting coalitions in the ECB will then lead to erratic behaviour, and a lot of volatility in the interest rate. As a result, risk premia will be high. This will not make the euro attractive. It will also prevent the development of a large and liquid euro bond market.

To conclude this part of the authors' analysis, it is worth stressing that the scenario presented by the authors in favour of the euro emerging as the major currency is a plausible one. However, uncertainty remains considerable. There is an equally plausible scenario that the euro will not be able to challenge the role of the dollar, and will acquire only a regional importance.

The second important conclusion reached by the authors is that the euro may appreciate in real terms during the transition. The argument is that the increased desire to hold euro assets will raise the price of the euro. If, as they recognize, euro liabilities increase at the same pace, one should not expect that the emergence of the euro as an international currency will lead to an appreciation. To the extent that the internationalization of the euro leads to a simultaneous increase in euro assets and euro liabilities, we simply do not know whether the euro will appreciate or depreciate. In order to strengthen their view that the first scenario (appreciation) is more plausible than the second one (simultaneous increase in demand and supply), the authors contend that the issue of euro liabilities will lag behind the increased demand for euro assets. It is unclear why this should be. Why does it take longer for borrowers to issue euro liabilities than for investors to hold more euro assets? The authors give no arguments to support this claim.

To conclude, I want to stress again that the authors provided us with the right framework to think about the future role of the euro. Not surprisingly, this framework can still lead to divergent conclusions.

Seppo Honkapohja
University of Helsinki

This paper takes up the key question of the future role of the euro in the world monetary system. While various opinionated writings already exist in this area, analytical studies on the subject are very scarce. The paper is among the very first such pieces and it is therefore most welcome. Most importantly, it tries to shed light on the question by means of explicit modelling, based to a large extent on the work of one of its authors (see Rey, 1997a, b). The topic is obviously both challenging and difficult, and the paper is bold and provocative. It provides a few alternative scenarios, of which the medium euro case is perhaps most likely on the basis of the numerical estimates provided in the paper. In this scenario the euro becomes of equal importance to the dollar as an international currency. If that is the case, the euro can become a reserve currency in the portfolios of both public and private institutions throughout the world. It is therefore important to consider the impact of this on the external value of the euro. The paper also takes up this issue and argues that there is a tendency for the euro to be relatively strong. My discussion will focus on some methodological aspects of the analysis.

I start with the modelling of the emergence of the euro as an international currency. The model of Rey (1997a) is quite stylized. One could obviously criticize the various simplifications and ask for additional features. I refrain from this and instead focus on its main theoretical feature: namely, that the model has multiple steady-state equilibria as a result of the externalities in transaction costs. The authors duly point out that multiple equilibria can result in possible inertia and hysteresis, or what is perhaps more commonly called path- or history-dependence. It is surprising that the paper does not make use of these implications. Instead the different scenarios are considered on the basis of empirical data on transaction costs and their elasticities with respect to transaction volumes. This is a possible first approach to use, since the alternative equilibria can be characterized in terms of sets of inequalities on transaction costs. The problem is that simply listing different outcomes is just a first result and one should try to go further into dynamic aspects. Indeed, history-dependence or inertia and hysteresis are inherently dynamic phenomena.

Although transaction costs are endogenous, the paper does not relate the data and elasticity estimates to the underlying structural parameters of the model. Had that been done, part of the way would have been cleared for possible sharper conclusions. Recent economic theory suggests that some equilibria are more plausible than others when there are multiple equilibria. Certain selection criteria for finding the plausible equilibria have been suggested. Some of these are based on dynamic stability analysis, and their use in this model could provide an explicit description of the emergence – or non-emergence – of the euro as an international currency, and of history-dependence in this process. While one can accept the paper as a first attempt, further work focusing on dynamics would be most interesting. This would be a major undertaking, since even the Rey model is rather complex. Nevertheless, I think it should be done.

The second part of the paper considers the possibility of a strong euro. I have two comments. First, I am worried about the change of the model. While the standard macroeconomic model implicitly used in this section can perhaps provide a first answer, it is potentially in direct conflict with the Rey model used in sections 2–4. For example, the macro model does not have multiple equilibria. Should one not try to use the same model for both questions? This is not done in the paper, partly because, as noted above, the Rey model cannot distinguish between dynamic scenarios. Second, if one thinks that the macroeconomic model is usable, it should be stressed that the analysis is based on continuous rational expectations. While rational expectations are the standard assumption in macroeconomics, one can raise doubts about this assumption when one is studying the adjustment of an economy to a change as fundamental as the introduction of the euro. As an alternative, one could use an approach based on transitorily non-rational expectations and learning in expectations formation. This kind of approach is becoming common, and it may provide a better account of the transition (for a recent survey, see Evans and Honkapohja (1997)). While I have not done the formal analysis, I would like to conjecture here that it would make the prediction about overshooting in the value of the euro much less pronounced, or even suggest monotone appreciation in the adjustment from the old equilibrium to the new. However, the long-run prediction about steady-state appreciation would not change.

Finally, I want to emphasize that the welfare predictions in the paper are very important. The result that the EMU area appears to gain and that the USA loses with the relative decline in the use of the dollar is most interesting. In practice, much can be at stake here. The paper is certainly very valuable in bringing out this implication in analytical terms. The implications for international policy making ought to be considered in future research, for which the sharper analytical approach suggested above might be useful.

General discussion

Rudi Dornbusch thought that the transaction cost approach used in the paper was useful as it stresses economies of scale in the use of an international currency. However, we must also consider the countervailing effect of exchange rate risk. Incorporating diversification in the analysis would rule out corner solutions, which are unrealistic. He wanted the authors to identify the determinants of the costs of international transactions. It was not so much the sheer volume of trade but its denomination in a single currency that would reduce transaction costs. Another important cause of low transaction costs was a competitive and deregulated market. Jacques Le Cacheux felt it was important to determine whether supply or demand effects are the real driving force in making the euro an international currency. He observed that supply-side factors may be quite important as many countries, especially in central and southern Europe, would soon issue bonds and equities denominated in the euro. What policies would speed up the internationalization of the euro? Robert McCauley suggested that the ECB could use an active strategy to transfer business from New York to London, in order to strengthen the role of the euro in international transactions. For instance, the Federal Reserve Act had exempted banks from reserve requirements early in the century to make the New York money market more attractive.

Marc Flandreau argued that the transaction cost approach misses an important feature: namely, the lender of last resort function in the creation of international or regional currencies. For instance, the Reichsmark was created because there was strong political support to repatriate the banking business from London to Germany. This move was motivated by the 1866 crisis in London, when German banks were left without lender of last resort facilities. Friedrich Schneider thought that monetary and political strength went hand in hand. The history of fiscal federalism in the USA, Germany and Switzerland shows that the importance of a currency as an international transaction vehicle always had strong effects on a country's political influence.

Maurice Obstfeld was doubtful about the welfare assessment in the paper, as it was very difficult to allocate welfare gains and losses geographically. For instance, a lot of dealing was done in London by non-US banks. If the transaction costs of dealing dollars increased, the welfare loss would accrue only partially to the USA.

Rudi Dornbusch argued that the anticipated portfolio shift towards the euro will not necessarily result in its appreciation. First, the ECB is likely to sterilize the portfolio demand for euro. Second, as the entire European public debt will be denominated in the euro, there would also be an immediate supply effect on the euro bond market. Alternatively, the US Treasury could make a one-time big issue of euro-denominated bonds to avoid a hard landing. Kenneth Rogoff felt that concern about the appreciation of the euro was understandable, but it was difficult to assess the likely extent of appreciation without an explicit portfolio model. It was important, for instance, to include the endogenous shift in the supply of other euro-denominated assets. Robert McCauley conjectured that this supply response is likely to be pretty rapid and would not lag behind the shift in demand. Given that many international assets were short term, there was no need to wait for a bond to mature to shift denomination. Patrick Honohan suggested that the authors estimate the elasticity of demand for high-powered money in response to changes in the volume of transactions in foreign exchange markets. Such estimates could help to obtain a better understanding of the likely pressure on the exchange rate due to the portfolio effect. Jürgen von Hagen argued that even the possibility of real appreciation is very relevant for policy making. For instance, the risk that the DM might become a reserve currency had been a recurrent theme in the protocols of the Bundesbank council during the 1970s, triggering concerns that the resulting appreciation would put German industry at a disadvantage. This suggests that, even when the economic reasoning is questionable, the fact that many people are concerned about appreciation may nevertheless make it a relevant issue. The importance of this argument for the ECB will depend largely on the degree to which the ECB responds to pressure from industry.

APPENDIX. COMPUTING POSSIBLE EQUILIBRIA

Our estimates in section 3 are based on a simplified static version of the general equilibrium model with thick market externalities derived in Rey (1997a, b). The key feature of this model is to represent the medium of exchange function of money through a transaction technology whose cost decreases with the liquidity of the market. In equilibrium, the transaction costs, prices and volumes exchanged are determined jointly.[13] We assume here that the transaction costs on each market are a decreasing function of the volumes exchanged and that volumes exchanged can be decomposed as in section 3.1. The different scenarios are the ones presented in section 2.5 and pictured in Figures 1–4. On each side of the triangles is the preferred currency of denomination of financial assets in which exporters or investors store their wealth when they have to acquire the currency of the other bloc one period hence. In the middle of the triangle is the international currency.

We proceed as follows. First, we make an assumption regarding the scenario we are in. Second, we compute the volumes exchanged under this scenario. Third, we use an assumed elasticity parameter to derive the various transaction costs. Finally, we check that the transaction cost structure we have just derived is compatible with the scenario initially assumed.

In the following, S stands for the USA with s for the dollar, E for EU countries with e for the euro, Y for Japan with y for the yen. We denote by T_{ij} the transaction costs on bilateral market ij: that is, the cost of exchanging one unit of currency i into currency j ($T_{ij} = T_{ji}$). T_{ii}

---

[13] When preferences of the three blocs are Cobb–Douglas, price and output effects cancel out, so that computing volumes exchanged becomes easier.

is the transaction cost on the bond market ii: that is, the cost of exchanging currency i against a bond denominated in currency i. In all the scenarios considered, the following inequalities hold, reflecting the home bias in domestic savings:

$$Tee \leqslant Tes + Tss + Tse \tag{A1}$$

$$Tee \leqslant Tey + Tyy + Tye \tag{A2}$$

These equations mean that it is cheaper for Europeans to save in euro assets than to save in foreign assets and therefore to go (at least) twice on the foreign exchange market. Similar equations are verified for the USA and Japan. The structure of fundamentals and the observed structure of transactions between customers and dealers are shown in Table 5.

A1. Quasi status quo scenario (Figure 2)

The following two equations state that the markets involving US dollar-denominated financial assets are the most liquid ones (more liquid than those involving the yen or the euro), so that when a financial intermediary holds euros or yen and needs dollars for a future date, he will use dollar-denominated assets rather than euro or yen securities.

$$Tes + Tss \leqslant Tee + Tes \quad \Leftrightarrow \quad Tss \leqslant Tee \tag{A3}$$

$$Tys + Tss \leqslant Tyy + Tys \quad \Leftrightarrow \quad Tss \leqslant Tyy \tag{A4}$$

The next equations state that the euro has replaced the dollar as the dominant currency for exchanges between Europe and the Asian bloc, but the dollar is still the vehicle currency on foreign exchange markets.

$$Tes + Tss + Tsy > Tee + Tye \tag{A5}$$

$$Tye \leqslant Tes + Tsy \tag{A6}$$

$$Tes \leqslant Tye \tag{A7}$$

$$Tsy \leqslant Tye \tag{A8}$$

The volumes exchanged on foreign exchange markets are the same as those shown in Table 5 (current structure of world payments) except that inter-dealer bond transactions between Japan and the EU are no longer on the yen/\$ and \$/euro markets, but on the yen/euro market. Let Bo be the inter-dealer share of the cross-border bond flows between Japan and the EU. Now we have $Bo = 274 \times 50\%$. The ms are the corresponding multipliers (they multiply the customer–dealer transactions to get the global volumes exchanged, as explained in section 3).

	euro	Yen
Dollar	$594 \times m - Bo$	$333 \times m - Bo$
euro		$38 \times m + Bo$

The transaction costs are then computed using volume data and the assumed elasticity of -0.03 for the foreign exchange markets and of -0.11 for the bond markets. They are shown in Tables 6 and 8. Relative to the current situation, costs increase in the dollar bond market because of a decrease in turnover. Euro bond markets are by assumption not integrated in this case, so the transaction costs remain at their DM level. Yen markets are not affected either. These transaction costs verify the above set of inequalities, in particular (A5), meaning that the *quasi status quo* scenario can be an equilibrium, but not the *status quo*.

A2. Medium euro scenario (Figure 4)

The conditions required for this scenario are (A6), (A7), (A8) and:

$$Tee \leqslant Tss \leqslant Tyy \tag{A9}$$

$$Tse + Tee + Tey \geqslant Tss + Tsy \tag{A10}$$

Volumes exchanged on foreign exchange markets are unchanged from the current ones (the structure of world payments is the same as in the status quo) except that inter-dealer bond transactions *Bo* between EU and Japan no longer appear on the yen/\$ and \$/euro markets, but appear on the yen/euro market:

	euro	Yen
Dollar	$594 \times m - Bo$	$333 \times m - Bo$
euro		$38 \times m + Bo$

The difference between the *medium euro* and *quasi status quo* cases therefore comes exclusively from the bond markets. The corresponding associated transaction costs are shown in Table 8. Transaction costs on the euro markets are equal to those on the dollar market by assumption (institutional change). Transaction costs on yen markets are unaffected. It is apparent that these transaction costs support the set of inequalities characterizing the *medium euro* case. Therefore this scenario is an equilibrium scenario.

A3. Big euro scenario (Figure 3)

The transaction costs structure must satisfy (A9) and (A10) as well as

$$Tse \leqslant Tsy \tag{A11}$$

$$Tey \leqslant Tsy \tag{A12}$$

For inter-dealer bond trading, the pattern is the same as in the *quasi status quo* and *medium euro* cases. However, the international currency is no longer the dollar, but the euro. Therefore, there is some additional turnover on the euro/yen and euro/\$ markets and fewer transactions on the yen/\$ market. Transactions on the yen/\$ market now reflect only the fundamentals ($F = 144$), and some of the turnover ($I = 128$) is lost to the other two markets involving the euro (the international currency). Symmetrically, the yen/euro market now reflects the fundamentals ($F = 166$) and the additional turnover brought by the international role of the euro ($I = 128$). $I = 128$ is the difference between fundamentals and actual turnover (as explained in section 3).

	euro	Yen
Dollar	$333 \times m - Bo$	$(F - I) \times m - Bo$
euro		$(F + I) \times m + Bo$

These transaction costs verify the set of inequalities defining the *big euro* scenario. Therefore, the *big euro* scenario is also an equilibrium scenario.

A4. Pan euro scenario (Figure 1 with *e* replacing *s*)

The transaction cost structure is defined as follows:

$$Tse + Tee \leqslant Tss + Tse \quad \Leftrightarrow \quad Tee \leqslant Tss \tag{A13}$$

$$Tye + Tee \leqslant Tyy + Tye \quad \Leftrightarrow \quad Tee \leqslant Tyy \tag{A14}$$

$$Tye + Tee + Tes \leqslant Tyy + Tys \tag{A15}$$

$$Tse + Tee + Tey \leqslant Tss + Tsy \tag{A16}$$

$$Tes + Tey \leqslant Tsy \tag{A17}$$

Provided that the post-euro \$/yen market is at least as liquid as the pre-euro DM/yen, it is possible to show that this last inequality cannot be verified. Therefore, we can exclude this equilibrium.

REFERENCES

Alogoskoufis, G.S. and R. Portes (1991). 'International costs and benefits of EMU', in 'The Economics of EMU', *European Economy*, Special Edition no.1.

—— (1992). 'European monetary union and international currencies in a tri-polar world', in M. Canzoneri, V. Grilli and P. Masson (eds.), *Establishing a Central Bank: Issues in Europe and Lessons from the US*, Cambridge University Press and CEPR, Cambridge.

—— (1997). 'The euro, the dollar, and the international monetary system', in T. Krueger, P. Masson and B. Turtleboom (eds.), *EMU and the International Monetary System*, IMF, Washington, DC.

Alogoskoufis, G.S., L. Papademos and R. Portes (eds.) (1991). *External Constraints on Macroeconomic Policy: The European Experience*, Cambridge University Press, Cambridge.

Amihud, Y. and H. Mendelson (1991). 'Liquidity, maturity, and the yields on US Treasury securities', *Journal of Finance*.

Ammer, J. and A. Brunner (1997). 'Are banks market timers or market makers?', *Journal of International Financial Markets, Institutions and Money*.

Artus, P. (1996). 'A strong euro or a weak euro?', Document de Travail 1996-02/EI, Caisse des Dépôts et Consignations, Paris.

—— (1997a). 'Comment change l'équilibre financier international s'il apparaît une seconde monnaie de reserve?', Document de Travail 1997-03/EI, Caisse des Dépôts et Consignations, Paris.

—— (1997b). 'L'euro, la diversification de portefeuille et la gestion des reserves', Document de Travail 1997-09/EI, Caisse des Dépôts et Consignations, Paris.

Begg, D., F. Giavazzi and C. Wyplosz (1997). 'Options for the future exchange-rate policy of the EMU', CEPR Occasional Paper no. 17.

Bénassy-Quéré, A. (1996). 'Potentialities and opportunities of the euro as an international currency', CEPII Working Paper no. 96-09.

Bergsten, F. (1997). 'The impact of the euro on exchange rates and international policy cooperation', in T. Krueger, P. Masson and B. Turtleboom (eds.), *EMU and the International Monetary System*, IMF, Washington, DC.

BIS (1996). *Central Bank Survey of Foreign Exchange and Derivatives Market Activity 1995*, Basle.

—— (1997). *International Banking and Financial Market Developments* (February and August).

Black, S. (1985). 'International money and international monetary arrangements', in P.B. Kenen and R.W. Jones (eds.), *Handbook of International Economics*, North-Holland, Amsterdam.

—— (1989). 'The international use of currencies', in Y. Suzuki, J. Miyake and M. Okabe (eds.), *The Evolution of the International Monetary System: How Can Stability and Efficiency Be Attained?*, University of Tokyo Press, Tokyo.

Cohen, B.J. (1997). 'The political economy of currency regions', in H. Milner (ed.), *The Political Economy of Regionalism*, Columbia University Press, New York.

Commission of the European Communities (1990). *One Market, One Money*, Brussels.

Dooley, M.P., J.S. Lizondo and D.J. Mathieson (1989). 'The currency composition of foreign exchange reserves', *IMF Staff Papers*.

ECU Institute (1995). *International Currency Competition and the Future Role of the Single European Currency*, Kluwer Law International, Dordrecht.

Eichengreen, B. (1987). 'Conducting the international orchestra: Bank of England leadership under the classical gold standard', *Journal of International Money and Finance*.

—— and J. Frankel (1996). 'The SDR, reserve currencies, and the future of the international monetary system', in M. Mussa *et al.* (eds.), *The Future of the SDR in the Light of Changes in International Financial System*, IMF, Washington, DC.

European Commission (1997a). *External Aspects of Economic and Monetary Union*, Directorate General II, Brussels.

—— (1997b). *The Impact of the Introduction of the Euro on Capital Markets*, Directorate General II, Brussels.

Evans, G.W. and S. Honkapohja (1997). 'Learning dynamics', in J.B. Taylor and M. Woodford (eds.), *Handbook of Macroeconomics*, Elsevier, Amsterdam.

Fleming, M. (1997). 'The round-the-clock market for US Treasury securities', *Economic Policy Review*, Federal Reserve Bank of New York.

Folkerts-Landau, D. and P. Garber (1992). 'The ECB: a bank or a monetary policy rule?', in M. Canzoneri, V. Grilli and P. Masson, (eds.), *Establishing a Central Bank: Issues in Europe and Lessons from the US*, Cambridge University Press and CEPR, Cambridge.

Frankel, J. (1995). 'Still the lingua franca: the exaggerated death of the dollar', *Foreign Affairs*.

Giovannini, A. and C. Mayer (eds.) (1991). *European Financial Integration*, Cambridge University Press and CEPR, Cambridge.

Goodhart, C. (1996). 'The two concepts of money and the future of Europe', manuscript, London School of Economics.

Hartmann, P. (1996a). 'The future of the euro as an international currency: a transactions perspective', Special Paper no. 91, Financial Markets Group, London School of Economics.

—— (1996b). 'Foreign exchange vehicles before and after EMU: from dollar/mark to dollar/euro?', manuscript, London School of Economics.

—— (1997). 'Do Reuters spreads reflect currencies' differences in global trading activity?' LSE FMG DP 265, London School of Economics.

Henning, R. (1994). *Currencies and Politics in the United States, Germany, and Japan*, Institute for International Economics, Washington, DC.

—— (1997). *Cooperating with Europe's Monetary Union*, Institute for International Economics, Washington, DC.

Kenen, P. (1995). *Economic and Monetary Union in Europe: Moving Beyond Maastricht*, Cambridge University Press, Cambridge.

—— (1996). 'Sorting out some EMU issues', *Reprints in International Finance*, International Finance Section, Princeton University.

Kindleberger, C. (1984). *A Financial History of Western Europe*, Allen and Unwin, London.

Krugman, P. (1980). 'Vehicle currencies and the structure of international exchange', *Journal of Money, Credit and Banking*.

—— (1984). 'The international role of the dollar: theory and prospect', in J.F.O. Bilson and R.C. Marston (eds.), *Exchange Rate Theory and Practice*, University of Chicago Press, Chicago, IL.

Kunz, D. (1995). 'The fall of the dollar order: the world the United States is losing', *Foreign Affairs*.

Lyons, R. (1995). 'Foreign exchange volume: sound and fury signifying nothing?' in J. Frankel *et al.* (eds.), *The Microstructure of Foreign Exchange Markets*, University of Chicago Press, Chicago, IL.

—— (1997a). 'A simultaneous trade model of the foreign exchange hot potato', *Journal of International Economics*.

—— (1997b). 'Profits and position control: a week of FX dealing', *Journal of International Money and Finance*.

McCauley, R. (1997). 'The euro and the dollar', BIS Working Paper, Basle.

—— and W. White (1997). 'The euro and European financial markets', BIS Working Paper, Basle.

McKinnon, R. (1993). 'International money in historical perspective', *Journal of Economic Literature*.

Miles, D. (1996). *The Future of Savings and Wealth Accumulation: Differences within the Developed Economies*, Merrill Lynch, London.

Morgan, J.P. (1997a). *Valuing Bonds in a Low-Inflation World*, London.

—— (1997b). *The Euro, FX Reserves and Vehicle Currencies*, London.

PDFM (1997). *Pension Fund Indicators*, Phillips and Drew Financial Markets, London.

Prati, A. and G. Schinasi (1997). 'European monetary union and international capital markets: structural implications and risks', IMF Working Paper.

Rey, H. (1997a). 'International trade and currency exchange', Discussion Paper, Centre for Economic Performance, London School of Economics.

—— (1997b). 'Inflation and the moneyness of currencies', manuscript, London School of Economics.

Takagi, S. (1989). 'Transaction costs and the term structure of interest rates in the OTC bond market in Japan', *Journal of Money, Credit and Banking*.

Tavlas, G. (1991). 'On the international use of currencies: the case of the Deutsche Mark', *Essays in International Finance*, International Finance Section, Princeton University.

—— (1997). 'The international use of the US dollar: an optimum currency area perspective', manuscript, IMF, Washington, DC.

—— and Y. Ozeki (1992). 'The internationalization of currencies: an appraisal of the Japanese yen', IMF Occasional Paper.

Yeager, L. (1976). *International Monetary Relations*, Harper and Row, New York.

Index